THE ESSENTIAL
JUNG

Selected and Introduced by
Anthony Storr

MJF BOOKS

NEW YORK

Published by MJF Books
Fine Communications
Two Lincoln Square
60 West 66th Street
New York, NY 10023

Library of Congress Catalog Card Number 96-77137
ISBN 1-56731-150-4

Selected from *The Collected Works of C. G. Jung* (translated by R. F. C. Hull), *The Freud/Jung Letters* (passage translated by R. F. C. Hull), *C. G. Jung: Letters*, and *C. G. Jung: Word and Image*, all published by Princeton University Press; and from *Memories, Dreams, Reflections* by C. G. Jung (translated by Richard and Clara Winston), copyright © 1961, 1962, 1963 by Random House, Inc., and published by Pantheon Books, New York.

This edition published by arrangement with Princeton University Press

Manufactured in the United States of America on acid-free paper ∞

MJF Books and the MJF colophon are trademarks of Fine Creative Media, Inc.

10   9   8   7   6   5   4   3   2   1

Contents

Note on the Text

Bibliographical details of the works from which I have taken extracts – *Collected Works* (CW), *Memories, Dreams, Reflections* (MDR), *Septem Sermones ad Mortuos*, *The Freud/Jung Letters* and *Letters* – are given on pages 434–5. English and American page or paragraph numbering diverges only in the case of MDR; when quoting from this book I have given the English hardback edition's pages followed by those of the American edition.

I have been selective about my inclusion of footnotes, keeping those of Jung's which illuminate the text or which refer to sources of interest to the non-specialist reader, but omitting his and his editors' references to works which, particularly in the case of the alchemical volumes, are unobtainable by all but the most dedicated scholars. Where editors' notes have been retained, they are within square brackets. I have used the bibliographies contained in CW to fill out Jung's footnotes where appropriate.

Preface

Throughout his long life, C. G. Jung was a prolific writer, so that his Collected Works run to no less than eighteen large volumes. In addition, there are two volumes of his letters, a separate volume of his correspondence with Freud, and his autobiography, *Memories, Dreams, Reflections*. Comparatively few people are prepared to read the whole corpus of this material; but many might welcome the opportunity to become acquainted with Jung's thought as he himself expounded it. This book is an attempt to distil the essential features of Jung's psychology as it developed during the course of his life by means of extracts from his own writings. Since Jung's way of thinking may be unfamiliar to contemporary readers, I have summarized the main features of his thought in an introduction; and I have prefaced the extracts which I have chosen with brief explanatory remarks. But, so far as is possible, I have let Jung present his ideas in his own words. My purpose has been exposition, not criticism; and it must not be assumed that I personally subscribe to everything that Jung wrote.

Anthony Storr

Introduction

Carl Gustav Jung was born on 26 July 1875 and died on 6 June 1961. The greater part of his early childhood was spent at Klein-Hüningen, near Basel, to which his family moved in 1879. Jung attended the local school from the age of six, and, in his eleventh year, was transferred to the Gymnasium in Basel. From here, he went on to study medicine at the University of Basel during the years 1895–1900. Concurrently, he read extensively in the fields of philosophy and theology.

In 1900, he moved to Zurich where he became an assistant physician to Eugen Bleuler at the Burghölzli mental hospital. He was later promoted to Senior Staff Physician. In 1902–3, he spent a term at the Salpêtrière in Paris in order to study psychopathology with Pierre Janet. During these first years in psychiatry, he wrote his MD dissertation, "On the Psychology and Pathology of So-called Occult Phenomena"; undertook experimental work in word association; and, in 1903, married Emma Rauschenbach, by whom he had a son and four daughters. In 1905, he was appointed a lecturer in the University of Zurich.

In 1907, Jung published a pioneering book on schizophrenia, *The Psychology of Dementia Praecox*, which he sent to Freud. This led to a meeting between the two men in Vienna, and to a close association between them which lasted until 1913. In 1909, Jung, in company with Freud and Ferenczi, paid his first visit to the USA, where he lectured on word-association experiments and received an honorary degree from Clark University, in Massachusetts. In the same year, Jung gave up his post at the Burghölzli in favour of his growing private practice which he conducted in his own house at Küsnacht on the Lake of Zurich. Although he travelled in various parts of the world and paid frequent visits to his country retreat in Bollingen, which was also on the Lake of Zurich, Jung continued to practise and to write in the same house in Küsnacht until his death in 1961. His last piece of writing was completed only ten days before he died.

Jung's earliest work and his later writings have more in common than is generally supposed. They are linked by the theme that mental illness is characterized by disunity of the personality, whilst mental health is manifested by unity. Jung's first study was conducted on a 15½-year-old girl who, claiming to be a medium, said that she was "controlled" by a variety of different personalities, which Jung interpreted as personifications of various unconscious parts of herself. Before Freud's concept of repression became widely employed, the term used to describe such phenomena was "dissociation"; and Jung, who at that time was as much influenced by Janet, with whom he had studied, as he was by Freud, whom he had only read, continued to think of personality as being capable of dissociation into a number of subsidiary personalities, any of which could temporarily "take over." Although Jung accepted the idea of repression in the Freudian sense of making the unacceptable unconscious, and thus inaccessible, he continued to think and write in terms of subsidiary, dissociated personalities, and it is important to bear this in mind when approaching his work. In hysteria, for example, the patient might behave as if she were two or more different persons, who were sometimes given different names and who had no cognizance of each other. Dissociation was a splitting of the personality in which the right hand did not know what the left was doing; and it followed that cure of this type of neurosis depended upon making the divided selves conscious of each other and thus creating a new unity. In schizophrenia, the personality appeared fragmented into many parts, rather than into two or three as in hysteria. Moreover, whereas the hysteric retained contact with reality by means of that part of the personality which was already being called the "ego," the schizophrenic lost contact with reality because the ego was overwhelmed by irruptions from the unconscious and became only one "voice" amongst many.

Jung's next group of studies was based upon the word-association test. A list of a hundred words is read out, and the subject is asked to respond to each with the first word that occurs to him. By timing the interval between stimulus and response, it becomes possible to show that, unknown to themselves, subjects are influenced by words which arouse emotion and slow down their responses. Often, groups of words were linked around a theme; and to such a collection of associations, Jung applied the word "complex," a term which he introduced into psychology. He regarded complexes as similar to, but lesser than, the subsidiary personalities referred to above. These experiments were important in that they demonstrated objectively, in ways which could be measured, the dynamic effects of unconscious mental contents. They will also remind the reader that Jung was trained in the natural sciences and had an accurate grasp of scientific method, although his later interests drew him into fields where scientific method cannot easily be applied.

Although Freud's writings were being eagerly discussed by the younger generation when Jung was working at the Burghölzli, psychiatry was dominated by German phenomenology. Psychiatrists were content to describe their patients' symptoms and behaviour, and to fit them into diagnostic categories, without attempting to understand them as individuals. Jung, by applying psychoanalytic ideas to the study of delusions and hallucinations, was able to demonstrate that such phenomena, hitherto dismissed as incomprehensible, could sometimes be shown to have a psychological origin and meaning. Jung remained keenly interested in schizophrenia, and was one of the first psychiatrists to attempt psychoanalytic treatment of the psychotic.

Jung was never dogmatic as to a single "cause" of schizophrenia, although he inclined to the belief that a psychological, rather than a physical, origin was probable. He was also modest in his therapeutic claims, recognizing that only a limited number of cases responded to analysis, and that partial alleviation was more common than cure. Jung considered that there were many schizophrenics who never came near a mental hospital. If such people consulted him, he was cautious and sometimes dismissed them without attempting psychotherapy. Jung was one of the first to recognize that a psychotic episode could be precipitated by analysis.

It was Jung's intimate acquaintance with the phenomena of schizophrenia which led him to postulate a "collective" unconscious. He found that delusions and hallucinations, which often seemed to be variations on similar themes, could seldom be entirely explained as products of the patient's personal history. Jung's extensive knowledge of comparative religion and of mythology led him to detect parallels with psychotic material which argued a common source: a myth-producing level of mind which was common to all men.

Jung described the collective unconscious as consisting of mythological motifs or primordial images to which he gave the name "archetypes." Archetypes are not inborn ideas, but "typical forms of behaviour which, once they become conscious, naturally present themselves *as ideas and images, like* everything else that becomes a content of consciousness." (CW 8, par. 435) Archetypes have an organizing influence on images and ideas. Archetypes are not themselves conscious, but seem to be like underlying ground themes upon which conscious manifestations are sets of variations. Their presence is felt as "numinous"; that is, of profound spiritual significance. Jung wrote:

All the most powerful ideas in history go back to archetypes. This is particularly true of religious ideas, but the central concepts of science, philosophy and ethics are no exception to this rule. In their present form they are variants of archetypal ideas, created by consciously applying and adapting these ideas to reality. For it is the function of consciousness not only to recognize and assimilate the external world through the gateway of the senses, but to translate into visible reality the world within us. [CW 8, par. 342]

Examples of archetypes as images of ideas are given in extracts which follow.

It was also Jung's study of schizophrenia which led him to formulate a different, and more general, view of psychic energy from that of Freud. Freud believed that schizophrenia, in common with other mental disturbances, was due to repression of sexuality and withdrawal of erotic interest from objects in the external world into the inner world of the subject. Jung considered that contact with the external world was maintained in other ways beside the sexual; and that the loss of contact with reality characteristic of schizophrenia could not be attributed to sexual withdrawal alone.

Because of this, he came to use the term "libido" for psychic energy in general, without limiting it to sexuality.

While Jung was still at the Burghölzli, his private practice was also growing, so that he became as familiar with the various types of neurosis as he was with schizophrenia and the other psychoses. His divergence from Freud became wider. Freud believed that neurosis invariably originated in early childhood, and that the incestuous fantasies and desires connected with the Oedipus complex were central factors. (Freud made an exception in the case of so-called "traumatic" neurosis; but this did not form a main part of his theory.) Jung thought that the cause of neurosis usually lay in the present; and that the infantile fantasies which Freud unearthed were secondary phenomena. When the natural course of a man's development through life was held up, either by misfortune or by his failure to face life's obligations, his libido became turned in upon himself and reactivated the attitudes and feelings of childhood which would normally have been left behind him. Jung believed that there was a natural and proper path of development for each individual; and that neurosis might actually be a valuable signal which indicated when, through intellectual arrogance, a false set of values or an evasion of responsibilities, a person was straying too far from his own true path. Neurotic symptoms, therefore, might be *compensatory*; part of a self-regulating mechanism whose aim was the achievement of a better balance within the psyche. Jung sometimes said of an individual: "Thank God, he became neurotic!" Just as pain might make a man realize that there was something wrong with his body, so neurotic symptoms could draw attention to psychological problems of which the individual was unaware.

The idea of self-regulation runs right through the whole of Jung's scheme of how the mind works, and largely accounts for his view of dreams. Freud considered that the majority of dreams had as their core an unacceptable wish which was striving, in the dream, to find indirect expression. He believed that the "manifest content" of a dream was merely a cloak concealing the "latent content," which was generally some repressed sexual desire of an infantile kind. Jung, on the other hand, regarded dreams as communications from the unconscious. Dreams might be couched in symbolic language which was hard to understand; but they were not necessarily concerned with wishes, nor ways of concealing the unacceptable. Most commonly, dreams were compensatory to the conscious point of view; expressions of aspects of the individual which were neglected or unrealized; or, like neurotic symptoms, warnings of divergence from the individual's proper path. Dreams from the collective level might sometimes be visions of vast significance, quite outside the range of conscious contrivance.

The idea of compensation and self-regulation also became linked with Jung's classification of "psychological types." It was Jung who introduced the terms "extravert" and "introvert" into psychology. Jung's observation of the very different ways in which Freud, Adler and he himself approached the same psychological material led him to postulate that individuals adopted differing habitual attitudes toward life which determined their interpretation of experience. The extravert's bias was toward the external world; the introvert's, toward the inner world of the psyche. Jung later proposed that the psyche operated by means of four functions: thinking, feeling, sensation and intuition. Any one of these functions could also be predominant in an individual's way of dealing with experience. For example, a man could be an introverted thinker or an extraverted intuitive or an introverted feeling type. The eight possible types are vividly described in volume 6 of the Collected Works, *Psychological Types.*

Compensation and self-regulation are integral parts of this type theory. Jung considered that habitual attitudes were nearly always carried too far, so that the thinker neglected his feelings, while the intuitive paid too little attention to the facts given by sensation. Introverts were caught up in their inner worlds; while extraverts lost themselves in the press of events. In Western man, because of the achievements of his culture, there was an especial tendency toward intellectual hubris; an overvaluation of thinking which could alienate a man from his emotional roots. Neurotic symptoms, dreams and other manifestations of the unconscious were often expressions of the "other side" trying to assert itself. There was, therefore, within every individual, a striving toward unity in which divisions would be replaced by consistency, opposites equally balanced, consciousness in reciprocal relation with the unconscious. Jung affirmed that personality was manifested by "definiteness, wholeness and ripeness". (CW 17, par. 288) He considered personality to be an achievement, not something given. Moreover, it was essentially an achievement of the second half of life. In the first half of life, a person is, and should be, concerned with emancipating himself from parents and with establishing himself in the world as spouse, parent and effective contributor. In the modern world, especially, a certain one-sidedness might be needed to fulfil these conventional demands; but, once a person had done so, then he could and should look inwards. Jung called the journey toward wholeness the "process of individuation," and it is toward the study of this process that the thrust of his later work is directed.

Jung's later writings are much concerned with alchemy. Although the ostensible purpose of alchemy was to find a way of changing base metals into gold, the early alchemists "sought not only to make gold, but *to perfect everything in its own nature*" (F. Sherwood Taylor, *The Alchemists*, London: Heinemann, 1951, p. 3). Moreover they linked change in matter with change in man, so that the alchemical "work" aimed at perfecting matter was, at the same time, a psychological process aimed at perfecting man. Some of the alchemists undoubtedly thought of their work as a meditative development of the inner personality; and this is why their writings appealed to Jung, who found parallels between the series of changes described by the alchemists and the process of individuation which he observed taking place within his patients. Individuation is essentially a spiritual journey. "Only the man who can consciously assent to the power of the inner voice becomes a personality." (CW 17, par. 308) By paying attention to the voice within, the individual achieves a new synthesis between conscious and unconscious, a sense of calm acceptance and detachment, and a realization of the meaning of life.

If the unconscious can be recognized as a co-determining factor along with consciousness, and if we can live in such a way that conscious and unconscious demands are taken into account as far as possible, then the centre of gravity of the total personality shifts its position. It is then no longer in the ego, which is merely the centre of consciousness, but in the hypothetical point between conscious and unconscious. This new centre might be called the self. [CW 13, par. 67]

Jung found that the new centre expressed itself in quaternity symbols and circular structures which he called "mandalas," the Sanskrit name applied to images of this kind which, in the East, are used for meditation. Mandalas symbolize an integrating factor. In cases where consciousness is confused, mandalas may appear as compensatory attempts at self-healing by imposing an ordered structure. The self, of which the mandala is a symbol, is the archetype of unity and totality. Jung believed that this archetype was the underlying reality manifesting itself in the various systems of monotheism. The self, therefore, is the God within; and the individual, in seeking self-realization and unity, becomes the means through which "God seeks his goal." (CW 10, par. 588) By fulfilling his own highest potential, the individual is not only realizing the meaning of life, but also fulfilling God's will.

Jung believed that only exceptional individuals reached the peaks of individual development. Individuation means parting company with the crowd; and this at first accentuates loneliness, and may seem alarming. Most human beings are content to remain safely with the majority, conforming to the conventions and beliefs shared by members of their family, church or political party. But exceptional individuals are impelled by their inner nature to seek their own path; and, although human psyches, like human bodies, share a basic structure, the individual psyche is "an endlessly varied recombination of age-old components". (MDR, p. 223/235) Jung continued to affirm that the highest ideals and values were carried by the individual, never by an ideology or the State.

Jung's major contribution to psychology, therefore, lies in the field of *adult* development. Freud and his followers were primarily interested in the earliest development of the young child, since they considered that the majority of neuroses originated in the first five years of life. Freudian analysis had as its aim the reconstruction and recall of the patient's earliest years. It was assumed that, when the repressed, infantile material had been made conscious, the patient would become free of the malign effects of his childhood and lose the neurotic symptoms which were its consequence. Freudian analysis, therefore, was, and is, primarily orientated toward the patient's past.

Jung, of course, was well aware of the importance of early childhood in determining personality development. Indeed, in cases in which it was clear that the patient's primary problem was emancipating himself from the influence of home and parents, Jung advocated proceeding along Freudian or Adlerian lines. But Jung was inclined to leave such analyses to others. The patients who interested him were those who had already freed themselves from the past sufficiently to become established in their own right; who were often successful in worldly terms; but who, in the mid-period of their lives, found that the world had become stale and unprofitable. Such people were seeking a meaning to their lives; and Jung's aim was to guide them along the path of individuation. Jungian analysis, therefore, was, and is, primarily orientated toward the patient's future.

The quest for a new synthesis of personality involves taking into account those parts of the whole which have been neglected. As pointed out above, Jung found that those who consulted him because of the emptiness of their lives were one-sided in their development: too much identified with their predominant attitude and function. Since everyone has both an extraverted and an introverted potential, and also needs all four functions (thinking, feeling, sensation and intuition) if he is to live life fully, it follows that one task of analysis is to help the patient become aware of neglected aspects of his personality. Such aspects appear in dreams; and the study of dreams became even more important in Jungian analysis than in its Freudian counterpart.

Another technique developed by Jung was that of "active imagination." Jung encouraged his patients to enter a state of reverie in which judgment was suspended but consciousness preserved. They were then enjoined to note what fantasies occurred to them, and to let these fantasies go their own way without interference. Jung encouraged his patients to draw and paint their fantasies, finding that this technique both helped the patient to rediscover hidden parts of himself and also portrayed the psychological journey upon which he was embarked. Jung was the first analyst to supplement verbal exchange in this way; and the increasing use of painting, modelling and music in therapy bears witness to Jung's prescience.

In times when so much importance is attributed to good or bad interpersonal relationships as determinants of mental health or illness, Jung's concentration upon the individual's relations with the different parts of his own psyche may seem puzzling. Jung was well aware of the importance of interpersonal relationships, but believed that it was only when the individual had come to terms with himself that satisfactory relationships with others could be achieved. Jung wrote: "Companionship thrives only when each individual remembers his individuality and does not identify himself with others." (MDR, p. 328/356)

Individuation is not the same as individualism, "which is essentially no more than a morbid reaction against an equally futile collectivism. In contrast to all this, the natural process of individuation brings to birth a consciousness of human community precisely because it makes us aware of the unconscious, which unites and is common to all mankind." (CW 16, par. 227)

Although Jung claimed that what he discovered were facts which anyone else who adopted the same technique would confirm, he was also aware that subjective factors were bound to influence his point of view. "Philosophical criticism has helped me to see that every psychology – my own included – has the character of a subjective confession ... Even when I am dealing with empirical data I am necessarily speaking about myself." (CW 4, par. 774) It may be helpful to glance at some of the influences which contributed to Jung's particular viewpoint.

For the first nine years of his life, Jung remained an only child who lived primarily in his imagination and who spent much of his time in solitary play. When he first went to school, he found that, in trying to adapt to his rural companions, he tended to become alienated from himself, as sensitive and imaginative people often do when trying too hard to "fit in." It became important to him to preserve his inner imaginative world from intrusion. In his autobiography, he describes various secret rituals by means of which he kept contact with his inner world and shielded it from others. In the "Late Thoughts" which form part of his autobiography, Jung wrote: "There is no better means of intensifying the treasured feeling of individuality than the possession of a secret which the individual is pledged to guard." (MDR, p. 315/342) In the last chapter of the same book, he wrote: "As a child I felt myself to be alone, and I am still, because I know things and must hint at things which others apparently know nothing of, and for the most part do not want to know." (MDR, p. 327/356) Jung's childhood discovery of the vital importance of remaining in touch with the inner world is one factor accounting for his emphasis on healing and the growth of personality as essentially an inner process, concentrating upon the individual's relation with the various aspects of his own psyche, rather than upon his relationships with other human beings.

From his earliest years, Jung was exposed to a great deal of discussion of religious matters. His father was a minister in the Swiss Reformed Church; two of his uncles were parsons; and there were no less than six parsons in his mother's family. Very early in his life, so Jung records, he experienced dreams and visions of a religious kind which convinced him not only that religious experience was a personal matter which might have little to do with established creeds, but also that God had a "dark" side which did not accord with the conventional Christian image of an ever-loving father. His own father was content to promulgate the teachings of his church, though Jung came to question the genuineness of his faith. He was unable, or unwilling, to discuss the doubts with which his more gifted son confronted him. Jung, therefore, found himself in the position of being unable to subscribe to the faith in which he had been reared, while at the same time continuing to think that individuals could neither be happy nor healthy unless they acknowledged their dependence upon some higher power than that of the ego. Jung himself became one of those exceptional individuals who so much interested him as patients: individuals who were compelled by their own natures to strike out on their own, abandon conventional beliefs and find what they were seeking within their own psyches. Although Jung continued to profess allegiance to what he called "the extreme left wing of Protestantism," his religious ideas became so unconventional that he gave offence to both Catholic and Protestant theologians, although some from both camps continued to find value in what Jung had to say.

Another important factor determining Jung's psychological standpoint was the period of mental upheaval through which he passed in the years of the First World War, just after his break with Freud. Although, as we shall see, Jung was never a disciple of Freud, and had carried out a good deal of original work before he had even met him, Freud was a powerful influence, and separating from him was extremely painful. It was because Jung felt that he had to be true to his own inner voice that the break occurred; for Freud's tolerance of any divergence from the "truths" which he believed he had discovered was limited. At the time of parting, Jung was thirty-eight. Jung's insistence that the mid-life period was a turning point in psychological development took origin from his own experience.

Like many solitary thinkers, Jung was always an avid reader, and, while still an adolescent, plunged into Kant and Schopenhauer. The latter's sombre view especially appealed to him. "Here at last was a philosopher who had the courage to see that all was not for the best in the fundaments of the universe." (MDR, p. 76/69) Although there are profound differences between Jung's thought and that of Schopenhauer, there are also striking similarities. Schopenhauer considered that individuals were the embodiments of an underlying Will which was outside space and time. Jung begins his autobiography by writing: "My life is a story of the self-realization of the unconscious." (MDR, p. 17/3) Schopenhauer considered that the very notion of individuality, the *principium individuationis*, is dependent on the human, subjective categories of space and time which force us to be conscious of individual objects, and prevent us from seeing the original unity of the Will of which individuals are a manifestation. Jung also believed that there was a realm outside space and time from which individuals become differentiated. Borrowing the Gnostic term, he referred to this spiritual realm transcending consciousness as the *pleroma*. "We are distinguished from the pleroma in our essence ... which is confined within time and space." *Septem Sermones ad Mortuos*, I) Whereas in the pleroma all is one and there is no differentiation between opposites like good and evil, light and darkness, time and space, or force and matter, the *principium individuationis* compels distinctiveness which is the essential characteristic of individuals. Whereas Schopenhauer's philosophy is governed by the ideal of deliverance from the bonds of individuality by means of self-denial and asceticism (an ideal which Schopenhauer himself was far from realizing), Jung's philosophy is ruled by the idea of affirmation of individuality. A man who understands and comes to terms with the different aspects of his inner being is enabled to live life more completely. Jung was also influenced by Nietzsche, who was a passionate individualist; but, whereas Nietzsche stated that God was dead, Jung rediscovered God as a guiding principle of unity within the depths of the individual psyche.

Jung's belief in the ultimate unity of all existence led him to suppose that physical and mental, as well as spatial and temporal, were human categories imposed upon reality which did not accurately reflect it. Human beings, because of the nature of thought and language, are bound to categorize things as opposites; that is, all human statements are antinomian. But these opposites may, in fact, be facets of the same reality. Through his collaboration with the physicist Wolfgang Pauli, Jung came to believe that the physicist's investigation of matter and the psychologist's investigation of the depths of the psyche might be different ways of approaching the same underlying reality. It had long been recognized that analytical psychology could never be wholly "objective," since the observer was bound to exert an effect on what he was observing by the fact of paying it attention. But the same point had also been reached in modern physics. At the subatomic level, it was recognized that it was impossible to determine a particle's momentum and its velocity at the same time. Moreover, the constituents of matter could be considered to behave as waves or particles, depending on the choice of the observer. Physicists came to realize that it was possible to look at one and the same event through two different frames of reference which, though mutually exclusive, were nevertheless complementary. The Principle of Complementarity, which became a cornerstone of modern physics, could also be applied to the mind-body problem. Perhaps mind and body were simply different aspects of a single reality as viewed through different frames of reference.

Jung claimed that there were "sufficient reasons" for believing that "the psychic lies embedded in something that appears to be of a nonpsychic nature." (CW 8, par. 437) Jung came to think of archetypes as existing in this reality outside space and time, but manifesting themselves in the individual psyche as organizers. "Archetypes, so far as we can observe and explain them at all, manifest themselves only through their ability to *organize* images and ideas, and this is always an unconscious process which cannot be detected until afterwards. By assimilating material whose provenance in the phenomenal world is not to be contested, they become visible and *psychic*." (CW 8, par. 440) One reason why Jung thought of archetypes as existing outside space and time was that he believed them responsible for what he called "meaningful coincidences," of which examples are given in the extracts which follow. Throughout his life, Jung had been impressed by clusters of significant events occurring together, and by the fact that these events might be physical as well as mental. The physical death of one individual, for example, might coincide with a disturbing dream referring to that death in the mind of another. Jung felt that such coincidences, which he considered "relatively common," demanded an explanatory principle in addition to causality. This principle he named *synchronicity*. Once again, Jung seems to have been influenced by Schopenhauer, who had postulated a link between simultaneous events which were causally unconnected. Jung's idea was that synchronicity was based on a universal order of *meaning*, complementary to causality. He thought that synchronistic phenomena were connected with archetypes which he referred to as *psychoid* factors of the collective unconscious, meaning by this that archetypes were neither physical nor mental but partaking of both realms, and able, therefore, to manifest themselves both physically and mentally simultaneously. Jung refers to the case of Swedenborg, who experienced a vision of a fire in Stockholm at the same time as an actual fire was raging. Jung considered that some change in Swedenborg's state of mind gave him temporary access to "absolute knowledge"; to an area in which the limits of space and time are transcended. Jung believed that causeless events were creative acts "as the continuous creation of a pattern that exists from all eternity, repeats itself sporadically, and is not derivable from any known antecedents." (CW 8, par. 967) The recognition of patterns of order affects human beings as *meaning*.

In Jung's view, changes in the collective unconscious, which might take centuries to complete themselves, were responsible for alterations in the way in which men viewed the world and thought about themselves. The decline in conventional Christian belief, for example, is related to the fact that the Christ-image, which excludes both evil and the feminine, can no longer symbolize wholeness for modern man. It was only in 1950 that the Pope proclaimed the Assumption of the Virgin Mary as part of divine revelation. Jung considered this as a significant step toward incorporating femininity into the image of the divine, and pointed out that the impulse to do this did not come from the ecclesiastical authorities but from the Catholic masses "who have insisted more and more vehemently on this development. Their insistence is, at bottom, the urge of the archetype to realize itself" (CW 9 ii, par. 142) and it took many years for this to be accomplished.

I hope that this brief introduction to Jung's thought will make it easier for the reader to find his way through the extracts which follow. Some may find Jung's later writings difficult or antipathetic; but Jung's valuable contributions to psychotherapy and to the understanding of individuals can be appreciated without subscribing to the whole of his system of belief.

Part 1. Jung's Early Work

Jung began his career in psychiatry in December 1900, when he was appointed as an assistant physician at the Burghölzli mental hospital in Zurich. Breuer and Freud had published their Studies on Hysteria *in 1895; and Freud's* The Interpretation of Dreams *had appeared in November 1899. But psychiatrists were still fascinated by the researches of Janet and Morton Prince into cases of "multiple personality," and it was this phenomenon which inspired Jung's first published work: his dissertation for his medical degree, "On the Psychology and Pathology of So-called Occult Phenomena." This was based on his observations during seances of a 15½-year-old cousin, Hélène Preiswerk (called S. W. in the paper), who was reputedly a medium. She claimed to be controlled by a variety of spirits, varying from her grandfather, who was deeply serious, to a figure called Ulrich von Gerbenstein, who was flirtatious and frivolous. Jung interpreted these various figures as "unconscious personalities."*

From "On the Psychology and Pathology of So-called Occult Phenomena" CW 1, par. 77

In our account of S. W.'s case, the following condition was indicated by the term "semi-somnambulism": For some time before and after the actual somnambulistic attack the patient found herself in a state whose most salient feature can best be described as "preoccupation". She lent only half an ear to the conversation around her, answered absent-mindedly, frequently lost herself in all manner of hallucinations; her face was solemn, her look ecstatic, visionary, ardent. Closer observation revealed a far-reaching alteration of her entire character. She was now grave, dignified; when she spoke, the theme was always an extremely serious one. In this state she could talk so seriously, so forcefully and convincingly, that one almost had to ask oneself: Is this really a girl of 15½? One had the impression that a mature woman was being acted with considerable dramatic talent.

Jung goes on to compare S. W. with a case of Janet's.

CW 1, pars. 92–3

Janet conducted the following conversation with the subconscious of Lucie, who, meanwhile, was engaged in conversation with another observer:

[Janet asks:] Do you hear me? [Lucie answers, in automatic writing:] *No.*
But one has to hear in order to answer. – *Absolutely.*
Then how do you do it? – *I don't know.*
There must be someone who hears me. – *Yes.*
Who is it? – *Somebody besides Lucie.*
All right. Somebody else. Shall we give the other person a name? – *No.*
Yes, it will be more convenient. – *All right. Adrienne.*
Well, Adrienne, do you hear me? – *Yes.*

One can see from these extracts how the unconscious personality builds itself up: it owes its existence simply to suggestive questions which strike an answering chord in the medium's own disposition. This disposition can be explained by the disaggregation of psychic complexes, and the feeling of strangeness evoked by these automatisms assists the process as soon as conscious attention is directed to the automatic act. Binet remarks on this experiment of Janet's: "Nevertheless it should be carefully noted that if the personality of 'Adrienne' could be created, it was because the suggestion encountered a *psychological possibility*; in other words, disaggregated phenomena were existing there apart from the normal consciousness of the subject."* The individualization of the subconscious is always a great step forward and has enormous suggestive influence on further development of the automatisms.

*Alfred Binet, *Alterations of Personality*, tr. Helen Green Baldwin, London: 1896, p. 147.

The formation of unconscious personalities in our case must also be regarded in this light.

Returning to his own case, Jung discusses the "Origin of the Unconscious Personalities."

CW 1, pars. 132–3

As we have seen, the various personalities are grouped round two types, the grandfather and Ulrich von Gerbenstein. The grandfather produces nothing but sanctimonious twaddle and edifying moral precepts. Ulrich von Gerbenstein is simply a silly schoolgirl, with nothing masculine about him except his name. We must here add, from the anamnesis, that the patient was confirmed at the age of fifteen by a very pietistic clergyman, and that even at home she had to listen to moral sermons. The grandfather represents this side of her past, Gerbenstein the other half; hence the curious contrast. So here we have, personified, the chief characters of the past: here the compulsorily educated bigot, there the boisterousness of a lively girl of fifteen who often goes too far. The patient herself is a peculiar mixture of both; sometimes timid, shy, excessively reserved, at other times boisterous to the point of indecency. She is often painfully conscious of these contrasts. This gives us the key to the origin of the two subconscious personalities. The patient is obviously seeking a middle way between two extremes; she endeavours to repress them and strives for a more ideal state. These strivings lead to the adolescent dream of the ideal Ivenes, beside whom the unrefined aspects of her character fade into the background. They are not lost; but as repressed thoughts, analogous to the idea of Ivenes, they begin to lead an independent existence as autonomous personalities.

This behaviour calls to mind Freud's dream investigations, which disclose the independent growth of repressed thoughts.

The idea that personality was not a unity, but might contain subsidiary personalities was familiar to Jung from his own experience, since he records his surprise, at the age of twelve, at finding that he himself was two different persons.

From "**School Years**" MDR, pp. 44–6/33–4

Around this time I was invited to spend the holidays with friends of the family who had a house on Lake Lucerne. To my delight the house was situated right on the lake, and there was a boat-house and a rowing boat. My host allowed his son and me to use the boat, although we were sternly warned not to be reckless. Unfortunately I also knew how to steer a *Waidling* (a boat of the gondola type) – that is to say, standing. At home we had such a punt, in which we had tried out every imaginable trick. The first thing I did, therefore, was to take my stand on the stern seat and with one oar push off into the lake. That was too much for the anxious master of the house. He whistled us back and gave me a first-class dressing-down. I was thoroughly crestfallen but had to admit that I had done exactly what he had said not to, and that his lecture was quite justified. At the same time I was seized with rage that this fat, ignorant boor should dare to insult ME. This ME was not only grown up, but important, an authority, a person with office and dignity, an old man, an object of respect and awe. Yet the contrast with reality was so grotesque that in the midst of my fury I suddenly stopped myself, for the question rose to my lips: "Who in the world are you, anyway? You are reacting as though you were the devil only knows how important! And yet you know he is perfectly right. You are barely twelve years old, a schoolboy, and he is a father and a rich, powerful man besides, who owns two houses and several splendid horses."

Then, to my intense confusion, it occurred to me that I was actually two different persons. One of them was the schoolboy who could not grasp algebra and was far from sure of himself; the other was important, a high authority, a man not to be trifled with, as powerful and influential as this manufacturer. This "Other" was an old man who lived in the eighteenth century, wore buckled shoes and a white wig and went driving in a fly with high, concave rear wheels between which the box was suspended on springs and leather straps.

This notion sprang from a curious experience I had had. When we were living in Klein-Hüningen an ancient green carriage from the Black Forest drove past our house one day. It was truly an antique, looking exactly as if it had come straight out of the eighteenth century. When I saw it, I felt with great excitement: "That's it! Sure enough, that comes from *my* times." It was as though I had recognized it because it was the same type as the one I had driven in myself. Then came a curious *sentiment écoeurant*, as though someone had stolen something from me, or as though I had been cheated – cheated out of my beloved past. The carriage was a relic of those times! I cannot describe what was happening in me or what it was that affected me so strongly: a longing, a nostalgia, or a recognition that kept saying "Yes, that's how it was! Yes, that's how it was!"

When Jung began work at the Burghölzli mental hospital, word-association tests were used as a means of studying the way in which mental contents are linked together by similarity, contrast or contiguity in space and time. Jung transformed their use into a tool for investigating emotional preoccupations; and his researches led him to formulate the notion of the "complex," a term which he introduced.

From "**Tavistock Lecture II**" CW 18, pars. 97–106

First of all I want to say something about *word-association tests*. To many of you perhaps these seem old-fashioned, but since they are still being used I have to refer to them. I use this test now not with patients but with criminal cases.

The experiment is made – I am repeating well-known things – with a list of say a hundred words. You instruct the test person to react with the first word that comes into his mind as quickly as possible after having heard and understood the stimulus word. When you have made sure that the test person has understood what you mean you start the experiment. You mark the time of each reaction with a stop-watch. When you have finished the hundred words you do another experiment. You repeat the stimulus words and the test person has to reproduce his former answers. In certain places his memory fails and reproduction becomes uncertain or faulty. These mistakes are important.

Originally the experiment was not meant for its present application at all; it was intended to be used for the study of mental association. That was of course a most Utopian idea. One can study nothing of the sort by such primitive means. But you can study something else when the experiment fails, when people make mistakes. You ask a simple word that a child can answer, and a highly intelligent person cannot reply. Why? That word has hit on what I call a complex, a conglomeration of psychic contents characterized by a peculiar or perhaps painful feeling-tone, something that is usually hidden from sight. It is as though a projectile struck through the thick layer of the *persona* into the dark layer. For instance, somebody with a money complex will be hit when you say: "To buy," "to pay," or "money." That is a disturbance of reaction.

We have about twelve or more categories of disturbance and I will mention a few of them so that you will get an idea of their practical value. The prolongation of the reaction time is of the greatest practical importance. You decide whether the reaction time is too long by taking the average mean of the reaction times of the test person. Other characteristic disturbances are: reaction with more than one word, against the instructions; mistakes in reproduction of the word; reaction expressed by facial expression, laughing, movement of the hands or feet or body, coughing, stammering, and such things; insufficient reactions like "yes" or "no"; not reacting to the real meaning of the stimulus word; habitual use of the same words; use of foreign languages – of which there is not a great danger in England, though with us it is a great nuisance; defective reproduction, when memory begins to fail in the reproduction experiment; total lack of reaction.

All these reactions are beyond the control of the will. If you submit to the experiment you are done for, and if you do not submit to it you are done for too, because one knows why you are unwilling to do so. If you put it to a criminal he can refuse, and that is fatal because one knows why he refuses. If he gives in he hangs himself. In Zurich I am called in by the Court when they have a difficult case; I am the last straw.

The results of the association test can be illustrated very neatly by a diagram (Figure 5). The height of the columns represents the actual reaction time of the test person. The dotted horizontal line represents the average mean of reaction times. The unshaded columns are those reactions which show no signs of disturbance.

The shaded columns show disturbed reactions. In reactions 7, 8, 9, 10, you observe for instance a whole series of disturbances: the stimulus word at 7 was a critical one, and without the test person noticing it at all three subsequent reaction times are overlong on account of the perseveration of the reaction to the stimulus

Figure 5. Association Test

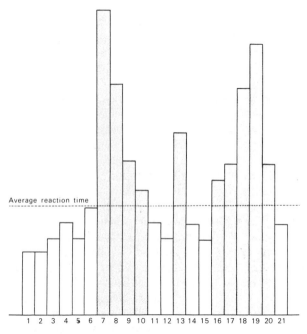

Average reaction time

1 2 3 4 5 6 7 8 9 10 11 12 13 14 15 16 17 18 19 20 21

Stimulus words
 7 knife
13 lance (= spear)
16 to beat
18 pointed
19 bottle

word. The test person was quite unconscious of the fact that he had an emotion. Reaction 13 shows an isolated disturbance, and in 16–20 the result is again a whole series of disturbances. The strongest disturbances are in reactions 18 and 19. In this particular case we have to do with a so-called intensification of sensitiveness through the sensitizing effect of an unconscious emotion: when a critical stimulus word has aroused a perseverating emotional reaction, and when the next critical stimulus word happens to occur within the range of that perseveration, then it is apt to produce a greater effect than it would have been expected to produce if it had occurred in a series of indifferent associations. This is called the sensitizing effect of a perseverating emotion.

In dealing with criminal cases we can make use of the sensitizing effect, and then we arrange the critical stimulus words in such a way that they occur more or less within the presumable range of perseveration. This can be done in order to increase the effect of critical stimulus words. With a suspected culprit as a test person, the critical stimulus words are words which have a direct bearing upon the crime.

The test person for Figure 5 was a man about 35, a decent individual, one of my normal test persons. I had of course to experiment with a great number of normal people before I could draw conclusions from pathological material. If you want to know what it was that disturbed this man, you simply have to read the words that caused the disturbances and fit them together. Then you get a nice story. I will tell you exactly what it was.

To begin with, it was the word *knife* that caused four disturbed reactions. The next disturbance was *lance* (or *spear*) and then *to beat*, then the word *pointed* and then *bottle*. That was in a short series of fifty stimulus words, which was enough for me to tell the man point-blank what the matter was. So I said: "I did not know you had had such a disagreeable experience." He stared at me and said: "I do not know what you are talking about." I said: "You know you were drunk and had a disagreeable affair with sticking your knife into somebody." He said: "How do you know?" Then he confessed the whole thing. He came of a respectable family, simple but quite nice people. He had been abroad and one day got into a drunken quarrel, drew a knife and stuck it into somebody, and got a year in prison. That is a great secret which he does not mention because it would cast a shadow on his life. Nobody in his town or surroundings knows anything about it and I am the only one who by chance stumbled upon it. In my seminar in Zurich I also make these experiments. Those who want to confess are of course welcome to. However, I always ask them to bring some material of a person *they* know and *I* do not know, and I show them how to read the story of that individual. It is quite interesting work; sometimes one makes remarkable discoveries.

I will give you other instances. Many years ago, when I was quite a young doctor, an old professor of criminology asked me about the experiment and said he did not believe in it. I said: "No, Professor? You can try it whenever you like." He invited me to his house and I began. After ten words he got tired and said: "What can you make of it? Nothing has come of it." I told him he could not expect a result with ten or twelve words; he ought to have a hundred and then we could see something. He said: "Can you do something with these words?" I said: "Little enough, but I can tell you something. Quite recently you have had worries about money, you have too little of it. You are afraid of dying of heart disease. You must have studied in France, where you had a love affair, and it has come back to your mind, as often, when one has thoughts of dying, old sweet memories come back from the womb of time." He said: "How do you know?" Any child could have seen it! He was a man of 72 and he had associated *heart* with *pain* – fear that he would die of heart failure. He associated *death* with *to die* – a natural reaction – and with *money* he associated *too little*, a very usual reaction. Then things became rather startling to me. To *pay*, after a long reaction time, he said *La Semeuse*, though our conversation was in German. That is the famous figure on the French coin. Now why on earth should this old man say *La Semeuse*? When he came to the word *kiss* there was a long reaction time and there was a light in his eyes and he said: *Beautiful*. Then of course I had the story. He would never have used French if it had not been associated with a particular feeling, and so we must think why he used it. Had he had losses with the French franc? There was no talk of inflation and devaluation in those days. That could not be the clue. I was in doubt whether it was money or love, but when he came to *kiss/beautiful* I knew it was love. He was not the kind of man to go to France in later life, but he had been a student in Paris, a lawyer, probably at the Sorbonne. It was relatively simple to stitch together the whole story.

Jung soon began to link the idea of complexes with that of "unconscious personalities."

From "**A Review of the Complex Theory**" CW 8, pars. 200–3

So far, I have purposely avoided discussing the nature of complexes, on the tacit assumption that their nature is generally known. The word "complex" in its psychological sense has passed into common speech both in German and in English. Everyone knows nowadays that people "have complexes." What is not so well known, though far more important theoretically, is that complexes *can have us*. The existence of complexes throws serious doubt on the naïve assumption of the unity of consciousness, which is equated with "psyche," and on the supremacy of the will. Every constellation of a complex postulates a disturbed state of consciousness. The unity of consciousness is disrupted and the intentions of the will are impeded or made impossible. Even memory is often noticeably affected, as we have seen. The complex must therefore be a psychic factor which, in terms of energy, possesses a value that sometimes exceeds that of our conscious intentions, otherwise such disruptions of the conscious order would not be possible at all. And in fact, an active complex puts us momentarily under a state of duress, of compulsive thinking and acting, for which under certain conditions the only appropriate term would be the judicial concept of diminished responsibility.

What then, scientifically speaking, is a "feeling toned complex"? It is the *image* of a certain psychic situation which is strongly accentuated emotionally and is, moreover, incompatible with the habitual attitude of consciousness. This image has a powerful inner coherence, it has its own wholeness and, in addition, a relatively high degree of autonomy, so that it is subject to the control of the conscious mind to only a limited extent, and therefore behaves like an animated foreign body in the sphere of consciousness. The complex can usually be suppressed with an effort of will, but not argued out of existence, and at the first suitable opportunity it reappears in all its original strength. Certain experimental investigations seem to indicate that its intensity or activity curve has a wavelike character, with a "wave-length" of hours, days, or weeks. This very complicated question remains as yet unclarified.

We have to thank the French psychopathologists, Pierre Janet in particular, for our knowledge today of the extreme *dissociability* of consciousness. Janet and Morton Prince both succeeded in producing four to five splittings of the personality, and it turned out that each fragment of personality had its own peculiar character and its own separate memory. These fragments subsist relatively independently of one another and can take one another's place at any time, which means that each fragment possesses a high degree of autonomy. My findings in regard to complexes corroborate this somewhat disquieting picture of the possibilities of psychic disintegration, for fundamentally there is no difference in principle between a fragmentary personality and a complex. They have all the essential features in common, until we come to the delicate question of fragmented consciousness. Personality fragments undoubtedly have their own consciousness, but whether such small psychic fragments as complexes are also capable of a consciousness of their own is a still unanswered question. I must confess that this question has often occupied my thoughts, for complexes behave like Descartes' devils and seem to delight in playing impish tricks. They slip just the wrong word into one's mouth, they make one forget the name of the person one is about to introduce, they cause a tickle in the throat just when the softest passage is being played on the piano at a concert, they make the tiptoeing latecomer trip over a chair with a resounding crash. They bid us congratulate the mourners at a burial instead of condoling with them, they are the instigators of all those maddening things which F. T. Vischer atributed to the "mischievousness of the object." They are the actors in our dreams, whom we confront so powerlessly; they are the elfin beings so aptly characterized in Danish folklore by the story of the clergyman who tried to teach the Lord's prayer to two elves. They took the greatest pains to repeat the words after him correctly, but at the very first sentence they could not avoid saying: "Our Father, who art not in heaven." As one might expect on theoretical grounds, these impish complexes are unteachable.

I hope that, taking it with a very large grain of salt, no one will mind this metaphorical paraphrase of a scientific problem. But even the soberest formulation of the phenomenology of complexes cannot get round the impressive fact of their autonomy, and the deeper one penetrates into their nature – I might almost say into their biology – the more clearly do they reveal their character as *splinter psyches*. Dream psychology shows us as plainly as could be wished how complexes appear in personified form when there is no inhibiting consciousness to suppress them, exactly like the hobgoblins of folklore who go crashing round the house at night. We observe the same phenomenon in certain psychoses when the complexes get "loud" and appear as "voices" having a thoroughly personal character.

In 1907, Jung published The Psychology of Dementia Praecox *(the current name for what is now called schizophrenia). He sent the book to Freud, and it was this which led to Freud's invitation to Jung to visit him in Vienna. Jung retained an interest in schizophrenia throughout his life, and wrote a paper on the condition as recently as 1957, only four years before his death.*

From "**Mental Disease and the Psyche**" CW 3, pars. 498–503

In 1907 I came before the scientific public with a book on the psychology of dementia praecox. By and large, I adopted a standpoint affirming the psychogenesis of schizophrenia, and emphasized that the symptoms (delusions and hallucinations) are not just meaningless chance happenings but, as regards their content, are in every respect significant psychic products. This means that schizophrenia has a "psychology," i.e., a psychic causality and finality, just as normal mental life has, though with this important difference: whereas in the healthy person the ego is the subject of his experience, in the schizophrenic the ego is only *one* of the experiencing subjects. In other words, in schizophrenia the normal subject has split into a plurality of subjects, or into a plurality of *autonomous complexes*.

The simplest form of schizophrenia, of the splitting of the personality, is paranoia, the classic persecution-mania of the "persécuteur persécuté." It consists in a simple doubling of the personality, which in milder cases is still held together by the identity of the two egos. The patient strikes us at first as completely normal; he may hold office, be in a lucrative position, we suspect nothing. We converse normally with him, and at some point we let fall the word "Freemason." Suddenly the jovial face before us changes, a piercing look full of abysmal mistrust and inhuman fanaticism meets us from his eye. He has become a hunted, dangerous animal, surrounded by invisible enemies: the other ego has risen to the surface.

What has happened? Obviously at some time or other the idea of being a persecuted victim gained the upper hand, became autonomous, and formed a second subject which at times completely replaces the healthy ego. It is characteristic that neither of the two subjects can fully experience the other, although the two personalities are not separated by a belt of unconsciousness as they are in an hysterical dissociation of the personality. They know each other intimately, but they have no valid arguments against one another. The healthy ego cannot counter the affectivity of the other, for at least half its affectivity has gone over into its opposite number. It is, so to speak, paralysed. This is the beginning of that schizophrenic "apathy" which can be observed in paranoid dementia. The patient can assure you with the greatest indifference: "I am the triple owner of the world, the finest Turkey, the Lorelei, Germania and Helvetia of exclusively sweet butter and Naples and I must supply the whole world with macaroni." All this without a blush, and with no flicker of a smile. Here there are countless subjects and no central ego to experience anything and react emotionally.

Turning back to our case of paranoia, we must ask: Is it psychologically meaningless that the idea of persecution has taken possession of him and usurped a part of his personality? Is it, in other words, simply a product of some chance organic disturbance of the brain? If that were so, the delusion would be "unpsychological"; it would lack psychological causality and finality, and would not be psychogenic. But should it be found that the pathological idea did not appear just by chance, that it appeared at a particular psychological moment, then we would have to speak of psychogenesis, even if we assumed that there had always been a predisposing factor in the brain which was partly responsible for the disease.

The psychological moment must certainly be something out of the ordinary; it must have something about it that would adequately explain why it had such a profound and dangerous effect. If someone is frightened by a mouse and then falls ill with schizophrenia, this is obviously not a psychic causation, which is always intricate and subtle. Thus our paranoiac fell ill long before anyone suspected his illness; and secondly, the pathological idea overwhelmed him at a psychological moment. This happened when his congenitally hypersensitive emotional life became warped, and the spiritual form which his emotions needed in order to live finally broke down. It did not break by itself, it was broken by the patient. It came about in the following way.

When still a sensitive youth, but already equipped with a powerful intellect, he developed a passionate love for his sister-in-law, until finally – and not unnaturally – it displeased her husband, his elder brother. His were boyish feelings, woven mostly out of moonshine, seeking the mother, like all psychic impulses that are immature. But these feelings really do need a mother, they need prolonged incubation in order to grow strong and to withstand the unavoidable clash with reality. In themselves there is nothing reprehensible about them, but to the simple, straightforward mind they arouse suspicion. The harsh interpretation which his brother put upon them had a devastating effect, because the patient's own mind admitted that it was right. His dream was destroyed, but this in itself would not have been harmful had it not also killed his feelings. For his intellect then took over the role of the brother and, with inquisitorial sternness, destroyed every trace of feeling, holding before him the ideal of cold-blooded heartlessness. A less passionate nature can put up with this for a time, but a highly-strung, sensitive nature in need of affection will be broken. Gradually it seemed to him that he had attained his ideal, when suddenly he discovered that waiters and suchlike people took a curious interest in him, smiling at one another understandingly, and one day he made the startling discovery that they took him for a homosexual. The paranoid idea had now become autonomous. It is easy to see the deeper connection between the pitilessness of his intellect, which cold-bloodedly destroyed every feeling, and his unshakable paranoid conviction. That is psychic causality, psychogenesis.

In some such way – naturally with endless variations – not only does paranoia arise, but also the paranoid form of schizophrenia characterized by delusions and hallucinations, and indeed all other forms of schizophrenia. (I would not class among the group of schizophrenias those schizophrenic syndromes, such as catatonias with a rapidly lethal outcome, which seem from the beginning to have an organic basis.) The microscopic lesions of the brain often found in schizophrenia I would, for the time being, regard as secondary symptoms of degeneration, like the atrophy of the muscles in hysterical paralyses. The psychogenesis of schizophrenia would explain why certain milder cases, which do not get as far as the mental hospital but only appear in the neurologist's consulting-room, can be cured by psychotherapeutic means. With regard to the possibility of cure, however, one should not be too optimistic. Such cases are rare. The very nature of the disease, involving as it does the disintegration of the personality, rules out the possibility of psychic influence, which is the essential agent in therapy. Schizophrenia shares this peculiarity with obsessional neurosis, its nearest relative in the realm of the neuroses.

From "On the Psychogenesis of Schizophrenia" CW 3, pars. 539–40

Two facts have impressed themselves on me during my career as a psychiatrist and psychotherapist. One is the enormous change that the average mental hospital has undergone in my lifetime. That whole desperate crowd of utterly degenerate catatonics has practically disappeared, simply because they have been given something to do. The other fact that impressed me is the discovery I made when I began my psychotherapeutic practice: I was amazed at the number of schizophrenics whom we almost never see in psychiatric hospitals. These cases are partially camouflaged as obsessional neuroses, compulsions, phobias, and hysterias, and they are very careful never to go near an asylum. These patients insist upon treatment, and I found myself, Bleuler's loyal disciple, trying my hand on cases we never would have dreamed of touching if we had had them in the clinic, cases unmistakably schizophrenic even before treatment – I felt hopelessly unscientific in treating them at all – and after the treatment I was told that they could never have been schizophrenic in the first place. There are numbers of latent psychoses – and quite a few that are not so latent – which, under favourable conditions, can be subjected to psychological analysis, sometimes with quite decent results. Even if I am not very hopeful about a patient, I try to give him as much psychology as he can stand, because I have seen plenty of cases where the later attacks were less severe, and the prognosis was better, as a result of increased psychological understanding. At least so it seemed to me. You know how difficult it is to judge these things correctly. In such doubtful matters, where you have to work as a pioneer, you must be able to put some trust in your intuition and to follow your feeling even at the risk of going wrong. To make a correct diagnosis, and to nod your head gravely at a bad prognosis, is the less important aspect of the medical art. It can even cripple your enthusiasm, and in psychotherapy enthusiasm is the secret of success.

The results of occupational therapy in mental hospitals have clearly shown that the status of hopeless cases can be enormously improved. And the much milder cases not in hospitals sometimes show encouraging results under psychotherapeutic treatment. I do not want to appear overoptimistic. Often enough one can do little or nothing at all; or again, one can have unexpected results. For about fourteen years I have been seeing a woman, who is now sixty-four years of age. I never see her more than fifteen times in the course of a year. She is a schizophrenic and has twice spent a number of months in hospital with an acute psychosis. She suffers from numberless voices distributed all over her body. I found one voice which was fairly reasonable and helpful. I tried to cultivate that voice, with the result that for about two years the right side of the body has been free of voices. Only the left side is still under the domination of the unconscious. No further attacks have occurred. Unfortunately, the patient is not intelligent. Her mentality is early medieval, and I was able to establish a fairly good rapport with her only by adapting my terminology to that of the early Middle Ages. There were no hallucinations then; it was all devils and witchcraft.

Part 2. Jung's Involvement with Freud and His Divergence from Freud's Theories

During the years 1907–13, Jung was closely associated with Freud, and deeply influenced by him. The story of the rise and fall of their relationship can be traced and studied in The Freud/Jung Letters. *But, although Jung always acknowledged his debt to Freud, and paid tribute to his originality, he was never a whole-hearted "Freudian." For example, in his introduction to* The Psychology of Dementia Praecox, *dated July 1906, Jung writes:*

Fairness to Freud, however, does not imply, as many fear, unqualified submission to a dogma; one can very well maintain an independent judgment. If I, for instance, acknowledge the complex mechanisms of dreams and hysteria, this does not mean that I attribute to the infantile sexual trauma the exclusive importance that Freud apparently does. Still less does it mean that I place sexuality so predominantly in the foreground, or that I grant it the psychological universality which Freud, it seems, postulates in view of the admittedly enormous role which sexuality plays in the psyche. As for Freud's therapy, it is at best but one of several possible methods, and perhaps does not always offer in practice what one expects from it in theory. [CW 3, Foreword, p. 4]

And, in a letter to Freud dated 5 October 1906, Jung wrote:

What I can appreciate, and what has helped us here in our psychopathological work, are your psychological views, whereas I am still pretty far from understanding the therapy and the genesis of hysteria because our material on hysteria is rather meagre. That is to say your therapy seems to me to depend not merely on the affects released by abreaction but also on certain personal rapports, and it seems to me that though the genesis of hysteria is predominantly, it is not exclusively sexual. I take the same view of your sexual theory. [*The Freud/Jung Letters*, pp. 4–5]

Freud originally supposed that hysteria was caused by trauma, and that the trauma was both literal and sexual. By the end of 1897, however, Freud realized that the stories which his hysterical patients told him of incestuous seduction were fantasies rather than actual occurrences. Freud then postulated that the cause of neurosis was the "fixation" of the patient at an early stage of emotional development, but continued to assume that the reason for this fixation was to be found in the events of the patient's early childhood without reference to the present. Jung took a different view.

"Psychoanalysis and Neurosis" CW 4, pars. 557–75

After many years' experience I now know that it is extremely difficult to discuss psychoanalysis at public meetings and at congresses. There are so many misconceptions of the matter, so many prejudices against certain psychoanalytic views, that it is an almost impossible task to reach mutual understanding in a public discussion. I have always found a quiet conversation on the subject much more useful and fruitful than heated arguments *coram publico*. However, having been honoured by an invitation from the Committee of this Congress to speak as a representative of the psychoanalytic movement, I will do my best to discuss some of the fundamental theoretical problems of psychoanalysis. I must limit myself to this aspect of the subject because I am quite unable to put before my audience all that psychoanalysis means and strives for, and its various applications in the fields of mythology, comparative religion, philosophy, etc. But if I am to discuss certain theoretical problems fundamental to psychoanalysis, I must presuppose that my audience is familiar with the development and the main results of psychoanalytic research. Unfortunately, it often happens that people think themselves entitled to judge psychoanalysis who have not even read the literature. It is my firm conviction that no one is competent to form an opinion on this matter until he has studied the basic writings of the psychoanalytic school.

In spite of the fact that Freud's theory of neurosis has been worked out in great detail, it cannot be said to be, on the whole, very clear or easy to understand. This justifies my giving you a short abstract of his fundamental views on the theory of neurosis.

You are aware that the original theory that hysteria and the related neuroses have their origin in a trauma or sexual shock in early childhood was given up about fifteen years ago. It soon became evident that the sexual trauma could not be the real cause of the neurosis, for the simple reason that the trauma was found to be almost universal. There is scarcely a human being who has not had some sexual shock in early youth, and yet comparatively few develop a neurosis in later life. Freud himself soon realized that many of the patients who related an early traumatic experience had only invented the story of the so-called trauma; it had never occurred in reality, but was a mere creation of fantasy. Moreover, on further investigation it became quite obvious that even if a trauma had actually occurred it was not always responsible for the whole of the neurosis, although it does sometimes look as if the structure of the neurosis depended entirely on the trauma. If a neurosis were the inevitable consequence of the trauma it would be quite incomprehensible why neurotics are not incomparably more numerous than they are.

The apparently heightened effect of the shock was clearly due to the exaggerated and morbid fantasy of the patient. Freud also saw that this same fantasy activity manifested itself relatively early in bad habits, which he called infantile perversions. His new conception of the aetiology of neurosis was based on this insight, and he traced the neurosis back to some sexual activity in early infancy. This conception led to his recent view that the neurotic is "fixated" to a certain period of his early infancy, because he seems to preserve some trace of it, direct or indirect, in his mental attitude. Freud also makes the attempt to classify or to differentiate the neuroses, as well as dementia praecox, according to the stage of infantile development in which the fixation took place. From the standpoint of this theory, the neurotic appears to be entirely dependent on his infantile past, and all his troubles in later life, his moral conflicts and his deficiencies, seem to be derived from the powerful influences of that period. Accordingly, the main task of the treatment is to resolve this infantile fixation, which is conceived as an unconscious attachment of the sexual libido to certain infantile fantasies and habits.

This, so far as I can see, is the essence of Freud's theory of neurosis. But it overlooks the following important question: What is the cause of this fixation of libido to the old infantile fantasies and habits? We have to remember that almost everyone has at some time had infantile fantasies and habits exactly corresponding to those of a neurotic, yet he does not become fixated to them; consequently, he does not become neurotic later on. The aetiological secret of the neurosis, therefore, does not lie in the mere *existence* of infantile fantasies but in the so-called *fixation*. The numerous statements of neurotics affirming the existence of infantile sexual fantasies are worthless in so far as they attribute an aetiological significance to them, for the same fantasies can be found in normal individuals as well, a fact which I have often proved. It is only the fixation which seems to be characteristic.

It is therefore necessary to demand proof of the reality of this infantile fixation. Freud, an absolutely sincere and painstaking empiricist, would never have evolved this hypothesis had he not had sufficient grounds for it. These grounds are furnished by the results of psychoanalytic investigations of the unconscious. Psychoanalysis reveals the unconscious presence of numerous fantasies which have their roots in the infantile past and are grouped round the so-called "nuclear complex," which in men may be designated as the Oedipus complex, in women as the Electra complex. These terms convey their own meaning exactly. The whole tragic fate of Oedipus and Electra was acted out within the narrow confines of the family, just as a child's fate lies wholly within the family boundaries. Hence the Oedipus complex, like the Electra complex, is very characteristic of an infantile conflict. The existence of these conflicts in infancy has been proved by means of psychoanalytic research. It is in the realm of this complex that the fixation is supposed to have taken place. The extremely potent and effective existence of the nuclear complex in the unconscious of neurotics led Freud to the hypothesis that the neurotic has a peculiar fixation or attachment to it. Not the mere existence of this complex – for everybody has it in the unconscious – but the very strong attachment to it is what is typical of the neurotic. He is far more influenced by this complex than the normal person; many examples in confirmation of this can be found in every one of the recent psychoanalytic histories of neurotic cases.

We must admit that this view is a very plausible one, because the hypothesis of fixation is based on the well-known fact that certain periods of human life, and particularly infancy, do sometimes leave determining traces behind them which are permanent. The only question is whether this is a sufficient explanation or not. If we examine persons who have been neurotic from infancy it seems to be confirmed, for we see the nuclear complex as a permanent and powerful agent throughout life. But if we take cases which never show any noticeable trace of neurosis except at the particular time when they break down, and there are many such, this explanation becomes doubtful. If there is such a thing as fixation, it is not permissible to erect upon it a new hypothesis, claiming that at times during certain periods of life the fixation becomes loosened and ineffective, while at others it suddenly becomes strengthened. In these cases we find that the nuclear complex is as active and potent as in those which apparently support the theory of fixation. Here a critical attitude is justifiable, especially when we consider the oft-repeated observation that the moment of the outbreak of neurosis is not just a matter of chance; as a rule it is most critical. It is usually *the moment when a new psychological adjustment, that is, a new adaptation, is demanded*. Such moments facilitate the outbreak of a neurosis, as every experienced neurologist knows.

This fact seems to me extremely significant. If the fixation were indeed real we should expect to find its influence constant: in other words, a neurosis lasting throughout life. This is obviously not the case. The psychological determination of a neurosis is only partly due to an early infantile predisposition; it must be due to some cause in the present as well. And if we carefully examine the kind of infantile fantasies and occurrences to which the neurotic is attached, we shall be obliged to agree that there is nothing in them that is specifically neurotic. Normal individuals have pretty much the same inner and outer experiences, and may be attached to them

[margin note, left side: "is he saying that Freud is neurotic?"]

to an astonishing degree without developing a neurosis. Primitive people, especially, are very much bound to their infantility. It now begins to look as if this so-called fixation were a normal phenomenon, and that the importance of infancy for the later mental attitude is natural and prevails everywhere. The fact that the neurotic seems to be markedly influenced by his infantile conflicts shows that it is less a matter of fixation than of the peculiar use which he makes of his infantile past. It looks as if he exaggerated its importance and attributed to it a wholly artificial value. Adler, a pupil of Freud's, expresses a very similar view.

It would be unjust to say that Freud limited himself to the hypothesis of fixation; he was also aware of the problem I have just discussed. He called this phenomenon of reactivation or secondary exaggeration of infantile reminiscences "regression." But in Freud's view it appears as if the incestuous desires of the Oedipus complex were the real cause of the regression to infantile fantasies. If this were the case, we should have to postulate an unexpected intensity of the primary incestuous tendencies. This view led Freud to his recent comparison between what he calls the psychological "incest barrier" in children and the "incest taboo" in primitive man. He supposes that a desire for real incest led primitive man to frame laws against it; while to me it looks as if the incest taboo were only one among numerous taboos of all kinds, and were due to the typical superstitious fear of primitive man – a fear existing independently of incest and its prohibition. I am able to attribute as little strength to incestuous desires in childhood as in primitive humanity. I do not even seek the reason for regression in primary incestuous or any other sexual desires. I must admit that a purely sexual aetiology of neurosis seems to me much too narrow. I base this criticism not on any prejudice against sexuality but on an intimate acquaintance with the whole problem.

I therefore suggest that psychoanalytic theory should be freed from the purely sexual standpoint. In place of it I should like to introduce an *energic viewpoint* into the psychology of neurosis.

[margin note, left side: "break from Freud."]

All psychological phenomena can be considered as manifestations of energy, in the same way that all physical phenomena have been understood as energic manifestations ever since Robert Mayer discovered the law of the conservation of energy. Subjectively and psychologically, this energy is conceived as *desire*. I call it *libido*, using the word in its original sense, which is by no means only sexual. Sallust uses it exactly as we do here when he says: "They took more pleasure [*libidinem*] in handsome arms and war horses than in harlots and revelry."

From a broader standpoint libido can be understood as vital energy in general, or as Bergson's *élan vital*. The first manifestation of this energy in the infant is the nutritive instinct. From this stage the libido slowly develops through numerous variants of the act of sucking into the sexual function. Hence I do not consider the act of sucking a sexual act. The pleasure in sucking can certainly not be considered as sexual pleasure, but as pleasure in nutrition, for it is nowhere proved that pleasure is sexual in itself. This process of development is continued into adult life and is accompanied by constantly increasing adaptation to the external world. Whenever the libido, in the process of adaptation, meets an obstacle, an accumulation takes place which normally gives rise to an increased effort to overcome the obstacle. But if the obstacle seems to be insurmountable, and the individual abandons the task of overcoming it, the stored-up libido makes a regression. Instead of being employed for an increased effort, the libido gives up its present task and reverts to an earlier and more primitive mode of adaptation.

The best examples of such regressions are found in hysterical cases where a disappointment in love or marriage has precipitated a neurosis. There we find those well-known digestive disorders, loss of appetite, dyspeptic symptoms of all sorts, etc. In these cases the regressive libido, turning back from the task of adaptation, gains power over the nutritive function and produces marked disturbances. Similar effects can be observed in cases where there is no disturbance of the nutritive function but, instead, a regressive revival of reminiscences from the distant past. We then find a reactivation of the parental imagos, of the Oedipus complex. Here the events of early infancy – never before important – suddenly become so. They have been regressively reactivated. Remove the obstacle from the path of life and this whole system of infantile fantasies at once breaks down and becomes as inactive and ineffective as before. But let us not forget that, to a certain extent, it is at work all the time, influencing us in unseen ways. This view, incidentally, comes very close to Janet's hypothesis that the "parties supérieures" of a function are replaced by its "parties inférieures." I would also remind you of Claparède's conception of neurotic symptoms as emotional reflexes of a primitive nature.

For these reasons I no longer seek the cause of a neurosis in the past, but in the present. I ask, what is the necessary task which the patient will not accomplish? The long list of his infantile fantasies does not give me any sufficient aetiological explanation, because I know that these fantasies are only puffed up by the regressive libido, which has not found its natural outlet in a new form of adaptation to the demands of life.

You may ask why the neurotic has a special tendency not to accomplish his necessary tasks. Here let me point out that no living creature adjusts itself easily and smoothly to new conditions. The law of inertia is valid everywhere.

A sensitive and somewhat unbalanced person, as a neurotic always is, will meet with special difficulties and perhaps with more unusual tasks in life than a normal individual, who as a rule has only to follow the well-worn path of an ordinary existence. For the neurotic there is no established way of life, because his aims and tasks are apt to be of a highly individual character. He tries to go the more or less uncontrolled and half-conscious way of normal people, not realizing that his own critical and very different nature demands of him more effort than the normal person is required to exert. There are neurotics who have shown their heightened sensitiveness and their resistance to adaptation in the very first weeks of life, in the difficulty they have in taking the mother's breast and in their exaggerated nervous reactions, etc. For this peculiarity in the neurotic predisposition it will always be impossible to find a psychological aetiology, because it is anterior to all psychology. This predisposition – you can call it "congenital sensitiveness" or what you like – is the cause of the first resistances to adaptation. As the way to adaptation is blocked, the biological energy we call libido does not find its appropriate outlet or activity, with the result that a suitable form of adaptation is replaced by an abnormal or primitive one.

In neurosis we speak of an infantile attitude or of the predominance of infantile fantasies and wishes. In so far as infantile impressions are of obvious importance in normal people they will be equally influential in neurosis, but they have no aetiological significance; they are reactions merely, being chiefly secondary and regressive phenomena. It is perfectly true, as Freud says, that infantile fantasies determine the form and the subsequent development of neurosis, but this is not an aetiology. Even when we find perverted sexual fantasies whose existence can be demonstrated in childhood, we cannot consider them of aetiological significance. A neurosis is not really caused by infantile sexual fantasies, and the same must be said of the sexualism of neurotic fantasy in general. It is not a primary phenomenon based on a perverted sexual disposition, but merely secondary and a consequence of the failure to apply the stored-up libido in a suitable way. I realize that this is a very old view, but this does not prevent it from being true. The fact that the patient himself very often believes that his infantile fantasies are the real cause of his neurosis does not prove that he is right in his belief, or that a theory based on this belief is right either. It may look as if it were so, and I must admit that very many cases do have that appearance. At all events, it is perfectly easy to understand how Freud arrived at this view. Everyone who has any psychoanalytic experience will agree with me here.

To sum up: I cannot see the real aetiology of neurosis in the various manifestations of infantile sexual development and the fantasies to which they give rise. The fact that these fantasies are exaggerated in neurosis and occupy the foreground is a consequence of the stored-up energy or libido. The psychological trouble in neurosis, and the neurosis itself, can be formulated as an act of adaptation that has failed. This formulation might reconcile certain views of Janet's with Freud's view that a neurosis is, in a sense, an attempt at self-cure – a view which can be and has been applied to many other illnesses.

Here the question arises as to whether it is still advisable to bring to light all the patient's fantasies by analysis, if we now consider them of no aetiological significance. Hitherto psychoanalysis has set about unravelling these fantasies because they were considered aetiologically important. My altered view of the theory of neurosis does not affect the psychoanalytic procedure. The technique remains the same. Though we no longer imagine we are unearthing the ultimate root of the illness, we have to pull up the sexual fantasies because the energy which the patient needs for his health, that is, for adaptation, is attached to them. By means of psychoanalysis the connection between his conscious mind and the libido in the unconscious is re-established. Thus the unconscious libido is brought under the control of the will. Only in this way can the split-off energy become available again for the accomplishment of the necessary tasks of life. Considered from this standpoint, psychoanalysis no longer appears as a mere reduction of the individual to his primitive sexual wishes, but, if rightly understood, as a highly moral task of immense educational value.

Another reason for Jung's divergence from Freud was disagreement about the psychopathology of schizophrenia. Freud tried to maintain that withdrawal of sexual involvement with the external world was at the root of schizophrenic withdrawal, whereas Jung considered that schizophrenia involved a more general failure in adaptation to reality. This led to Jung's use of the word "libido" as a synonym for psychic energy in general; whereas Freud used the term to signify only sexual energy. It must be remembered that Freud had little experience of schizophrenic patients, since most such cases were to be found in mental hospitals rather than in private practice. Freud's only experience of mental hospital work was three weeks as a locum tenens (at Oberdöbling in June 1885), whereas Jung stayed at the Burghölzli from 1900 until 1909.

From "The Theory of Psychoanalysis" CW 4, pars. 271–8

THE PROBLEM OF LIBIDO IN DEMENTIA PRAECOX

In my book *Wandlungen und Symbole der Libido* I tried to furnish proof of these transgressions and at the same time to show the need for a new conception of libido which took account only of the energic view. Freud himself was forced to admit that his original conception of libido might possibly be too narrow when he tried to apply the energic view consistently to a famous case of dementia praecox – the so-called Schreber case. This case is concerned among other things with that well-known problem in the psychology of dementia praecox, the loss of adaptation to reality, a peculiar phenomenon consisting in the special tendency of these patients to construct an inner fantasy world of their own, surrendering for this purpose their adaptation to reality.

One aspect of this phenomenon, the absence of emotional rapport, will be well known to you, as this is a striking disturbance of the reality function. By dint of much psychoanalytic work with these patients we established that this lack of adaptation to reality is compensated by a progressive increase in the creation of fantasies, which goes so far that the dream world becomes more real for the patient than external reality. Schreber found an excellent figurative description for this phenomenon in his delusion about the "end of the world." He thus depicts the loss of reality in a very concrete way. The dynamic explanation is simple: we say that libido has withdrawn more and more from the external world into the inner world of fantasy, and there had to create, as a substitute for the lost world, a so-called reality equivalent. This substitute is built up piece by piece, so to speak, and it is most interesting to see out of what psychological material this inner world is constructed.

This way of looking at the displacement of libido is based on the everyday use of the term, its original, purely sexual connotation being very rarely remembered. In actual practice we speak simply of *libido*, and this is understood in so innocuous a sense that Claparède once remarked to me that one could just as well use the word "interest." The customary use of the term has developed, quite naturally and spontaneously, into a usage which makes it possible to explain Schreber's end of the world simply as a withdrawal of libido. On this occasion Freud remembered his original sexual definition of libido and tried to come to terms with the change of meaning that had quietly taken place in the meantime. In his paper on Schreber he asks himself whether *what the psychoanalytic school calls libido and conceives as "interest from erotic sources" coincides with interest in general.* You see that, putting the problem in this way, Freud asks himself the question which Claparède had already answered in practice.

Freud thus broaches the question of whether the loss of reality in schizophrenia, to which I drew attention in my "Psychology of Dementia Praecox," is due entirely to the withdrawal of erotic interest, or whether this coincides with objective interest in general. We can hardly suppose that the normal "fonction du réel" (Janet) is maintained solely by erotic interest. The fact is that in very many cases reality disappears altogether, so that not a trace of psychological adaptation can be found in these patients. (In these states reality is replaced by complex contents.) We are therefore compelled to admit that not only the erotic interest, but all interest whatsoever, has got lost, and with it the whole adaptation to reality.

Earlier, in my "Psychology of Dementia Praecox," I tried to get round this difficulty by using the expression "psychic energy," because I could not base the theory of dementia praecox on the theory of displacements of libido sexually defined. My experience – at that time chiefly psychiatric – did not permit me to understand this latter theory: only later did I come to realize its partial correctness as regards the neuroses, thanks to increased experiences in the field of hysteria and obsessional neurosis. Abnormal displacements of libido, quite definitely sexual, do in fact play a great role in these illnesses. But although very characteristic repressions of sexual libido do take place in the neuroses, the loss of reality so typical of dementia praecox never occurs. In dementia praecox the loss of the reality function is so extreme that it must involve the loss of other instinctual forces whose sexual character must be denied absolutely, for no one is likely to maintain that reality is a function of sex. Moreover, if it were, the withdrawal of erotic interest in the neuroses would necessarily entail a loss of reality comparable to that which occurs in dementia praecox. But, as I said before, this is not the case.

(Another thing to be considered – as Freud also pointed out in his work on the Schreber case – is that the introversion of sexual libido leads to an investment of the ego which might conceivably produce that effect of loss of reality. It is indeed tempting to explain the psychology of the loss in this way. But when we examine more closely the various things that can arise from the withdrawal and introversion of sexual libido, we come to see that though it can produce the psychology of an ascetic anchorite, it cannot produce dementia praecox. The anchorite's whole endeavour is to exterminate every trace of sexual interest, and this is something that cannot be asserted of dementia praecox.*)

These facts have made it impossible for me to apply Freud's libido theory to dementia praecox. I am also of the opinion that Abraham's essay on this subject is theoretically untenable from the standpoint of Freud's conception of libido. Abraham's belief that the paranoid system, or the schizophrenic symptomatology, is produced by the withdrawal of sexual libido from the outside world cannot be justified in terms of our present knowledge. For, as Freud has clearly shown, a mere introversion or regression of libido invariably leads to a neurosis and not to dementia praecox. It seems to me impossible simply to transfer the libido theory to dementia praecox, because this disease shows a loss of reality which cannot be explained solely by the loss of erotic interest.

THE GENETIC CONCEPTION OF LIBIDO

The attitude of reserve which I adopted towards the ubiquity of sexuality in my foreword to "The Psychology of Dementia Praecox," despite the fact that I recognized the psychological mechanisms pointed out by Freud, was dictated by the position of the libido theory at that time. Its sexual definition did not permit me to explain functional disturbances which affect the indefinite sphere of the hunger drive just as much as that of sex solely in the light of a sexual libido theory. Freud's libido theory had long seemed to me inapplicable to dementia praecox. In my analytical work I noticed that, with growing experience, a slow change in my conception of libido had taken place. Instead of the descriptive definition set forth in Freud's *Three Essays*, there gradually took shape a genetic definition of libido, which enabled me to replace the expression "psychic energy" by "libido."

*It might be objected that dementia praecox is characterized not only by the introversion of sexual libido but also by a regression to the infantile level, and that this constitutes the difference between the anchorite and the schizophrenic. This is certainly correct, but it would still have to be proved that in dementia praecox it is regularly and exclusively the erotic interest which goes into a regression. It seems to me rather difficult to prove this, because erotic interest would then have to be understood as the "Eros" of the old philosophers. But that can hardly be meant. I know cases of dementia praecox where all regard for self-preservation disappears, but not the very lively erotic interests.

A very important divergence of view with Freud was over the question of incest. Freud, with his insistence on the literal, believed that neurosis was connected with the persistence of incestuous desires connected with the Oedipus complex. As a previous extract demonstrated, Jung believed that incestuous fantasies were not causal factors in neurosis, but became reactivated as a result of regression in the face of a failure of adaptation in the present. He also began to realize that regression might be a necessary prelude to finding a new and better adaptation. Incest, therefore, could have the symbolic significance of a new synthesis taking place within the individual which pointed toward a creative solution to his problems.

From "**Sigmund Freud**" MDR, p. 162/167

When I was working on my book about the libido and approaching the end of the chapter "The Sacrifice," I knew in advance that its publication would cost me my friendship with Freud. For I planned to set down in it my own conception of incest, the decisive transformation of the concept of libido, and various other ideas in which I differed from Freud. To me incest signified a personal complication only in the rarest cases. Usually incest has a highly religious aspect, for which reason the incest theme plays a decisive part in almost all cosmogonies and in numerous myths. But Freud clung to the literal interpretation of it and could not grasp the spiritual significance of incest as a symbol. I knew that he would never be able to accept any of my ideas on this subject.

I spoke with my wife about this, and told her of my fears. She attempted to reassure me, for she thought that Freud would magnanimously raise no objections, although he might not accept my views. I myself was convinced that he could not do so. For two months I was unable to touch my pen, so tormented was I by the conflict. Should I keep my thoughts to myself, or should I risk the loss of so important a friendship? At last I resolved to go ahead with the writing – and it did indeed cost me Freud's friendship.

In the following passage, Jung elaborates the idea that regression occurs when inner conflict prevents the individual's adaptation to the external world. He goes on to show that the unconscious contents reactivated by regression contain the germs of a new and better adaptation. (The balance of opposites and the notion of compensation which Jung touches on in the passage below will be reviewed in more detail later.)

what is the word to mi. s? the back and forth ring...?

From "**On Psychic Energy**" CW 8, pars. 60–9

FUNDAMENTAL CONCEPTS OF THE LIBIDO THEORY

Progression and Regression

One of the most important energic phenomena of psychic life is the progression and regression of libido. Progression could be defined as the daily advance of the process of psychological adaptation. We know that adaptation is not something that is achieved once and for all, though there is a tendency to believe the contrary. This is due to mistaking a person's psychic attitude for actual adaptation. We can satisfy the demands of adaptation only by means of a suitably directed attitude. Consequently, the achievement of adaptation is completed in two stages: (1) attainment of attitude, (2) completion of adaptation by means of the attitude. A man's attitude to reality is something extraordinarily persistent, but the more persistent his mental habitus is, the less permanent will be his effective achievement of adaptation. This is the necessary consequence of the continual changes in the environment and the new adaptations demanded by them.

The progression of libido might therefore be said to consist in a continual satisfaction of the demands of environmental conditions. This is possible only by means of an attitude, which as such is necessarily directed and therefore characterized by a certain one-sidedness. Thus it may easily happen that an attitude can no longer satisfy the demands of adaptation because changes have occurred in the environmental conditions which require a different attitude. For example, a feeling-attitude that seeks to fulfil the demands of reality by means of empathy may easily encounter a situation that can only be solved through thinking. In this case the feeling-attitude breaks down and the progression of libido also ceases. The vital feeling that was present before disappears, and in its place the psychic value of certain conscious contents increases in an unpleasant way; subjective contents and reactions press to the fore and the situation becomes full of affect and ripe for explosions. These symptoms indicate a damming up of libido, and the stoppage is always marked by the breaking up of the pairs of opposites. During the progression of libido the pairs of opposites are united in the co-ordinated flow of psychic processes. Their working together makes possible the balanced regularity of these processes, which without this inner polarity would become one-sided and unreasonable. We are therefore justified in regarding all extravagant and exaggerated behaviour as a loss of balance, because the co-ordinating effect of the opposite impulse is obviously lacking. Hence it is essential for progression, which is the successful achievement of adaptation, that impulse and counter-impulse, positive and negative, should reach a state of regular interaction and mutual influence. This balancing and combining of pairs of opposites can be seen, for instance, in the process of reflection that precedes a difficult decision. But in the stoppage of libido that occurs when progression has become impossible, positive and negative can no longer unite in co-ordinated action, because both have attained an equal value which keeps the scales balanced. The longer the stoppage lasts, the more the value of the opposed positions increases; they become enriched with more and more associations and attach to themselves an ever-widening range of psychic material. The tension leads to conflict, the conflict leads to attempts at mutual repression, and if one of the opposing forces is successfully repressed a dissociation ensues, a splitting of the personality, or disunion with oneself. The stage is then set for a neurosis. The acts that follow from such a condition are unco-ordinated, sometimes pathological, having the appearance of symptomatic actions. Although in part normal, they are based partly on the repressed opposite which, instead of working as an equilibrating force, has an obstructive effect, thus hindering the possibility of further progress.

The struggle between the opposites would persist in this fruitless way if the process of regression, the backward movement of libido, did not set in with the outbreak of the conflict. Through their collision the opposites are gradually deprived of value and depotentiated. This loss of value steadily increases and is the only thing perceived by consciousness. It is synonymous with regression, for in proportion to the decrease in value of the conscious opposites there is an increase in the value of all those psychic processes which are not concerned with outward adaptation and therefore are seldom or never employed consciously. These psychic factors are for the most part unconscious. As the value of the subliminal elements and of the unconscious increases, it is to be expected that they will gain influence over the conscious mind. On account of the inhibiting influence which the conscious exercises over the unconscious, the unconscious values assert themselves at first only indirectly. The inhibition to which they are subjected is a result of the exclusive directedness of conscious contents. (This inhibition is identical with what Freud calls the "censor.") The indirect manifestation of the unconscious takes the form of disturbances of conscious behaviour. In the association experiment they appear as complex-indicators, in daily life as the "symptomatic actions" first described by Freud, and in neurotic conditions they appear as symptoms.

Since regression raises the value of contents that were previously excluded from the conscious process of adaptation, and hence are either totally unconscious or only "dimly conscious," the psychic elements now being forced over the threshold are momentarily useless from the standpoint of adaptation, and for this reason are invariably kept at a distance by the directed psychic function. The nature of these contents is for all the world to read in Freudian literature. They are not only of an infantile-sexual character, but are altogether incompatible contents and tendencies, partly immoral, partly unaesthetic, partly again of an irrational, imaginary nature. The obviously inferior character of these contents as regards adaptation has given rise to that depreciatory view of the psychic background which is habitual in psychoanalytic writings.*
What the regression brings to the surface certainly seems at first sight to be slime from the depths; but if one does not stop short at a superficial evaluation and refrains from passing judgment on the basis of a preconceived dogma, it will be found that this "slime" contains not merely incompatible and rejected remnants of everyday life, or inconvenient and objectionable animal tenden-

*Somewhat after the manner of Hudibras, whose opinion is quoted by Kant (*Träume eines Geistersehers*, III): "When a hypochondriacal wind is roaring in the bowels, everything depends on the direction it takes. If it goes downwards, it turns into a fart, but if it mounts upwards, it is a vision or a divine inspiration."

cies, but also germs of new life and vital possibilities for the future.* This is one of the great merits of psychoanalysis, that it is not afraid to dredge up the incompatible elements, which would be a thoroughly useless and indeed reprehensible undertaking were it not for the possibilities of new life that lie in the repressed contents. That this is and must be so is not only proved by a wealth of practical experience but can also be deduced from the following considerations.

The process of adaptation requires a directed conscious function characterized by inner consistency and logical coherence. Because it is directed, everything unsuitable must be excluded in order to maintain the integrity of direction. The unsuitable elements are subjected to inhibition and thereby escape attention. Now experience shows that there is only *one* consciously directed function of adaptation. If, for example, I have a thinking orientation I cannot at the same time orient myself by feeling, because thinking and feeling are two quite different functions. In fact, I must carefully exclude feeling if I am to satisfy the logical laws of thinking, so that the thought-process will not be disturbed by feeling. In this case I withdraw as much libido as possible from the feeling process, with the result that this function becomes relatively unconscious. Experience shows, again, that the orientation is largely habitual; accordingly the other unsuitable functions, so far as they are incompatible with the prevailing attitude, are relatively unconscious, and hence unused, untrained, and undifferentiated. Moreover, on the principle of coexistence they necessarily become associated with other contents of the unconscious, the inferior and incompatible quality of which I have already pointed out. Consequently, when these functions are activated by regression and so reach consciousness, they appear in a somewhat incompatible form, disguised and covered up with the slime of the deep.

If we remember that the stoppage of libido was due to the failure of the conscious attitude, we can now understand what valuable seeds lie in the unconscious contents activated by regression. They contain the elements of that other function which was excluded by

*Though professional satiety with neurotic unrealities makes the analyst sceptical, a generalized judgment from the pathological angle has the disadvantage of being always biased.

the conscious attitude and which would be capable of effectively complementing or even of replacing the inadequate conscious attitude. If thinking fails as the adapted function, because it is dealing with a situation to which one can adapt only by feeling, then the unconscious material activated by regression will contain the missing feeling function, although still in embryonic form, archaic and undeveloped. Similarly, in the opposite type, regression would activate a thinking function that would effectively compensate the inadequate feeling.

By activating an unconscious factor, regression confronts consciousness with the problem of the psyche as opposed to the problem of outward adaptation. It is natural that the conscious mind should fight against accepting the regressive contents, yet it is finally compelled by the impossibility of further progress to submit to the regressive values. In other words, regression leads to the necessity of adapting to the inner world of the psyche.

Just as adaptation to the environment may fail because of the one-sidedness of the adapted function, so adaptation to the inner world may fail because of the one-sidedness of the function in question. For instance, if the stoppage of libido was due to the failure of the thinking attitude to cope with the demands of outward adaptation, and if the unconscious feeling function is activated by regression, there is only a feeling attitude towards the inner world. This may be sufficient at first, but in the long run it will cease to be adequate, and the thinking function will have to be enlisted too, just as the reverse was necessary when dealing with the outer world. Thus a complete orientation towards the inner world becomes necessary until such time as inner adaptation is attained. Once the adaptation is achieved, progression can begin again.

The principle of progression and regression is portrayed in the myth of the whale-dragon worked out by Frobenius, as I have shown in detail in my book *Symbols of Transformation* (pars. 307ff.). The hero is the symbolical exponent of the movement of libido. Entry into the dragon is the regressive direction, and the journey to the East (the "night sea journey") with its attendant events symbolizes the effort to adapt to the conditions of the psychic inner world. The complete swallowing up and disappearance of the hero in the belly of the dragon represents the complete withdrawal of interest from the outer world. The overcoming of the monster from within is the achievement of adaptation to the conditions of the inner world, and the emergence ("slipping out") of the hero from the monster's belly with the help of a bird, which happens at the moment of sunrise, symbolizes the recommencement of progression.

It is characteristic that the monster begins the night sea journey to the East, i.e., towards sunrise, while the hero is engulfed in its belly. This seems to me to indicate that regression is not necessarily a retrograde step in the sense of a backwards development or degeneration, but rather represents a necessary phase of development. The individual is, however, not consciously aware that he is developing; he feels himself to be in a compulsive situation that resembles an early infantile state or even an embryonic condition within the womb. It is only if he remains stuck in this condition that we can speak of involution or degeneration.

Part 3. The Development of the Idea of the Collective Unconscious and of Archetypes

Jung's deep involvement with schizophrenic patients and his endeavour to understand their psychology led him to conclude that their fantasies and delusional systems could not be explained in terms of their personal biographies.

From "**Recent Thoughts on Schizophrenia**" CW 3, par. 549

But unlike the contents of a neurosis, which can be satisfactorily explained by biographical data, psychotic contents show peculiarities that defy reduction to individual determinants, just as there are dreams where the symbols cannot be properly explained with the aid of personal data. By this I mean that neurotic contents can be compared with those of normal complexes, whereas psychotic contents, especially in paranoid cases, show close analogies with the type of dream that the primitive aptly calls a "big dream." Unlike ordinary dreams, such a dream is highly impressive, numinous, and its imagery frequently makes use of motifs analogous to or even identical with those of mythology. I call these structures *archetypes* because they function in a way similar to instinctual patterns of behaviour. Moreover, most of them can be found everywhere and at all times. They occur in the folklore of primitive races, in Greek, Egyptian, and ancient Mexican myths, as well as in the dreams, visions, and delusions of modern individuals entirely ignorant of all such traditions.

As an example of the kind of observation which led him to this conclusion, Jung quotes a particular case.

From "**The Structure of the Psyche**" CW 8, pars. 317–21

But as to whether this supra-individual psychic activity actually exists, I have so far given no proof that satisfies all the requirements. I should now like to do this once more in the form of an example. The case is that of a man in his thirties, who was suffering from a paranoid form of schizophrenia. He became ill in his early twenties. He had always presented a strange mixture of intelligence, wrong-headedness, and fantastic ideas. He was an ordinary clerk, employed in a consulate. Evidently as a compensation for his very modest existence he was seized with megalomania and believed himself to be the Saviour. He suffered from frequent hallucinations and was at times very much disturbed. In his quiet periods he was allowed to go unattended in the corridor. One day I came across him there, blinking through the window up at the sun, and moving his head from side to side in a curious manner. He took me by the arm and said he wanted to show me something. He said I must look at the sun with eyes half shut, and then I could see the sun's phallus. If I moved my head from side to side the sun-phallus would move too, and that was the origin of the wind.

I made this observation about 1906. In the course of the year 1910, when I was engrossed in mythological studies, a book of Dieterich's came into my hands. It was part of the so-called Paris magic papyrus and was thought by Dieterich to be a liturgy of the Mithraic cult.* It consisted of a series of instructions, invocations, and visions. One of these visions is described in the following words: "And likewise the so-called tube, the origin of the ministering wind. For you will see hanging down from the disc of the sun something that looks like a tube. And towards the regions westward it is as though there were an infinite east wind. But if the other wind should prevail towards the regions of the east, you will in like manner see the vision veering in that direction." The Greek word for "tube," $αὐλός$, means a wind-instrument, and the combination $αὐλός παχύς$ in Homer means "a thick jet of blood." So evidently a stream of wind is blowing through the tube out of the sun.

*As the author subsequently learned, the 1910 edition was actually the second, there having been a first edition in 1903.

how to
past lives
and archetypes
relate?

The vision of my patient in 1906, and the Greek text first edited in 1910, should be sufficiently far apart to rule out the possibility of cryptomnesia on his side and of thought-transference on mine. The obvious parallelism of the two visions cannot be disputed, though one might object that the similarity is purely fortuitous. In that case we should expect the vision to have no connections with analogous ideas, nor any inner meaning. But this expectation is not fulfilled, for in certain medieval paintings this tube is actually depicted as a sort of hose-pipe reaching down from heaven under the robe of Mary. In it the Holy Ghost flies down in the form of a dove to impregnate the Virgin. As we know from the miracle of Pentecost, the Holy Ghost was originally conceived as a mighty rushing wind, the $\pi\nu\varepsilon\tilde{\upsilon}\mu\alpha$, "the wind that bloweth where it listeth." In a Latin text we read: "Animo descensus per orbem solis tribuitur" (They say that the spirit descends through the disc of the sun). This conception is common to the whole of late classical and medieval philosophy.

I cannot, therefore, discover anything fortuitous in these visions, but simply the revival of possibilities of ideas that have always existed, that can be found again in the most diverse minds and in all epochs, and are therefore not to be mistaken for inherited ideas.

I have purposely gone into the details of this case in order to give you a concrete picture of that deeper psychic activity which I call the collective unconscious. Summing up, I would like to emphasize that we must distinguish three psychic levels: (1) consciousness, (2) the personal unconscious, and (3) the collective unconscious. The personal unconscious consists firstly of all those contents that became unconscious either because they lost their intensity and were forgotten or because consciousness was withdrawn from them (repression), and secondly of contents, some of them sense-impressions, which never had sufficient intensity to reach consciousness but have somehow entered the psyche. The collective unconscious, however, as the ancestral heritage of possibilities of representation, is not individual but common to all men, and perhaps even to all animals, and is the true basis of the individual psyche.

Since the collective unconscious is common to all men, archetypal manifestations can be demonstrated in the normal as well as in the insane.

From "**On the Psychology of the Unconscious**" *Two Essays*, CW 7, pars. 106–9

THE PERSONAL AND THE COLLECTIVE UNCONSCIOUS

Let us take as an example one of the greatest thoughts which the nineteenth century brought to birth: the idea of the conservation of energy. Robert Mayer, the real creator of this idea, was a physician, and not a physicist or natural philosopher, for whom the making of such an idea would have been more appropriate. But it is very important to realize that the idea was not, strictly speaking, "made" by Mayer. Nor did it come into being through the fusion of ideas or scientific hypotheses then extant, but grew in its creator like a plant. Mayer wrote about it in the following way to Griesinger, in 1844:

I am far from having hatched out the theory at my writing desk. [He then reports certain physiological observations he had made in 1840 and 1841 as ship's doctor.] Now, if one wants to be clear on matters of physiology, some knowledge of physical processes is essential, unless one prefers to work at things from the metaphysical side, which I find infinitely disgusting. I therefore held fast to physics and stuck to the subject with such fondness that, although many may laugh at me for this, I paid but little attention to that remote quarter of the globe in which we were, preferring to remain on board where I could work without intermission, and where I passed many an hour as though *inspired*, the like of which I cannot remember either before or since. Some flashes of thought that passed through me while in the roads of Surabaya were at once assiduously followed up, and in their turn led to fresh subjects. Those times have passed, but the quiet examination of that which then came to the surface in me has taught me that it is a truth, which can not only be subjectively felt, but objectively proved. It remains to be seen whether this can be accomplished by a man so little versed in physics as I am.*

In his book on energetics,† Helm expresses the view that "Robert Mayer's new idea did not detach itself gradually from the traditional concepts of energy by deeper reflection on them, but belongs to those intuitively apprehended ideas which, arising in other realms of a spiritual nature, as it were take possession of the mind and compel it to reshape the traditional conceptions in their own likeness."

The question now arises: Whence this new idea that thrusts itself upon consciousness with such elemental force? And whence did it derive the power that could so seize upon consciousness that it completely eclipsed the multitudinous impressions of a first voyage to the tropics? These questions are not so easy to answer. But if we apply our theory here, the explanation can only be this: the idea of energy and its conservation must be a primordial image that was dormant in the collective unconscious. Such a conclusion naturally obliges us to prove that a primordial image of this kind really did exist in the mental history of mankind and was operative through the ages. As a matter of fact, this proof can be produced without much difficulty: the most primitive religions in the most widely separated parts of the earth are founded upon this image. These are the so-called dynamistic religions whose sole and determining thought is that there exists a universal magical power** about which everything revolves. Tylor, the well-known English investigator, and Frazer likewise, misunderstood this idea as animism. In reality primitives do not mean, by their power-concept, souls or spirits at all, but something which the American investigator Lovejoy has appropriately termed "primitive energetics." This concept is equivalent to the idea of soul, spirit, God, health, bodily strength, fertility, magic, influence, power, prestige, medicine, as well as certain states of feeling which are characterized by the release of affects. Among certain Polynesians *mulungu* – this same

*Robert Mayer, *Kleinere Schriften und Briefe* (Stuttgart, 1893), p. 213 (letter to Wilhelm Griesinger, June 16, 1844).
†G. F. Helm, *Die Energetik nach ihrer geschichtlichen Entwicklung* (Leipzig, 1898), p. 20.
**Generally called *mana*.

primitive power-concept – means spirit, soul, daemonism, magic, prestige; and when anything astonishing happens, the people cry out "Mulungu!" This power-concept is also the earliest form of a concept of God among primitives, and is an image which has undergone countless variations in the course of history. In the Old Testament the magic power glows in the burning bush and in the countenance of Moses; in the Gospels it descends with the Holy Ghost in the form of fiery tongues from heaven. In Heraclitus it appears as world energy, as "ever-living fire"; among the Persians it is the fiery glow of "haoma," divine grace; among the Stoics it is the original heat, the power of fate. Again, in medieval legend it appears as the aura or halo, and it flares up like a flame from the roof of the hut in which the saint lies in ecstasy. In their visions the saints behold the sun of this power, the plenitude of its light. According to the old view, the soul itself is this power; in the idea of the soul's immortality there is implicit its conservation, and in the Buddhist and primitive notion of metempsychosis – transmigration of souls – is implicit its unlimited changeability together with its constant preservation.

So this idea has been stamped on the human brain for aeons. That is why it lies ready to hand in the unconscious of every man. Only, certain conditions are needed to cause it to appear. These conditions were evidently fulfilled in the case of Robert Mayer. The greatest and best thoughts of man shape themselves upon these primordial images as upon a blueprint. I have often been asked where the archetypes or primordial images come from. It seems to me that their origin can only be explained by assuming them to be deposits of the constantly repeated experiences of humanity. One of the commonest and at the same time most impressive experiences is the apparent movement of the sun every day. We certainly cannot discover anything of the kind in the unconscious, so far as the known physical process is concerned. What we do find, on the other hand, is the myth of the sun-hero in all its countless modifications. It is this myth, and not the physical process, that forms the sun archetype. The same can be said of the phases of the moon. The archetype is a kind of readiness to produce over and over again the same or similar mythical ideas. Hence it seems as though what is impressed upon the unconscious were exclusively the subjective fantasy-ideas aroused by the physical process. Therefore we may take it that archetypes are recurrent impressions made by subjective reactions. Naturally this assumption only pushes the problem further back without solving it. There is nothing to prevent us from assuming that certain archetypes exist even in animals, that they are grounded in the peculiarities of the living organism itself and are therefore direct expressions of life whose nature cannot be further explained. Not only are the archetypes, apparently, impressions of ever-repeated typical experiences, but, at the same time, they behave empirically like agents that tend towards the repetition of these same experiences. For when an archetype appears in a dream, in a fantasy, or in life, it always brings with it a certain influence or power by virtue of which it either exercises a numinous or a fascinating effect, or impels to action.

Jung's conception of archetypes and the collective unconscious sprang not only from his observation of patients, but from his own experience. After the break with Freud, Jung passed through a period of mental upheaval which was so intense that he decided that he was "menaced by a psychosis." Part of this upheaval was connected with Jung's need to develop his own, independent point of view.

From "Confrontation with the Unconscious" MDR, p. 165/170

After the parting of the ways with Freud, a period of inner uncertainty began for me. It would be no exaggeration to call it a state of disorientation. I felt totally suspended in mid-air, for I had not yet found my own footing. Above all, I felt it necessary to develop a new attitude towards my patients. I resolved for the present not to bring any theoretical premises to bear upon them, but to wait and see what they would tell of their own accord. My aim became to leave things to chance. The result was that the patients would spontaneously report their dreams and fantasies to me, and I would merely ask, "What occurs to you in connection with that?" or, "How do you mean that, where does that come from, what do you think about it?" The interpretations seemed to follow of their own accord from the patients' replies and associations. I avoided all theoretical points of view and simply helped the patients to understand the dream-images by themselves, without application of rules and theories.

Jung's disturbance was also connected with something which later became a cornerstone in Jung's delineation of the stages of life. In July 1913, Jung attained the age of thirty-eight; a time of life at which "mid-life crises" often occur. By this time, Jung had married and fathered a family, and had achieved professional recognition and a position in the world. His conscious attitude had been that, together with Freud, he could develop a new science of the mind which would benefit the world. Now, against his conscious will, his libido was being forced away from involvement in the external world into an exploration of the inner depths of his own psyche.

From "**The Stages of Life**" CW 8, pars. 772–7

The nearer we approach to the middle of life, and the better we have succeeded in entrenching ourselves in our personal attitudes and social positions, the more it appears as if we had discovered the right course and the right ideals and principles of behaviour. For this reason we suppose them to be eternally valid, and make a virtue of unchangeably clinging to them. We overlook the essential fact that the social goal is attained only at the cost of a diminution of personality. Many – far too many – aspects of life which should also have been experienced lie in the lumber-room among dusty memories; but sometimes, too, they are glowing coals under grey ashes.

Statistics show a rise in the frequency of mental depressions in men about forty. In women the neurotic difficulties generally begin somewhat earlier. We see that in this phase of life – between thirty-five and forty – an important change in the human psyche is in preparation. At first it is not a conscious and striking change; it is rather a matter of indirect signs of a change which seems to take its rise in the unconscious. Often it is something like a slow change in a person's character; in another case certain traits may come to light which had disappeared since childhood; or again, one's previous inclinations and interests begin to weaken and others take their place. Conversely – and this happens very frequently – one's cherished convictions and principles, especially the moral ones, begin to harden and to grow increasingly rigid until, somewhere around the age of fifty, a period of intolerance and fanaticism is reached. It is as if the existence of these principles were endangered and it were therefore necessary to emphasize them all the more.

The wine of youth does not always clear with advancing years; sometimes it grows turbid. All the phenomena mentioned above can best be seen in rather one-sided people, turning up sometimes sooner and sometimes later. Their appearance, it seems to me, is often delayed by the fact that the parents of the person in question are still alive. It is then as if the period of youth were being unduly drawn out. I have seen this especially in the case of men whose fathers were long-lived. The death of the father then has the effect of a precipitate and almost catastrophic ripening.

I know of a pious man who was a churchwarden and who, from the age of forty onward, showed a growing and finally unbearable intolerance in matters of morality and religion. At the same time his moods grew visibly worse. At last he was nothing more than a darkly lowering pillar of the Church. In this way he got along until the age of fifty-five, when suddenly, sitting up in bed in the middle of the night, he said to his wife: 'Now at last I've got it! I'm just a plain rascal." Nor did this realization remain without results. He spent his declining years in riotous living and squandered a goodly part of his fortune. Obviously quite a likable fellow, capable of both extremes!

The very frequent neurotic disturbances of adult years all have one thing in common: they want to carry the psychology of the youthful phase over the threshold of the so-called years of discretion. Who does not know those touching old gentlemen who must always warm up the dish of their student days, who can fan the flame of life only by reminiscences of their heroic youth, but who, for the rest, are stuck in a hopelessly wooden Philistinism? As a rule, to be sure, they have this one merit which it would be wrong to undervalue: they are not neurotic, but only boring and stereotyped. The neurotic is rather a person who can never have things as he would like them in the present, and who can therefore never enjoy the past either.

As formerly the neurotic could not escape from childhood, so now he cannot part with his youth. He shrinks from the grey thoughts of approaching age, and, feeling the prospect before him unbearable, is always straining to look behind him. Just as the childish person shrinks back from the unknown in the world and in human existence, so the grown man shrinks back from the second half of life. It is as if unknown and dangerous tasks awaited him, or as if he were threatened with sacrifices and losses which he does not wish to accept, or as if his life up to now seemed to him so fair and precious that he could not relinquish it.

Jung's "confrontation with the unconscious," as he termed it, turned out to be both extremely disturbing and highly rewarding.

From "**Confrontation with the Unconscious**" MDR, pp. 167–74/172–81

One fantasy kept returning: there was something dead present, but it was also still alive. For example, corpses were placed in crematory ovens, but were then discovered to be still living. These fantasies came to a head and were simultaneously resolved in a dream.

I was in a region like the Alyscamps near Arles. There they have a lane of sarcophagi which go back to Merovingian times. In the dream I was coming from the city, and saw before me a similar lane with a long row of tombs. They were pedestals with stone slabs on which the dead lay. They reminded me of old church burial vaults, where knights in armour lie outstretched. Thus the dead lay in my dream, in their antique clothes, with hands clasped, the difference being that they were not hewn out of stone, but in a curious fashion mummified. I stood still in front of the first grave and looked at the dead man, who was a person of the eighteen-thirties. I looked at his clothes with interest, whereupon he suddenly moved and came to life. He unclasped his hands; but that was only because I was looking at him. I had an extremely unpleasant feeling, but walked on and came to another body. He belonged to the eighteenth century. There exactly the same thing happened: when I looked at him, he came to life and moved his hands. So I went down the whole row, until I came to the twelfth century – that is, to a crusader in chain mail who lay there with clasped hands. His figure seemed carved out of wood. For a long time I looked at him and thought he was really dead. But suddenly I saw that a finger of his left hand was beginning to stir gently.

Of course, I had originally held to Freud's view that vestiges of old experiences exist in the unconscious.* But dreams like this, and my actual experiences of the unconscious, taught me that such contents are not dead, outmoded forms, but belong to our living being. My work had confirmed this assumption, and in the course of years there developed from it the theory of archetypes.

The dreams, however, could not help me over my feeling of disorientation. On the contrary, I lived as if under constant inner pressure. At times this became so strong that I suspected there was some psychic disturbance in myself. Therefore I twice went over all the details of my entire life, with particular attention to childhood memories; for I thought there might be something in my past which I could not see and which might possibly be the cause of the disturbance. But this retrospection led to nothing but a fresh acknowledgment of my own ignorance. Thereupon I said to myself, "Since I know nothing at all, I shall simply do whatever occurs to me." Thus I consciously submitted myself to the impulses of the unconscious.

The first thing that came to the surface was a childhood memory from perhaps my tenth or eleventh year. At that time I had had a spell of playing passionately with building blocks. I distinctly recalled how I had built little houses and castles, using bottles to form the sides of gates and vaults. Somewhat later I had used ordinary stones, with mud for mortar. These structures had fascinated me for a long time. To my astonishment, this memory was accompanied by a good deal of emotion. "Aha," I said to myself, "there is still life in these things. The small boy is still around, and possesses a creative life which I lack. But how can I make my way to it?" For as a grown man it seemed impossible to

*Freud speaks of "archaic vestiges."

me that I should be able to bridge the distance from the present back to my eleventh year. Yet if I wanted to re-establish contact with that period, I had no choice but to return to it and take up once more that child's life with his childish games. This moment was a turning point in my fate, but I gave in only after endless resistances and with a sense of resignation. For it was a painfully humiliating experience to realize that there was nothing to be done except play childish games.

Nevertheless, I began accumulating suitable stones, gathering them partly from the lake shore and partly from the water. And I started building: cottages, a castle, a whole village. The church was still missing, so I made a square building with a hexagonal drum on top of it, and a dome. A church also requires an altar, but I hesitated to build that.

Preoccupied with the question of how I could approach this task, I was walking along the lake as usual one day, picking stones out of the gravel on the shore. Suddenly I caught sight of a red stone, a four-sided pyramid about an inch and a half high. It was a fragment of stone which had been polished into this shape by the action of the water – a pure product of chance. I knew at once: this was the altar! I placed it in the middle under the dome, and as I did so, I recalled the underground phallus of my childhood dream. This connection gave me a feeling of satisfaction.

I went on with my building game after the noon meal every day, whenever the weather permitted. As soon as I was through eating, I began playing, and continued to do so until the patients arrived; and if I was finished with my work early enough in the evening, I went back to building. In the course of this activity my thoughts clarified, and I was able to grasp the fantasies whose presence in myself I dimly felt.

Naturally, I thought about the significance of what I was doing, and asked myself, "Now, really, what are you about? You are building a small town, and doing it as if it were a rite!" I had no answer to my question, only the inner certainty that I was on the way to discovering my own myth. For the building game was only a beginning. It released a stream of fantasies which I later carefully wrote down.

This sort of thing has been consistent with me, and at any time in my later life when I came up against a blank wall, I painted a

picture or hewed stone. Each such experience proved to be a *rite
d'entrée* for the ideas and works that followed hard upon it.
Everything that I have written this year* and last year, "The
Undiscovered Self," "Flying Saucers: A Modern Myth," "A
Psychological View of Conscience," has grown out of the stone
sculptures I did after my wife's death.† The close of life, the end,
and what it made me realize, wrenched me violently out of myself.
It cost me a great deal to regain my footing, and contact with stone
helped me.

Towards the autumn of 1913 the pressure which I had felt was in
me seemed to be moving outwards, as though there were something
in the air. The atmosphere actually seemed to me darker than it
had been. It was as though the sense of oppression no longer sprang
exclusively from a psychic situation, but from concrete reality.
This feeling grew more and more intense.

In October, while I was alone on a journey, I was suddenly seized
by an overpowering vision: I saw a monstrous flood covering all
the northern and low-lying lands between the North Sea and the
Alps. When it came up to Switzerland I saw that the mountains
grew higher and higher to protect our country. I realized that a
frightful catastrophe was in progress. I saw the mighty yellow
waves, the floating rubble of civilization, and the drowned bodies
of uncounted thousands. Then the whole sea turned to blood. This
vision lasted about one hour. I was perplexed and nauseated, and
ashamed of my weakness.

Two weeks passed; then the vision recurred, under the same
conditions, even more vividly than before, and the blood was more
emphasized. An inner voice spoke. "Look at it well; it is wholly
real and it will be so. You cannot doubt it." That winter someone
asked me what I thought were the political prospects of the world
in the near future. I replied that I had no thoughts on the matter,
but that I saw rivers of blood.

I asked myself whether these visions pointed to a revolution, but
could not really imagine anything of the sort. And so I drew the
conclusion that they had to do with me myself, and decided that

*1957.
†27th November, 1955.

I was menaced by a psychosis. The idea of war did not occur to me at all.

Soon afterwards, in the spring and early summer of 1914, I had a thrice-repeated dream that in the middle of summer an Arctic cold wave descended and froze the land to ice. I saw, for example, the whole of Lorraine and its canals frozen and the entire region totally deserted by human beings. All living green things were killed by frost. This dream came in April and May, and for the last time in June, 1914.

In the third dream frightful cold had again descended from out of the cosmos. This dream, however, had an unexpected end. There stood a leaf-bearing tree, but without fruit (my tree of life, I thought), whose leaves had been transformed by the effects of the frost into sweet grapes full of healing juices. I plucked the grapes and gave them to a large, waiting crowd.

At the end of July 1914 I was invited by the British Medical Association to deliver a lecture, "On the Importance of the Unconscious in Psychopathology," at a congress in Aberdeen. I was prepared for something to happen, for such visions and dreams are fateful. In my state of mind just then, with the fears that were pursuing me, it seemed fateful to me that I should have to talk on the importance of the unconscious at such a time!

On 1st August the world war broke out. Now my task was clear: I had to try to understand what had happened and to what extent my own experience coincided with that of mankind in general. Therefore my first obligation was to probe the depths of my own psyche. I made a beginning by writing down the fantasies which had come to me during my building game. This work took precedence over everything else.

An incessant stream of fantasies had been released, and I did my best not to lose my head but to find some way to understand these strange things. I stood helpless before an alien world; everything in it seemed difficult and incomprehensible. I was living in a constant state of tension; often I felt as if gigantic blocks of stone were tumbling down upon me. One thunderstorm followed another. My enduring these storms was a question of brute strength. Others have been shattered by them – Nietzsche, and Hölderlin, and many others. But there was a demonic strength in me, and from the beginning there was no doubt in my mind that I must find the meaning of what I was experiencing in these fantasies. When I endured these assaults of the unconscious I had an unswerving conviction that I was obeying a higher will, and that feeling continued to uphold me until I had mastered the task.

I was frequently so wrought up that I had to do certain yoga exercises in order to hold my emotions in check. But since it was my purpose to know what was going on within myself, I would do these exercises only until I had calmed myself enough to resume my work with the unconscious. As soon as I had the feeling that I was myself again, I abandoned this restraint upon the emotions and allowed the images and inner voices to speak afresh. The Indian, on the other hand, does yoga exercises in order to obliterate completely the multitude of psychic contents and images.

To the extent that I managed to translate the emotions into images – that is to say, to find the images which were concealed in the emotions – I was inwardly calmed and reassured. Had I left those images hidden in the emotions, I might have been torn to pieces by them. There is a chance that I might have succeeded in splitting them off; but in that case I would inexorably have fallen into a neurosis and so been ultimately destroyed by them anyhow. As a result of my experiment I learned how helpful it can be, from the therapeutic point of view, to find the particular images which lie behind emotions.

I wrote down the fantasies as well as I could, and made an earnest effort to analyse the psychic conditions under which they had arisen. But I was able to do this only in clumsy language. First I formulated the things as I had observed them, usually in "high-flown language," for that corresponds to the style of the archetypes. Archetypes speak the language of high rhetoric, even of bombast. It is a style I find embarrassing; it grates on my nerves, as when someone draws his nails down a plaster wall, or scrapes his knife against a plate. But since I did not know what was going on, I had no choice but to write everything down in the style selected by the unconscious itself. Sometimes it was as if I were hearing it with my ears, sometimes feeling it with my mouth, as if my tongue were formulating words; now and then I heard myself whispering aloud. Below the threshold of consciousness everything was seething with life.

From the beginning I had conceived my voluntary confrontation with the unconscious as a scientific experiment which I myself was conducting and in whose outcome I was vitally interested. To-day I might equally well say that it was an experiment which was being conducted on *me*. One of the greatest difficulties for me lay in dealing with my negative feelings. I was voluntarily submitting myself to emotions of which I could not really approve, and I was writing down fantasies which often struck me as nonsense, and towards which I had strong resistances. For as long as we do not understand their meaning, such fantasies are a diabolical mixture of the sublime and the ridiculous. It cost me a great deal to undergo them, but I had been challenged by fate. Only by extreme effort was I finally able to escape from the labyrinth.

In order to grasp the fantasies which were stirring in me "underground," I knew that I had to let myself plummet down into them, as it were. I felt not only violent resistance to this, but a distinct fear. For I was afraid of losing command of myself and becoming a prey to the fantasies – and as a psychiatrist I realized only too well what that meant. After prolonged hesitation, however, I saw that there was no other way out. I had to take the chance, had to try to gain power over them; for I realized that if I did not do so, I ran the risk of their gaining power over me. A cogent motive for my making the attempt was the conviction that I could not expect of my patients something I did not dare to do myself. The excuse that a helper stood at their side would not pass muster, for I was well aware that the so-called helper – that is, myself – could not help them unless he knew their fantasy material from his own direct experience, and that at present all he possessed were a few theoretical prejudices of dubious value. This idea – that I was committing myself to a dangerous enterprise not for myself alone, but also for the sake of my patients – helped me over several critical phases.

It was during Advent of the year 1913 – 12th December, to be exact – that I resolved upon the decisive step. I was sitting at my desk once more, thinking over my fears. Then I let myself drop. Suddenly it was as though the ground literally gave way beneath my feet, and I plunged down into dark depths. I could not fend off a feeling of panic. But then, abruptly, at not too great a depth, I landed on my feet in a soft, sticky mass. I felt great relief, although I was apparently in complete darkness. After a while my eyes grew accustomed to the gloom, which was rather like a deep twilight. Before me was the entrance to a dark cave, in which stood a dwarf with a leathery skin, as if he were mummified. I squeezed past him through the narrow entrance and waded knee deep through icy water to the other end of the cave where, on a projecting rock, I saw a glowing red crystal. I grasped the stone, lifted it, and discovered a hollow underneath. At first I could make out nothing, but then I saw that there was running water. In it a corpse floated by, a youth with blond hair and a wound in the head. He was followed by a gigantic black scarab and then by a red, newborn sun, rising up out of the depths of the water. Dazzled by the light, I wanted to replace the stone upon the opening, but then a fluid welled out. It was blood. A thick jet of it leaped up, and I felt nauseated. It seemed to me that the blood continued to spurt for an unendurably long time. At last it ceased, and the vision came to an end.

I was stunned by this vision. I realized, of course, that it was a hero and solar myth, a drama of death and renewal, the rebirth symbolized by the Egyptian scarab. At the end, the dawn of the new day should have followed, but instead came that intolerable outpouring of blood – an altogether abnormal phenomenon, so it seemed to me. But then I recalled the vision of blood that I had had in the autumn of that same year, and I abandoned all further attempt to understand.

Six days later (18th December, 1913), I had the following dream. I was with an unknown, brown-skinned man, a savage, in a lonely, rocky mountain landscape. It was before dawn; the eastern sky was already bright, and the stars fading. Then I heard Siegfried's horn sounding over the mountains and I knew that we had to kill him. We were armed with rifles and lay in wait for him on a narrow path over the rocks.

Then Siegfried appeared high up on the crest of the mountain, in the first ray of the rising sun. On a chariot made of the bones of the dead he drove at furious speed down the precipitous slope. When he turned a corner, we shot at him, and he plunged down, struck dead.

Filled with disgust and remorse for having destroyed something so great and beautiful, I turned to flee, impelled by the fear that the murder might be discovered. But a tremendous downfall of rain began, and I knew that it would wipe out all traces of the dead. I had escaped the danger of discovery; life could go on, but an unbearable feeling of guilt remained.

When I awoke from the dream, I turned it over in my mind, but was unable to understand it. I tried therefore to fall asleep again, but a voice within me said, "You *must* understand the dream, and must do so at once!" The inner urgency mounted until the terrible moment came when the voice said, "If you do not understand the dream, you must shoot yourself!" In the drawer of my night table lay a loaded revolver, and I became frightened. Then I began pondering once again, and suddenly the meaning of the dream dawned on me. "Why, that is the problem that is being played out in the world." Siegfried, I thought, represents what the Germans want to achieve, heroically to impose their will, have their own way. "Where there is a will there is a way!" I had wanted to do the same. But now that was no longer possible. The dream showed that the attitude embodied by Siegfried, the hero, no longer suited me. Therefore it had to be killed.

After the deed I felt an overpowering compassion, as though I myself had been shot: a sign of my secret identity with Siegfried, as well as of the grief a man feels when he is forced to sacrifice his ideal and his conscious attitudes. This identity and my heroic idealism had to be abandoned, for there are higher things than the ego's will, and to these one must bow.

These thoughts sufficed for the present, and I fell asleep again.

The small, brown-skinned savage who accompanied me and had actually taken the initiative in the killing was an embodiment of the primitive shadow. The rain showed that the tension between consciousness and the unconscious was being resolved. Although at the time I was not able to understand the meaning of the dream beyond these few hints, new forces were released in me which helped me to carry the experiment with the unconscious to a conclusion.

This dream is typical of dreams occurring in middle life when a change in attitude is demanded. It was about this time (1913) that Jung gave up his position as lecturer (Privatdozent) *in the University of Zurich, thus abandoning his academic career. Jung felt that this sacrifice was required of him as surely as the sacrifice of Siegfried was demanded in the dream; but it nevertheless cost him a great deal to make it.*

From "**Confrontation with the Unconscious**" MDR, pp. 185–6/193–4

In the midst of this period when I was so preoccupied with the images of the unconscious, I came to the decision to withdraw from the university, where I had lectured for eight years as *Privatdozent* (since 1905). My experience and experiments with the unconscious had brought my intellectual activity to a standstill. After the completion of *The Psychology of the Unconscious* I found myself utterly incapable of reading a scientific book. This went on for three years. I felt I could no longer keep up with the world of the intellect, nor would I have been able to talk about what really preoccupied me. The material brought to light from the unconscious had, almost literally, struck me dumb. I could neither understand it nor give it form. At the university I was in an exposed position, and felt that in order to go on giving courses there I would first have to find an entirely new and different orientation. It would be unfair to continue teaching young students when my own intellectual situation was nothing but a mass of doubts.

I therefore felt that I was confronted with the choice of either continuing my academic career, whose road lay smooth before me, or following the laws of my inner personality, of a higher reason, and forging ahead with this curious task of mine, this experiment in confrontation with the unconscious. But until it was completed I could not appear before the public.

Consciously, deliberately, then, I abandoned my academic career. For I felt that something great was happening to me, and I put my trust in the thing which I felt to be more important *sub specie æternitatis*. I knew that it would fill my life, and for the sake of that goal I was ready to take any kind of risk.

Siegfried is one characteristic personification of the archetype of the hero. Hero myths are found all over the world; and, from whatever culture they originate, show striking similarities. The archetype does not correspond to the actual manifestation produced by any particular culture; yet it underlies all manifestations produced by all cultures.

From "**Psychological Aspects of the Mother Archetype**" CW 9 i, par. 155

Again and again I encounter the mistaken notion that an archetype is determined in regard to its content, in other words that it is a kind of unconscious idea (if such an expression be admissible). It is necessary to point out once more that archetypes are not determined as regards their content, but only as regards their form and then only to a very limited degree. A primordial image is determined as to its content only when it has become conscious and is therefore filled out with the material of conscious experience. Its form, however, as I have explained elsewhere, might perhaps be compared to the axial system of a crystal, which, as it were, preforms the crystalline structure in the mother liquid, although it has no material existence of its own. This first appears according to the specific way in which the ions and molecules aggregate. The archetype in itself is empty and purely formal, nothing but a *facultas praeformandi*, a possibility of representation which is given *a priori*. The representations themselves are not inherited, only the forms, and in that respect they correspond in every way to the instincts, which are also determined in form only. The existence of the instincts can no more be proved than the existence of the archetypes, so long as they do not manifest themselves concretely. With regard to the definiteness of the form, our comparison with the crystal is illuminating inasmuch as the axial system determines only the stereometric structure but not the concrete form of the individual crystal. This may be either large or small, and it may vary endlessly by reason of the different size of its planes or by the growing together of two crystals. The only thing that remains constant is the axial system, or rather, the invariable geometric proportions underlying it. The same is true of the archetype. In principle, it can be named and has an invariable nucleus of meaning – but always only in principle, never as regards its concrete manifestation. In the same way, the specific appearance of the mother-image at any given time cannot be deduced from the mother archetype alone, but depends on innumerable other factors.

Part 4. Archetypes: Shadow; Anima; Animus; the Persona; the Old Wise Man

In Jung's dream about Siegfried (quoted in Part 3), it will be recalled that he was accompanied by a "small, brown-skinned savage" who initiated the killing. This figure, Jung affirms, "was an embodiment of the primitive shadow."

> By shadow I mean the "negative" side of the personality, the sum of all those unpleasant qualities we like to hide, together with the insufficiently developed functions and the contents of the personal unconscious. [CW 7, par. 103n]

The shadow is one example of an "unconscious personality" which possesses a certain measure of autonomy. The shadow might be said to be responsible for those slips of the tongue and other "mistakes" which Freud catalogues in The Psychopathology of Everyday Life; *mistakes which reveal feelings and motives which the conscious self disowns. The shadow is also often projected on to others. Examination of those attributes which a man most condemns in other people (greed, intolerance, disregard for others etc.) usually shows that, unacknowledged, he himself possesses them.*

The shadow is usually the first archetype to be encountered during analysis. In the dreams of Europeans, the shadow appears as a figure of the same sex as the dreamer; usually as dark-skinned, alien or primitive, as in Jung's own dream. Jung makes the point that making conscious the repressed tendencies and confessing the less desirable aspects of personality which the shadow portrays does not rid us of them.

From *Psychology and Religion*, CW 11, pars. 130–4

If one discounts the "statistical criminal," there still remains the vast domain of inferior qualities and primitive tendencies which belong to the psychic structure of the man who is less ideal and more primitive than we should like to be. We have certain ideas as to how a civilized or educated or moral being should live, and we occasionally do our best to fulfil these ambitious expectations. But since nature has not bestowed the same blessings upon each of her children, some are more and others less gifted. Thus there are people who can just afford to live properly and respectably; that is to say, no manifest flaw is discoverable. They either commit minor sins, if they sin at all, or their sins are concealed from them by a thick layer of unconciousness. One is rather inclined to be lenient with sinners who are unconscious of their sins. But nature is not at all lenient with unconscious sinners. She punishes them just as severely as if they had committed a conscious offence. Thus we find, as the pious Henry Drummond* once observed, that it is highly moral people, unaware of their other side, who develop particularly hellish moods which make them insupportable to their relatives. The odour of sanctity may be far reaching, but to live with a saint might well cause an inferiority complex or even a wild outburst of immorality in individuals less morally gifted. Morality seems to be a gift like intelligence. You cannot pump it into a system to which it is not indigenous.

Unfortunately there can be no doubt that man is, on the whole, less good than he imagines himself or wants to be. Everyone carries a shadow, and the less it is embodied in the individual's conscious life, the blacker and denser it is. If an inferiority is conscious, one always has a chance to correct it. Furthermore, it is constantly in contact with other interests, so that it is continually subjected to modifications. But if it is repressed and isolated from consciousness, it never gets corrected, and is liable to burst forth suddenly in a moment of unawareness. At all events, it forms an unconscious snag, blocking the most well-meant attempts.

We carry our past with us, to wit, the primitive and inferior man with his desires and emotions, and it is only with an enormous effort that we can detach ourselves from this burden. If it comes to a neurosis, we invariably have to deal with a considerably

*Widely known because of his book *Natural Law in the Spiritual World*. The quotation comes from *The Greatest Thing in the World*.

intensified shadow. <u>And if such a person wants to be cured</u> it is necessary to find a way in which his conscious personality and his shadow can live together.

This is a very serious problem for all those who are themselves in such a predicament or have to help sick people back to normal life. Mere suppression of the shadow is as little of a remedy as beheading would be for headache. To destroy a man's morality does not help either, because it would kill his better self, without which even the shadow makes no sense. The reconciliation of these opposites is a major problem, and even in antiquity it bothered certain minds. Thus we know of an otherwise legendary personality of the second century, Carpocrates, a Neoplatonist philosopher whose school, according to Irenaeus, taught that good and evil are merely human opinions and that the soul, before its departure from the body, must pass through the whole gamut of human experience to the very end if it is not to fall back into the prison of the body. It is as if the soul could only ransom itself from imprisonment in the somatic world of the demiurge by complete fulfilment of all life's demands. The bodily existence in which we find ourselves is a kind of hostile brother whose conditions must first be known. It was in this sense that the Carpocratians interpreted Matthew 5:25f. (also Luke 12:58f.): "Agree with thine adversary quickly, whiles thou art in the way with him; lest at any time the adversary deliver thee to the judge, and the judge deliver thee to the officer, and thou be cast into prison. Verily I say unto thee, Thou shalt by no means come out thence, till thou hast paid the uttermost farthing." Remembering the other Gnostic doctrine that no man can be redeemed from a sin he has not committed, we are here confronted with a problem of the very greatest importance, obscured though it is by the Christian abhorrence of anything Gnostic. Inasmuch as the somatic man, the "adversary," is none other than "the other in me," it is plain that the Carpocratian mode of thought would lead to the following interpretation of Matthew 5:22f.: "But I say unto you, That whosoever is angry with *himself* without a cause shall be in danger of the judgment: and whosoever shall say to *himself*, Raca, shall be in danger of the council: but whosoever shall say, Thou fool, shall be in danger of hell fire. Therefore if thou bring thy gift to the altar, and there rememberest that *thou hast aught against thyself*, leave there thy gift before the altar, and go thy way; first be reconciled to *thyself*, and then come and offer thy gift. Agree with *thyself* quickly, whiles thou art in the way with *thyself*; lest at any time *thou deliverest thyself* to the judge." From here it is but a step to the uncanonical saying: "Man, if indeed thou knowest what thou doest, thou art blessed; but if thou knowest not, thou art cursed, and a transgressor of the law." But the problem comes very close indeed in the parable of the unjust steward, which is a stumbling-block in more senses than one. "And the lord commended the unjust steward, because he had done wisely" (Luke 16:8). In the Vulgate the word for "wisely" is *prudenter*, and in the Greek text it is φρονίμως (prudently, sensibly, intelligently). There's no denying that practical intelligence functions here as a court of ethical decision. Perhaps, despite Irenaeus, we may credit the Carpocratians with this much insight, and allow that they too, like the unjust steward, were commendably aware of how to save face. It is natural that the more robust mentality of the Church Fathers could not appreciate the delicacy and the merit of this subtle and, from a modern point of view, immensely practical argument. It was also dangerous, and it is still the most vital and yet the most ticklish ethical problem of a civilization that has forgotten why man's life should be sacrificial, that is, offered up to an idea greater than himself. Man can live the most amazing things if they make sense to him. But the difficulty is to create that sense. It must be a conviction, naturally; but you find that the most convincing things man can invent are cheap and ready-made, and are never able to convince him against his personal desires and fears.

If the repressed tendencies, the shadow as I call them, were obviously evil, there would be no problem whatever. But the shadow is merely somewhat inferior, primitive, unadapted, and awkward; not wholly bad. It even contains childish or primitive qualities which would in a way vitalize and embellish human existence, but convention forbids!

Jung goes on to show that confrontation with, and at least partial acceptance of, the shadow leads on to deeper problems and further encounters with other archetypal figures.

From "**The Shadow**" *Aion*, CW 9 ii, pars. 13–19

Whereas the contents of the personal unconscious are acquired during the individual's lifetime, the contents of the collective unconscious are invariably archetypes that were present from the beginning. Their relation to the instincts has been discussed elsewhere. The archetypes most clearly characterized from the empirical point of view are those which have the most frequent and the most disturbing influence on the ego. These are the *shadow*, the *anima*, and the *animus*. The most accessible of these, and the easiest to experience, is the shadow, for its nature can in large measure be inferred from the contents of the personal unconscious. The only exceptions to this rule are those rather rare cases where the positive qualities of the personality are repressed, and the ego in consequence plays an essentially negative or unfavourable role.

The shadow is a moral problem that challenges the whole ego-personality, for no one can become conscious of the shadow without considerable moral effort. To become conscious of it involves recognizing the dark aspects of the personality as present and real. This act is the essential condition for any kind of self-knowledge, and it therefore, as a rule, meets with considerable resistance. Indeed, self-knowledge as a psychotherapeutic measure frequently requires much painstaking work extending over a long period.

Closer examination of the dark characteristics – that is, the inferiorities constituting the shadow – reveals that they have an *emotional* nature, a kind of autonomy, and accordingly an obsessive or, better, possessive quality. Emotion, incidentally, is not an activity of the individual but something that happens to him. Affects occur usually where adaptation is weakest, and at the same time they reveal the reason for its weakness, namely a certain degree of inferiority and the existence of a lower level of personality. On this lower level with its uncontrolled or scarcely controlled emotions one behaves more or less like a primitive, who is not only the passive victim of his affects but also singularly incapable of moral judgment.

Although, with insight and good will, the shadow can to some extent be assimilated into the conscious personality, experience shows that there are certain features which offer the most obstinate resistance to moral control and prove almost impossible to influence. These resistances are usually bound up with *projections*, which are not recognized as such, and their recognition is a moral achievement beyond the ordinary. While some traits peculiar to the shadow can be recognized without too much difficulty as one's own personal qualities, in this case both insight and good will are unavailing because the cause of the emotion appears to lie, beyond all possibility of doubt, in the *other person*. No matter how obvious it may be to the neutral observer that it is a matter of projections, there is little hope that the subject will perceive this himself. He must be convinced that he throws a very long shadow before he is willing to withdraw his emotionally-toned projections from their object.

Let us suppose that a certain individual shows no inclination whatever to recognize his projections. The projection-making factor then has a free hand and can realize its object – if it has one – or bring about some other situation characteristic of its power. As we know, it is not the conscious subject but the unconscious which does the projecting. Hence one meets with projections, one does not make them. The effect of projection is to isolate the subject from his environment, since instead of a real relation to it there is now only an illusory one. Projections change the world into the replica of one's own unknown face. In the last analysis, therefore, they lead to an autoerotic or autistic condition in which one dreams a world whose reality remains forever unattainable. The resultant *sentiment d'incomplétude* and the still worse feeling of sterility are in their turn explained by projection as the malevolence of the environment, and by means of this vicious circle the isolation is intensified. The more projections are thrust in between the subject and the environment, the harder it is for the ego to see through its illusions. A forty-five-year-old patient who had suffered from a compulsion neurosis since he was twenty and had become completely cut off from the world once said to me: "But I can never admit to myself that I've wasted the best twenty-five years of my life!"

It is often tragic to see how blatantly a man bungles his own life and the lives of others yet remains totally incapable of seeing how much the whole tragedy originates in himself, and how he continually feeds it and keeps it going. Not *consciously*, of course – for consciously he is engaged in bewailing and cursing a faithless world that recedes further and further into the distance. Rather, it is an unconscious factor which spins the illusions that veil his world. And what is being spun is a cocoon, which in the end will completely envelop him.

One might assume that projections like these, which are so very difficult if not impossible to dissolve, would belong to the realm of the shadow – that is, to the negative side of the personality. This assumption becomes untenable after a certain point, because the symbols that then appear no longer refer to the same but to the opposite sex, in a man's case to a woman and vice versa. The source of projections is no longer the shadow – which is always of the same sex as the subject – but a contrasexual figure. Here we meet the animus of a woman and the anima of a man, two corresponding archetypes whose autonomy and unconsciousness explain the stubbornness of their projections. Though the shadow is a motif as well known to mythology as anima and animus, it represents first and foremost the personal unconscious, and its content can therefore be made conscious without too much difficulty. In this it differs from anima and animus, for whereas the shadow can be seen through and recognized fairly easily, the anima and animus are much further away from consciousness and in normal circumstances are seldom if ever realized. With a little self-criticism one can see through the shadow – so far as its nature is personal. But when it appears as an archetype, one encounters the same difficulties as with anima and animus. In other words, it is quite within the bounds of possibility for a man to recognize the relative evil of his nature, but it is a rare and shattering experience for him to gaze into the face of absolute evil.

Before proceeding to what Jung has to say about the contrasexual archetypes of animus and anima, it is necessary to outline his conception of the persona, *since "a compensatory relationship exists between persona and anima."*

From "**The Relations between the Ego and the Unconscious**"
Two Essays, CW 7, pars. 305–9

The persona is a complicated system of relations between
individual consciousness and society, fittingly enough a kind of
mask, designed on the one hand to make a definite impression
upon others, and, on the other, to conceal the true nature of the
individual. That the latter function is superfluous could be
maintained only by one who is so identified with his persona that
he no longer knows himself; and that the former is unnecessary
could only occur to one who is quite unconscious of the true nature
of his fellows. Society expects, and indeed must expect, every
individual to play the part assigned to him as perfectly as possible,
so that a man who is a parson must not only carry out his official
functions objectively, but must at all times and in all circumstances
play the role of parson in a flawless manner. Society demands this
as a kind of surety; each must stand at his post, here a cobbler,
there a poet. No man is expected to be both. Nor is it advisable
to be both, for that would be "queer." Such a man would be
"different" from other people, not quite reliable. In the academic
world he would be a dilettante, in politics an "unpredictable"
quantity, in religion a free-thinker – in short, he would always be
suspected of unreliability and incompetence, because society is
persuaded that only the cobbler who is not a poet can supply
workmanlike shoes. To present an unequivocal face to the world
is a matter of practical importance: the average man – the only kind
society knows anything about – must keep his nose to one thing
in order to achieve anything worth while, two would be too much.
Our society is undoubtedly set on such an ideal. It is therefore not
surprising that everyone who wants to get on must take these
expectations into account. Obviously no one could completely
submerge his individuality in these expectations; hence the
construction of an artificial personality becomes an unavoidable
necessity. The demands of propriety and good manners are an
added inducement to assume a becoming mask. What goes on
behind the mask is then called "private life." This painfully
familiar division of consciousness into two figures, often preposter-
ously different, is an incisive psychological operation that is bound
to have repercussions on the unconscious.

The construction of a collectively suitable persona means a formidable concession to the external world, a genuine self-sacrifice which drives the ego straight into identification with the persona, so that people really do exist who believe they are what they pretend to be. The "soullessness" of such an attitude is, however, only apparent, for under no circumstances will the unconscious tolerate this shifting of the centre of gravity. When we examine such cases critically, we find that the excellence of the mask is compensated by the "private life" going on behind it. The pious Drummond once lamented that "bad temper is the vice of the virtuous." Whoever builds up too good a persona for himself naturally has to pay for it with irritability. Bismarck had hysterical weeping fits, Wagner indulged in correspondence about the belts of silk dressing-gowns, Nietzsche wrote letters to his "dear lama," Goethe held conversations with Eckermann, etc. But there are subtler things than the banal lapses of heroes. I once made the acquaintance of a very venerable personage – in fact, one might easily call him a saint. I stalked round him for three whole days, but never a mortal failing did I find in him. My feeling of inferiority grew ominous, and I was beginning to think seriously of how I might better myself. Then, on the fourth day, his wife came to consult me . . . Well, nothing of the sort has ever happened to me since. But this I did learn: that any man who becomes one with his persona can cheerfully let all disturbances manifest themselves through his wife without her noticing it, though she pays for her self-sacrifice with a bad neurosis.

These identifications with a social role are a very fruitful source of neuroses. A man cannot get rid of himself in favour of an artificial personality without punishment. Even the attempt to do so brings on, in all ordinary cases, unconscious reactions in the form of bad moods, affects, phobias, compulsive ideas, backslidings, vices, etc. The socially "strong man" is in his private life often a mere child where his own states of feeling are concerned; his public discipline (which he demands quite particularly of others) goes miserably to pieces in private. His "happiness in his work" assumes a woeful countenance at home; his "spotless" public morality looks strange indeed behind the mask – we will not mention deeds, but only fantasies, and the wives of such men would have a pretty tale to tell. As to his selfless altruism, his children have decided views about that.

To the degree that the world invites the individual to identify with the mask, he is delivered over to influences from within. "High rests on low," says Lao-tzu. An opposite forces its way up from inside; it is exactly as though the unconscious suppressed the ego with the very same power which drew the ego into the persona. The absence of resistance outwardly against the lure of the persona means a similar weakness inwardly against the influence of the unconscious. Outwardly an effective and powerful role is played, while inwardly an effeminate weakness develops in face of every influence coming from the unconscious. Moods, vagaries, timidity, even a limp sexuality (culminating in impotence), gradually gain the upper hand.

The persona, the ideal picture of a man as he should be, is inwardly compensated by feminine weakness, and as the individual outwardly plays the strong man, so he becomes inwardly a woman, i.e., the anima, for it is the anima that reacts to the persona. But because the inner world is dark and invisible to the extraverted consciousness, and because a man is all the less capable of conceiving his weaknesses the more he is identified with the persona, the persona's counterpart, the anima, remains completely in the dark and is at once projected, so that our hero comes under the heel of his wife's slipper. If this results in a considerable increase of her power, she will acquit herself none too well. She becomes inferior, thus providing her husband with the welcome proof that it is not he, the hero, who is inferior in private, but his wife. In return the wife can cherish the illusion, so attractive to many, that at least she has married a hero, unperturbed by her own uselessness. This little game of illusion is often taken to be the whole meaning of life.

The ideal individual, one might postulate, would be consistently the same whatever the circumstances. In practice, most human beings adopt attitudes in public which are different from their attitudes in private. There is a dissociation of personality into "outer" and "inner"; into "mask" and "soul." Jung affirms that, in men, the inner personality or soul is feminine, and represented as such by female figures in dreams and fantasies; whereas the opposite is true for women.

(The words preceding "q.v." in the following passage are defined by Jung elsewhere in "Definitions.")

From "**Definitions**" *Psychological Types*, CW 6, pars. 797–811

48. SOUL [Psyche, personality, persona, anima]. I have been compelled, in my investigations into the structure of the unconscious, to make a conceptual distinction between *soul* and *psyche*. By psyche I understand the totality of all psychic processes, conscious as well as unconscious. By soul, on the other hand, I understand a clearly demarcated functional complex that can best be described as a "personality." In order to make clear what I mean by this, I must introduce some further points of view. It is, in particular, the phenomena of somnambulism, double consciousness, split personality, etc., whose investigation we owe primarily to the French school, that have enabled us to accept the possibility of a plurality of personalities in one and the same individual.

[Soul as a functional complex or "personality"]

It is at once evident that such a plurality of personalities can never appear in a normal individual. But, as the above-mentioned phenomena show, the possibility of a dissociation of personality must exist, at least in the germ, within the range of the normal. And, as a matter of fact, any moderately acute psychological observer will be able to demonstrate, without much difficulty, traces of character-splitting in normal individuals. One has only to observe a man rather closely, under varying conditions, to see that a change from one milieu to another brings about a striking alteration of personality, and on each occasion a clearly defined character emerges that is noticeably different from the previous one. "Angel abroad, devil at home" is a formulation of the phenomenon of character-splitting derived from everyday experience. A particular milieu necessitates a particular *attitude* (q.v.). The longer this attitude lasts, and the more often it is required, the more habitual it becomes. Very many people from the educated classes have to move in two totally different milieus – the domestic circle and the world of affairs. These two totally different environments demand two totally different attitudes, which, depending on the degree of the ego's *identification* (q.v.) with the attitude of the moment, produce a duplication of character. In accordance with social conditions and requirements, the social character is oriented on the one hand by the expectations and demands of society, and on the other by the social aims and aspirations of the individual. The domestic character is, as a rule, moulded by emotional demands and an easy-going acquiescence for the sake of comfort and convenience; whence it frequently happens that men who in public life are extremely energetic, spirited, obstinate, wilful and ruthless appear good-natured, mild, compliant, even weak, when at home and in the bosom of the family. Which is the true character, the real personality? This question is often impossible to answer.

These reflections show that even in normal individuals character-splitting is by no means an impossibility. We are, therefore, fully justified in treating personality dissociation as a problem of normal psychology. In my view the answer to the above question should be that such a man has no real character at all: he is not *individual* (q.v.) but *collective* (q.v.), the plaything of circumstance and general expectations. Were he individual, he would have the same character despite the variation of attitude. He would not be identical with the attitude of the moment, and he neither would nor could prevent his *individuality* (q.v.) from expressing itself just as clearly in one state as in another. Naturally he is individual, like every living being, but unconsciously so. Because of his more or less complete identification with the attitude of the moment, he deceives others, and often himself, as to his real character. He puts on a *mask*, which he knows is in keeping with his conscious intentions, while it also meets the requirements and fits the opinions of society, first one motive and then the other gaining the upper hand.

[Soul as persona]

This mask, i.e., the *ad hoc* adopted attitude, I have called the *persona*, which was the name for the masks worn by actors in antiquity. The man who identifies with this mask I would call "personal" as opposed to "individual."

The two above-mentioned attitudes represent two collective personalities, which may be summed up quite simply under the name "personae." I have already suggested that the real individuality is different from both. The persona is thus a functional complex that comes into existence for reasons of adaptation or personal convenience, but is by no means identical with the individuality. The persona is exclusively concerned with the relation to objects. The relation of the individual to the object must be sharply distinguished from the relation to the subject. By the "subject" I mean first of all those vague, dim stirrings, feelings, thoughts, and sensations which flow in on us not from any demonstrable continuity of conscious experience of the object, but well up like a disturbing, inhibiting, or at times helpful, influence from the dark inner depths, from the background and underground vaults of consciousness, and constitute, in their totality, our perception of the life of the unconscious. The subject, conceived as the "inner object," *is* the unconscious. Just as there is a relation to the outer object, an outer attitude, there is a relation to the inner object, an inner attitude. It is readily understandable that this inner attitude, by reason of its extremely intimate and inaccessible nature, is far more difficult to discern than the outer attitude, which is immediately perceived by everyone. Nevertheless, it does not seem to me impossible to formulate it as a concept. All those allegedly accidental inhibitions, fancies, moods, vague feelings, and scraps of fantasy that hinder concentration and disturb the peace of mind even of the most normal man, and that are rationalized away as being due to bodily causes and suchlike, usually have their origin, not in the reasons consciously ascribed to them, but in perceptions of unconscious processes. Dreams naturally belong to this class of phenomena, and, as we all know, are often traced back to such external and superficial causes as indigestion, sleeping on one's back, and so forth, in spite of the fact that these explanations can never stand up to searching criticism. The attitude of the individual in these matters is extremely varied. One man will not allow himself to be disturbed in the slightest by his inner processes – he can ignore them completely; another man is just as completely at their mercy – as soon as he wakes up some fantasy or other, or a disagreeable feeling, spoils his mood for the whole day; a vaguely unpleasant sensation puts the idea into his head that he is suffering from a secret disease, a dream fills him with gloomy forebodings, although ordinarily he is not superstitious. Others, again, have only periodic access to these unconscious stirrings, or only to a certain category of them. For one man they may never have reached consciousness at all as anything worth thinking about, for another they are a worrying problem he broods on daily. One man takes them as physiological, another attributes them to the behaviour of his neighbours, another finds in them a religious revelation.

These entirely different ways of dealing with the stirrings of the unconscious are just as habitual as the attitudes to the outer object. The inner attitude, therefore, is correlated with just as definite a functional complex as the outer attitude. People who, it would seem, entirely overlook their inner psychic processes no more lack a typical inner attitude than the people who constantly overlook the outer object and the reality of facts lack a typical outer one. In all the latter cases, which are by no means uncommon, the persona is characterized by a lack of relatedness, at times even a blind inconsiderateness, that yields only to the harshest blows of fate. Not infrequently, it is just these people with a rigid persona who possess an attitude to the unconscious processes which is extremely susceptible and open to influence. Inwardly they are as weak, malleable, and "soft-centred" as they are inflexible and unapproachable outwardly. Their inner attitude, therefore, corresponds to a personality that is diametrically opposed to the outer personality. I know a man, for instance, who blindly and pitilessly destroyed the happiness of those nearest to him, and yet would interrupt important business journeys just to enjoy the beauty of a forest scene glimpsed from the carriage window. Cases of this kind are doubtless familiar to everyone, so I need not give further examples.

[Soul as anima]

We can, therefore, speak of an inner personality with as much justification as, on the grounds of daily experience, we speak of an outer personality. The inner personality is the way one behaves in relation to one's inner psychic processes; it is the inner attitude, the characteristic face, that is turned towards the unconscious. I call the outer attitude, the outward face, the *persona*; the inner attitude, the inward face, I call the *anima*. To the degree that an attitude is habitual, it is a well-knit functional complex with which the ego can identify itself more or less. Common speech expresses this very graphically: when a man has an habitual attitude to certain situations, an habitual way of doing things, we say he is quite *another man* when doing this or that. This is a practical demonstration of the autonomy of the functional complex represented by the habitual attitude: it is as though another personality had taken possession of the individual, as though "another spirit had got into him." The same autonomy that very often characterizes the outer attitude is also claimed by the inner attitude, the anima. It is one of the most difficult educational feats to change the persona, the outer attitude, and it is just as difficult to change the anima, since its structure is usually quite as well-knit as the persona's. Just as the persona is an entity that often seems to constitute the whole character of a man, and may even accompany him unaltered throughout his entire life, the anima is a clearly defined entity with a character that, very often, is autonomous and immutable. It therefore lends itself very readily to characterization and description.

As to the character of the anima, my experience confirms the rule that it is, by and large, *complementary* to the character of the persona. The anima usually contains all those common human qualities which the conscious attitude lacks. The tyrant tormented by bad dreams, gloomy forebodings, and inner fears is a typical figure. Outwardly ruthless, harsh, and unapproachable, he jumps inwardly at every shadow, is at the mercy of every mood, as though he were the feeblest and most impressionable of men. Thus his anima contains all those fallible human qualities his persona lacks. If the persona is intellectual, the anima will quite certainly be sentimental. The complementary character of the anima also affects the sexual character, as I have proved to myself beyond a doubt. A very feminine woman has a masculine soul, and a very masculine man has a feminine soul. This contrast is due to the fact that a man is not in all things wholly masculine, but also has certain feminine traits. The more masculine his outer attitude is, the more his feminine traits are obliterated: instead, they appear in his unconscious. This explains why it is just those very virile men who are most subject to characteristic weaknesses; their attitude to the unconscious has a womanish weakness and impressionability. Conversely, it is often just the most feminine women who, in their inner lives, display an intractability, an obstinacy, and a wilfulness that are to be found with comparable intensity only in a man's outer attitude. These are masculine traits which, excluded from the womanly outer attitude, have become qualities of her soul.

If, therefore, we speak of the *anima* of a man, we must logically speak of the *animus* of a woman, if we are to give the soul of a woman its right name. Whereas logic and objectivity are usually the predominant features of a man's outer attitude, or are at least regarded as ideals, in the case of a woman it is feeling. But in the soul it is the other way round: inwardly it is the man who feels, and the woman who reflects. Hence a man's greater liability to total despair, while a woman can always find comfort and hope; accordingly a man is more likely to put an end to himself than a woman. However much a victim of social circumstances a woman may be, as a prostitute for instance, a man is no less a victim of impulses from the unconscious, taking the form of alcoholism and other vices.

As to its common human qualities, the character of the anima can be deduced from that of the persona. Everything that should normally be in the outer attitude, but is conspicuously absent, will invariably be found in the inner attitude. This is a fundamental rule which my experience has borne out over and over again. But as regards its individual qualities, nothing can be deduced about them in this way. We can only be certain that when a man is identical with his persona, his individual qualities will be associated with the anima. This association frequently gives rise in dreams to the symbol of psychic pregnancy, a symbol that goes back to the *primordial image* (q.v.) of the hero's birth. The child that is to be born signifies the individuality, which, though present, is not yet conscious. For in the same way as the persona, the instrument of adaptation to the environment, is strongly influenced by environmental conditions, the anima is shaped by the unconscious and its qualities. In a primitive milieu the persona necessarily takes on primitive features, and the anima similarly takes over the *archaic* (q.v.) features of the unconscious as well as its symbolic, prescient character. Hence the "pregnant," "creative" qualities of the inner attitude.

Identity (q.v.) with the persona automatically leads to an unconscious identity with the anima because, when the ego is not differentiated from the persona, it can have no conscious relation to the unconscious processes. Consequently, it *is* these processes, it is identical with them. Anyone who is himself his outward role will infallibly succumb to the inner processes; he will either frustrate his outward role by absolute inner necessity or else reduce it to absurdity, by a process of *enantiodromia* (q.v.). He can no longer keep to his individual way, and his life runs into one deadlock after another. Moreover, the anima is inevitably projected upon a real object, with which he gets into a relation of almost total dependence. Every reaction displayed by this object has an immediate, inwardly enervating effect on the subject. Tragic ties are often formed in this way (v. *Soul-image*).

49. SOUL-IMAGE [Anima / Animus]. The soul-image is a specific *image* (q.v.) among those produced by the unconscious. Just as the *persona* (v. *Soul*), or outer attitude, is represented in dreams by images of definite persons who possess the outstanding qualities of the persona in especially marked form, so in a man the soul, i.e., anima, or inner attitude, is represented in the unconscious by definite persons with the corresponding qualities. Such an image is called a "soul-image." Sometimes these images are of quite unknown or mythological figures. With men the anima is usually personified by the unconscious as a woman; with women the animus is personified as a man. In every case where the *individuality* (q.v.) is unconscious, and therefore associated with the soul, the soul-image has the character of the same sex. In all cases where there is an *identity* (q.v.) with the persona, and the soul accordingly is unconscious, the soul-image is transferred to a real person. This person is the object of intense love or equally intense hate (or fear). The influence of such a person is immediate and absolutely compelling, because it always provokes an affective response. The *affect* (q.v.) is due to the fact that a real, conscious adaptation to the person representing the soul-image is impossible. Because an objective relationship is non-existent and out of the question, the *libido* (q.v.) gets dammed up and explodes in an outburst of affect. Affects always occur where there is a failure of adaptation. Conscious adaptation to the person representing the

soul-image is impossible precisely because the subject is unconscious of the soul. Were he conscious of it, it could be distinguished
from the object, whose immediate effects might then be mitigated,
since the potency of the object depends on the *projection* (q.v.) of
the soul-image.

For a man, a woman is best fitted to be the real bearer of his
soul-image, because of the feminine quality of his soul; for a
woman it will be a man. Wherever an impassioned, almost magical,
relationship exists between the sexes, it is invariably a question of
a projected soul-image. Since these relationships are very common,
the soul must be unconscious just as frequently – that is, vast
numbers of people must be quite unaware of the way they are
related to their inner psychic processes. Because this unconsciousness is always coupled with complete identification with the
persona, it follows that this identification must be very frequent
too. And in actual fact very many people are wholly identified with
their outer attitude and therefore have no conscious relation to
their inner processes. Conversely, it may also happen that the
soul-image is not projected but remains with the subject, and this
results in an identification with the soul because the subject is then
convinced that the way he relates to his inner processes is his real
character. In that event the persona, being unconscious, will be
projected on a person of the same sex, thus providing a foundation
for many cases of open or latent homosexuality, and of father-
transferences in men or mother-transferences in women. In such
cases there is always a defective adaptation to external reality and
a lack of relatedness, because identification with the soul produces
an attitude predominantly oriented to the perception of inner
processes, and the object is deprived of its determining power.

If the soul-image is projected, the result is an absolute affective
tie to the object. If it is not projected, a relatively unadapted state
develops, which Freud has described as *narcissism*. The projection
of the soul-image offers a release from preoccupation with one's
inner processes so long as the behaviour of the object is in harmony
with the soul-image. The subject is then in a position to live out
his persona and develop it further. The object, however, will
scarcely be able to meet the demands of the soul-image indefinitely, although there are many women who, by completely
disregarding their own lives, succeed in representing their

husband's soul-image for a very long time. The biological feminine instinct assists them in this. A man may unconsciously do the same for his wife, though this will prompt him to deeds which finally exceed his capacities whether for good or evil. Here again the biological masculine instinct is a help.

If the soul-image is not projected, a thoroughly morbid relation to the unconscious gradually develops. The subject is increasingly overwhelmed by unconscious contents, which his inadequate relation to the object makes him powerless to assimilate or put to any kind of use, so that the whole subject-object relation only deteriorates further. Naturally these two attitudes represent the two extremes between which the more normal attitudes lie. In a normal man the soul-image is not distinguished by any particular clarity, purity, or depth, but is apt to be rather blurred. In men with a good-natured and unaggressive persona, the soul-image has a rather malevolent character. A good literary example of this is the daemonic woman who is the companion of Zeus in Spitteler's *Olympian Spring*. For an idealistic woman, a depraved man is often the bearer of the soul-image; hence the "saviour fantasy" so frequent in such cases. The same thing happens with men, when the prostitute is surrounded with the halo of a soul crying for succour.

From "**The Relations between the Ego and the Unconscious**" *Two Essays*, CW 7, pars. 296–301, 314–16

ANIMA AND ANIMUS

Among all possible spirits the spirits of the parents are in practice the most important; hence the universal incidence of the ancestor cult. In its original form it served to conciliate the *revenants*, but on a higher level of culture it became an essentially moral and educational institution, as in China. For the child, the parents are his closest and most influential relations. But as he grows older this influence is split off; consequently the parental imagos become increasingly shut away from consciousness, and on account of the restrictive influence they sometimes continue to exert, they easily acquire a negative aspect. In this way the parental imagos remain as alien elements somewhere "outside" the psyche.

In place of the parents, woman now takes up her position as the most immediate environmental influence in the life of the adult man. She becomes his companion, she belongs to him in so far as she shares his life and is more or less of the same age. She is not of a superior order, either by virtue of age, authority, or physical strength. She is, however, a very influential factor and, like the parents, she produces an imago of a relatively autonomous nature – not an imago to be split off like that of the parents, but one that has to be kept associated with consciousness. Woman, with her very dissimilar psychology, is and always has been a source of information about things for which a man has no eyes. She can be his inspiration; her intuitive capacity, often superior to man's, can give him timely warning, and her feeling, always directed towards the personal, can show him ways which his own less personally accented feeling would never have discovered. What Tacitus says about the Germanic women is exactly to the point in this respect.*

Here, without a doubt, is one of the main sources for the feminine quality of the soul. But it does not seem to be the only source. No man is so entirely masculine that he has nothing feminine in him. The fact is, rather, that very masculine men have – carefully guarded and hidden – a very soft emotional life, often incorrectly described as "feminine." A man counts it a virtue to repress his feminine traits as much as possible, just as a woman, at least until recently, considered it unbecoming to be "mannish." The repression of feminine traits and inclinations naturally causes these contrasexual demands to accumulate in the unconscious. No less naturally, the imago of woman (the soul-image) becomes a receptacle for these demands, which is why a man, in his love-choice, is strongly tempted to win the woman who best corresponds to his own unconscious femininity – a woman, in short, who can unhesitatingly receive the projection of his soul. Although such a choice is often regarded and felt as altogether ideal, it may turn out that the man has manifestly married his own worst weakness. This would explain some highly remarkable conjunctions.

It seems to me, therefore, that apart from the influence of

*Cf. Tacitus, *Germania* (Loeb Classical Library), pars. 18, 19.

woman there is also the man's own femininity to explain the feminine nature of the soul complex. There is no question here of any linguistic "accident," of the kind that makes the sun feminine in German and masculine in other languages. We have, in this matter, the testimony of art from all ages, and besides that the famous question: *habet mulier animam?* Most men, probably, who have any psychological insight at all will know what Rider Haggard means by "She-who-must-be-obeyed," and will also recognize the chord that is struck when they read Benoît's description of Antinéa.* Moreover they know at once the kind of woman who most readily embodies this mysterious factor, of which they have so vivid a premonition.

The wide recognition accorded to such books shows that there must be some supra-individual quality in this image of the anima, something that does not owe a fleeting existence simply to its individual uniqueness, but is far more typical, with roots that go deeper than the obvious surface attachments I have pointed out. Both Rider Haggard and Benoît give unmistakable utterance to this supposition in the *historical* aspect of their anima figures.

As we know, there is no human experience, nor would experience be possible at all, without the intervention of a subjective aptitude. What is this subjective aptitude? Ultimately it consists in an innate psychic structure which allows man to have experiences of this kind. Thus the whole nature of man presupposes woman, both physically and spiritually. His system is tuned in to woman from the start, just as it is prepared for a quite definite world where there is water, light, air, salt, carbohydrates, etc. The form of the world into which he is born is already inborn in him as a virtual image. Likewise parents, wife, children, birth, and death are inborn in him as virtual images, as psychic aptitudes. These *a priori* categories have by nature a collective character; they are images of parents, wife, and children in general, and are not individual predestinations. We must therefore think of these images as lacking in solid content, hence as unconscious. They only acquire solidity, influence, and eventual consciousness in the encounter with empirical facts, which touch the unconscious

*Cf. H. Rider Haggard, *She* (London, 1887), and Pierre Benoît, *L'Atlantide* (Paris, 1920; trans. by Mary C. Tongue and Mary Ross as *Atlantida*, New York, 1920).

aptitude and quicken it to life. They are in a sense the deposits of all our ancestral experiences, but they are not the experiences themselves. So at least it seems to us, in the present limited state of our knowledge. (I must confess that I have never yet found infallible evidence for the inheritance of memory images, but I do not regard it as positively precluded that in addition to these collective deposits which contain nothing specifically individual, there may also be inherited memories that are individually determined.)

An inherited collective image of woman exists in a man's unconscious, with the help of which he apprehends the nature of woman. This inherited image is the third important source for the femininity of the soul.

. . . .

Now, everything that is true of the persona and of all autonomous complexes in general also holds true of the anima. She likewise is a personality, and this is why she is so easily projected upon a woman. So long as the anima is unconscious she is always projected, for everything unconscious is projected. The first bearer of the soul-image is always the mother; later it is borne by those women who arouse the man's feelings, whether in a positive or a negative sense. Because the mother is the first bearer of the soul-image, separation from her is a delicate and important matter of the greatest educational significance. Accordingly among primitives we find a large number of rites designed to organize this separation. The mere fact of becoming adult, and of outward separation, is not enough; impressive initiations into the "men's house" and ceremonies of rebirth are still needed in order to make the separation from the mother (and hence from childhood) entirely effective.

Just as the father acts as a protection against the dangers of the external world and thus serves his son as a model persona, so the mother protects him against the dangers that threaten from the darkness of his psyche. In the puberty rites, therefore, the initiate receives instruction about these things of "the other side," so that he is put in a position to dispense with his mother's protection.

The modern civilized man has to forgo this primitive but nonetheless admirable system of education. The consequence is that the anima, in the form of the mother-imago, is transferred to the wife; and the man, as soon as he marries, becomes childish, sentimental, dependent, and subservient, or else truculent, tyrannical, hypersensitive, always thinking about the prestige of his superior masculinity. The last is of course merely the reverse of the first. The safeguard against the unconscious, which is what his mother meant to him, is not replaced by anything in the modern man's education; unconsciously, therefore, his ideal of marriage is so arranged that his wife has to take over the magical role of the mother. Under the cloak of the ideally exclusive marriage he is really seeking his mother's protection, and thus he plays into the hands of his wife's possessive instincts. His fear of the dark incalculable power of the unconscious gives his wife an illegitimate authority over him, and forges such a dangerously close union that the marriage is permanently on the brink of explosion from internal tension – or else, out of protest, he flies to the other extreme, with the same results.

From "**The Syzygy: Anima and Animus**" *Aion*, CW 9 ii, pars. 24–40

In the case of the son, the projection-making factor is identical with the mother-imago, and this is consequently taken to be the real mother. The projection can only be dissolved when the son sees that in the realm of his psyche there is an imago not only of the mother but of the daughter, the sister, the beloved, the heavenly goddess, and the chthonic Baubo. Every mother and every beloved is forced to become the carrier and embodiment of this omnipresent and ageless image, which corresponds to the deepest reality in a man. It belongs to him, this perilous image of Woman; she stands for the loyalty which in the interests of life he must sometimes forgo; she is the much needed compensation for the risks, struggles, sacrifices that all end in disappointment; she is the solace for all the bitterness of life. And, at the same time, she is the great illusionist, the seductress, who draws him into life with her Maya – and not only into life's reasonable and useful aspects, but into its frightful paradoxes and ambivalences where good and evil, success and ruin, hope and despair, counterbalance one another. Because she is his greatest danger she demands from a man his greatest, and if he has it in him she will receive it.

This image is "My Lady Soul," as Spitteler called her. I have suggested instead the term "anima," as indicating something specific, for which the expression "soul" is too general and too vague. The empirical reality summed up under the concept of the anima forms an extremely dramatic content of the unconscious. It is possible to describe this content in rational, scientific language, but in this way one entirely fails to express its living character. Therefore, in describing the living processes of the psyche, I deliberately and consciously give preference to a dramatic, mythological way of thinking and speaking, because this is not only more expressive but also more exact than an abstract scientific terminology, which is wont to toy with the notion that its theoretic formulations may one fine day be resolved into algebraic equations.

The projection-making factor is the anima, or rather the unconscious as represented by the anima. Whenever she appears, in dreams, visions, and fantasies, she takes on personified form, thus demonstrating that the factor she embodies possesses all the outstanding characteristics of a feminine being.* She is not an invention of the conscious, but a spontaneous product of the unconscious. Nor is she a substitute figure for the mother. On the contrary, there is every likelihood that the numinous qualities which make the mother-imago so dangerously powerful derive from the collective archetype of the anima, which is incarnated anew in every male child.

Since the anima is an archetype that is found in men, it is reasonable to suppose that an equivalent archetype must be present in women; for just as the man is compensated by a feminine element, so woman is compensated by a masculine one. I do not, however, wish this argument to give the impression that these compensatory relationships were arrived at by deduction. On the contrary, long and varied experience was needed in order to grasp

---

*Naturally, she is a typical figure in *belles-lettres*. Recent publications on the subject of the anima include Linda Fierz-David, *The Dream of Poliphilo*, and my "Psychology of the Transference." The anima as a psychological idea first appears in the 16th-cent. humanist Richardus Vitus. Cf. my *Mysterium Coniunctionis*, pars. 91ff.

the nature of anima and animus empirically. Whatever we have to say about these archetypes, therefore, is either directly verifiable or at least rendered probable by the facts. At the same time, I am fully aware that we are discussing pioneer work which by its very nature can only be provisional.

Just as the mother seems to be the first carrier of the projection-making factor for the son, so is the father for the daughter. Practical experience of these relationships is made up of many individual cases presenting all kinds of variations on the same basic theme. A concise description of them can, therefore, be no more than schematic.

Woman is compensated by a masculine element and therefore her unconscious has, so to speak, a masculine imprint. This results in a considerable psychological difference between men and women, and accordingly I have called the projection-making factor in women the animus, which means mind or spirit. The animus corresponds to the paternal Logos just as the anima corresponds to the maternal Eros. But I do not wish or intend to give these two intuitive concepts too specific a definition. I use Eros and Logos merely as conceptual aids to describe the fact that woman's consciousness is characterized more by the connective quality of Eros than by the discrimination and cognition associated with Logos. In men, Eros, the function of relationship, is usually less developed than Logos. In women, on the other hand, Eros is an expression of their true nature, while their Logos is often only a regrettable accident. It gives rise to misunderstandings and annoying interpretations in the family circle and among friends. This is because it consists of _opinions_ instead of reflections, and by opinions I mean _a priori_ assumptions that lay claim to absolute truth. Such assumptions, as everyone knows, can be extremely irritating. As the animus is partial to argument, he can best be seen at work in disputes where both parties know they are right. Men can argue in a very womanish way, too, when they are anima-possessed and have thus been transformed into the animus of their own anima. With them the question becomes one of personal vanity and touchiness (as if they were females); with women it is a question of _power_, whether of truth or justice or some other "ism" – for the dressmaker and hairdresser have already taken care of their vanity. The "Father" (i.e., the sum of conventional opinions)

domestic violence cycle

always plays a great role in female argumentation. No matter how friendly and obliging a woman's Eros may be, no logic on earth can shake her if she is ridden by the animus. Often the man has the feeling – and he is not altogether wrong – that only seduction or a beating or rape would have the necessary power of persuasion. He is unaware that this highly dramatic situation would instantly come to a banal and unexciting end if he were to quit the field and let a second woman carry on the battle (his wife, for instance, if she herself is not the fiery war horse). This sound idea seldom or never occurs to him, because no man can converse with an animus for five minutes without becoming the victim of his own anima. Anyone who still had enough sense of humour to listen objectively to the ensuing dialogue would be staggered by the vast number of commonplaces, misapplied truisms, clichés from newspapers and novels, shop-soiled platitudes of every description interspersed with vulgar abuse and brain-splitting lack of logic. It is a dialogue which, irrespective of its participants, is repeated millions and millions of times in all the languages of the world and always remains essentially the same.

This singular fact is due to the following circumstance: when animus and anima meet, the animus draws his sword of power and the anima ejects her poison of illusion and seduction. The outcome need not always be negative, since the two are equally likely to fall in love (a special instance of love at first sight). The language of love is of astonishing uniformity, using the well-worn formulas with the utmost devotion and fidelity, so that once again the two partners find themselves in a banal collective situation. Yet they live in the illusion that they are related to one another in a most individual way.

In both its positive and its negative aspects the anima/animus relationship is always full of "animosity," i.e., it is emotional, and hence collective. Affects lower the level of the relationship and bring it closer to the common instinctual basis, which no longer has anything individual about it. Very often the relationship runs its course heedless of its human performers, who afterwards do not know what happened to them.

Whereas the cloud of "animosity" surrounding the man is composed chiefly of sentimentality and resentment, in woman it expresses itself in the form of opinionated views, interpretations, insinuations, and misconstructions, which all have the purpose (sometimes attained) of severing the relation between two human beings. The woman, like the man, becomes wrapped in a veil of illusions by her demon-familiar, and, as the daughter who alone understands her father (that is, is eternally right in everything), she is translated to the land of sheep, where she is put to graze by the shepherd of her soul, the animus.

Like the anima, the animus too has a positive aspect. Through the figure of the father he expresses not only conventional opinion but – equally – what we call "spirit," philosophical or religious ideas in particular, or rather the attitude resulting from them. Thus the animus is a psychopomp, a mediator between the conscious and the unconscious and a personification of the latter. Just as the anima becomes, through integration, the Eros of consciousness, so the animus becomes a Logos; and in the same way that the anima gives relationship and relatedness to a man's consciousness, the animus gives to woman's consciousness a capacity for reflection, deliberation, and self-knowledge.

The effect of anima and animus on the ego is in principle the same. This effect is extremely difficult to eliminate because, in the first place, it is uncommonly strong and immediately fills the ego-personality with an unshakable feeling of rightness and righteousness. In the second place, the cause of the effect is projected and appears to lie in objects and objective situations. Both these characteristics can, I believe, be traced back to the peculiarities of the archetype. For the archetype, of course, exists *a priori*. This may possibly explain the often totally irrational yet undisputed and indisputable existence of certain moods and opinions. Perhaps these are so notoriously difficult to influence because of the powerfully suggestive effect emanating from the archetype. Consciousness is fascinated by it, held captive, as if hypnotized. Very often the ego experiences a vague feeling of moral defeat and then behaves all the more defensively, defiantly, and self-righteously, thus setting up a vicious circle which only increases its feeling of inferiority. The bottom is then knocked out of the human relationship, for, like megalomania, a feeling of inferiority makes mutual recognition impossible, and without this there is no relationship.

As I said, it is easier to gain insight into the shadow than into the anima or animus. With the shadow, we have the advantage of being prepared in some sort by our education, which has always endeavoured to convince people that they are not one-hundred-per-cent pure gold. So everyone immediately understands what is meant by "shadow," "inferior personality," etc. And if he has forgotten, his memory can easily be refreshed by a Sunday sermon, his wife, or the tax collector. With the anima and animus, however, things are by no means so simple. Firstly, there is no moral education in this respect, and secondly, most people are content to be self-righteous and prefer mutual vilification (if nothing worse!) to the recognition of their projections. Indeed, it seems a very natural state of affairs for men to have irrational moods and women irrational opinions. Presumably this situation is grounded on instinct and must remain as it is to ensure that the Empedoclean game of the hate and love of the elements shall continue for all eternity. Nature is conservative and does not easily allow her courses to be altered; she defends in the most stubborn way the inviolability of the preserves where anima and animus roam. Hence it is much more difficult to become conscious of one's anima/animus projections than to acknowledge one's shadow side. One has, of course, to overcome certain moral obstacles, such as vanity, ambition, conceit, resentment, etc., but in the case of projections all sorts of purely intellectual difficulties are added, quite apart from the contents of the projection which one simply doesn't know how to cope with. And on top of all this there arises a profound doubt as to whether one is not meddling too much with nature's business by prodding into consciousness things which it would have been better to leave asleep.

Although there are, in my experience, a fair number of people who can understand without special intellectual or moral difficulties what is meant by anima and animus, one finds very many more who have the greatest trouble in visualizing these empirical concepts as anything concrete. This shows that they fall a little outside the usual range of experience. They are unpopular precisely because they seem unfamiliar. The consequence is that they mobilize prejudice and become taboo like everything else that is unexpected.

So if we set it up as a kind of requirement that projections should be dissolved, because it is wholesomer that way and in every respect more advantageous, we are entering upon new ground. Up till now everybody has been convinced that the idea "my father," "my mother," etc., is nothing but a faithful reflection of the real parent, corresponding in every detail to the original, so that when someone says "my father" he means no more and no less than what his father is in reality. This is actually what he supposes he does mean, but a supposition of identity by no means brings that identity about. This is where the fallacy of the *enkekalymmenos* ("the veiled one") comes in.* If one includes in the psychological equation X's picture of his father, which he takes for the real father, the equation will not work out, because the unknown quantity he has introduced does not tally with reality. X has overlooked the fact that his idea of a person consists, in the first place, of the possibly very incomplete picture he has received of the real person and, in the second place, of the subjective modifications he has imposed upon this picture. X's idea of his father is a complex quantity for which the real father is only in part responsible, an indefinitely larger share falling to the son. So true is this that every time he criticizes or praises his father he is unconsciously hitting back at himself, thereby bringing about those psychic consequences that overtake people who habitually disparage or overpraise themselves. If, however, X carefully compares his reactions with reality, he stands a chance of noticing that he has miscalculated somewhere by not realizing long ago from his father's behaviour that the picture he has of him is a false one. But as a rule X is convinced that he is right, and if anybody is wrong it must be the other fellow. Should X have a poorly developed Eros, he will be either indifferent to the inadequate relationship he has with his father or else annoyed by the inconsistency and general incomprehensibility of a father whose behaviour never really corresponds to the picture X has of him. Therefore X thinks he has every right to feel hurt, misunderstood, and even betrayed.

One can imagine how desirable it would be in such cases to dissolve the projection. And there are always optimists who believe that the golden age can be ushered in simply by telling people the

*The fallacy, which stems from Eubulides the Megarian, runs: "Can you recognize your father?" Yes. "Can you recognize this veiled one?" No. "This veiled one is your father. Hence you can recognize your father and not recognize him."

right way to go. But just let them try to explain to these people that they are acting like a dog chasing its own tail. To make a person see the shortcomings of his attitude considerably more than mere "telling" is needed, for more is involved than ordinary common sense can allow. What one is up against here is the kind of fateful misunderstanding which, under ordinary conditions, remains forever inaccessible to insight. It is rather like expecting the average respectable citizen to recognize himself as a criminal.

I mention all this just to illustrate the order of magnitude to which the anima/animus projections belong, and the moral and intellectual exertions that are needed to dissolve them. Not all the contents of the anima and animus are projected, however. Many of them appear spontaneously in dreams and so on, and many more can be made conscious through active imagination. In this way we find that thoughts, feelings, and affects are alive in us which we would never have believed possible. Naturally, possibilities of this sort seem utterly fantastic to anyone who has not experienced them himself, for a normal person "knows what he thinks." Such a childish attitude on the part of the "normal person" is simply the rule, so that no one without experience in this field can be expected to understand the real nature of anima and animus. With these reflections one gets into an entirely new world of psychological experience, provided of course that one succeeds in realizing it in practice. Those who do succeed can hardly fail to be impressed by all that the ego does not know and never has known. This increase in self-knowledge is still very rare nowadays and is usually paid for in advance with a neurosis, if not with something worse.

The autonomy of the collective unconscious expresses itself in the figures of anima and animus. They personify those of its contents which, when withdrawn from projection, can be integrated into consciousness. To this extent, both figures represent *functions* which filter the contents of the collective unconscious through to the conscious mind. They appear or behave as such, however, only so long as the tendencies of the conscious and unconscious do not diverge too greatly. Should any tension arise, these functions, harmless till then, confront the conscious mind in personified form and behave rather like systems split off from the personality, or like part souls. This comparison is inadequate in so far as nothing previously belonging to the ego-personality has split off from it; on the contrary, the two figures represent a disturbing accretion. The reason for their behaving in this way is that though the *contents* of anima and animus can be integrated they themselves cannot, since they are archetypes. As such they are the foundation stones of the psychic structure, which in its totality exceeds the limits of consciousness and therefore can never become the object of direct cognition. Though the effects of anima and animus can be made conscious, they themselves are factors transcending consciousness and beyond the reach of perception and volition. Hence they remain autonomous despite the integration of their contents, and for this reason they should be borne constantly in mind. This is extremely important from the therapeutic standpoint, because constant observation pays the unconscious a tribute that more or less guarantees its co-operation. The unconscious as we know can never be "done with" once and for all. It is, in fact, one of the most important tasks of psychic hygiene to pay continual attention to the symptomatology of unconscious contents and processes, for the good reason that the conscious mind is always in danger of becoming one-sided, of keeping to well-worn paths and getting stuck in blind alleys. The complementary and compensating function of the unconscious ensures that these dangers, which are especially great in neurosis, can in some measure be avoided. It is only under ideal conditions, when life is still simple and unconscious enough to follow the serpentine path of instinct without hesitation or misgiving, that the compensation works with entire success. The more civilized, the more unconscious and complicated a man is, the less he is able to follow his instincts. His complicated living conditions and the influence of his environment are so strong that they drown the quiet voice of nature. Opinions, beliefs, theories, and collective tendencies appear in its stead and back up all the aberrations of the conscious mind. Deliberate attention should then be given to the unconscious so that the compensation can set to work. Hence it is especially important to picture the archetypes of the unconscious not as a rushing phantasmagoria of fugitive images but as constant, autonomous factors, which indeed they are.

In his "Confrontation with the Unconscious," Jung encountered figures who represented superior wisdom; personifications of "intelligence and knowledge."

From "Confrontation with the Unconscious" MDR, pp. 174–8/181–5

In order to seize hold of the fantasies, I frequently imagined a steep descent. I even made several attempts to get to the very bottom. The first time I reached, as it were, a depth of about a thousand feet; the next time I found myself at the edge of a cosmic abyss. It was like a voyage to the moon, or a descent into empty space. First came the image of a crater, and I had the feeling that I was in the land of the dead. The atmosphere was that of the other world. Near the steep slope of a rock I caught sight of two figures, an old man with a white beard and a beautiful young girl. I summoned up my courage and approached them as though they were real people, and listened attentively to what they told me. The old man explained that he was Elijah, and that gave me a shock. But the girl staggered me even more, for she called herself Salome! She was blind. What a strange couple: Salome and Elijah. But Elijah assured me that he and Salome had belonged together from all eternity, which completely astounded me . . . They had a black serpent living with them which displayed an unmistakable fondness for me. I stuck close to Elijah because he seemed to be the most reasonable of the three, and to have a clear intelligence. Of Salome I was distinctly suspicious. Elijah and I had a long conversation which, however, I did not understand.

Naturally I tried to find a plausible explanation for the appearance of Biblical figures in my fantasy by reminding myself that my father had been a clergyman. But that really explained nothing at all. For what did the old man signify? What did Salome signify? Why were they together? Only many years later, when I knew a great deal more than I knew then, did the connection between the old man and the young girl appear perfectly natural to me.

In such dream wanderings one frequently encounters an old man who is accompanied by a young girl, and examples of such couples are to be found in many mythic tales. Thus, according to Gnostic tradition, Simon Magus went about with a young girl whom he had picked up in a brothel. Her name was Helen, and she was regarded as the reincarnation of the Trojan Helen. Klingsor and Kundry, Lao-tzu and the dancing girl, likewise belong to this category.

I have mentioned that there was a third figure in my fantasy besides Elijah and Salome: the large black snake. In myths the snake is a frequent counterpart of the hero. There are numerous accounts of their affinity. For example, the hero has eyes like a snake, or after his death he is changed into a snake and revered as such, or the snake is his mother, etc. In my fantasy, therefore, the presence of the snake was an indication of a hero-myth.

Salome is an anima figure. She is blind because she does not see the meaning of things. Elijah is the figure of the wise old prophet and represents the factor of intelligence and knowledge; Salome, the erotic element. One might say that the two figures are personifications of Logos and Eros. But such a definition would be excessively intellectual. It is more meaningful to let the figures be what they were for me at the time – namely, events and experiences.

Soon after this fantasy another figure rose out of the unconscious. He developed out of the Elijah figure. I called him Philemon. Philemon was a pagan and brought with him an Egypto-Hellenistic atmosphere with a Gnostic colouration. His figure first appeared to me in the following dream.

There was a blue sky, like the sea, covered not by clouds but by flat brown clods of earth. It looked as if the clods were breaking apart and the blue water of the sea were becoming visible between them. But the water was the blue sky. Suddenly there appeared from the right a winged being sailing across the sky. I saw that it was an old man with the horns of a bull. He held a bunch of four keys, one of which he clutched as if he were about to open a lock. He had the wings of the kingfisher with its characteristic colours.

Since I did not understand this dream-image, I painted it in order to impress it upon my memory. During the days when I was occupied with the painting, I found in my garden, by the lake shore, a dead kingfisher! I was thunderstruck, for kingfishers are quite rare in the vicinity of Zürich and I have never since found a dead one. The body was recently dead – at the most, two or three days – and showed no external injuries.

Philemon and other figures of my fantasies brought home to me the crucial insight that there are things in the psyche which I do not produce, but which produce themselves and have their own life. Philemon represented a force which was not myself. In my fantasies I held conversations with him, and he said things which I had not consciously thought. For I observed clearly that it was he who spoke, not I. He said I treated thoughts as if I generated them myself, but in his view thoughts were like animals in the forest, or people in a room, or birds in the air, and added, "If you should see people in a room, you would not think that you had made those people, or that you were responsible for them." It was he who taught me psychic objectivity, the reality of the psyche. Through him the distinction was clarified between myself and the object of my thought. He confronted me in an objective manner, and I understood that there is something in me which can say things that I do not know and do not intend, things which may even be directed against me.

Psychologically, Philemon represented superior insight. He was a mysterious figure to me. At times he seemed to me quite real, as if he were a living personality. I went walking up and down the garden with him, and to me he was what the Indians call a guru.

Whenever the outlines of a new personification appeared, I felt it almost as a personal defeat. It meant: "Here is something else you didn't know until now!" Fear crept over me that the succession of such figures might be endless, that I might lose myself in bottomless abysses of ignorance. My ego felt devalued – although the successes I had been having in worldly affairs might have reassured me. In my darknesses (*horridas nostrae mentis purga tenebras* – "cleanse the horrible darknesses of our mind" – the *Aurora Consurgens**** says) I could have wished for nothing better than a real, live guru, someone possessing superior knowledge and ability, who would have disentangled for me the involuntary creations of my imagination. This task was undertaken by the figure of Philemon, whom in this respect I had willy-nilly to

*An alchemical treatise ascribed to Thomas Aquinas.

recognize as my psychagogue. And the fact was that he conveyed to me many an illuminating idea.

More than fifteen years later a highly cultivated elderly Indian visited me, a friend of Gandhi's, and we talked about Indian education – in particular, about the relationship between guru and chela. I hesitantly asked him whether he could tell me anything about the person and character of his own guru, whereupon he replied in a matter-of-fact tone, "Oh yes, he was Shankaracharya."

"You don't mean the commentator on the Vedas who died centuries ago?" I asked.

"Yes, I mean him," he said, to my amazement.

"Then you are referring to a spirit?" I asked.

"Of course it was his spirit," he agreed.

At that moment I thought of Philemon.

"There are ghostly gurus too," he added. "Most people have living gurus. But there are always some who have a spirit for teacher."

This information was both illuminating and reassuring to me. Evidently, then, I had not plummeted right out of the human world, but had only experienced the sort of thing that could happen to others who made similar efforts.

Later, Philemon became relativized by the emergence of yet another figure, whom I called Ka. In ancient Egypt the "king's ka" was his earthly form, the embodied soul. In my fantasy the ka-soul came from below, out of the earth as if out of a deep shaft. I did a painting of him, showing him in his earth-bound form, as a herm with base of stone and upper part of bronze. High up in the painting appears a kingfisher's wing, and between it and the head of Ka floats a round, glowing nebula of stars. Ka's expression has something demonic about it – one might also say, Mephistophelian. In one hand he holds something like a coloured pagoda, or a reliquary, and in the other a stylus with which he is working on the reliquary. He is saying, "I am he who buries the gods in gold and gems."

Philemon had a lame foot, but was a winged spirit, whereas Ka represented a kind of earth demon or metal demon. Philemon was the spiritual aspect, or "meaning." Ka, on the other hand, was a spirit of nature like the Anthroparion of Greek alchemy – with which at the time I was still unfamiliar.* Ka was he who made everything real, but who also obscured the halcyon spirit, Meaning, or replaced it by beauty, the "eternal reflection."

In time I was able to integrate both figures through the study of alchemy.

The archetype of the wise old man, also called the "Mana-personality," tends to be projected upon human beings who set themselves up as leaders, secular or spiritual. This may have disastrous results, as when religious sects or political movements are led by charlatans or madmen. Alternatively, the subject may identify himself with the archetype, believing that he himself has superior wisdom. Analysts and priests, as well as politicians, sometimes succumb to this danger, referred to by Jung as "inflation."

From "The Relations between the Ego and the Unconscious"
Two Essays, CW 7, pars. 387–90

THE MANA-PERSONALITY

The immediate goal of the analysis of the unconscious, therefore, is to reach a state where the unconscious contents no longer remain unconscious and no longer express themselves indirectly as animus and anima phenomena; that is to say, a state in which animus and anima become functions of relationship to the unconscious. So long as they are not this, they are autonomous complexes, disturbing factors that disrupt conscious control and act like true "disturbers of the peace." Because this is such a well-known fact my term "complex," as used in this sense, has passed into common speech. The more "complexes" a man has, the more he is possessed; and when we try to form a picture of the personality which expresses itself through its complexes we must admit that it resembles nothing so much as an hysterical woman

---

*[The Anthroparion is a tiny man, a kind of homunculus. He is found, for example, in the visions of Zosimos of Panopolis, an important alchemist of the third century. To the group which includes the Anthroparion belong the gnomes, the Dactyls of classical antiquity, and the homunculi of the alchemists. As the spirit of quicksilver, the alchemical Mercurius was also an Anthroparion.]

– i.e., the anima! But if such a man makes himself conscious of his unconscious contents, as they appear firstly in the factual contents of his personal unconscious, and then in the fantasies of the collective unconscious, he will get to the roots of his complexes, and in this way rid himself of his possession. With that the anima phenomenon comes to a stop.

That superior power, however, which caused the possession – for what I cannot shake off must in some sense be superior to me – should, logically, disappear with the anima. One should then be "complex-free," psychologically house-trained, so to speak. Nothing more should happen that is not sanctioned by the ego, and when the ego wants something, nothing should be capable of interfering. The ego would thus be assured of an impregnable position, the steadfastness of a superman or the sublimity of a perfect sage. Both figures are ideal images: Napoleon on the one hand, Lao-tzu on the other. Both are consistent with the idea of "the extraordinarily potent," which is the term that Lehmann, in his celebrated monograph,* uses for his definition of mana. I therefore call such a personality simply the *mana-personality*. It corresponds to a dominant of the collective unconscious, to an archetype which has taken shape in the human psyche through untold ages of just that kind of experience. Primitive man does not analyse and does not work out why another is superior to him. If another is cleverer and stronger than he, then he has mana, he is possessed of a stronger power; and by the same token he can lose this power, perhaps because someone has walked over him in his sleep, or stepped on his shadow.

Historically, the mana-personality evolves into the hero and the godlike being,† whose earthly form is the priest. How very much the doctor is still mana is the whole plaint of the analyst! But in so far as the ego apparently draws to itself the power belonging to the anima, the ego does become a mana-personality. This development is an almost regular phenomenon. I have never yet seen a fairly advanced development of this kind where at least a temporary identification with the archetype of the mana-personality did not take place. It is the most natural thing in the

*F. R. Lehmann, *Mana* (Leipzig, 1922).
†According to popular belief, the Most Christian King could cure epilepsy with his mana by the laying on of hands.

world that this should happen, for not only does one expect it oneself, but everybody else expects it too. One can scarcely help admiring oneself a little for having seen more deeply into things than others, and the others have such an urge to find a tangible hero somewhere, or a superior wise man, a leader and father, some undisputed authority, that they build temples to little tin gods with the greatest promptitude and burn incense upon the altars. This is not just the lamentable stupidity of idolaters incapable of judging for themselves, but a natural psychological law which says that what has once been will always be in the future. And so it will be, unless consciousness puts an end to the naïve concretization of primordial images. I do not know whether it is desirable that consciousness should alter the eternal laws; I only know that occasionally it does alter them, and that this measure is a vital necessity for some people – which, however, does not always prevent these same people from setting themselves up on the father's throne and making the old rule come true. It is indeed hard to see how one can escape the sovereign power of the primordial images.

Actually I do not believe it can be escaped. One can only alter one's attitude and thus save oneself from naïvely falling into an archetype and being forced to act a part at the expense of one's humanity. Possession by an archetype turns a man into a flat collective figure, a mask behind which he can no longer develop as a human being, but becomes increasingly stunted. One must therefore beware of the danger of falling victim to the dominant of the mana-personality. The danger lies not only in oneself becoming a father-mask, but in being overpowered by this mask when worn by another. Master and pupil are in the same boat in this respect.

In a lecture on "The Phenomenology of the Spirit in Fairytales," Jung defines the spirit (Geist) as "the principle that stands in opposition to matter." He goes on to link spirit with paternal authority and the archetype of the wise old man.

From **"The Phenomenology of the Spirit in Fairytales"** CW 9 i, pars. 396–9

SELF-REPRESENTATION OF THE SPIRIT IN DREAMS

The psychic manifestations of the spirit indicate at once that they are of an archetypal nature – in other words, the phenomenon we call spirit depends on the existence of an autonomous primordial image which is universally present in the preconscious makeup of the human psyche. As usual, I first came up against this problem when investigating the dreams of my patients. It struck me that a certain kind of father-complex has a "spiritual" character, so to speak, in the sense that the father-image gives rise to statements, actions, tendencies, impulses, opinions, etc., to which one could hardly deny the attribute "spiritual." In men, a positive father-complex very often produces a certain credulity with regard to authority and a distinct willingness to bow down before all spiritual dogmas and values; while in women, it induces the liveliest spiritual aspirations and interests. In dreams, it is always the father-figure from whom the decisive convictions, prohibitions, and wise counsels emanate. The invisibility of this source is frequently emphasized by the fact that it consists simply of an authoritative voice which passes final judgments. Mostly, therefore, it is the figure of a "wise old man" who symbolizes the spiritual factor. Sometimes the part is played by a "real" spirit, namely the ghost of one dead, or, more rarely, by grotesque gnomelike figures or talking animals. The dwarf forms are found, at least in my experience, mainly in women; hence it seems to me logical that in Ernst Barlach's play *Der tote Tag* (1912), the gnomelike figure of Steissbart ("Rumpbeard") is associated with the mother, just as Bes is associated with the mother-goddess at Karnak. In both sexes the spirit can also take the form of a boy or a youth. In women he corresponds to the so-called "positive" animus who indicates the possibility of conscious spiritual effort. In men his meaning is not so simple. He can be positive, in which case he signifies the "higher" personality, the self or *filius regius* as conceived by the alchemists.* But he can also be negative, and then

*Cf. the vision of the "naked boy" in Meister Eckhart (trans. by Evans, I, p. 438).

he signifies the infantile shadow. In both cases the boy means some form of spirit. Graybeard and boy belong together. The pair of them play a considerable role in alchemy as symbols of Mercurius.

It can never be established with one-hundred-per-cent certainty whether the spirit-figures in dreams are morally good. Very often they show all the signs of duplicity, if not of outright malice. I must emphasize, however, that the grand plan on which the unconscious life of the psyche is constructed is so inaccessible to our understanding that we can never know what evil may not be necessary in order to produce good by enantiodromia, and what good may very possibly lead to evil. Sometimes the *probate spiritus* recommended by John cannot, with the best will in the world, be anything other than a cautious and patient waiting to see how things will finally turn out.

The figure of the wise old man can appear so plastically, not only in dreams but also in visionary meditation (or what we call "active imagination"), that, as is sometimes apparently the case in India, it takes over the role of a guru.* The wise old man appears in dreams in the guise of a magician, doctor, priest, teacher, professor, grandfather, or any other person possessing authority. The archetype of spirit in the shape of a man, hobgoblin, or animal always appears in a situation where insight, understanding, good advice, determination, planning, etc., are needed but cannot be mustered on one's own resources. The archetype compensates this state of spiritual deficiency by contents designed to fill the gap. An excellent example of this is the dream about the white and black magicians, which tried to compensate the spiritual difficulties of a young theological student. I did not know the dreamer myself, so the question of my personal influence is ruled out. He dreamed *he was standing in the presence of a sublime hieratic figure called the "white magician," who was nevertheless clothed in a long black robe. This magician had just ended a lengthy discourse with the words "And for that we require the help of the black magician." Then the door*

---

*Hence the many miraculous stories about rishis and mahatmas. A cultured Indian with whom I once conversed on the subject of gurus told me, when I asked him who his guru had been, that it was Shankaracharya (who lived in the 8th and 9th cents.). "But that's the celebrated commentator," I remarked in amazement. Whereupon he replied, "Yes, so he was; but naturally it was his spirit," not in the least perturbed by my Western bewilderment.

suddenly opened and another old man came in, the "black magician," who however was dressed in a white robe. He too looked noble and sublime. The black magician evidently wanted to speak with the white, but hesitated to do so in the presence of the dreamer. At that the white magician, pointing to the dreamer, said, "Speak, he is an innocent." So the black magician began to relate a strange story of how he had found the lost keys of Paradise and did not know how to use them. He had, he said, come to the white magician for an explanation of the secret of the keys. He told him that the king of the country in which he lived was seeking a suitable tomb for himself. His subjects had chanced to dig up an old sarcophagus containing the mortal remains of a virgin. The king opened the sarcophagus, threw away the bones, and had the empty sarcophagus buried again for later use. But no sooner had the bones seen the light of day than the being to whom they once had belonged – the virgin – changed into a black horse that galloped off into the desert. The black magician pursued it across the sandy wastes and beyond, and there after many vicissitudes and difficulties he found the lost keys of Paradise. That was the end of his story, and also, unfortunately, of the dream.

Here the compensation certainly did not fall out as the dreamer would wish, by handing him a solution on a plate; rather it confronted him with a problem to which I have already alluded, and one which life is always bringing us up against: namely, the uncertainty of all moral valuation, the bewildering interplay of good and evil, and the remorseless concatenation of guilt, suffering, and redemption. This path to the primordial religious experience is the right one, but how many can recognize it? It is like a still small voice, and it sounds from afar. It is ambiguous, questionable, dark, presaging danger and hazardous adventure; a razor-edged path, to be trodden for God's sake only, without assurance and without sanction.

Part 5. Psychological Types and the Self-regulating Psyche

At the same time that Jung was engaged in his own confrontation with the unconscious, he was also concerned with defining the difference in his approach to the problems of psychology from those adopted by Freud and Adler. How was it, he asked, that each could interpret the same material so differently? He concluded that human beings belonged to different psychological types; and, in 1921, his book Psychological Types *was first published in Zurich. The terms "extravert" and "introvert" were introduced by Jung, and are still in current use as descriptive of personality differences.*

"Introduction" *Psychological Types*, CW 6, pars. 1–7

In my practical medical work with nervous patients I have long been struck by the fact that besides the many individual differences in human psychology there are also typical differences. Two types especially become clear to me; I have termed them the introverted and the extraverted types.

When we consider the course of human life, we see how the fate of one individual is determined more by the objects of his interest, while in another it is determined more by his own inner self, by the subject. Since we all swerve rather more towards one side or the other, we naturally tend to understand everything in terms of our own type.

I mention this circumstance at once in order to avoid possible misunderstandings. It will be apparent that it is one which considerably aggravates the difficulty of a general description of types. I must presume unduly upon the goodwill of the reader if I may hope to be rightly understood. It would be relatively simple if every reader knew to which category he belonged. But it is often very difficult to find out whether a person belongs to one type or the other, especially in regard to oneself. In respect of one's own personality one's judgment is as a rule extraordinarily clouded. This subjective clouding of judgment is particularly common because in every pronounced type there is a special tendency to compensate the one-sidedness of that type, a tendency which is biologically purposive since it strives constantly to maintain the psychic equilibrium. The compensation gives rise to secondary characteristics, or secondary types, which present a picture that is extremely difficult to interpret, so difficult that one is inclined to deny the existence of types altogether and to believe only in individual differences.

I must emphasize this difficulty in order to justify certain peculiarities in my presentation. It might seem as if the simplest way would be to describe two concrete cases and to dissect them side by side. But everyone possesses both mechanisms, extraversion as well as introversion, and only the relative predominance of one or the other determines the type. Hence, in order to throw the picture into the necessary relief, one would have to retouch it rather vigorously, and this would amount to a more or less pious fraud. Moreover, the psychological reactions of a human being are so complicated that my powers of description would hardly suffice to draw an absolutely correct picture. From sheer necessity, therefore, I must confine myself to a presentation of principles which I have abstracted from a wealth of facts observed in many different individuals. In this there is no question of a *deductio a priori*, as it might appear; it is rather a deductive presentation of empirically gained insights. These insights will, I hope, help to clarify a dilemma which, not only in analytical psychology but in other branches of science as well, and especially in the personal relations of human beings with one another, has led and still continues to lead to misunderstanding and discord. For they explain how the existence of two distinct types is actually a fact that has long been known: a fact that in one form or another has struck the observer of human nature or dawned upon the brooding reflection of the thinker, presenting itself to Goethe's intuition, for instance, as the all-embracing principle of systole and diastole. The names and concepts by which the mechanisms of extraversion and introversion have been grasped are extremely varied, and each of them is adapted to the standpoint of the observer in question. But despite the diversity of the formulations the fundamental idea common to them all constantly shines through: in one case an outward movement of interest towards the object, and in the other a movement of interest away from the object to the subject and his own psychological processes. In the first case the object works like a magnet upon the tendencies of the subject; it determines the subject to a large extent and even alienates him from himself. His qualities may become so transformed by assimilation to the object that one might think it possessed some higher and decisive significance for him. It might almost seem as if it were an absolute determinant, a special purpose of life or fate that he should abandon himself wholly to the object. But in the second case the subject is and remains the centre of every interest. It looks, one might say, as though all the life-energy were ultimately seeking the subject, and thus continually prevented the object from exercising any overpowering influence. It is as though the energy were flowing away from the object, and the subject were a magnet drawing the object to itself.

It is not easy to give a clear and intelligible description of this two-way relationship to the object without running the risk of paradoxical formulations which would create more confusion than clarity. But in general one could say that the introverted standpoint is one which sets the ego and the subjective psychological process above the object and the objective process, or at any rate seeks to hold its ground against the object. This attitude, therefore, gives the subject a higher value than the object, and the object accordingly has a lower value. It is of secondary importance; indeed, sometimes the object represents no more than an outward token of a subjective content, the embodiment of an idea, the idea being the essential thing. If it is the embodiment of a feeling, then again the feeling is the main thing and not the object in its own right. The extraverted standpoint, on the contrary, subordinates the subject to the object, so that the object has the higher value. In this case the subject is of secondary importance, the subjective process appearing at times as no more than a disturbing or superfluous appendage of objective events. It is clear that the psychology resulting from these contrary standpoints must be classed as two totally different orientations. The one sees everything in terms of his own situation, the other in terms of the objective event.

These contrary attitudes are in themselves no more than correlative mechanisms: a diastolic going out and seizing of the object, and a systolic concentration and detachment of energy from the object seized. Every human being possesses both mechanisms as an expression of his natural life-rhythm, a rhythm which Goethe, surely not by chance, described physiologically in terms of the heart's activity. A rhythmical alternation of both forms of psychic activity would perhaps correspond to the normal course of life. But the complicated outer conditions under which we live and the even more complicated conditions of our individual psychic make-up seldom permit a completely undisturbed flow of psychic energy. Outer circumstances and inner disposition frequently favour one mechanism and restrict or hinder the other. One mechanism will naturally predominate, and if this condition becomes in any way chronic a *type* will be produced; that is, an habitual attitude in which one mechanism predominates permanently, although the other can never be completely suppressed since it is an integral part of the psychic economy. Hence there can never be a pure type in the sense that it possesses only one mechanism with the complete atrophy of the other. A typical attitude always means merely the relative predominance of one mechanism.

The hypothesis of introversion and extraversion allows us, first of all, to distinguish two large groups of psychological individuals. Yet this grouping is of such a superficial and general nature that it permits no more than this very general distinction. Closer investigation of the individual psychologies that fall into one group or the other will at once show great differences between individuals who nevertheless belong to the same group. If, therefore, we wish to determine wherein lie the differences between individuals belonging to a definite group, we must take a further step. Experience has taught me that in general individuals can be distinguished not only according to the broad distinction between introversion and extraversion, but also according to their basic psychological functions. For in the same measure as outer circumstances and inner disposition cause either introversion or extraversion to predominate, they also favour the predominance of one definite basic function in the individual. I have found from experience that the basic psychological functions, that is, functions which are genuinely as well as essentially different from other functions, prove to be *thinking, feeling, sensation*, and *intuition*. If one of these functions habitually predominates, a corresponding type results. I therefore distinguish a thinking, a feeling, a sensation, and an intuitive type. *Each of these types may moreover be either introverted or extraverted*, depending on its relation to the object as we have described above. In my preliminary work on psychological types I did not carry out this differentiation, but identified the thinking type with the introvert and the feeling type with the extravert. A deeper study of the problem has shown this equation to be untenable. In order to avoid misunderstandings, I would ask the reader to bear in mind the differentiation I have developed here. For the sake of clarity, which is essential in such complicated matters, I have devoted the last chapter of this book to the definition of my psychological concepts.

Psychological Types *is a long and interesting book in which Jung draws on his extensive knowledge of literature and history to demonstrate that his typology has various ancestors. In a work presenting the essentials of Jung's own thought, these historical parallels must be omitted. However, a paper of 1936 which is published as an appendix to* Psychological Types *gives a good summary of Jung's conceptions, and also mentions in passing some of his predecessors in the field.*

"Psychological Typology" CW 6, pars. 960–87

Ever since the early days of science, it has been a notable endeavour of the reflective intellect to interpose gradations between the two poles of the absolute similarity and dissimilarity of human beings. This resulted in a number of types, or "temperaments" as they were then called, which classified similarities and dissimilarities into regular categories. The Greek philosopher Empedocles attempted to impose order on the chaos of natural phenomena by dividing them into the four elements: earth, water, air, and fire. It was above all the physicians of ancient times who applied this principle of order, in conjunction with the related doctrine of the four qualities, dry, moist, cold, warm, to human beings, and thus tried to reduce the bewildering diversity of mankind to orderly groups. Of these physicians one of the most important was Galen, whose use of these teachings influenced medical science and the treatment of the sick for nearly seventeen hundred years. The very names of the Galenic temperaments betray their origin in the pathology of the four "humours." *Melancholic* denotes a preponderance of black bile, *phlegmatic* a preponderance of phlegm or mucus (the Greek word *phlegma* means fire, and phlegm was regarded as the end-product of inflammation), *sanguine* a preponderance of blood, and *choleric* a preponderance of choler, or yellow bile.

Our modern conception of "temperament" has certainly become much more psychological, since in the course of man's development over the last two thousand years the "soul" has freed itself from any conceivable connection with cold agues and fevers, or secretions of mucus and bile. Not even the doctors of today would equate a temperament, that is, a certain kind of emotional state or excitability, directly with the constitution of the blood or lymph, although their profession and their exclusive approach to human beings from the side of physical illness tempt them, more often than the layman, to regard the psyche as an end-product dependent on the physiology of the glands. The "humours" of present-day medicine are no longer the old body-secretions, but the more subtle hormones, which influence "temperament" to an outstanding degree, if we define this as the sum-total of emotional reactions. The whole make-up of the body, its constitution in the broadest sense, has in fact a very great deal to do with the psychological temperament, so much that we cannot blame the doctors if they regard psychic phenomena as largely dependent on the body. Somewhere the psyche is living body, and the living body is animated matter; somehow and somewhere there is an undiscoverable unity of psyche and body which would need investigating psychically as well as physically; in other words, this unity must be as dependent on the body as it is on the psyche so far as the investigator is concerned. The materialism of the nineteenth century gave the body first place and relegated the psyche to the rank of something secondary and derived, allowing it no more substantiality than that of a so-called "epiphenomenon." What proved to be a good working hypothesis, namely, that psychic phenomena are conditioned by physical processes, became a philosophical presumption with the advent of materialism. Any serious science of the living organism will reject this presumption; for on the one hand it will constantly bear in mind that living matter is an as yet unsolved mystery, and on the other hand it will be objective enough to recognize that for us there is a completely unbridgeable gulf between physical and psychic phenomena, so that the psychic realm is no less mysterious than the physical.

The materialistic presumption became possible only in recent times, after man's conception of the psyche had, in the course of many centuries, emancipated itself from the old view and developed in an increasingly abstract direction. The ancients could still see body and psyche together, as an undivided unity, because they were closer to that primitive world where no moral rift yet ran through the personality, and the pagan could still feel himself indivisibly one, childishly innocent and unburdened by responsibility. The ancient Egyptians could still enjoy the naïve luxury of a negative confession of sin: "I have not let any man go hungry. I have not made anyone weep. I have not committed murder," and so on. The Homeric heroes wept, laughed, raged, outwitted and killed each other in a world where these things were taken as natural and self-evident by men and gods alike, and the Olympians amused themselves by passing their days in a state of amaranthine irresponsibility.

It was on this archaic level that pre-philosophical man lived and experienced the world. He was entirely in the grip of his emotions. All passions that made his blood boil and his heart pound, that accelerated his breathing or took his breath away, that "turned his bowels to water" – all this was a manifestation of the "soul." Therefore he localized the soul in the region of the diaphragm (in Greek *phren*, which also means mind) and the heart. It was only with the first philosophers that the seat of reason began to be assigned to the head. There are still Negroes today whose "thoughts" are localized principally in the belly, and the Pueblo Indians "think" with their hearts – "only madmen think with their heads," they say. On this level consciousness is essentially passion and the experience of oneness. Yet, serene and tragic at once, it was just this archaic man who, having started to think, invented that dichotomy which Nietzsche laid at the door of Zarathustra: the discovery of pairs of opposites, the division into odd and even, above and below, good and evil. It was the work of the old Pythagoreans, and it was their doctrine of moral responsibility and the grave metaphysical consequences of sin that gradually, in the course of the centuries, percolated through to all strata of the population, chiefly owing to the spread of the Orphic and Pythagorean mysteries. Plato even used the parable of the white and black horses to illustrate the intractability and polarity of the human psyche, and, still earlier, the mysteries proclaimed the doctrine of the good rewarded in the Hereafter and of the wicked punished in hell. These teachings cannot be dismissed as the mystical humbug of "backwoods" philosophers, as Nietzsche claimed, or as so much sectarian cant, for already in the sixth century B.C. Pythagoreanism was something like a state religion throughout Graecia Magna. Also, the ideas underlying its mysteries never died out, but underwent a philosophical renaissance in the second century B.C., when they exercised the strongest influence on the Alexandrian world of thought. Their collision with Old Testament prophecy then led to what one can call the beginnings of Christianity as a world religion.

From Hellenistic syncretism there now arose a classification of man into types which was entirely alien to the "humoral" psychology of Greek medicine. In the philosophical sense, it established gradations between the Parmenidean poles of light and darkness, of above and below. It classified men into *hylikoi*, *psychikoi*, and *pneumatikoi* – material, psychic, and spiritual beings. This classification is not, of course, a scientific formulation of similarities and dissimilarities; it is a critical system of values based not on the behaviour and outward appearance of man as a phenotype, but on definitions of an ethical, mystical, and philosophic kind. Although it is not exactly a "Christian" conception it nevertheless forms an integral part of early Christianity at the time of St. Paul. Its very existence is incontrovertible proof of the split that had occurred in the original unity of man as a being entirely in the grip of his emotions. Before this, he was merely alive and there, the plaything of experience, incapable of any reflective analysis concerning his origins and his destination. Now, suddenly, he found himself confronted by three fateful factors and endowed with body, soul, and spirit, to each of which he had moral obligations. Presumably it was already decided at birth whether he would pass his life in the hylic or the pneumatic state, or in the indeterminate centre between the two. The ingrained dichotomy of the Greek mind had now become acute, with the result that the accent shifted significantly to the psychic and spiritual, which was unavoidably split off from the hylic realm of the body. All the highest and ultimate goals lay in man's moral destination, in a spiritual, supramundane end-state, and the separation of the hylic realm broadened into a cleavage between world and spirit. Thus the original, suave wisdom expressed in the Pythagorean pairs of opposites became a passionate moral conflict. Nothing, however, is so apt to challenge our self-awareness and alertness as being at war with oneself. One can hardly think of any other or more effective means of waking humanity out of the irresponsible and innocent half-sleep of the primitive mentality and bringing it to a state of conscious responsibility.

This process is called cultural development. It is, at any rate, a development of man's powers of discrimination and capacity for judgment, and of consciousness in general. With the increase of knowledge and enhanced critical faculties the foundations were laid for the whole subsequent development of the human mind in terms of intellectual achievement. The particular mental product that far surpassed all the achievements of the ancient world was science. It closed the rift between man and nature in the sense that, although he was separated from nature, science enabled him to find his rightful place again in the natural order. His special metaphysical position, however, had to be jettisoned – so far as it was not secured by belief in the traditional religion – whence arose the notorious conflict between "faith and knowledge." At all events, science brought about a splendid rehabilitation of matter, and in this respect materialism may even be regarded as an act of historical justice.

But one absolutely essential field of experience, the hun .n psyche itself, remained for a very long time the preserve of metaphysics, although increasingly serious attempts were made after the Enlightenment to open it up to scientific investigation. They began, tentatively, with the sense perceptions, and gradually ventured into the domain of associations. This line of research paved the way for experimental psychology, and it culminated in the "physiological psychology" of Wundt. A more descriptive kind of psychology, with which the medical men soon made contact, developed in France. Its chief exponents were Taine, Ribot, and Janet. It was characteristic of this scientific approach that it broke down the psyche into particular mechanisms or processes. In face of these attempts, there were some who advocated what we today would call a "holistic" approach – the systematic observation of the psyche as a whole. It seems as if this trend originated in a certain type of biography, more particularly the kind that an earlier age, which also had its good points, used to describe as "curious lives." In this connection I think of Justinus Kerner and his *Seeress of Prevorst*, and the case of the elder Blumhardt and his medium Gottliebin Dittus. To be historically fair, however, I should not forget the medieval *Acta Sanctorum*.

This line of research has been continued in more recent investigations associated with the names of William James, Freud, and Theodore Flournoy. James and his friend Flournoy, a Swiss psychologist, made an attempt to describe the whole phenomenology of the psyche and also to view it as a totality. Freud, too, as a doctor, took as his point of departure the wholeness and indivisibility of the human personality, though, in keeping with the spirit of the age, he restricted himself to the investigation of instinctive mechanisms and individual processes. He also narrowed the picture of man to the wholeness of an essentially "bourgeois" collective person, and this necessarily led to philosophically one-sided interpretations. Freud, unfortunately, succumbed to the medical man's temptation to trace everything psychic to the body, in the manner of the old "humoral" psychologists, not without rebellious gestures at those metaphysical preserves of which he had a holy dread.

Unlike Freud, who after a proper psychological start reverted to the ancient assumption of the sovereignty of the physical constitution, trying to turn everything back in theory into instinctual processes conditioned by the body, I start with the assumption of the sovereignty of the psyche. Since body and psyche somewhere form a unity, although in their manifest natures they are so utterly different, we cannot but attribute to the one as to the other a substantiality of its own. So long as we have no way of knowing that unity, there is no alternative but to investigate them separately and, for the present, treat them as though they were independent of each other, at least in their structure. That they are not so, we can see for ourselves every day. But if we were to stop at that, we would never be in a position to make out anything about the psyche at all.

Now if we assume the sovereignty of the psyche, we exempt ourselves from the – at present – insoluble task of reducing everything psychic to something definitely physical. We can then take the manifestations of the psyche as expressions of its intrinsic being, and try to establish certain conformities or types. So when I speak of a psychological typology, I mean by this the formulation of the structural elements of the psyche and not a description of the psychic emanations of a particular type of constitution. This is covered by, for instance, Kretschmer's researches into body-structure and character.

I have given a detailed description of a purely psychological typology in my book *Psychological Types*. My investigation was based on twenty years of work as a doctor, which brought me into contact with people of all classes from all the great nations. When one begins as a young doctor, one's head is still full of clinical pictures and diagnoses. In the course of the years, impressions of quite another kind accumulate. One is struck by the enormous diversity of human individuals, by the chaotic profusion of individual cases, the special circumstances of whose lives and whose special characters produce clinical pictures that, even supposing one still felt any desire to do so, can be squeezed into the straitjacket of a diagnosis only by force. The fact that the disturbance can be given such and such a name appears completely irrelevant beside the overwhelming impression one has that all clinical pictures are so many mimetic or histrionic demonstrations of certain definite character traits. The pathological problem upon which everything turns has virtually nothing to do with the clinical picture, but is essentially an expression of character. Even the complexes, the "nuclear elements" of a neurosis, are beside the point, being mere concomitants of a certain characterological disposition. This can be seen most easily in the relation of the patient to his parental family. He is, let us say, one of four siblings, is neither the eldest nor the youngest, has had the same education and conditioning as the others. Yet he is sick and they are sound. The anamnesis shows that a whole series of influences to which the others were exposed as well as he, and from which indeed they all suffered, had a pathological effect on him alone – at least to all appearances. In reality these influences were not aetiological factors in his case either, but prove to be false explanations. The real cause of the neurosis lies in the peculiar way he responded to and assimilated the influences emanating from the environment.

By comparing many such cases it gradually became clear to me that there must be two fundamentally different general attitudes which would divide human beings into two groups – provided the whole of humanity consisted of highly differentiated individuals. Since this is obviously not the case, one can only say that this difference of attitude becomes plainly observable only when we are confronted with a comparatively well-differentiated personality; in other words, it becomes of practical importance only after a certain degree of differentiation has been reached. Pathological cases of this kind are almost always people who deviate from the familial type and, in consequence, no longer find sufficient security in their inherited instinctual foundation. Weak instincts are one of the prime causes of the development of an habitual one-sided attitude, though in the last resort it is conditioned or reinforced by heredity.

I have called these two fundamentally different attitudes *extraversion* and *introversion*. Extraversion is characterized by interest in the external object, responsiveness, and a ready acceptance of external happenings, a desire to influence and be influenced by events, a need to join in and get "with it," the capacity to endure bustle and noise of every kind, and actually find them enjoyable, constant attention to the surrounding world, the cultivation of friends and acquaintances, none too carefully selected, and finally by the great importance attached to the figure one cuts, and hence by a strong tendency to make a show of oneself. Accordingly, the extravert's philosophy of life and his ethics are as a rule of a highly collective nature with a strong streak of altruism, and his conscience is in large measure dependent on public opinion. Moral misgivings arise mainly when "other people know." His religious convictions are determined, so to speak, by majority vote.

The actual subject, the extravert as a subjective entity, is, so far as possible, shrouded in darkness. He hides it from himself under veils of unconsciousness. The disinclination to submit his own motives to critical examination is very pronounced. He has no secrets he has not long since shared with others. Should something unmentionable nevertheless befall him, he prefers to forget it. Anything that might tarnish the parade of optimism and positivism is avoided. Whatever he thinks, intends, and does is displayed with conviction and warmth.

The psychic life of this type of person is enacted, as it were, outside himself, in the environment. He lives in and through others; all self-communings give him the creeps. Dangers lurk there which are better drowned out by noise. If he should ever have a "complex," he finds refuge in the social whirl and allows himself to be assured several times a day that everything is in order. Provided he is not too much of a busy-body, too pushing, and too superficial, he can be a distinctly useful member of the community.

In this short essay I have to content myself with an allusive sketch. It is intended merely to give the reader some idea of what extraversion is like, something he can bring into relationship with his own knowledge of human nature. I have purposely started with a description of extraversion because this attitude is familiar to everyone; the extravert not only lives in this attitude, but parades it before his fellows on principle. Moreover it accords with certain popular ideals and moral requirements.

Introversion, on the other hand, being directed not to the object but to the subject, and not being oriented by the object, is not so easy to put into perspective. The introvert is not forthcoming, he is as though in continual retreat before the object. He holds aloof from external happenings, does not join in, has a distinct dislike of society as soon as he finds himself among too many people. In a large gathering he feels lonely and lost. The more crowded it is, the greater becomes his resistance. He is not in the least "with it," and has no love of enthusiastic get-togethers. He is not a good mixer. What he does, he does in his own way, barricading himself against influences from outside. He is apt to appear awkward, often seeming inhibited, and it frequently happens that, by a certain brusqueness of manner, or by his glum unapproachability, or some kind of malapropism, he causes unwitting offence to people. His better qualities he keeps to himself, and generally does everything he can to dissemble them. He is easily mistrustful, self-willed, often suffers from inferiority feelings and for this reason is also envious. His apprehensiveness of the object is not due to fear, but to the fact that it seems to him negative, demanding, overpowering or even menacing. He therefore suspects all kinds of bad motives, has an everlasting fear of making a fool of himself, is usually very touchy and surrounds himself with a barbed wire entanglement so dense and impenetrable that finally he himself would rather do anything than sit behind it. He confronts the world with an elaborate defensive system compounded of scrupulosity, pedantry, frugality, cautiousness, painful conscientiousness, stiff-lipped rectitude, politeness, and open-eyed distrust. His picture of the world lacks rosy hues, as he is over-critical and finds a hair in every soup. Under normal conditions he is pessimistic and worried, because the world and human beings are not in the least good but crush him, so he never feels accepted and taken to their bosom. Yet he himself does not accept the world either, at any rate not outright, for everything has first to be judged by his own critical standards. Finally only those things are accepted which, for various subjective reasons, he can turn to his own account.

For him self-communings are a pleasure. His own world is a safe harbour, a carefully tended and walled-in garden, closed to the public and hidden from prying eyes. His own company is the best. He feels at home in his world, where the only changes are made by himself. His best work is done with his own resources, on his own initiative, and in his own way. If ever he succeeds, after long and often wearisome struggles, in assimilating something alien to himself, he is capable of turning it to excellent account. Crowds, majority views, public opinion, popular enthusiasm never convince him of anything, but merely make him creep still deeper into his shell.

His relations with other people become warm only when safety is guaranteed, and when he can lay aside his defensive distrust. All too often he cannot, and consequently the number of friends and acquaintances is very restricted. Thus the psychic life of this type is played out wholly within. Should any difficulties and conflicts arise in this inner world, all doors and windows are shut tight. The introvert shuts himself up with his complexes until he ends in complete isolation.

In spite of these peculiarities the introvert is by no means a social loss. His retreat into himself is not a final renunciation of the world, but a search for quietude, where alone it is possible for him to make his contribution to the life of the community. This type of person is the victim of numerous misunderstandings – not unjustly, for he actually invites them. Nor can he be acquitted of the charge of taking a secret delight in mystification, and that being misunderstood gives him a certain satisfaction, since it reaffirms his pessimistic outlook. That being so, it is easy to see why he is accused of being cold, proud, obstinate, selfish, conceited, cranky, and what not, and why he is constantly admonished that devotion to the goals of society, clubbableness, imperturbable urbanity, and selfless trust in the powers-that-be are true virtues and the marks of a sound and vigorous life.

The introvert is well enough aware that such virtues exist, and that somewhere, perhaps – only not in his circle of acquaintances – there are divinely inspired people who enjoy undiluted possession of these ideal qualities. But his self-criticism and his awareness of his own motives have long since disabused him of the illusion that he himself would be capable of such virtues; and his mistrustful gaze, sharpened by anxiety, constantly enables him to detect on his fellow men the ass's ear sticking up from under the lion's mane. The world and men are for him a disturbance and a danger, affording no valid standard by which he could ultimately orient himself. What alone is valid for him is his subjective world, which he sometimes believes, in moments of delusion, to be the objective one. We could easily charge these people with the worst kind of subjectivism, indeed with morbid individualism, if it were certain beyond a doubt that only one objective world existed. But this truth, if such it be, is not axiomatic; it is merely a half truth, the other half of which is the fact that the world *also* is as it is seen by human beings, and in the last resort by the individual. There is simply no world at all without the knowing subject. This, be it never so small and inconspicuous, is always the other pier supporting the bridge of the phenomenal world. The appeal to the subject therefore has the same validity as the appeal to the so-called objective world, for it is grounded on psychic reality itself. But this is a reality with its own peculiar laws which are not of a secondary nature.

The two attitudes, extraversion and introversion, are opposing modes that make themselves felt not least in the history of human thought. The problems to which they give rise were very largely anticipated by Friedrich Schiller, and they underlie his *Letters on the Aesthetic Education of Man*. But since the concept of the unconscious was still unknown to him, he was unable to reach a satisfactory solution. Moreover philosophers, who would be the best equipped to go more closely into this question, do not like having to submit their thinking function to a thorough psychological criticism, and therefore hold aloof from such discussions. It should, however, be obvious that the intrinsic polarity of such an attitude exerts a very great influence on the philosopher's own point of view.

For the extravert the object is interesting and attractive *a priori*, as is the subject, or psychic reality, for the introvert. We could therefore use the expression "numinal accent" for this fact, by which I mean that for the extravert the quality of positive significance and value attaches primarily to the object, so that it plays the predominant, determining, and decisive role in all psychic processes from the start, just as the subject does for the introvert.

But the numinal accent does not decide only between subject and object; it also selects the conscious function of which the individual makes the principal use. I distinguish four functions: *thinking, feeling, sensation,* and *intuition*. The essential function of sensation is to establish that something exists, thinking tells us what it means, feeling what its value is, and intuition surmises whence it comes and whither it goes. Sensation and intuition I call irrational functions, because they are both concerned simply with what happens and with actual or potential realities. Thinking and feeling, being discriminative functions, are rational. Sensation, the *fonction du réel*, rules out any simultaneous intuitive activity, since the latter is not concerned with the present but is rather a sixth sense for hidden possibilities, and therefore should not allow itself to be unduly influenced by existing reality. In the same way, thinking is opposed to feeling, because thinking should not be influenced or deflected from its purpose by feeling values, just as feeling is usually vitiated by too much reflection. The four functions therefore form, when arranged diagrammatically, a cross with a rational axis at right angles to an irrational axis.

The four orienting functions naturally do not contain everything that is in the conscious psyche. Will and memory, for instance, are not included. The reason for this is that the differentiation of the four orienting functions is, essentially, an empirical consequence of typical differences in the functional attitude. There are people for whom the numinal accent falls on sensation, on the perception of actualities, and elevates it into the sole determining and all-overriding principle. These are the fact-minded men, in whom intellectual judgment, feeling, and intuition are driven into the background by the paramount importance of actual facts. When the accent falls on thinking, judgment is reserved as to what significance should be attached to the facts in question. And on this significance will depend the way in which the individual deals with the facts. If feeling is numinal, then his adaptation will depend entirely on the feeling value he attributes to them. Finally, if the numinal accent falls on intuition, actual reality counts only in so far as it seems to harbour possibilities which then become the supreme motivating force, regardless of the way things actually are in the present.

The localization of the numinal accent thus gives rise to four function-types, which I encountered first of all in my relations with people and formulated systematically only very much later. In practice these four types are always combined with the attitude-type, that is, with extraversion or introversion, so that the functions appear in an extraverted or introverted variation. This produces a set of eight demonstrable function-types. It is naturally impossible to present the specific psychology of these types within the confines of an essay, and to go into its conscious and unconscious manifestations. I must therefore refer the interested reader to the aforementioned study.

It is not the purpose of a psychological typology to classify human beings into categories – this in itself would be pretty pointless. Its purpose is rather to provide a critical psychology which will make a methodical investigation and presentation of the empirical material possible. First and foremost, it is a critical tool for the research worker, who needs definite points of view and guidelines if he is to reduce the chaotic profusion of individual experiences to any kind of order. In this respect we could compare typology to a trigonometric net or, better still, to a crystallographic axial system. Secondly, a typology is a great help in understanding the wide variations that occur among individuals, and it also furnishes a clue to the fundamental differences in the psychological theories now current. Last but not least, it is an essential means for determining the "personal equation" of the practising psychologist, who, armed with an exact knowledge of his differentiated and inferior functions, can avoid many serious blunders in dealing with his patients.

The typological system I have proposed is an attempt, grounded on practical experience, to provide an explanatory basis and theoretical framework for the boundless diversity that has hitherto prevailed in the formation of psychological concepts. In a science as young as psychology, limiting definitions will sooner or later become an unavoidable necessity. Some day psychologists will have to agree upon certain basic principles secure from arbitrary interpretation if psychology is not to remain an unscientific and fortuitous conglomeration of individual opinions.

In "On the Psychology of the Unconscious," the first of the Two Essays on Analytical Psychology which constitute volume 7 of the Collected Works, Jung gives an outline of Freudian theory and Adlerian theory, and goes on to show that the psychopathology of a particular case can be interpreted equally validly from either standpoint. He then presents these two "psychologies" as examples of extraversion versus introversion; affirms that both attitudes are present in human beings; and suggests that neurosis occurs when either attitude is exaggerated. At the end of this passage, he states an important principle of Jungian thought: the psyche is self-regulating.

From "**On the Psychology of the Unconscious**" *Two Essays*, CW 7, pars. 56–92

THE PROBLEM OF THE ATTITUDE-TYPE

The incompatibility of the two theories discussed in the preceding chapters requires a standpoint superordinate to both, in which they could come together in unison. We are certainly not entitled to discard one in favour of the other, however convenient this expedient might be. For, if we examine the two theories without prejudice, we cannot deny that both contain significant truths, and, contradictory as these are, they should not be regarded as mutually exclusive. The Freudian theory is attractively simple, so much so that it almost pains one if anybody drives in the wedge of a contrary assertion. But the same is true of Adler's theory. It too is of illuminating simplicity and explains just as much as the Freudian theory. No wonder, then, that the adherents of both schools obstinately cling to their one-sided truths. For humanly understandable reasons they are unwilling to give up a beautiful, rounded theory in exchange for a paradox, or, worse still, lose themselves in the confusion of contradictory points of view.

Now, since both theories are in a large measure correct – that is to say, since they both appear to explain their material – it follows that a neurosis must have two opposite aspects, one of which is grasped by the Freudian, the other by the Adlerian theory. But how comes it that each investigator sees only one side, and why does each maintain that he has the only valid view? It must come from the fact that, owing to his psychological peculiarity, each investigator most readily sees that factor in the neurosis which corresponds to his peculiarity. It cannot be assumed that the cases of neurosis seen by Adler are totally different from those seen by Freud. Both are obviously working with the same material; but because of personal peculiarities they each see things from a different angle, and thus they evolve fundamentally different views and theories. Adler sees how a subject who feels suppressed and inferior tries to secure an illusory superiority by means of "protests," "arrangements," and other appropriate devices directed equally against parents, teachers, regulations, authorities, situations, institutions, and such. Even sexuality may figure among these devices. This view lays undue emphasis upon the subject, before which the idiosyncrasy and significance of objects entirely vanishes. Objects are regarded at best as vehicles of suppressive tendencies. I shall probably not be wrong in assuming that the love relation and other desires directed upon objects exist equally in Adler as essential factors; yet in his theory of neurosis they do not play the principal role assigned to them by Freud.

Freud sees his patient in perpetual dependence on, and in relation to, significant objects. Father and mother play a large part here; whatever other significant influences or conditions enter into the life of the patient go back in a direct line of causality to these prime factors. The *pièce de résistance* of his theory is the concept of transference, i.e., the patient's relation to the doctor. Always a specifically qualified object is either desired or met with resistance, and this reaction always follows the pattern established in earliest childhood through the relation to father and mother. What comes from the subject is essentially a blind striving after pleasure; but this striving always acquires its quality from specific objects. With Freud objects are of the greatest significance and possess almost exclusively the determining power, while the subject remains remarkably insignificant and is really nothing more than the source of desire for pleasure and a "seat of anxiety." As already pointed out, Freud recognizes ego-instincts, but this term alone is enough to show that his conception of the subject differs *toto coelo* from Adler's, where the subject figures as the determining factor.

Certainly both investigators see the subject in relation to the object; but how differently this relation is seen! With Adler the emphasis is placed on a subject who, no matter what the object, seeks his own security and supremacy; with Freud the emphasis is placed wholly upon objects, which, according to their specific character, either promote or hinder the subject's desire for pleasure.

This difference can hardly be anything else but a difference of temperament, a contrast between two types of human mentality, one of which finds the determining agency pre-eminently in the subject, the other in the object. A middle view, it may be that of common sense, would suppose that human behaviour is conditioned as much by the subject as by the object. The two investigators would probably assert, on the other hand, that their theory does not envisage a psychological explanation of the normal man, but is a theory of neurosis. But in that case Freud would have to explain and treat some of his patients along Adlerian lines, and Adler condescend to give earnest consideration in certain instances to his former teacher's point of view – which has occurred neither on the one side nor on the other.

The spectacle of this dilemma made me ponder the question: are there at least two different human types, one of them more interested in the object, the other more interested in himself? And does that explain why the one sees only the one and the other only the other, and thus each arrives at totally different conclusions? As we have said, it was hardly to be supposed that fate selected the patients so meticulously that a definite group invariably reached a definite doctor. For some time it had struck me, in connection both with myself and with my colleagues, that there are some cases which make a distinct appeal, while others somehow refuse to "click." It is of crucial importance for the treatment whether a good relationship between doctor and patient is possible or not. If some measure of natural confidence does not develop within a short period, then the patient will do better to choose another doctor. I myself have never shrunk from recommending to a colleague a patient whose peculiarities were not in my line or were unsympathetic to me, and indeed this is in the patient's own interests. I am positive that in such a case I would not do good work. Everyone has his personal limitations, and the psychotherapist in particular is well advised never to disregard them. Excessive personal differences and incompatibilities cause resistances that are disproportionate and out of place, though they are not altogether unjustified. The Freud-Adler controversy is simply a paradigm and one single instance among many possible attitude-types.

I have long busied myself with this question and have finally, on the basis of numerous observations and experiences, come to postulate two fundamental attitudes, namely introversion and extraversion. The first attitude is normally characterized by a hesitant, reflective, retiring nature that keeps itself to itself, shrinks from objects, is always slightly on the defensive and prefers to hide behind mistrustful scrutiny. The second is normally characterized by an outgoing, candid, and accommodating nature that adapts easily to a given situation, quickly forms attachments, and, setting aside any possible misgivings, will often venture forth with careless confidence into unknown situations. In the first case obviously the subject, and in the second the object, is all-important.

Naturally these remarks sketch the two types only in the roughest outlines.* As a matter of empirical fact the two attitudes, to which I shall come back shortly, can seldom be observed in their pure state. They are infinitely varied and compensated, so that often the type is not at all easy to establish. The reason for variation – apart from individual fluctuations – is the predominance of one of the conscious functions, such as thinking or feeling, which then gives the basic attitude a special character. The numerous compensations of the basic type are generally due to experiences which teach a man, perhaps in a very painful way, that he cannot give free rein to his nature. In other cases, for instance with neurotics, one frequently does not know whether one is dealing with a conscious or an unconscious attitude because, owing to the dissociation of the personality, sometimes one half of it and sometimes the other half occupies the foreground and confuses one's judgment. This is what makes it so excessively trying to live with neurotic persons.

The actual existence of far-reaching type-differences, of which I have described eight groups† in the above-mentioned book, has enabled me to conceive the two controversial theories of neurosis as manifestations of a type-antagonism.

This discovery brought with it the need to rise above the opposition and to create a theory which should do justice not merely to one or the other side, but to both equally. For this purpose a critique of both the aforementioned theories is essential. Both are painfully inclined to reduce high-flown ideals, heroic attitudes, nobility of feeling, deep convictions, to some banal reality, if applied to such things as these. On no account should they be so applied, for both theories are properly therapeutic instruments from the armoury of the doctor, whose knife must be

---

*A complete study of the type problem is to be found in my *Psychological Types, Coll. Works*, Vol. 6.
†Naturally this does not include all the existing types. Further points of difference are age, sex, activity, emotionality, and level of development. My type-psychology is based on the four orienting functions of consciousness: thinking, feeling, sensation, and intuition.

sharp and pitiless for excising what is diseased and injurious. This was what Nietzsche wanted with his destructive criticism of ideals, which he held to be morbid overgrowths in the soul of humanity (as indeed they sometimes are). In the hand of a good doctor, of one who really knows the human soul – who, to use Nietzsche's phrase, has a "finger for nuances" – both theories, when applied to the really sick part of a soul, are wholesome caustics, of great help in dosages measured to the individual case, but harmful and dangerous in the hand that knows not how to measure and weigh. They are critical methods, having, like all criticism, the power to do good when there is something that must be destroyed, dissolved, or reduced, but capable only of harm when there is something to be built.

Both theories may therefore be allowed to pass with no ill consequences provided that, like medical poisons, they are entrusted to the sure hand of the physician, for it requires an uncommon knowledge of the human psyche to apply these caustics with advantage. One must be capable of distinguishing the pathological and the useless from what is valuable and worth preserving, and that is one of the most difficult things. Anyone who wishes to get a vivid impression of how irresponsibly a psychologizing doctor can falsify his subject from narrow, pseudo-scientific prejudice, should turn to the writings of Möbius on Nietzsche, or, better still, to the various "psychiatric" writings on the "case" of Christ. He will not hesitate to cry a "threefold lamentation" over the patient who meets with such "understanding."

The two theories of neurosis are not universal theories: they are caustic remedies to be applied, as it were, locally. They are destructive and reductive. They say to everything, "You are nothing but . . ." They explain to the sufferer that his symptoms come from here and from there and are nothing but this or that. It would be unjust to assert that this reduction is wrong in a given case; but, exalted to the status of a general explanation of the healthy psyche as well as the sick, a reductive theory by itself is impossible. For the human psyche, be it sick or healthy, cannot be explained *solely* by reduction. Eros is certainly always and everywhere present, the urge to power certainly pervades the heights and depths of the psyche, but the psyche is not *just* the one or the other, nor for that matter both together. It is *also* what it has made and will make out of them. A man is only half understood when we know how everything in him came into being. If that were all, he could just as well have been dead years ago. As a living being he is not understood, for life does not have only a yesterday, nor is it explained by reducing today to yesterday. Life has also a tomorrow, and today is understood only when we can add to our knowledge of what was yesterday the beginnings of tomorrow. This is true of all life's psychological expressions, even of pathological symptoms. The symptoms of a neurosis are not simply the effects of long-past causes, whether "infantile sexuality" or the infantile urge to power; they are also attempts at a new synthesis of life – unsuccessful attempts, let it be added in the same breath, yet attempts nevertheless, with a core of value and meaning. They are seeds that fail to sprout owing to the inclement conditions of inner and outer nature.

The reader will doubtless ask: What in the world is the value and meaning of a neurosis, this most useless and pestilent curse of humanity? To be neurotic – what good can that do? As much good, possibly, as flies and other pests, which the good Lord created so that man might exercise the useful virtue of patience. However stupid this thought is from the point of view of natural science, it may yet be sensible enough from the point of view of psychology, if we put "nervous symptoms" instead of "pests." Even Nietzsche, a rare one for scorning stupid and banal thoughts, more than once acknowledged how much he owed to his malady. I myself have known more than one person who owed his entire usefulness and reason for existence to a neurosis, which prevented all the critical follies in his life and *forced* him to a mode of living that developed his valuable potentialities. These might have been stifled had not the neurosis, with iron grip, held him to the place where he belonged. There are actually people who have the whole meaning of their life, their true significance, in the unconscious, while in the conscious mind is nothing but inveiglement and error. With others the case is reversed, and here neurosis has a different meaning. In these cases, but not in the former, a thorough-going reduction is indicated.

At this point the reader may be inclined to grant the possibility that the neurosis has such a meaning in certain cases, while denying it so far-reaching a purposiveness in ordinary everyday cases. What, for instance, could be the value of a neurosis in the above-mentioned case of asthma with its hysterical anxiety-states? I admit that the value is not so obvious here, especially when the case is considered from the theoretical reductive standpoint, that is, from the shadow-side of individual development.

The two theories we have been discussing evidently have this much in common: they pitilessly unveil everything that belongs to man's shadow-side. They are theories or, more correctly, hypotheses which explain in what the pathogenic factor consists. They are accordingly concerned not with a man's positive values, but with his negative values which make themselves so disturbingly conspicuous.

A "value" is a possibility for the display of energy. But in so far as a negative value is likewise a possibility for the display of energy – which can be seen most clearly in the notable manifestations of neurotic energy – it too is properly a "value," but one that makes possible useless and harmful manifestations of energy. Energy in itself is neither good nor bad, neither useful nor harmful, but neutral, since everything depends on the *form* into which energy passes. Form gives energy its quality. On the other hand, mere form without energy is equally neutral. For the creation of a real value, therefore, both energy and valuable form are needed. In neurosis psychic energy* is present, but undoubtedly it is there in an inferior and unserviceable form. The two reductive theories act as solvents of this inferior form. They are approved caustic remedies, by means of which we obtain free but neutral energy. Now, it has hitherto been supposed that this newly disengaged energy is at the conscious disposal of the patient, so that he can apply it at his pleasure. Since it was thought that the energy is nothing but the instinctual power of sex, people talked of a "sublimated" application of it, on the assumption that the patient could, with the help of analysis, canalize the sexual energy into a "sublimation," in other words, could apply it non-sexually, in the practice of an art, perhaps, or in some other good or useful activity. According to this view, it is possible for the patient, from free

*I refer the reader to my essay "On Psychic Energy," *Coll. Works*, Vol. 8.

choice or inclination, to achieve the sublimation of his instinctual forces.

We may allow that this view has a certain justification in so far as man is at all capable of marking out a definite line along which his life has to go. But we know that there is no human foresight or wisdom that can prescribe direction to our life, except for small stretches of the way. This is of course true only of the "ordinary" type of life, not of the "heroic" type. The latter kind also exists, though it is much rarer. Here we are certainly not entitled to say that no marked direction can be given to life, or only for short distances. The heroic conduct of life is absolute – that is, it is oriented by fateful decisions, and the decision to go in a certain direction holds, sometimes, to the bitter end. Admittedly the doctor has to do, in the main, only with human beings, seldom with voluntary heroes, and then they are mostly of a type whose surface heroism is an infantile defiance of a fate greater than they, or else a pomposity meant to cover up some touchy inferiority. In this overpoweringly humdrum existence, alas, there is little out of the ordinary that is healthy, and not much room for conspicuous heroism. Not that heroic demands are never put to us: on the contrary – and this is just what is so irritating and irksome – the banal everyday makes banal demands upon our patience, our devotion, perseverance, self-sacrifice; and for us to fulfil these demands (as we must) humbly and without courting applause through heroic gestures, a heroism is needed that cannot be seen from the outside. It does not glitter, is not belauded, and it always seeks concealment in everyday attire. These are the demands which, if not fulfilled, are the cause of neurosis. In order to evade them, many a man has dared the great decision of his life and carried it through, even if in the common human estimation it was a great error. Before a fate such as this one can only bow one's head. But, as I say, such cases are rare; the others are in the vast majority. For them the direction of their life is not a simple, straight line; fate confronts them like an intricate labyrinth, all too rich in possibilities, and yet of these many possibilities only one is their own right way. Who would presume – even though armed with the completest knowledge of his own character – to designate in advance that single possibility? Much indeed can be attained by the will, but, in view of the fate of certain markedly strong-willed personalities, it is a fundamental error to try to subject our own fate at all costs to our will. Our will is a function regulated by reflection; hence it is dependent on the quality of that reflection. This, if it really is reflection, is supposed to be rational, i.e., in accord with reason. But has it ever been shown, or will it ever be, that life and fate are in accord with reason, that they too are rational? We have on the contrary good grounds for supposing that they are irrational, or rather that in the last resort they are grounded beyond human reason. The irrationality of events is shown in what we call chance, which we are obviously compelled to deny, because we cannot in principle think of any process that is not causal and necessary, whence it follows that it cannot happen by chance.* In practice, however, chance reigns everywhere, and so obtrusively that we might as well put our causal philosophy in our pocket. The plenitude of life is governed by law and yet not governed by law, rational and yet irrational. Hence reason and the will that is grounded in reason are valid only up to a point. The further we go in the direction selected by reason, the surer we may be that we are excluding the irrational possibilities of life which have just as much right to be lived. It was indeed highly expedient for man to become somewhat more capable of directing his life. It may justly be maintained that the acquisition of reason is the greatest achievement of humanity; but that is not to say that things must or will always continue in that direction. The frightful catastrophe of the first World War drew a very thick line through the calculations of even the most optimistic rationalizers of culture. In 1913, Ostwald wrote:

> The whole world is agreed that the present state of armed peace is untenable and is gradually becoming impossible. It demands tremendous sacrifices from each single nation, far exceeding the expenditure for cultural purposes, yet without securing any positive values. If mankind could discover ways and means for doing away with these preparations for wars *which never take place*, together with the immobilization of a large part of the nation's manhood, at the age of maximum strength and

---

*Modern physics has put an end to this strict causality. Now there is only "statistical probability." As far back as 1916, I had pointed out the limitations of the causal view in psychology, for which I was heavily censured at the time.

efficiency, for the furtherance of warlike aims, and all the other innumerable evils which the present state of affairs creates, such an immense economy of energy would be effected that from this moment onwards we could look forward to a blossoming of culture hitherto undreamed of. For war, like personal combat, although the oldest of all possible means of settling contests of will, is on that very account the most inept, and entails the most grievous waste of energy. Hence the complete abolition of warfare, potential no less than actual, is the categorical imperative of efficiency and one of the supremely important cultural tasks of our day.*

The irrationality of fate, however, did not concur with the rationality of well-meaning thinkers; it ordained not only the destruction of the accumulated arms and armies, but, far beyond that, a mad and monstrous devastation, a mass murder without parallel – from which humanity may possibly draw the conclusion that only one side of fate can be mastered with rational intentions.

What is true of humanity in general is also true of each individual, for humanity consists only of individuals. And as is the psychology of humanity so also is the psychology of the individual. The World War brought a terrible reckoning with the rational intentions of civilization. What is called "will" in the individual is called "imperialism" in nations; for all will is a demonstration of power over fate, i.e., the exclusion of chance. Civilization is the rational, "purposeful" sublimation of free energies, brought about by will and intention. It is the same with the individual; and just as the idea of a world civilization received a fearful correction at the hands of war, so the individual must often learn in his life that so-called "disposable" energies are not his to dispose.

Once, in America, I was consulted by a business man of about forty-five, whose case is a good illustration of what has been said. He was a typical American self-made man who had worked his way up from the bottom. He had been very successful and had founded an immense business. He had also succeeded in organizing it in such a way that he was able to think of retiring. Two years before

*Wilhelm Ostwald, *Die Philosophie der Werte* (Leipzig, 1913), pp. 312f.

I saw him he had in fact taken his farewell. Until then he had lived entirely for his business and concentrated all his energies on it with the incredible intensity and one-sidedness peculiar to successful American business men. He had purchased a splendid estate where he thought of "living," by which he meant horses, automobiles, golf, tennis, parties and what not. But he had reckoned without his host. The energy which should have been at his disposal would not enter into these alluring prospects, but went capering off in quite another direction. A few weeks after the initiation of the longed-for life of bliss, he began brooding over peculiar, vague sensations in his body, and a few weeks more sufficed to plunge him into a state of extreme hypochondria. He had a complete nervous collapse. From a healthy man, of uncommon physical strength and abounding energy, he became a peevish child. That was the end of all his glories. He fell from one state of anxiety to the next and worried himself almost to death with hypochondriacal mopings. He then consulted a famous specialist, who recognized at once that there was nothing wrong with the man but lack of work. The patient saw the sense of this, and returned to his former position. But, to his immense disappointment, no interest in the business could be aroused. Neither patience nor resolution was of any use. His energy could not by any means be forced back into the business. His condition naturally became worse than before. All that had formerly been living, creative energy in him now turned against him with terrible destroying force. His creative genius rose up, as it were, in revolt against him; and just as before he had built up great organizations in the world, so now his daemon spun equally subtle systems of hypochondriacal delusion that completely annihilated him. When I saw him he was already a hopeless moral ruin. Nevertheless I tried to make clear to him that though such a gigantic energy might be withdrawn from the business, the question remained, where should it go? The finest horses, the fastest cars, and the most amusing parties may very likely fail to allure the energy, although it would be rational enough to think that a man who had devoted his whole life to serious work had a sort of natural right to enjoy himself. Yes, if fate behaved in a humanly rational way, it would certainly be so: first work, then well-earned rest. But fate behaves irrationally, and the energy of life inconveniently demands a gradient agreeable to itself; otherwise it simply gets dammed up and turns destructive. It regresses to former situations – in the case of this man, to the memory of a syphilitic infection contracted twenty-five years before. Yet even this was only a stage on the way to the resuscitation of infantile reminiscences which had all but vanished in the meantime. It was the original relation to his mother that mapped the course of his symptoms: they were an "arrangement" whose purpose it was to compel the attention and interest of his long-dead mother. Nor was this stage the last; for the ultimate goal was to drive him back, as it were, into his own body, after he had lived since his youth only in his head. He had differentiated one side of his being; the other side remained in an inert physical state. He would have needed this other side in order to "live." The hypochondriacal "depression" pushed him down into the body he had always overlooked. Had he been able to follow the direction indicated by his depression and hypochondriacal illusion, and make himself conscious of the fantasies which proceed from such a condition, that would have been the road to salvation. My argument naturally met with no response, as was to be expected. A case so far advanced can only be cared for until death; it can hardly be cured.

This example clearly shows that it does not lie in our power to transfer "disposable" energy at will to a rationally chosen object. The same is true in general of the apparently disposable energy which is disengaged when we have destroyed its unserviceable forms through the corrosive of reductive analysis. This energy, as we have said, can at best be applied voluntarily for only a short time. But in most cases it refuses to seize hold, for any length of time, of the possibilities rationally presented to it. Psychic energy is a very fastidious thing which insists on fulfilment of its own conditions. However much energy may be present, we cannot make it serviceable until we have succeeded in finding the right gradient.

This question of the gradient is an eminently practical problem which crops up in most analyses. For instance, when in a favourable case the disposable energy, the so-called libido,* does

*From the foregoing it will have become clear to the reader that the term "libido," coined by Freud and very suitable for practical usage, is used by me in a much wider sense. Libido for me means psychic energy, which is equivalent to the intensity with which psychic contents are charged.

seize hold of a rational object, we think we have brought about the transformation through conscious exertion of the will. But in that we are deluded, because even the most strenuous exertions would not have sufficed had there not been present at the same time a gradient in that direction. How important the gradient is can be seen in cases when, despite the most desperate exertions, and despite the fact that the object chosen or the form desired impresses everybody with its reasonableness, the transformation still refuses to take place, and all that happens is a new repression.

It has become abundantly clear to me that life can flow forward only along the path of the gradient. But there is no energy unless there is a tension of opposites; hence it is necessary to discover the opposite to the attitude of the conscious mind. It is interesting to see how this compensation by opposites also plays its part in the historical theories of neurosis: Freud's theory espoused Eros, Adler's the will to power. Logically, the opposite of love is hate, and of Eros, Phobos (fear); but psychologically it is the will to power. Where love reigns, there is no will to power; and where the will to power is paramount, love is lacking. The one is but the shadow of the other: the man who adopts the standpoint of Eros finds his compensatory opposite in the will to power, and that of the man who puts the accent on power is Eros. Seen from the one-sided point of view of the conscious attitude, the shadow is an inferior component of the personality and is consequently re-pressed through intensive resistance. But the repressed content must be made conscious so as to produce a tension of opposites, without which no forward movement is possible. The conscious mind is on top, the shadow underneath, and just as high always longs for low and hot for cold, so all consciousness, perhaps without being aware of it, seeks its unconscious opposite, lacking which it is doomed to stagnation, congestion, and ossification. Life is born only of the spark of opposites.

It was a concession to intellectual logic on the one hand and to psychological prejudice on the other that impelled Freud to name the opposite of Eros the destructive or death instinct. For in the first place, Eros is not equivalent to life; but for anyone who thinks it is, the opposite of Eros will naturally appear to be death. And in the second place, we all feel that the opposite of our own highest principle must be purely destructive, deadly, and evil. We refuse to endow it with any positive life-force; hence we avoid and fear it.

As I have already indicated, there are many highest principles both of life and of philosophy, and accordingly there are just as many different forms of compensation by opposition. Earlier on I singled out the two – as it seems to me – main opposite types, which I have called introverted and extraverted. William James* had already been struck by the existence of both these types among thinkers. He distinguished them as "tender-minded" and "tough-minded." Similarly Ostwald† found an analogous division into "classical" and "romantic" types among men of learning. So I am not alone in my idea of types, to mention only these two well-known names among many others. Inquiries into history have shown me that not a few of the great spiritual controversies rest upon the opposition of the two types. The most significant case of this kind is the opposition between nominalism and realism which, beginning with the difference between the Platonic and Megaric schools, became the heritage of scholastic philosophy, where it is Abelard's great merit to have hazarded at least the attempt to unite the two opposed standpoints in his "conceptualism." This controversy has continued right into our own day, as is shown in the opposition between idealism and materialism. And again, not only the human mind in general, but each individual has a share in this opposition of types. It has come to light on closer investigation that either type has a predilection to marry its opposite, each being unconsciously complementary to the other. The reflective nature of the introvert causes him always to think and consider before acting. This naturally makes him slow to act. His shyness and distrust of things induces hesitation, and so he always has difficulty in adapting to the external world. Conversely the extravert has a positive relation to things. He is, so to speak, attracted by them. New, unknown situations fascinate him. In order to make closer acquaintance with the unknown he will jump into it with both feet. As a rule he acts first and thinks afterwards. Thus his action is swift, subject to no misgivings and hesitations.

*Pragmatism (London and Cambridge, Mass., 1907).
†Grosse Männer (Leipzig, 1910).

The two types therefore seem created for a symbiosis. The one takes care of reflection and the other sees to the initiative and practical action. When the two types marry they may effect an ideal union. So long as they are fully occupied with their adaptation to the manifold external needs of life they fit together admirably. But when the man has made enough money, or if a fine legacy should drop from the skies and external necessity no longer presses, then they have time to occupy themselves with one another. Hitherto they stood back to back and defended themselves against necessity. But now they turn face to face and look for understanding – only to discover that they have never understood one another. Each speaks a different language. Then the conflict between the two types begins. This struggle is envenomed, brutal, full of mutual depreciation, even when conducted quietly and in the greatest intimacy. For the value of the one is the negation of value for the other. It might reasonably be supposed that each, conscious of his own value, could peaceably recognize the other's value, and that in this way any conflict would be superfluous. I have seen a good number of cases where this line of argument was adopted, without, however, arriving at a satisfactory goal. Where it is a question of normal people, such critical periods of transition will be overcome fairly smoothly. By "normal" I mean a person who can somehow exist under all circumstances which afford him the minimum needs of life. But many people cannot do this; therefore not so very many people are normal. What we commonly mean by a "normal person" is actually an ideal person whose happy blend of character is a rare occurrence. By far the greater number of more or less differentiated persons demand conditions of life which afford considerably more than the certainty of food and sleep. For these the ending of a symbiotic relationship comes as a severe shock.

It is not easy to understand why this should be so. Yet if we consider that no man is simply introverted or simply extraverted, but has both attitudes potentially in him – although he has developed only one of them as a function of adaptation – we shall immediately conjecture that with the introvert extraversion lies dormant and undeveloped somewhere in the background, and that introversion leads a similar shadowy existence in the extravert. And this is indeed the case. The introvert does possess an extraverted attitude, but it is unconscious, because his conscious gaze is always turned to the subject. He sees the object, of course, but has false or inhibiting ideas about it, so that he keeps his distance as much as possible, as though the object were something formidable and dangerous. I will make my meaning clear by a simple illustration:

Let us suppose two youths rambling in the country. They come to a fine castle; both want to see inside it. The introvert says, "I'd like to know what it's like inside." The extravert answers, "Right, let's go in," and makes for the gateway. The introvert draws back – "Perhaps we aren't allowed in," says he, with visions of policemen, fines, and fierce dogs in the background. Whereupon the extravert answers, "Well, we can ask. They'll let us in all right" – with visions of kindly old watchmen, hospitable seigneurs, and the possibility of romantic adventures. On the strength of extraverted optimism they at length find themselves in the castle. But now comes the dénouement. The castle has been rebuilt inside, and contains nothing but a couple of rooms with a collection of old manuscripts. As it happens, old manuscripts are the chief joy of the introverted youth. Hardly has he caught sight of them when he becomes as one transformed. He loses himself in contemplation of the treasures, uttering cries of enthusiasm. He engages the keeper in conversation so as to extract from him as much information as possible, and when the result is meagre the youth asks to see the curator in order to propound his questions to him. His shyness has vanished, objects have taken on a seductive glamour, and the world wears a new face. But meanwhile the spirits of the extraverted youth are ebbing lower and lower. His face grows longer and he begins to yawn. No kindly watchmen are forthcoming here, no knightly hospitality, not a trace of romantic adventure – only a castle made over into a museum. There are manuscripts enough to be seen at home. While the enthusiasm of the one rises, the spirits of the other fall, the castle bores him, the manuscripts remind him of a library, library is associated with university, university with studies and menacing examinations. Gradually a veil of gloom descends over the once so interesting and enticing castle. The object becomes negative. "Isn't it marvellous," cries the introvert, "to have stumbled on this wonderful collection?" "The place bores me to extinction," replies the other with undisguised ill humour. This annoys the introvert, who secretly vows never again to go rambling with an extravert. The latter is annoyed with the other's annoyance, and he thinks to himself that he always knew the fellow was an inconsiderate egotist who would, in his own selfish interest, waste all the lovely spring day that could be enjoyed so much better out of doors.

What has happened? Both were wandering together in happy symbiosis until they discovered the fatal castle. Then the forethinking, or Promethean, introvert said it might be seen from the inside, and the afterthinking, or Epimethean, extravert opened the door. At this point the types invert themselves: the introvert, who at first resisted the idea of going in, cannot now be induced to go out, and the extravert curses the moment when he set foot inside the castle. The former is now fascinated by the object, the latter by his negative thoughts. When the introvert spotted the manuscripts, it was all up with him. His shyness vanished, the object took possession of him, and he yielded himself willingly. The extravert, however, felt a growing resistance to the object and was eventually made the prisoner of his own ill-humoured subjectivity. The introvert became extraverted, the extravert introverted. But the extraversion of the introvert is different from the extraversion of the extravert, and vice versa. So long as both were wandering along in joyous harmony, neither fell foul of the other, because each was in his natural character. Each was positive to the other, because their attitudes were complementary. They were complementary, however, only because the attitude of the one included the other. We can see this from the short conversation at the gateway. Both wanted to enter the castle. The doubt of the introvert as to whether an entry were possible also held good for the other. The initiative of the extravert likewise held good for the other. Thus the attitude of the one included the other, and this is always in some degree true if a person happens to be in the attitude natural to him, for this attitude has some degree of collective adaptation. The same is true of the introvert's attitude, although this always comes from the subject. It simply goes from subject to object, while the extravert's attitude goes from object to subject.

But the moment when, in the case of the introvert, the object overpowers and attracts the subject, his attitude loses its social character. He forgets the presence of his friend, he no longer includes him, he becomes absorbed into the object and does not see how very bored his friend is. In the same way the extravert loses all consideration for the other as soon as his expectations are disappointed and he withdraws into subjectivity and moodiness.

We can therefore formulate the occurrence as follows: in the introvert the influence of the object produces an inferior extraversion, while in the extravert an inferior introversion takes the place of his social attitude. And so we come back to the proposition from which we started: "The value of the one is the negation of value for the other."

Positive as well as negative occurrences can constellate the inferior counter-function. When this happens, sensitiveness appears. Sensitiveness is a sure sign of the presence of inferiority. This provides the psychological basis for discord and misunderstanding, not only as between two people, but also in ourselves. The essence of the inferior function is autonomy: it is independent, it attacks, it fascinates and so spins us about that we are no longer masters of ourselves and can no longer rightly distinguish between ourselves and others.

And yet it is necessary for the development of character that we should allow the other side, the inferior function, to find expression. We cannot in the long run allow one part of our personality to be cared for symbiotically by another; for the moment when we might have need of the other function may come at any time and find us unprepared, as the above example shows. And the consequences may be bad: the extravert loses his indispensable relation to the object, and the introvert loses his to the subject. Conversely, it is equally indispensable for the introvert to arrive at some form of action not constantly bedevilled by doubts and hesitations, and for the extravert to reflect upon himself, yet without endangering his relationships.

In extraversion and introversion it is clearly a matter of two antithetical, natural attitudes or trends, which Goethe once referred to as diastole and systole. They ought, in their harmonious alternation, to give life a rhythm, but it seems to require a high degree of art to achieve such a rhythm. Either one must do it quite unconsciously, so that the natural law is not disturbed by any conscious act, or one must be conscious in a much higher sense, to be capable of willing and carrying out the antithetical movements. Since we cannot develop backwards into animal unconsciousness, there remains only the more strenuous way forwards into higher consciousness. Certainly that consciousness, which would enable us to live the great Yea and Nay of our own free will and purpose, is an altogether superhuman ideal. Still, it is a goal. Perhaps our present mentality only allows us consciously to will the Yea and to bear with the Nay. When that is the case, much is already achieved.

The problem of opposites, as an inherent principle of human nature, forms a further stage in our process of realization. As a rule it is one of the problems of maturity. The practical treatment of a patient will hardly ever begin with this problem, especially not in the case of young people. The neuroses of the young generally come from a collision between the forces of reality and an inadequate, infantile attitude, which from the causal point of view is characterized by an abnormal dependence on the real or imaginary parents, and from the teleological point of view by unrealizable fictions, plans, and aspirations. Here the reductive methods of Freud and Adler are entirely in place. But there are many neuroses which either appear only at maturity or else deteriorate to such a degree that the patients become incapable of work. Naturally one can point out in these cases that an unusual dependence on the parents existed even in youth, and that all kinds of infantile illusions were present; but all that did not prevent them from taking up a profession, from practising it successfully, from keeping up a marriage of sorts until that moment in riper years when the previous attitude suddenly failed. In such cases it is of little help to make them conscious of their childhood fantasies, dependence on the parents, etc., although this is a necessary part of the procedure and often has a not unfavourable result. But the real therapy only begins when the patient sees that it is no longer father and mother who are standing in his way, but himself – i.e., an unconscious part of his personality which carries on the role of father and mother. Even this realization, helpful as it is, is still negative; it simply says, "I realize that it is not father and mother who are against me, but I myself." But *who* is it in him that is against him? What is this mysterious part of his personality that hides under the father- and mother-imagos, making him believe for years that the cause of his trouble must somehow have got into him from outside? This part is the counterpart to his conscious attitude; and it will leave him no peace and will continue to plague him until it has been accepted. For young people a liberation from the past may be enough: a beckoning future lies ahead, rich in possibilities. It is sufficient to break a few bonds; the life-urge will do the rest. But we are faced with another task in the case of people who have left a large part of their life behind them, for whom the future no longer beckons with marvellous possibilities, and nothing is to be expected but the endless round of familiar duties and the doubtful pleasures of old age.

If ever we succeed in liberating young people from the past, we see that they always transfer the imagos of their parents to more suitable substitute figures. For instance, the feeling that clung to the mother now passes to the wife, and the father's authority passes to respected teachers and superiors or to institutions. Although this is not a fundamental solution, it is yet a practical road which the normal man treads unconsciously and therefore with no notable inhibitions and resistances.

The problem for the adult is very different. He has put this part of the road behind him with or without difficulty. He has cut loose from his parents, long since dead perhaps, and has sought and found the mother in the wife, or, in the case of a woman, the father in the husband. He has duly honoured his fathers and their institutions, has himself become a father, and, with all this in the past, has possibly come to realize that what originally meant advancement and satisfaction has now become a boring mistake, part of the illusion of youth, upon which he looks back with mingled regret and envy, because nothing now awaits him but old age and the end of all illusions. Here there are no more fathers and mothers; all the illusions he projected upon the world and upon things gradually come home to him, jaded and way-worn. The energy streaming back from these manifold relationships falls into the unconscious and activates all the things he had neglected to develop.

In a young man, the instinctual forces tied up in the neurosis give him, when released, buoyancy and hope and the chance to extend the scope of his life. To the man in the second half of life the development of the function of opposites lying dormant in the unconscious means a renewal; but this development no longer proceeds via the solution of infantile ties, the destruction of infantile illusions and the transference of old imagos to new figures: it proceeds via the problem of opposites.

The principle of opposition is, of course, fundamental even in adolescence, and a psychological theory of the adolescent psyche is bound to recognize this fact. Hence the Freudian and Adlerian viewpoints contradict each other only when they claim to be generally applicable theories. But so long as they are content to be technical, auxiliary concepts, they do not contradict or exclude one another. A psychological theory, if it is to be more than a technical makeshift, must base itself on the principle of opposition; for without this it could only re-establish a neurotically unbalanced psyche. There is no balance, no system of self-regulation, without opposition. The psyche is just such a self-regulating system.

If the psyche is regarded as a self-regulating system, it follows that the attitude of consciousness is compensated by the attitude of the unconscious. In Jungian analysis, the principal, though not the only, way of discovering the attitude of the unconscious is through the study and interpretation of the patient's dreams.

Neurotic symptoms, also, can be compensatory to a distorted, one-sided conscious attitude, and may thus be valuable pointers toward a new adaptation rather than being simply disagreeable. In a discussion following one of his Tavistock Lectures, Jung says:

I am not altogether pessimistic about neurosis. In many cases we have to say: "Thank heaven he could make up his mind to be neurotic." Neurosis is really an attempt at self-cure, just as any physical disease is in part an attempt at self-cure. We cannot understand a disease as an *ens per se* any more, as something detached which not so long ago it was believed to be. Modern medicine – internal medicine, for instance – conceives of disease as a system composed of a harmful factor and a healing factor. It is exactly the same with neurosis. It is an attempt of the self-regulating psychic system to restore the balance, in no way different from the function of dreams – only rather more forceful and drastic. [CW 18, par. 389]

Jung's view of dreams as generally compensatory is clearly stated in a paper which he first read in Dresden in 1931, "The Practical Use of Dream-analysis."

"The Practical Use of Dream-analysis"   CW 16, pars. 294–352

The use of dream-analysis in psychotherapy is still a much debated question. Many practitioners find it indispensable in the treatment of neuroses, and consider that the dream is a function whose psychic importance is equal to that of the conscious mind itself. Others, on the contrary, dispute the value of dream-analysis and regard dreams as a negligible by-product of the psyche. Obviously, if a person holds the view that the unconscious plays a decisive part in the aetiology of neuroses, he will attribute a high practical importance to dreams as direct expressions of the unconscious. Equally obviously, if he denies the unconscious or at least thinks it aetiologically insignificant, he will minimize the importance of dream-analysis. It might be considered regrettable that in this year of grace 1931, more than half a century after Carus formulated the concept of the unconscious, more than a century after Kant spoke of the "illimitable field of obscure ideas," and nearly two hundred years after Leibniz postulated an unconscious psychic activity, not to mention the achievements of Janet, Flournoy, Freud, and many more – that after all this, the actuality of the unconscious should still be a matter for controversy. But, since it is my intention to deal exclusively with practical questions, I will not advance in this place an apology for the unconscious, although our special problem of dream-analysis stands or falls with such an hypothesis. Without it, the dream is a mere freak of nature, a meaningless conglomeration of fragments left over from the day. Were that really so, there would be no excuse for the present discussion. We cannot treat our theme at all unless we recognize the unconscious, for the avowed aim of dream-analysis is not only to exercise our wits, but to uncover and realize those hitherto unconscious contents which are considered to be of importance in the elucidation or treatment of a neurosis. Anyone who finds this hypothesis unacceptable must simply rule out the question of the applicability of dream-analysis.

But since, according to our hypothesis, the unconscious possesses an aetiological significance, and since dreams are the direct expression of unconscious psychic activity, the attempt to analyse and interpret dreams is theoretically justified from a scientific standpoint. If successful, we may expect this attempt to give us scientific insight into the structure of psychic causality, quite apart from any therapeutic results that may be gained. The practitioner, however, tends to consider scientific discoveries as, at most, a gratifying by-product of his therapeutic work, so he is hardly likely to take the bare possibility of theoretical insight into the aetiological background as a sufficient reason for, much less an indication of, the practical use of dream-analysis. He may believe, of course, that the explanatory insight so gained is of therapeutic value, in which case he will elevate dream-analysis to a professional duty. It is well known that the Freudian school is of the firm opinion that very valuable therapeutic results are achieved by throwing light upon the unconscious causal factors – that is, by explaining them to the patient and thus making him fully conscious of the sources of his trouble.

Assuming for the moment that this expectation is justified by the facts, then the only question that remains is whether dream-analysis can or cannot be used, alone or in conjunction with other methods, to discover the unconscious aetiology. The Freudian answer to this question is, I may assume, common knowledge. I can confirm this answer inasmuch as dreams, particularly the initial dreams which appear at the very outset of the treatment, often bring to light the essential aetiological factor in the most unmistakable way. The following example may serve as an illustration:

I was consulted by a man who held a prominent position in the world. He was afflicted with a sense of anxiety and insecurity, and complained of dizziness sometimes resulting in nausea, heaviness in the head, and constriction of breath – a state that might easily be confused with mountain sickness. He had had an extraordinarily successful career, and had risen, by dint of ambition, industry, and native talent, from his humble origins as the son of a poor peasant. Step by step he had climbed, attaining at last a leading position which held every prospect of further social advancement. He had now in fact reached the spring-board from which he could have commenced his flight into the empyrean, had not his neurosis suddenly intervened. At this point in his story the patient could not refrain from that familiar exclamation which begins with the stereotyped words: "And just now, when . . ." The fact that he had all the symptoms of mountain sickness seemed highly appropriate as a drastic illustration of his peculiar impasse. He had also brought to the consultation two dreams from the preceding night. The first dream was as follows: "*I am back again in the small village where I was born. Some peasant lads who went to school with me are standing together in the street. I walk past, pretending not to know them. Then I hear one of them say, pointing at me: 'He doesn't often come back to our village.'*"

It requires no feat of interpretation to see in this dream a reference to the humble beginnings of the dreamer's career and to understand what this reference means. The dream says quite clearly: "You forgot how far down you began."

Here is the second dream: "*I am in a great hurry because I want to go on a journey. I keep on looking for things to pack, but can find nothing. Time flies, and the train will soon be leaving. Having finally succeeded in getting all my things together, I hurry along the street, only to discover that I have forgotten a brief-case containing important papers. I dash back all out of breath, find it at last, then race to the station, but I make hardly any headway. With a final effort I rush on to the platform only to see the train just steaming out of the station yard. It is very long, and it runs in a curious S-shaped curve, and it occurs to me that if the engine-driver does not look out, and puts on steam when he comes into the straight, the rear coaches will still be on the curve and will be thrown off the rails by the gathering speed. And this is just what happens: the engine-driver puts on steam, I try to cry out, the rear coaches give a frightful lurch and are thrown off the rails. There is a terrible catastrophe. I wake up in terror.*"

Here again no effort is needed to understand the message of the dream. It describes the patient's frantic haste to advance himself still further. But since the engine-driver in front steams relentlessly ahead, the neurosis happens at the back: the coaches rock and the train is derailed.

It is obvious that, at the present phase of his life, the patient has reached the highest point of his career; the strain of the long ascent from his lowly origin has exhausted his strength. He should have rested content with his achievements, but instead of that his ambition drives him on and on, and up and up into an atmosphere that is too thin for him and to which he is not accustomed. Therefore his neurosis comes upon him as a warning.

Circumstances prevented me from treating the patient further, nor did my view of the case satisfy him. The upshot was that the fate depicted in the dream ran its course. He tried to exploit the professional openings that tempted his ambition, and ran so violently off the rails that the catastrophe was realized in actual life.

Thus, what could only be inferred from the conscious anamnesis – namely that the mountain sickness was a symbolical representation of the patient's inability to climb any further – was confirmed by the dreams as a fact.

Here we come upon something of the utmost importance for the applicability of dream-analysis: the dream describes the inner situation of the dreamer, but the conscious mind denies its truth and reality, or admits it only grudgingly. Consciously the dreamer could not see the slightest reason why he should not go steadily forward; on the contrary, he continued his ambitious climbing and refused to admit his own inability which subsequent events made all too plain. So long as we move in the conscious sphere, we are always unsure in such cases. The anamnesis can be interpreted in various ways. After all, the common soldier carries the marshal's baton in his knapsack, and many a son of poor parents has achieved the highest success. Why should it not be the case here? Since my judgment is fallible, why should my conjecture be better than his? At this point the dream comes in as the expression of an involuntary, unconscious psychic process beyond the control of the conscious mind. It shows the inner truth and reality of the patient as it really is: not as I conjecture it to be, and not as he would like it to be, but *as it is*. I have therefore made it a rule to regard dreams as I regard physiological facts: if sugar appears in the urine, then the urine contains sugar, and not albumen or urobilin or something else that might fit in better with my expectations. That is to say, I take dreams as diagnostically valuable facts.

As is the way of all dreams, my little dream example gives us rather more than we expected. It gives us not only the aetiology of the neurosis but a prognosis as well. What is more, we even know exactly where the treatment should begin: we must prevent the patient from going full steam ahead. This is just what he tells himself in the dream.

Let us for the time being content ourselves with this hint and return to our consideration of whether dreams enable us to throw light on the aetiology of a neurosis. The dreams I have cited actually do this. But I could equally well cite any number of initial dreams where there is no trace of an aetiological factor, although they are perfectly transparent. I do not wish for the present to consider dreams which call for searching analysis and interpretation.

The point is this: there are neuroses whose real aetiology becomes clear only right at the end of an analysis, and other neuroses whose aetiology is relatively unimportant. This brings me back to the hypothesis from which we started, that for the purposes of therapy it is absolutely necessary to make the patient conscious of the aetiological factor. This hypothesis is little more than a hang-over from the old trauma theory. I do not of course deny that many neuroses are traumatic in origin; I simply contest the notion that all neuroses are of this nature and arise without exception from some crucial experience in childhood. Such a view necessarily results in the causalistic approach. The doctor must give his whole attention to the patient's past; he must always ask "Why?" and ignore the equally pertinent question "What for?" Often this has a most deleterious effect on the patient, who is thereby compelled to go searching about in his memory – perhaps for years – for some hypothetical event in his childhood, while things of immediate importance are grossly neglected. The purely causalistic approach is too narrow and fails to do justice to the true significance either of the dream or of the neurosis. Hence an approach that uses dreams for the sole purpose of discovering the aetiological factor is biased and overlooks the main point of the dream. Our example indeed shows the aetiology clearly enough, but it also offers a prognosis or anticipation of the future as well as a suggestion about the treatment. There are in addition large numbers of initial dreams which do not touch the aetiology at all, but deal with quite other matters, such as the patient's attitude to the doctor. As an example of this I would like to tell you three dreams, all from the same patient, and each dreamt at the beginning of a course of treatment under three different analysts. Here is the first: "*I have to cross the frontier into another country, but cannot find the frontier and nobody can tell me where it is.*"

The ensuing treatment proved unsuccessful and was broken off after a short time. The second dream is as follows: "*I have to cross the frontier, but the night is pitch-black and I cannot find the customs-house. After a long search I see a tiny light far off in the distance, and assume that the frontier is over there. But in order to get there, I have to pass through a valley and a dark wood in which I lose my way. Then I notice that someone is near me. Suddenly he clings to me like a madman and I awake in terror.*"

This treatment, too, was broken off after a few weeks because the analyst unconsciously identified himself with the patient and the result was complete loss of orientation on both sides.

The third dream took place under my treatment: "*I have to cross a frontier, or rather, I have already crossed it and find myself in a Swiss customs-house. I have only a handbag with me and think I have nothing to declare. But the customs official dives into my bag and, to my astonishment, pulls out a pair of twin beds.*"

The patient had got married while under my treatment, and at first she developed the most violent resistance to her marriage. The aetiology of the neurotic resistance came to light only many months afterwards and there is not a word about it in the dreams. They are without exception anticipations of the difficulties she is to have with the doctors concerned.

These examples, like many others of the kind, may suffice to show that dreams are often anticipatory and would lose their specific meaning completely on a purely causalistic view. They afford unmistakable information about the analytical situation, the correct understanding of which is of the greatest therapeutic importance. Doctor A understood the situation correctly and handed the patient over to Doctor B. Under him she drew her own conclusions from the dream and decided to leave. My interpretation of the third dream was a disappointment to her, but the fact that the dream showed the frontier as already crossed encouraged her to go on in spite of all difficulties.

Initial dreams are often amazingly lucid and clear-cut. But as the work of analysis progresses, the dreams tend to lose their clarity. If, by way of exception, they keep it we can be sure that the analysis has not yet touched on some important layer of the personality. As a rule, dreams get more and more opaque and blurred soon after the beginning of the treatment, and this makes the interpretation increasingly difficult. A further difficulty is that a point may soon be reached where, if the truth be told, the doctor no longer understands the situation as a whole. That he does not understand is proved by the fact that the dreams become increasingly obscure, for we all know that their "obscurity" is a purely subjective opinion of the doctor. To the understanding nothing is obscure; it is only when we do not understand that things appear unintelligible and muddled. In themselves dreams are naturally clear; that is, they are just what they must be under the given circumstances. If, from a later stage of treatment or from a distance of some years, we look back at these unintelligible dreams, we are often astounded at our own blindness. Thus when, as the analysis proceeds, we come upon dreams that are strikingly obscure in comparison with the illuminating initial dreams, the doctor should not be too ready to accuse the dreams of confusion or the patient of deliberate resistance; he would do better to take these findings as a sign of his own growing inability to understand – just as the psychiatrist who calls his patient "confused" should recognize that this is a projection and should rather call himself confused, because in reality it is he whose wits are confused by the patient's peculiar behaviour. Moreover it is therapeutically very important for the doctor to admit his lack of understanding in time, for nothing is more unbearable to the patient than to be always understood. He relies far too much anyway on the mysterious powers of the doctor and, by appealing to his professional vanity, lays a dangerous trap for him. By taking refuge in the doctor's self-confidence and "profound" understanding, the patient loses all sense of reality, falls into a stubborn transference, and retards the cure.

Understanding is clearly a very subjective process. It can be extremely one-sided, in that the doctor understands but not the patient. In such a case the doctor conceives it to be his duty to convince the patient, and if the latter will not allow himself to be convinced, the doctor accuses him of resistance. When the understanding is all on my side, I say quite calmly that I do not understand, for in the end it makes very little difference whether the doctor understands or not, but it makes all the difference whether the patient understands. Understanding should therefore be understanding in the sense of an agreement which is the fruit of joint reflection. The danger of a one-sided understanding is that the doctor may judge the dream from the standpoint of a preconceived opinion. His judgment may be in line with orthodox theory, it may even be fundamentally correct, but it will not win the patient's assent, he will not come to an understanding with him, and that is in the practical sense incorrect – incorrect because it anticipates and thus cripples the patient's development. The patient, that is to say, does not need to have a truth inculcated into him – if we do that, we only reach his head; he needs far more to grow up to this truth, and in that way we reach his heart, and the appeal goes deeper and works more powerfully.

When the doctor's one-sided interpretation is based on mere agreement as to theory or on some other preconceived opinion, his chances of convincing the patient or of achieving any therapeutic results depend chiefly upon *suggestion*. Let no one deceive himself about this. In itself, suggestion is not to be despised, but it has serious limitations, not to speak of the subsidiary effects upon the patient's independence of character which, in the long run, we could very well do without. A practising analyst may be supposed to believe implicitly in the significance and value of conscious realization, whereby hitherto unconscious parts of the personality are brought to light and subjected to conscious discrimination and criticism. It is a process that requires the patient to face his problems and that taxes his powers of conscious judgment and decision. It is nothing less than a direct challenge to his ethical sense, a call to arms that must be answered by the whole personality. As regards the maturation of personality, therefore, the analytical approach is of a higher order than suggestion, which is a species of magic that works in the dark and makes no ethical demands upon the personality. Methods of treatment based on suggestion are deceptive makeshifts; they are incompatible with the principles of analytical therapy and should be avoided if at all possible. Naturally suggestion can only be avoided if the doctor is conscious of its possibility. There is at the best of times always enough – and more than enough – unconscious suggestion.

The analyst who wishes to rule out conscious suggestion must therefore consider every dream-interpretation invalid until such time as a formula is found which wins the assent of the patient.

The observance of this rule seems to me imperative when dealing with those dreams whose obscurity is evidence of the lack of understanding of both doctor and patient. The doctor should regard every such dream as something new, as a source of information about conditions whose nature is unknown to him, concerning which he has as much to learn as the patient. It goes without saying that he should give up all his theoretical assumptions and should in every single case be ready to construct a totally new theory of dreams. There are still boundless opportunities for pioneer work in this field. The view that dreams are merely the imaginary fulfilments of repressed wishes is hopelessly out of date. There are, it is true, dreams which manifestly represent wishes or fears, but what about all the other things? Dreams may contain ineluctable truths, philosophical pronouncements, illusions, wild fantasies, memories, plans, anticipations, irrational experiences, even telepathic visions, and heaven knows what besides. One thing we ought never to forget: almost half our life is passed in a more or less unconscious state. The dream is specifically the utterance of the unconscious. Just as the psyche has a diurnal side which we call consciousness, so also it has a nocturnal side: the unconscious psychic activity which we apprehend as dreamlike fantasy. It is certain that the conscious mind consists not only of wishes and fears, but of vastly more besides; and it is highly probable that our dream psyche possesses a wealth of contents and living forms equal to or even greater than those of the conscious mind, which is characterized by concentration, limitation, and exclusion.

This being so, it is imperative that we should not pare down the meaning of the dream to fit some narrow doctrine. We must remember that there are not a few patients who imitate the technical or theoretical jargon of the doctor, and do this even in their dreams, in accordance with the old tag, *Canis panem somniat, piscator pisces.* This is not to say that the fishes of which the fisherman dreams are fishes and nothing more. There is no language that cannot be misused. As may easily be imagined, the misuse often turns the tables on us; it even seems as if the unconscious had a way of strangling the doctor in the coils of his own theory. Therefore I leave theory aside as much as possible when analysing dreams – not entirely, of course, for we always need some theory to make things intelligible. It is on the basis of theory, for instance, that I expect dreams to have a meaning. I cannot prove in every case that this is so, for there are dreams which the doctor and the patient simply do not understand. But I have to make such an hypothesis in order to find courage to deal with dreams at all. To say that dreams add something important to our conscious knowledge, and that a dream which fails to do so has not been properly interpreted – that, too, is a theory. But I must make this hypothesis as well in order to explain to myself why I analyse dreams in the first place. All other hypotheses, however, about the function and the structure of dreams are merely rules of thumb and must be subjected to constant modification. In dream-analysis we must never forget, even for a moment, that we move on treacherous ground where nothing is certain but uncertainty. If it were not so paradoxical, one would almost like to call out to the dream interpreter: "Do anything you like, only don't try to understand!"

When we take up an obscure dream, our first task is not to understand and interpret, but to establish the context with minute care. By this I do *not* mean unlimited "free association" starting from any and every image in the dream, but a careful and conscious illumination of the interconnected associations objectively grouped round particular images. Many patients have first to be educated to this, for they resemble the doctor in their insuperable desire to understand and interpret offhand, especially when they have been primed by ill-digested reading or by a previous analysis that went wrong. They begin by associating in accordance with a theory, that is, they try to understand and interpret, and they nearly always get stuck. Like the doctor, they want to get behind the dream at once in the false belief that the dream is a mere façade concealing the true meaning. But the so-called façade of most houses is by no means a fake or a deceptive distortion; on the contrary, it follows the plan of the building and often betrays the interior arrangement. The "manifest" dream-picture is the dream itself and contains the whole meaning of the dream. When I find sugar in the urine, it is sugar and not just a façade for albumen. What Freud calls the "dream-façade" is the dream's obscurity, and this is really only a projection of our own lack of understanding.

We say that the dream has a false front only because we fail to see into it. We would do better to say that we are dealing with something like a text that is unintelligible not because it has a façade – a text has no façade – but simply because we cannot read it. We do not have to get behind such a text, but must first learn to read it.

The best way to do this, as I have already remarked, is to establish the context. Free association will get me nowhere, any more than it would help me to decipher a Hittite inscription. It will of course help me to uncover all my own complexes, but for this purpose I have no need of a dream – I could just as well take a public notice or a sentence in a newspaper. Free association will bring out all my complexes, but hardly ever the meaning of a dream. To understand the dream's meaning I must stick as close as possible to the dream-images. When somebody dreams of a "deal table," it is not enough for him to associate it with his writing-desk which does not happen to be made of deal. Supposing that nothing more occurs to the dreamer, this blocking has an objective meaning, for it indicates that a particular darkness reigns in the immediate neighbourhood of the dream-image, and that is suspicious. We would expect him to have dozens of associations to a deal table, and the fact that there is apparently nothing is itself significant. In such cases I keep on returning to the image, and I usually say to my patient, "Suppose I had no idea what the words 'deal table' mean. Describe this object and give me its history in such a way that I cannot fail to understand what sort of a thing it is."

In this way we manage to establish almost the whole context of the dream-image. When we have done this for all the images in the dream we are ready for the venture of interpretation.

Every interpretation is an hypothesis, an attempt to read an unknown text. An obscure dream, taken in isolation, can hardly ever be interpreted with any certainty. For this reason I attach little importance to the interpretation of single dreams. A relative degree of certainty is reached only in the interpretation of a series of dreams, where the later dreams correct the mistakes we have made in handling those that went before. Also, the basic ideas and themes can be recognized much better in a dream-series, and I therefore urge my patients to keep a careful record of their dreams and of the interpretations given. I also show them how to work out their dreams in the manner described, so that they can bring the dream and its context with them in writing to the consultation. At a later stage I get them to work out the interpretation as well. In this way the patient learns how to deal correctly with his unconscious without the doctor's help.

Were dreams nothing more than sources of information about factors of aetiological importance, the whole work of dream-interpretation could safely be left to the doctor. Again, if their only use was to provide the doctor with a collection of useful hints and psychological tips, my own procedure would be entirely superfluous. But since, as my examples have shown, dreams contain something more than practical helps for the doctor, dream-analysis deserves very special attention. Sometimes, indeed, it is a matter of life and death. Among many instances of this sort, there is one that has remained particularly impressive. It concerns a colleague of mine, a man somewhat older than myself, whom I used to see from time to time and who always teased me about my dream-interpretations. Well, I met him one day in the street and he called out to me, "How are things going? Still interpreting dreams? By the way, I've had another idiotic dream. Does that mean something too?" This is what he had dreamed: "*I am climbing a high mountain, over steep snow-covered slopes. I climb higher and higher, and it is marvellous weather. The higher I climb the better I feel. I think, 'If only I could go on climbing like this for ever!' When I reach the summit my happiness and elation are so great that I feel I could mount right up into space. And I discover that I can actually do so: I mount upwards on empty air, and awake in sheer ecstasy.*"

After some discussion, I said, "My dear fellow, I know you can't give up mountaineering, but let me implore you not to go alone from now on. When you go, take two guides, and promise on your word of honour to follow them absolutely." "Incorrigible!" he replied, laughing, and waved good-bye. I never saw him again. Two months later the first blow fell. When out alone, he was buried by an avalanche, but was dug out in the nick of time by a military patrol that happened to be passing. Three months afterwards the end came. He went on a climb with a younger friend, but without guides. A guide standing below saw him literally step out into the air while descending a rock face. He fell on the head of his friend, who was waiting lower down, and both were dashed to pieces far below. That was *ecstasis* with a vengeance!

No amount of scepticism and criticism has yet enabled me to regard dreams as negligible occurrences. Often enough they appear senseless, but it is obviously we who lack the sense and ingenuity to read the enigmatic message from the nocturnal realm of the psyche. Seeing that at least half our psychic existence is passed in that realm, and that consciousness acts upon our nightly life just as much as the unconscious overshadows our daily life, it would seem all the more incumbent on medical psychology to sharpen its senses by a systematic study of dreams. Nobody doubts the importance of conscious experience; why then should we doubt the significance of unconscious happenings? They also are part of our life, and sometimes more truly a part of it for weal or woe than any happenings of the day.

Since dreams provide information about the hidden inner life and reveal to the patient those components of his personality which, in his daily behaviour, appear merely as neurotic symptoms, it follows that we cannot effectively treat him from the side of consciousness alone, but must bring about a change in and through the unconscious. In the light of our present knowledge this can be achieved only by the thorough and conscious assimilation of unconscious contents.

"Assimilation" in this sense means mutual penetration of conscious and unconscious, and not – as is commonly thought and practised – a one-sided evaluation, interpretation, and deformation of unconscious contents by the conscious mind. As to the value and significance of unconscious contents in general, very mistaken views are current. It is well known that the Freudian school presents the unconscious in a thoroughly negative light, much as it regards primitive man as little better than a monster. Its nursery-tales about the terrible old man of the tribe and its teachings about the "infantile-perverse-criminal" unconscious have led people to make a dangerous ogre out of something perfectly natural. As if all that is good, reasonable, worth while, and beautiful had taken up its abode in the conscious mind! Have the horrors of the World War done nothing to open our eyes, so that we still cannot see that the conscious mind is even more devilish and perverse than the naturalness of the unconscious?

The charge has recently been laid at my door that my teaching about the assimilation of the unconscious would undermine civilization and deliver up our highest values to sheer primitivity. Such an opinion can only be based on the totally erroneous supposition that the unconscious is a monster. It is a view that springs from fear of nature and the realities of life. Freud invented the idea of sublimation to save us from the imaginary claws of the unconscious. But what is real, what actually exists, cannot be alchemically sublimated, and if anything is apparently sublimated it never was what a false interpretation took it to be.

The unconscious is not a demoniacal monster, but a natural entity which, as far as moral sense, aesthetic taste, and intellectual judgment go, is completely neutral. It only becomes dangerous when our conscious attitude to it is hopelessly wrong. To the degree that we repress it, its danger increases. But the moment the patient begins to assimilate contents that were previously unconscious, its danger diminishes. The dissociation of personality, the anxious division of the day-time and the night-time sides of the psyche, cease with progressive assimilation. What my critic feared – the overwhelming of the conscious mind by the unconscious – is far more likely to ensue when the unconscious is excluded from life by being repressed, falsely interpreted, and depreciated.

The fundamental mistake regarding the nature of the unconscious is probably this: it is commonly supposed that its contents have only one meaning and are marked with an unalterable plus or minus sign. In my humble opinion, this view is too naïve. The psyche is a self-regulating system that maintains its equilibrium just as the body does. Every process that goes too far immediately and inevitably calls forth compensations, and without these there would be neither a normal metabolism nor a normal psyche. In this sense we can take the theory of compensation as a basic law of psychic behaviour. Too little on one side results in too much on the other. Similarly, the relation between conscious and unconscious is compensatory. This is one of the best-proven rules of dream-interpretation. When we set out to interpret a dream, it is always helpful to ask: What conscious attitude does it compensate?

Compensation is not as a rule merely an illusory wish-fulfilment, but an actual fact that becomes still more actual the more we repress it. We do not stop feeling thirsty by repressing our thirst. In the same way, the dream-content is to be regarded with due seriousness as an actuality that has to be fitted into the conscious attitude as a codetermining factor. If we fail to do this, we merely persist in that eccentric frame of mind which evoked the unconscious compensation in the first place. It is then difficult to see how we can ever arrive at a sane judgment of ourselves or at a balanced way of living.

If it should occur to anyone to replace the conscious content by an unconscious one – and this is the prospect which my critics find so alarming – he would only succeed in repressing it, and it would then reappear as an unconscious compensation. The unconscious would thus have changed its face completely: it would now be timidly reasonable, in striking contrast to its former tone. It is not generally believed that the unconscious operates in this way, yet such reversals constantly take place and constitute its proper function. That is why every dream is an organ of information and control, and why dreams are our most effective aid in building up the personality.

The unconscious does not harbour in itself any explosive materials unless an overweening or cowardly conscious attitude has secretly laid up stores of explosives there. All the more reason, then, for watching our step.

From all this it should now be clear why I make it an heuristic rule, in interpreting a dream, to ask myself: What conscious attitude does it compensate? By so doing, I relate the dream as closely as possible to the conscious situation; indeed, I would even assert that without knowledge of the conscious situation the dream can never be interpreted with any degree of certainty. Only in the light of this knowledge is it possible to make out whether the unconscious content carries a plus or a minus sign. The dream is not an isolated event completely cut off from daily life and lacking its character. If it seems so to us, that is only the result of our lack of understanding, a subjective illusion. In reality the relation between the conscious mind and the dream is strictly causal, and they interact in the subtlest of ways.

I should like to show by means of an example how important it is to evaluate the unconscious contents correctly. A young man brought me the following dream: "*My father is driving away from the house in his new car. He drives very clumsily, and I get very annoyed over his apparent stupidity. He goes this way and that, forwards and backwards, and manoeuvres the car into a dangerous position. Finally he runs into a wall and damages the car badly. I shout at him in a perfect fury that he ought to behave himself. My father only laughs, and then I see that he is dead drunk.*" This dream has no foundation in fact. The dreamer is convinced that his father would never behave like that, even when drunk. As a motorist he himself is very careful and extremely moderate in the use of alcohol, especially when he has to drive. Bad driving, and even slight damage to the car, irritate him greatly. His relation to his father is positive. He admires him for being an unusually successful man. We can say, without any great feat of interpretation, that the dream presents a most unfavourable picture of the father. What, then, should we take its meaning to be for the son? Is his relation to his father good only on the surface, and does it really consist in over-compensated resistances? If so, we should have to give the dream-content a positive sign; we should have to tell the young man: "That is your real relation to your father." But since I could find nothing neurotically ambivalent in the son's real relation to his father, I had no warrant for upsetting the young man's feelings with such a destructive pronouncement. To do so would have been a bad therapeutic blunder.

But, if his relation to his father is in fact good, why must the dream manufacture such an improbable story in order to discredit the father? In the dreamer's unconscious there must be some tendency to produce such a dream. Is that because he has resistances after all, perhaps fed by envy or some other inferior motive? Before we go out of our way to burden his conscience – and with sensitive young people this is always rather a dangerous proceeding – we would do better to inquire not *why* he had this dream, but what its purpose is. The answer in this case would be that his unconscious is obviously trying to take the father down a peg. If we regard this as a compensation, we are forced to the conclusion that his relation to his father is not only good, but actually too good. In fact he deserves the French soubriquet of *fils à papa*. His father is still too much the guarantor of his existence, and the dreamer is still living what I would call a provisional life. His particular danger is that he cannot see his own reality on account of his father; therefore the unconscious resorts to a kind of artificial blasphemy so as to lower the father and elevate the son. "An immoral business," we may be tempted to say. An unintelligent father would probably take umbrage, but the compensation is entirely to the point, since it forces the son to contrast himself with his father, which is the only way he could become conscious of himself.

The interpretation just outlined was apparently the correct one, for it struck home. It won the spontaneous assent of the dreamer, and no real values were damaged, either for the father or for the son. But this interpretation was only possible when the whole conscious phenomenology of the father-son relationship had been carefully studied. Without a knowledge of the conscious situation the real meaning of the dream would have remained in doubt.

For dream-contents to be assimilated, it is of overriding importance that no real values of the conscious personality should be damaged, much less destroyed, otherwise there is no one left to do the assimilating. The recognition of the unconscious is not a Bolshevist experiment which puts the lowest on top and thus re-establishes the very situation it intended to correct. We must see to it that the values of the conscious personality remain intact, for unconscious compensation is only effective when it co-operates with an integral consciousness. Assimilation is never a question of "this *or* that," but always of "this *and* that."

Just as the interpretation of dreams requires exact knowledge of the conscious status quo, so the treatment of dream symbolism demands that we take into account the dreamer's philosophical, religious, and moral convictions. It is far wiser in practice not to regard dream-symbols semiotically, i.e., as signs or symptoms of a fixed character, but as true symbols, i.e., as expressions of a content not yet consciously recognized or conceptually formulated. In addition, they must be considered in relation to the dreamer's immediate state of consciousness. I say that this procedure is advisable *in practice* because in theory relatively fixed symbols do exist whose meaning must on no account be referred to anything known and formulable as a concept. If there were no such relatively fixed symbols it would be impossible to determine the structure of the unconscious, for there would be nothing that could in any way be laid hold of or described.

It may seem strange that I should attribute an as it were indefinite content to these relatively fixed symbols. Yet if their content were not indefinite, they would not be symbols at all, but signs or symptoms. We all know how the Freudian school operates with hard-and-fast sexual "symbols" – which in this case I would call "signs" – and endows them with an apparently definitive content, namely sexuality. Unfortunately Freud's idea of sexuality is incredibly elastic and so vague that it can be made to include almost anything. The word sounds familiar enough, but what it denotes is no more than an indeterminable x that ranges from the physiological activity of the glands at one extreme to the sublime reaches of the spirit at the other. Instead of yielding to a dogmatic conviction based on the illusion that we know something because we have a familiar word for it, I prefer to regard the symbol as an unknown quantity, hard to recognize and, in the last resort, never quite determinable. Take, for instance, the so-called phallic symbols which are supposed to stand for the *membrum virile* and nothing more. Psychologically speaking, the *membrum* is itself – as Kranefeldt points out in a recent work* – an emblem of something whose wider content is not at all easy to determine. But primitive people, who, like the ancients, make the freest use of phallic symbols, would never dream of confusing the phallus, as a ritualistic symbol, with the penis. The phallus always means the creative mana, the power of healing and fertility, the "extraordin- arily potent," to use Lehmann's expression, whose equivalents in mythology and in dreams are the bull, the ass, the pomegranate, the yoni, the he-goat, the lightning, the horse's hoof, the dance, the magical cohabitation in the furrow, and the menstrual fluid, to mention only a few of the thousand other analogies. That which underlies all the analogies, and sexuality itself, is an archetypal image whose character is hard to define, but whose nearest psychological equivalent is perhaps the primitive mana-symbol.

All these symbols are relatively fixed, but in no single case can we have the *a priori* certainty that in practice the symbol must be interpreted in that way.

*"Komplex und Mythos" (1950).

Practical necessity may call for something quite different. Of course, if we had to give an exhaustive scientific interpretation of a dream, in accordance with a theory, we should have to refer every such symbol to an archetype. But in practice that can be a positive mistake, for the patient's psychological state at the moment may require anything but a digression into dream theory. It is therefore advisable to consider first and foremost the meaning of the symbol in relation to the conscious situation – in other words, to treat the symbol as if it were not fixed. This is as much as to say that we must renounce all preconceived opinions, however knowing they make us feel, and try to discover what things mean for the patient. In so doing, we shall obviously not get very far towards a theoretical interpretation; indeed we shall probably get stuck at the very beginning. But if the practitioner operates too much with fixed symbols, there is a danger of his falling into mere routine and pernicious dogmatism, and thus failing his patient. Unfortunately I must refrain from illustrating this point, for I should have to go into greater detail than space here permits. Moreover I have published sufficient material elsewhere in support of my statements.

It frequently happens at the very beginning of the treatment that a dream will reveal to the doctor, in broad perspective, the whole programme of the unconscious. But for practical reasons it may be quite impossible to make clear to the patient the deeper meaning of the dream. In this respect, too, we are limited by practical considerations. Such insight is rendered possible by the doctor's knowledge of relatively fixed symbols. It can be of the greatest value in diagnosis as well as in prognosis. I was once consulted about a seventeen-year-old girl. One specialist had conjectured that she might be in the first stages of progressive muscular atrophy, while another thought that it was a case of hysteria. In view of the second opinion, I was called in. The clinical picture made me suspect an organic disease, but there were signs of hysteria as well. I asked for dreams. The patient answered at once: "Yes, I have terrible dreams. Only recently I dreamt *I was coming home at night. Everything is as quiet as death. The door into the living-room is half open, and I see my mother hanging from the chandelier, swinging to and fro in the cold wind that blows in through the open windows.* Another time I dreamt that *a terrible noise broke out in the house at night. I get up and discover that a frightened horse is tearing through the rooms. At last it finds the door into the hall, and jumps through the hall window from the fourth floor into the street below. I was terrified when I saw it lying there, all mangled."*

The gruesome character of the dreams is alone sufficient to make one pause. All the same, other people have anxiety dreams now and then. We must therefore look more closely into the meaning of the two main symbols, "mother" and "horse." They must be equivalents, for they both do the same thing: they commit suicide. "Mother" is an archetype and refers to the place of origin, to nature, to that which passively creates, hence to substance and matter, to materiality, the womb, the vegetative functions. It also means the unconscious, our natural and instinctive life, the physiological realm, the body in which we dwell or are contained; for the "mother" is also the matrix, the hollow form, the vessel that carries and nourishes, and it thus stands psychologically for the foundations of consciousness. Being inside or contained in something also suggests darkness, something nocturnal and fearful, hemming one in. These allusions give the idea of the mother in many of its mythological and etymological variants; they also represent an important part of the Yin idea in Chinese philosophy. This is no individual acquisition of a seventeen-year-old girl; it is a collective inheritance, alive and recorded in language, inherited along with the structure of the psyche and therefore to be found at all times and among all peoples.

The word "mother," which sounds so familiar, apparently refers to the best-known, the individual mother – to "my mother." But the mother-symbol points to a darker background which eludes conceptual formulation and can only be vaguely apprehended as the hidden, nature-bound life of the body. Yet even this is too narrow and excludes too many vital subsidiary meanings. The underlying, primary psychic reality is so inconceivably complex that it can be grasped only at the farthest reach of intuition, and then but very dimly. That is why it needs symbols.

If we apply our findings to the dream, its interpretation will be: The unconscious life is destroying itself. That is the dream's message to the conscious mind of the dreamer and to anybody who has ears to hear.

"Horse" is an archetype that is widely current in mythology and folklore. As an animal it represents the non-human psyche, the subhuman, animal side, the unconscious. That is why horses in folklore sometimes see visions, hear voices, and speak. As a beast of burden it is closely related to the mother-archetype (witness the Valkyries that bear the dead hero to Valhalla, the Trojan horse, etc.). As an animal lower than man it represents the lower part of the body and the animal impulses that rise from there. The horse is dynamic and vehicular power: it carries one away like a surge of instinct. It is subject to panics like all instinctive creatures who lack higher consciousness. Also it has to do with sorcery and magical spells – especially the black night-horses which herald death.

It is evident, then, that "horse" is an equivalent of "mother" with a slight shift of meaning. The mother stands for life at its origin, the horse for the merely animal life of the body. If we apply this meaning to the text of our dream, its interpretation will be: The animal life is destroying itself.

The two dreams make nearly identical statements, but, as is usually the case, the second is the more specific. Note the peculiar subtlety of the dream: there is no mention of the death of the individual. It is notorious that one often dreams of one's own death, but that is no serious matter. When it is really a question of death, the dream speaks another language.

Both dreams point to a grave organic disease with a fatal outcome. This prognosis was soon confirmed.

As for the relatively fixed symbols, this example gives a fair idea of their general nature. There are a great many of them, and all are individually marked by subtle shifts of meaning. It is only through comparative studies in mythology, folklore, religion, and philology that we can evaluate their nature scientifically. The evolutionary stratification of the psyche is more clearly discernible in the dream than in the conscious mind. In the dream, the psyche speaks in images, and gives expression to instincts, which derive from the most primitive levels of nature. Therefore, through the assimilation of unconscious contents, the momentary life of consciousness can once more be brought into harmony with the law of nature from which it all too easily departs, and the patient can be led back to the natural law of his own being.

I have not been able, in so short a space, to deal with anything but the elements of the subject. I could not put together before your eyes, stone by stone, the edifice that is reared in every analysis from the materials of the unconscious and finally reaches completion in the restoration of the total personality. The way of successive assimilations goes far beyond the curative results that specifically concern the doctor. It leads in the end to that distant goal which may perhaps have been the first urge to life: the complete actualization of the whole human being, that is, individuation. We physicians may well be the first conscious observers of this dark process of nature. As a rule we see only the pathological phase of development, and we lose sight of the patient as soon as he is cured. Yet it is only after the cure that we would really be in a position to study the normal process, which may extend over years and decades. Had we but a little knowledge of the ends toward which the unconscious development is tending, and were the doctor's psychological insight not drawn exclusively from the pathological phase, we should have a less confused idea of the processes mediated to the conscious mind by dreams and a clearer recognition of what the symbols point to. In my opinion, every doctor should understand that every procedure in psychotherapy, and particularly the analytical procedure, breaks into a purposeful and continuous process of development, now at this point and now at that, and thus singles out separate phases which seem to follow opposing courses. Each individual analysis by itself shows only one part or one aspect of the deeper process, and for this reason nothing but hopeless confusion can result from comparative case histories. For this reason, too, I have preferred to confine myself to the rudiments of the subject and to practical considerations; for only in closest contact with the everyday facts can we come to anything like a satisfactory understanding.

Part 6. The Development of the Individual

Jung of course accepted that man is a social animal, and realized that the majority of mankind are content to live in accordance with the collective, social conventions of their time. But the people who really interested him were not those who were thus adapted, but the exceptional individuals whose own nature compelled them to reject conventional ways and discover their own path. In Jung's view, "Nature is aristocratic, and one person of value outweighs ten lesser ones." (CW 7, par. 236) It is the individual who is the carrier of culture. "All the highest achievements of virtue, as well as the blackest villainies, are individual." (CW 7, par. 240) The development of individuality, the discovery of what an individual really thinks and feels and believes, as opposed to the collective thoughts, feelings and beliefs imposed on him by society, becomes a quest of vital significance.

[handwritten margin note: 1) evolution]

[handwritten note: without this society would not change → evolve]

"The Development of Personality" CW 17, pars. 284–323

In somewhat free-handed fashion the last two lines of Goethe's stanza are often quoted:

> The Highest bliss on earth shall be
> The joys of personality!

This gives expression to the view that the ultimate aim and strongest desire of all mankind is to develop that fulness of life which is called personality. Nowadays, "personality training" has become an educational ideal that turns its back upon the standardized, mass-produced, "normal" human being demanded by the machine age. It thus pays tribute to the historical fact that the great liberating deeds of world history have sprung from leading personalities and never from the inert mass, which is at all

[handwritten note: we are out of machine age — human must evolve into something other than a cog, bolt turner, because machines do this for us]

times secondary and can only be prodded into activity by the demagogue. The huzzahs of the Italian nation go forth to the personality of the Duce, and the dirges of other nations lament the absence of strong leaders.* The yearning for personality has therefore become a real problem that occupies many minds today, whereas in former times there was only one man who had a glimmering of this question – Friedrich Schiller, whose letters on aesthetic education have lain dormant, like a Sleeping Beauty of literature, for more than a century. We may confidently assert that the "Holy Roman Empire of the German Nation" has not taken much notice of Schiller as an educator. On the other hand, the *furor teutonicus* has hurled itself upon pedagogics (in the strict sense of the education of children), delved into child psychology, ferreted out the infantilism of the adult, and made of childhood such a portentous condition of life and human fate that it completely overshadows the creative meaning and potentialities of adult existence. Our age has been extravagantly praised as the "century of the child." This boundless expansion of the kindergarten amounts to complete forgetfulness of the problems of adult education divined by the genius of Schiller. Nobody will deny or underestimate the importance of childhood; the severe and often life-long injuries caused by stupid upbringing at home or in school are too obvious, and the need for more reasonable pedagogic methods is far too urgent. But if this evil is to be attacked at the root, one must in all seriousness face the question of how such idiotic and bigoted methods of education ever came to be employed, and still are employed. Obviously, for the sole reason that there are half-baked educators who are not human beings at all, but walking personifications of method. Anyone who wants to educate must himself be educated. But the parrot-like book-learning and mechanical use of methods that is still practised today is no education either for the child or for educator. People are everlastingly saying that the child's personality must be trained. While I admire this lofty ideal, I can't help asking who it is that trains the personality? In the first and foremost place we have the parents, ordinary, incompetent folk who, more often than not, are half children themselves and remain so all their lives. How could

*Since this sentence was written, Germany too has found her Führer.

anyone expect all these ordinary parents to be "personalities," and who has ever given a thought to devising methods for inculcating "personality" into them? Naturally, then, we expect great things of the pedagogue, of the trained professional, who, heaven help us, has been stuffed full of "psychology" and is bursting with ill-assorted views as to how the child is supposed to be constituted and how he ought to be handled. It is presumed that the youthful persons who have picked on education as a career are themselves educated; but nobody, I daresay, will venture to assert that they are all "personalities" as well. By and large, they suffer from the same defective education as the hapless children they are supposed to instruct, and as a rule are as little "personalities" as their charges. Our whole educational problem suffers from a one-sided approach to the child who is to be educated, and from an equally one-sided lack of emphasis on the uneducatedness of the educator. Everyone who has finished his course of studies feels himself to be fully educated; in a word, he feels grown up. He must feel this, he must have this solid conviction of his own competence in order to survive the struggle for existence. Any doubt or feeling of uncertainty would hinder and cripple him, undermining the necessary faith in his own authority and unfitting him for a professional career. People expect him to be efficient and good at his job and not to have doubts about himself and his capabilities. The professional man is irretrievably condemned to be competent.

Everyone knows that these conditions are not ideal. But, with reservations, we can say that they are the best possible under the circumstances. We cannot imagine how they could be different. We cannot expect more from the average educator than from the average parent. If he is good at his job, we have to be content with that, just as we have to be content with parents bringing up their children as best they can.

The fact is that the high ideal of educating the personality is not for children: for what is usually meant by personality – a well-rounded psychic whole that is capable of resistance and abounding in energy – is an *adult ideal*. It is only in an age like ours, when the individual is unconscious of the problems of adult life, or – what is worse – when he consciously shirks them, that people could wish to foist this ideal on to childhood. I suspect our contemporary pedagogical and psychological enthusiasm for the child of dishonourable intentions: we talk about the child, but we should mean the child in the adult. For in every adult there lurks a child – an eternal child, something that is always becoming, is never completed, and calls for unceasing care, attention, and education. That is the part of the human personality which wants to develop and become whole. But the man of today is far indeed from this wholeness. Dimly suspecting his own deficiencies, he seizes upon child education and fervently devotes himself to child psychology, fondly supposing that something must have gone wrong in his own upbringing and childhood development that can be weeded out in the next generation. This intention is highly commendable, but comes to grief on the psychological fact that we cannot correct in a child a fault that we ourselves still commit. Children are not half as stupid as we imagine. They notice only too well what is genuine and what is not. Hans Andersen's story of the emperor's clothes contains a perennial truth. How many parents have come to me with the laudable intention of sparing their children the unhappy experiences they had to go through in their own childhood! And when I ask, "Are you quite sure you have overcome these mistakes yourself?" they are firmly convinced that the damage has long since been repaired. In actual fact it has not. If as children they were brought up too strictly, then they spoil their own children with a tolerance bordering on bad taste; if certain matters were painfully concealed from them in childhood, these are revealed with a lack of reticence that is just as painful. They have merely gone to the opposite extreme, the strongest evidence for the tragic survival of the old sin – a fact which has altogether escaped them.

If there is anything that we wish to change in our children, we should first examine it and see whether it is not something that could better be changed in ourselves. Take our enthusiasm for pedagogics. It may be that the boot is on the other leg. It may be that we misplace the pedagogical need because it would be an uncomfortable reminder that we ourselves are still children in many respects and still need a vast amount of educating.

At any rate this doubt seems to me to be extremely pertinent when we set out to train our children's "personalities." Personality is a seed that can only develop by slow stages throughout life.

There is no personality without definiteness, wholeness, and ripeness. These three qualities cannot and should not be expected of the child, as they would rob it of childhood. It would be nothing but an abortion, a premature pseudo-adult; yet our modern education has already given birth to such monsters, particularly in those cases where parents set themselves the fanatical task of always "doing their best" for the children and "living only for them." This clamant ideal effectively prevents the parents from doing anything about their own development and allows them to thrust their "best" down their children's throats. This so-called "best" turns out to be the very things the parents have most badly neglected in themselves. In this way the children are goaded on to achieve their parents' most dismal failures, and are loaded with ambitions that are never fulfilled. Such methods and ideals only engender educational monstrosities.

No one can train the personality unless he has it himself. And it is not the child, but only the adult, who can achieve personality as the fruit of a full life directed to this end. The achievement of personality means nothing less than the optimum development of the whole individual human being. It is impossible to foresee the endless variety of conditions that have to be fulfilled. A whole lifetime, in all its biological, social, and spiritual aspects, is needed. Personality is the supreme realization of the innate idiosyncrasy of a living being. It is an act of high courage flung in the face of life, the absolute affirmation of all that constitutes the individual, the most successful adaptation to the universal conditions of existence coupled with the greatest possible freedom for self-determination. To educate a man to *this* seems to me no light matter. It is surely the hardest task the modern mind has set itself. And it is dangerous too, dangerous to a degree that Schiller never imagined, though his prophetic insight made him the first to venture upon these problems. It is as dangerous as the bold and hazardous undertaking of nature to let women bear children. Would it not be sacrilege, a Promethean or even Luciferian act of presumption, if a superman ventured to grow an homunculus in a bottle and then found it sprouting into a Golem? And yet he would not be doing anything that nature does not do every day. There is no human horror or fairground freak that has not lain in the womb of a loving mother. As the sun shines upon the just and the unjust, and as women who bear and give suck tend God's children and the devil's brood with equal compassion, unconcerned about the possible consequences, so we also are part and parcel of this amazing nature, and, like it, carry within us the seeds of the unpredictable.

Our personality develops in the course of our life from germs that are hard or impossible to discern, and it is only our deeds that reveal who we are. We are like the sun, which nourishes the life of the earth and brings forth every kind of strange, wonderful, and evil thing; we are like the mothers who bear in their wombs untold happiness and suffering. At first we do not know what deeds or misdeeds, what destiny, what good and evil we have in us, and only the autumn can show what the spring has engendered, only in the evening will it be seen what the morning began.

Personality, as the complete realization of our whole being, is an unattainable ideal. But unattainability is no argument against the ideal, for ideals are only signposts, never the goal.

Just as the child must develop in order to be educated, so the personality must begin to sprout before it can be trained. And this is where the danger begins. For we are handling something unpredictable, we do not know how and in what direction the budding personality will develop, and we have learned enough of nature and the world to be somewhat chary of both. On top of that, we were brought up in the Christian belief that human nature is intrinsically evil. But even those who no longer adhere to the Christian teaching are by nature mistrustful and not a little frightened of the possibilities lurking in the subterranean chambers of their being. Even enlightened psychologists like Freud give us an extremely unpleasant picture of what lies slumbering in the depths of the human psyche. So it is rather a bold venture to put in a good word for the development of personality. Human nature, however, is full of the strangest contradictions. We praise the "sanctity of motherhood," yet would never dream of holding it responsible for all the human monsters, the homicidal maniacs, dangerous lunatics, epileptics, idiots and cripples of every description who are born every day. At the same time we are tortured with doubts when it comes to allowing the free development of personality. "Anything might happen then," people say. Or they dish up the old, feeble-minded objection to "individualism." But individualism is not and never has been a natural development; it is nothing but an unnatural usurpation, a freakish, impertinent pose that proves its hollowness by crumpling up before the least obstacle. What we have in mind is something very different.

Clearly, no one develops his personality because somebody tells him that it would be useful or advisable to do so. Nature has never yet been taken in by well-meaning advice. The only thing that moves nature is causal necessity, and that goes for human nature too. Without necessity nothing budges, the human personality least of all. It is tremendously conservative, not to say torpid. Only acute necessity is able to rouse it. The developing personality obeys no caprice, no command, no insight, only brute necessity; it needs the motivating force of inner or outer fatalities. Any other development would be no better than individualism. That is why the cry of "individualism" is a cheap insult when flung at the natural development of personality.

The words "many are called, but few are chosen" are singularly appropriate here, for the development of personality from the germ-state to full consciousness is at once a charisma and a curse, because its first fruit is the conscious and unavoidable segregation of the single individual from the undifferentiated and unconscious herd. This means isolation, and there is no more comforting word for it. Neither family nor society nor position can save him from this fate, nor yet the most successful adaptation to his environment, however smoothly he fits in. The development of personality is a favour that must be paid for dearly. But the people who talk most loudly about developing their personalities are the very ones who are least mindful of the results, which are such as to frighten away all weaker spirits.

Yet the development of personality means more than just the fear of hatching forth monsters, or of isolation. It also means fidelity to the law of one's own being.

For the word "fidelity" I should prefer, in this context, the Greek word used in the New Testament, πίστις, which is erroneously translated "faith." It really means "trust," "trustful loyalty." Fidelity to the law of one's own being is a trust in this law, a loyal perseverance and confident hope; in short, an attitude such as a religious man should have towards God. It can now be seen how portentous is the dilemma that emerges from behind our problem:

personality can never develop unless the individual chooses his own way, consciously and with moral deliberation. Not only the causal motive – necessity – but conscious moral decision must lend its strength to the process of building the personality. If the first is lacking, then the alleged development is a mere acrobatics of the will; if the second, it will get stuck in unconscious automatism. But a man can make a moral decision to go his own way only if he holds that way to be the best. If any other way were held to be better, then he would live and develop that other personality instead of his own. The other ways are conventionalities of a moral, social, political, philosophical, or religious nature. The fact that the conventions always flourish in one form or another only proves that the vast majority of mankind do not choose their own way, but convention, and consequently develop not themselves but a method and a collective mode of life at the cost of their own wholeness.

Just as the psychic and social life of mankind at the primitive level is exclusively a group life with a high degree of unconsciousness among the individuals composing it, so the historical process of development that comes afterwards is in the main collective and will doubtless remain so. That is why I believe convention to be a collective necessity. It is a stopgap and not an ideal, either in the moral or in the religious sense, for submission to it always means renouncing one's wholeness and running away from the final consequences of one's own being.

To develop one's own personality is indeed an unpopular undertaking, a deviation that is highly uncongenial to the herd, an eccentricity smelling of the cenobite, as it seems to the outsider. Small wonder, then, that from earliest times only the chosen few have embarked upon this strange adventure. Had they all been fools, we could safely dismiss them as ἰδιῶται, mentally "private" persons who have no claim on our interest. But, unfortunately, these personalities are as a rule the legendary heroes of mankind, the very ones who are looked up to, loved, and worshipped, the true sons of God whose names perish not. They are the flower and the fruit, the ever fertile seeds of the tree of humanity. This allusion to historical personalities makes it abundantly clear why the development of personality is an ideal, and why the cry of individualism is an insult. Their greatness has never lain in their abject submission _to_ convention, but, on the contrary, in their deliverance _from_ convention. They towered up like mountain peaks above the mass that still clung to its collective fears, its beliefs, laws, and systems, and boldly chose their own way. To the man in the street it has always seemed miraculous that anyone should turn aside from the beaten track with its known destinations, and strike out on the steep and narrow path leading into the unknown. Hence it was always believed that such a man, if not actually crazy, was possessed by a daemon or a god; for the miracle of a man being able to act otherwise than as humanity has always acted could only be explained by the gift of daemonic power or divine spirit. How could anyone but a god counterbalance the dead weight of humanity in the mass, with its everlasting convention and habit? From the beginning, therefore, the heroes were endowed with godlike attributes. According to the Nordic view they had snake's eyes, and there was something peculiar about their birth or descent; certain heroes of ancient Greece were snake-souled, others had a personal daemon, were magicians or the elect of God. All these attributes, which could be multiplied at will, show that for the ordinary man the outstanding personality is something _supernatural_, a phenomenon that can only be explained by the intervention of some daemonic factor.

What is it, in the end, that induces a man to go his own way and to rise out of unconscious identity with the mass as out of a swathing mist? Not necessity, for necessity comes to many, and they all take refuge in convention. Not moral decision, for nine times out of ten we decide for convention likewise. What is it, then, that inexorably tips the scales in favour of the _extra-ordinary_?

It is what is commonly called _vocation_: an irrational factor that destines a man to emancipate himself from the herd and from its well-worn paths. True personality is always a vocation and puts its trust in it as in God, despite its being, as the ordinary man would say, only a personal feeling. But vocation acts like a law of God from which there is no escape. The fact that many a man who goes his own way ends in ruin means nothing to one who has a vocation. He _must_ obey his own law, as if it were a daemon whispering to him of new and wonderful paths. Anyone with a vocation hears the voice of the inner man: he is _called_. That is why the legends say that he possesses a private daemon who counsels him and whose mandates he must obey. The best known example of this is Faust, and an historical instance is provided by the daemon of Socrates. Primitive medicine-men have their snake spirits, and Aesculapius, the tutelary patron of physicians, has for his emblem the Serpent of Epidaurus. He also had, as his private daemon, the Cabir Telesphoros, who is said to have dictated or inspired his medical prescriptions.

The original meaning of "to have a vocation" is "to be addressed by a voice." The clearest examples of this are to be found in the avowals of the Old Testament prophets. That it is not just a quaint old-fashioned way of speaking is proved by the confessions of historical personalities such as Goethe and Napoleon, to mention only two familiar examples, who made no secret of their feeling of vocation.

Vocation, or the feeling of it, is not, however, the prerogative of great personalities; it is also appropriate to the small ones all the way down to the "midget" personalities, but as the size decreases the voice becomes more and more muffled and unconscious. It is as if the voice of the daemon within were moving further and further off, and spoke more rarely and more indistinctly. The smaller the personality, the dimmer and more unconscious it becomes, until finally it merges indistinguishably with the surrounding society, thus surrendering its own wholeness and dissolving into the wholeness of the group. In the place of the inner voice there is the voice of the group with its conventions, and vocation is replaced by collective necessities. But even in this unconscious social condition there are not a few who are called awake by the summons of the voice, whereupon they are at once set apart from the others, feeling themselves confronted with a problem about which the others know nothing. In most cases it is impossible to explain to the others what has happened for any understanding is walled off by impenetrable prejudices. "You are no different from anybody else," they will chorus, or, "there's no such thing," and even if there is such a thing, it is immediately branded as "morbid" and "most unseemly." For it is "a monstrous presumption to suppose anything of that sort could be of the slightest significance" – it is "purely psychological." This last objection is extremely popular nowadays. It stems from a curious underestimation of anything psychic, which people apparently regard as personal, arbitrary, and therefore completely futile. And this, paradoxically enough, despite their enthusiasm for psychology. The unconscious, after all, is "nothing but fantasy." We "merely imagined" so and so, etc. People think themselves magicians who can conjure the psyche hither and thither and fashion it to suit their moods. They deny what strikes them as inconvenient, sublimate anything nasty, explain away their phobias, correct their faults, and feel in the end that they have arranged everything beautifully. In the meantime they have forgotten the essential point, which is that only the tiniest fraction of the psyche is identical with the conscious mind and its box of magic tricks, while for much the greater part it is sheer unconscious *fact*, hard and immitigable as granite, immovable, inaccessible, yet ready at any time to come crashing down upon us at the behest of unseen powers. The gigantic catastrophes that threaten us today are not elemental happenings of a physical or biological order, but psychic events. To a quite terrifying degree we are threatened by wars and revolutions which are nothing other than psychic epidemics. At any moment several millions of human beings may be smitten with a new madness, and then we shall have another world war or devastating revolution. Instead of being at the mercy of wild beasts, earthquakes, landslides, and inundations, modern man is battered by the elemental forces of his own psyche. This is the World Power that vastly exceeds all other powers on earth. The Age of Enlightenment, which stripped nature and human institutions of gods, overlooked the God of Terror who dwells in the human soul. If anywhere, fear of God is justified in face of the overwhelming supremacy of the psychic.

But all this is so much abstraction. Everyone knows that the intellect, that clever jackanapes, can put it this way or any other way he pleases. It is a very different thing when the psyche, as an objective fact, hard as granite and heavy as lead, confronts a man as an inner experience and addresses him in an audible voice, saying, "This is what will and must be." Then he feels himself called, just as the group does when there's a war on, or a revolution, or any other madness. It is not for nothing that our age calls for the redeemer personality, for the one who can emancipate himself from the inescapable grip of the collective and save at least his own soul, who lights a beacon of hope for others, proclaiming that here is at least *one* man who has succeeded in extricating himself from that fatal identity with the group psyche. For the group, because of its unconsciousness, has no freedom of choice, and so psychic activity runs on in it like an uncontrolled law of nature. There is thus set going a chain reaction that comes to a stop only in catastrophe. The people always long for a hero, a slayer of dragons, when they feel the danger of psychic forces; hence the cry for personality.

But what has the individual personality to do with the plight of the many? In the first place he is part of the people as a whole, and is as much at the mercy of the power that moves the whole as anybody else. The only thing that distinguishes him from all the others is his vocation. He has been called by that all-powerful, all-tyrannizing psychic necessity that is his own and his people's affliction. If he hearkens to the voice, he is at once set apart and isolated as he has resolved to obey the law that commands him from within. "His *own* law!" everybody will cry. But he knows better: it is *the* law, *the* vocation for which he is destined, no more "his own" than the lion that fells him, although it is undoubtedly this particular lion that kills him and not any other lion. Only in this sense is he entitled to speak of "his" vocation, "his" law.

With the decision to put his way above all other possible ways he has already fulfilled the greater part of his vocation as a redeemer. He has invalidated all other ways for himself, exalting his law above convention and thus making a clean sweep of all those things that not only failed to prevent the great danger but actually accelerated it. For conventions in themselves are soulless mechanisms that can never understand more than the mere routine of life. Creative life always stands outside convention. That is why, when the mere routine of life predominates in the form of convention and tradition, there is bound to be a destructive outbreak of creative energy. This outbreak is a catastrophe only when it is a mass phenomenon, but never in the individual who consciously submits to these higher powers and serves them with all his strength. The mechanism of convention keeps people unconscious, for in that state they can follow their accustomed tracks like blind brutes, without the need for conscious decision. This unintended result of even the best conventions is unavoidable but is no less a terrible danger for that. For when new conditions arise that are not provided for under the old conventions, then, just as with animals, panic is liable to break out among human beings kept unconscious by routine, and with equally unpredictable results.

Personality, however, does not allow itself to be seized by the panic terror of those who are just waking to consciousness, for it has put all its terrors behind it. It is able to cope with the changing times, and has unknowingly and involuntarily become a *leader*.

All human beings are much alike, otherwise they could not succumb to the same delusion, and the psychic substratum upon which the individual consciousness is based is universally the same, otherwise people could never reach a common understanding. So, in this sense, personality and its peculiar psychic make-up are not something absolutely unique. The uniqueness holds only for the *individual* nature of the personality, as it does for each and every individual. To become a personality is not the absolute prerogative of the genius, for a man may be a genius without being a personality. In so far as every individual has the law of his life inborn in him, it is theoretically possible for any man to follow this law and so become a personality, that is, to achieve wholeness. But since life only exists in the form of living units, i.e., individuals, the law of life always tends towards a life individually lived. So although the objective psyche can only be conceived as a universal and uniform datum, which means that all men share the same primary, psychic condition, this objective psyche must nevertheless individuate itself if it is to become actualized, for there is no other way in which it could express itself except through the individual human being. The only exception to this is when it seizes hold of a group, in which case it must, of its own nature, precipitate a catastrophe, because it can only operate unconsciously and is not assimilated by any consciousness or assigned its place among the existing conditions of life.

Only the man who can consciously assent to the power of the inner voice becomes a personality; but if he succumbs to it he will be swept away by the blind flux of psychic events and destroyed. That is the great and liberating thing about any genuine personality: he voluntarily sacrifices himself to his vocation, and consciously translates into his own individual reality what would only lead to ruin if it were lived unconsciously by the group.

archetype of the redeemer

One of the most shining examples of the meaning of personality that history has preserved for us is the life of Christ. In Christianity, which, be it mentioned in passing, was the only religion really persecuted by the Romans, there rose up a direct opponent of the Caesarean madness that afflicted not only the emperor, but every Roman as well: *civis Romanus sum*. The opposition showed itself wherever the worship of Caesar clashed with Christianity. But, as we know from what the evangelists tell us about the psychic development of Christ's personality, this opposition was fought out just as decisively in the soul of its founder. The story of the Temptation clearly reveals the nature of the psychic power with which Jesus came into collision: it was the power-intoxicated devil of the prevailing Caesarean psychology that led him into dire temptation in the wilderness. This devil was the objective psyche that held all the peoples of the Roman Empire under its sway, and that is why it promised Jesus all the kingdoms of the earth, as if it were trying to make a Caesar of him. Obeying the inner call of his vocation, Jesus voluntarily exposed himself to the assaults of the imperialistic madness that filled everyone, conqueror and conquered alike. In this way he recognized the nature of the objective psyche which had plunged the whole world into misery and had begotten a yearning for salvation that found expression even in the pagan poets. Far from suppressing or allowing himself to be suppressed by this psychic onslaught, he let it act on him consciously, and assimilated it. Thus was world-conquering Caesarism transformed into spiritual kingship, and the Roman Empire into the universal kingdom of God that was not of this world. While the whole Jewish nation was expecting an imperialistically minded and politically active hero as a Messiah, Jesus fulfilled the Messianic mission not so much for his own nation as for the whole Roman world, and pointed out to humanity the old truth that where force rules there is no love, and where love reigns force does not count. The religion of love was the exact psychological counterpart to the Roman devil-worship of power.

The example of Christianity is perhaps the best illustration of my previous abstract argument. This apparently unique life became a sacred symbol because it is the psychological prototype of the only meaningful life, that is, of a life that strives for the individual realization – absolute and unconditional – of its own particular law. Well may we exclaim with Tertullian: *anima naturaliter christiana!*

The deification of Jesus, as also of the Buddha, is not surprising, for it affords a striking example of the enormous valuation that humanity places upon these hero figures and hence upon the ideal of personality. Though it seems at present as if the blind and destructive dominance of meaningless collective forces would thrust the ideal of personality into the background, yet this is only a passing revolt against the dead weight of history. Once the revolutionary, unhistorical, and therefore uneducated inclinations of the rising generation have had their fill of tearing down tradition, new heroes will be sought and found. Even the Bolsheviks, whose radicalism leaves nothing to be desired, have embalmed Lenin and made a saviour of Karl Marx. The ideal of personality is one of the ineradicable needs of the human soul, and the more unsuitable it is the more fanatically it is defended. Indeed, the worship of Caesar was itself a misconceived cult of personality, and modern Protestantism, whose critical theology has reduced the divinity of Christ to vanishing point, has found its last refuge in the personality of Jesus.

Yes, this thing we call personality is a great and mysterious problem. Everything that can be said about it is curiously unsatisfactory and inadequate, and there is always a danger of the discussion losing itself in pomposity and empty chatter. The very idea of personality is, in common usage, so vague and ill-defined that one hardly ever finds two people who take the word in the same sense. If I put forward a more definite conception of it, I do not imagine that I have uttered the last word. I should like to regard all I say here only as a tentative attempt to approach the problem of personality without making any claim to solve it. Or rather, I should like my attempt to be regarded as a description of the psychological problems raised by personality. All the usual explanations and nostrums of psychology are apt to fall short here, just as they do with the man of genius or the creative artist. Inferences from heredity or from environment do not quite come off; inventing fictions about childhood, so popular today, ends – to put it mildly – in unreality; explanations from necessity – "he had no money," "he was a sick man," etc. – remain caught in externals. There is always something irrational to be added, something that simply cannot be explained, a *deus ex machina* or an *asylum ignorantiae*, that well-known sobriquet for God. The problem thus seems to border on the extrahuman realm, which has always been known by a divine name. As you can see, I too have had to refer to the "inner voice," the vocation, and define it as a powerful objective-psychic factor in order to characterize the way in which it functions in the developing personality and how it appears subjectively. Mephistopheles, in *Faust*, is not personified merely because this creates a better dramatic or theatrical effect, as though Faust were his own moralist and painted his private devil on the wall. The opening words of the Dedication – "Once more you hover near me, forms and faces" – are more than just an aesthetic flourish. Like the concretism of the devil, they are an admission of the objectivity of psychic experience, a whispered avowal that this was what *actually happened*, not because of subjective wishes, or fears, or personal opinions, but somehow quite of itself. Naturally only a numskull thinks of ghosts, but something like a primitive numskull seems to lurk beneath the surface of our reasonable daytime consciousness.

Hence the eternal doubt whether what appears to be the objective psyche is really objective, or whether it might not be imagination after all. But then the question at once arises: have I imagined such and such a thing on purpose, or has it been imagined by something in me? It is a similar problem to that of the neurotic who suffers from an imaginary carcinoma. He knows, and has been told a hundred times before, that it is all imagination, and yet he asks me brokenly, "But why do I imagine such a thing? I don't want to do it!" To which the answer is: the idea of the carcinoma has imagined itself in him without his knowledge and without his consent. The reason is that a psychic growth, a "proliferation," is taking place in his unconscious without his being able to make it conscious. In the face of this interior activity he feels afraid. But since he is entirely persuaded that there can be nothing in his own soul that he does not know about, he must relate his fear to a physical carcinoma which he knows does not exist. And if he should still be afraid of it, there are a hundred doctors to convince him that his fear is entirely groundless. The neurosis is thus a defence against the objective, inner activity of the psyche, or an attempt, somewhat dearly paid for, to escape from the inner voice and hence from the vocation. For this "growth" is the objective activity of the psyche, which, independently of conscious volition, is trying to speak to the conscious mind through the inner voice and lead him towards wholeness. Behind the neurotic perversion is concealed his vocation, his destiny: the growth of personality, the full realization of the life-will that is born with the individual. It is the man without *amor fati* who is the neurotic; he, truly, has missed his vocation, and never will he be able to say with Cromwell, "None climbeth so high as he who knoweth not whither his destiny leadeth him."

To the extent that a man is untrue to the law of his being and does not rise to personality, he has failed to realize his life's meaning. Fortunately, in her kindness and patience, Nature never puts the fatal question as to the meaning of their lives into the mouths of most people. And where no one asks, no one need answer.

The neurotic's fear of carcinoma is therefore justified: it is not imagination, but the consistent expression of a psychic fact that exists in a sphere outside consciousness, beyond the reach of his will and understanding. If he withdrew into the wilderness and listened to his inner life in solitude, he might perhaps hear what the voice has to say. But as a rule the miseducated, civilized human being is quite incapable of perceiving the voice, which is something not guaranteed by the current shibboleths. Primitive people have a far greater capacity in this respect; at least the medicine-men are able, as part of their professional equipment, to talk with spirits, trees, and animals, these being the forms in which they encounter the objective psyche or psychic non-ego.

Because neurosis is a developmental disturbance of the personality, we physicians of the soul are compelled by professional necessity to concern ourselves with the problem of personality and the inner voice, however remote it may seem to be. In practical psychotherapy these psychic facts, which are usually so vague and have so often degenerated into empty phrases, emerge from obscurity and take visible shape. Nevertheless, it is extremely rare for this to happen spontaneously as it did with the Old Testament prophets; generally the psychic conditions that have caused the disturbance have to be made conscious with considerable effort. But the contents that then come to light are wholly in accord with

redemption of society/ self

the inner voice and point to a predestined vocation, which, if accepted and assimilated by the conscious mind, conduces to the development of personality.

Just as the great personality acts upon society to liberate, to redeem, to transform, and to heal, so the birth of personality in oneself has a therapeutic effect. It is as if a river that had run to waste in sluggish side-streams and marshes suddenly found its way back to its proper bed, or as if a stone lying on a germinating seed were lifted away so that the shoot could begin its natural growth.

The inner voice is the voice of a fuller life, of a wider, more comprehensive consciousness. That is why, in mythology, the birth of the hero or the symbolic rebirth coincides with sunrise, for the growth of personality is synonymous with an increase of self-consciousness. For the same reason most heroes are character-ized by solar attributes, and the moment of birth of their greater personality is known as illumination.

The fear that most people naturally have of the inner voice is not so childish as might be supposed. The contents that rise up and confront a limited consciousness are far from harmless, as is shown by the classic example of the temptation of Christ, or the equally significant Mara episode in the Buddha legend. As a rule, they signify the specific danger to which the person concerned is liable to succumb. What the inner voice whispers to us is generally something negative, if not actually evil. This must be so, first of all because we are usually not as unconscious of our virtues as of our vices, and then because we suffer less from the good than from the bad in us. The inner voice, as I have explained above, makes us conscious of the evil from which the whole community is suffering, whether it be the nation or the whole human race. But it presents this evil in an individual form, so that one might at first suppose it to be only an individual characteristic. The inner voice brings the evil before us in a very tempting and convincing way in order to make us succumb. If we do not partially succumb, nothing of this apparent evil enters into us, and no regeneration or healing can take place. (I say "apparent," though this may sound too optimistic.) If we succumb completely, then the contents expressed by the inner voice act as so many devils, and a catastrophe ensues. But if we can succumb only in part, and if by self-assertion the ego can save itself from being completely swallowed, then it can assimilate the voice, and we realize that the evil was, after all, only a semblance of evil, but in reality a bringer of healing and illumination. In fact, the inner voice is a "Lucifer" in the strictest and most unequivocal sense of the word, and it faces people with ultimate moral decisions without which they can never achieve full consciousness and become personalities. The highest and the lowest, the best and the vilest, the truest and the most deceptive things are often blended together in the inner voice in the most baffling way, thus opening up in us an abyss of confusion, falsehood, and despair.

It is naturally absurd for people to accuse the voice of Nature, the all-sustainer and all-destroyer, of evil. If she appears inveterately evil to us, this is mainly due to the old truth that the good is always the enemy of the better. We would be foolish indeed if we did not cling to the traditional good for as long as possible. But as Faust says:

> When we the good things of this world attain
> We call the better all a lie and sham.

A good thing is unfortunately not a good forever, for otherwise there would be nothing better. If better is to come, good must stand aside. Therefore Meister Eckhart says, "God is not good, or else he could be better."

There are times in the world's history – and our own time may be one of them – when good must stand aside, so that anything destined to be better first appears in evil form. This shows how extremely dangerous it is even to touch these problems, for evil can so easily slip in on the plea that it is, potentially, the better! The problems of the inner voice are full of pitfalls and hidden snares. Treacherous, slippery ground, as dangerous and pathless as life itself once one lets go of the railings. But he who cannot lose his life, neither shall he save it. The hero's birth and the heroic life are always threatened. The serpents sent by Hera to destroy the infant Hercules, the python that tries to strangle Apollo at birth, the massacre of the innocents, all these tell the same story. To develop the personality is a gamble, and the tragedy is that the daemon of the inner voice is at once our greatest danger and an

what of the voice calling us back to nature? Does it place us in danger?

indispensable help. It is tragic, but logical, for it is the nature of things to be so.

Can we, therefore, blame humanity, and all the well-meaning shepherds of the flock and worried fathers of families, if they erect protective barriers, hold up wonder-working images, and point out the roads that wind safely past the abyss?

But, in the end, the hero, the leader, the saviour, is one who discovers a new way to greater certainty. Everything could be left undisturbed did not the new way demand to be discovered, and did it not visit humanity with all the plagues of Egypt until it finally is discovered. The undiscovered vein within us is a living part of the psyche; classical Chinese philosophy names this interior way "Tao," and likens it to a flow of water that moves irresistibly towards its goal. To rest in Tao means fulfilment, wholeness, one's destination reached, one's mission done; the beginning, end, and perfect realization of the meaning of existence innate in all things. Personality is Tao.

As analysis proceeds, and the individual becomes more aware of the compensatory activity of the unconscious, he may lose his symptoms, become relatively well adapted, and feel no need to pursue any further development of his personality. However, many of Jung's patients wanted, or felt compelled, to go beyond the point of "adaptation."

From "**The Aims of Psychotherapy**" CW 16, pars. 81–4

The human psyche is a thing of enormous ambiguity. In every single case we have to ask ourselves whether an attitude or a so-called *habitus* is authentic, or whether it may not be just a compensation for its opposite. I must confess that I have so often been deceived in this matter that in any concrete case I am at pains to avoid all theoretical presuppositions about the structure of the neurosis and about what the patient can and ought to do. As far as possible I let pure experience decide the therapeutic aims. This may perhaps seem strange, because it is commonly supposed that the therapist has an aim. But in psychotherapy it seems to me positively advisable for the doctor not to have too fixed an aim. He can hardly know better than the nature and will to live of the patient. The great decisions in human life usually have far more to do with the instincts and other mysterious unconscious factors than with conscious will and well-meaning reasonableness. The shoe that fits one person pinches another; there is no universal recipe for living. Each of us carries his own life-form within him – an irrational form which no other can outbid.

All this naturally does not prevent us from doing our utmost to make the patient normal and reasonable. If the therapeutic results are satisfactory, we can probably let it go at that. If not, then for better or worse the therapist must be guided by the patient's own irrationalities. Here we must follow nature as a guide, and what the doctor then does is less a question of treatment than of developing the creative possibilities latent in the patient himself.

What I have to say begins where the treatment leaves off and this development sets in. Thus my contribution to psychotherapy confines itself to those cases where rational treatment does not yield satisfactory results. The clinical material at my disposal is of a peculiar composition: new cases are decidedly in the minority. Most of them already have some form of psychotherapeutic treatment behind them, with partial or negative results. About a third of my cases are not suffering from any clinically definable neurosis, but from the senselessness and aimlessness of their lives. I should not object if this were called the general neurosis of our age. Fully two thirds of my patients are in the second half of life.

This peculiar material sets up a special resistance to rational methods of treatment, probably because most of my patients are socially well-adapted individuals, often of outstanding ability, to whom normalization means nothing. As for so-called normal people, there I really am in a fix, for I have no ready-made philosophy of life to hand out to them. In the majority of my cases the resources of the conscious mind are exhausted (or, in ordinary English, they are "stuck"). It is chiefly this fact that forces me to look for hidden possibilities. For I do not know what to say to the patient when he asks me, "What do you advise? What shall I do?" I don't know either. I only know one thing: when my conscious mind no longer sees any possible road ahead and consequently gets stuck, my unconscious psyche will react to the unbearable standstill.

This further development of personality was named by Jung "the process of individuation." It is the central concept of his psychology, and his major original contribution.

"Conscious, Unconscious, and Individuation" CW 9 i, pars. 489–524

The relation between the conscious and the unconscious on the one hand, and the individuation process on the other, are problems that arise almost regularly during the later stages of analytical treatment. By "analytical" I mean a procedure that takes account of the existence of the unconscious. These problems do not arise in a procedure based on suggestion. A few preliminary words may not be out of place in order to explain what is meant by "individuation."

I use the term "individuation" to denote the process by which a person becomes a psychological "in-dividual," that is, a separate, indivisible unity or "whole."* It is generally assumed that consciousness is the whole of the psychological individual. But knowledge of the phenomena that can only be explained on the hypothesis of unconscious psychic processes makes it doubtful whether the ego and its contents are in fact identical with the "whole." If unconscious processes exist at all, they must surely belong to the totality of the individual, even though they are not components of the conscious ego. If they were part of the ego they would necessarily be conscious, because everything that is directly related to the ego is conscious. Consciousness can even be equated with the relation between the ego and the psychic contents. But unconscious phenomena are so little related to the ego that most people do not hesitate to deny their existence outright. Nevertheless, they manifest themselves in an individual's behaviour. An attentive observer can detect them without difficulty, while the

*Modern physicists (Louis de Broglie, for instance) use instead of this the concept of something "discontinuous."

observed person remains quite unaware of the fact that he is betraying his most secret thoughts or even things he has never thought consciously. It is, however, a great prejudice to suppose that something we have never thought consciously does not exist in the psyche. There is plenty of evidence to show that consciousness is very far from covering the psyche in its totality. Many things occur semiconsciously, and a great many more remain entirely unconscious. Thorough investigation of the phenomena of dual and multiple personalities, for instance, has brought to light a mass of material with observations to prove this point. (I would refer the reader to the writings of Pierre Janet, Théodore Flournoy, Morton Prince, and others.)

The importance of such phenomena has made a deep impression on medical psychology, because they give rise to all sorts of psychic and physiological symptoms. In these circumstances, the assumption that the ego expresses the totality of the psyche has become untenable. It is, on the contrary, evident that the whole must necessarily include not only consciousness but the illimitable field of unconscious occurrences as well, and that the ego can be no more than the centre of the field of consciousness.

You will naturally ask whether the unconscious possesses a centre too. I would hardly venture to assume that there is in the unconscious a ruling principle analogous to the ego. As a matter of fact, everything points to the contrary. If there were such a centre, we could expect almost regular signs of its existence. Cases of dual personality would then be frequent occurrences instead of rare curiosities. As a rule, unconscious phenomena manifest themselves in fairly chaotic and unsystematic form. Dreams, for instance, show no apparent order and no tendency to systematization, as they would have to do if there were a personal consciousness at the back of them. The philosophers Carus and von Hartmann treat the unconscious as a metaphysical principle, a sort of universal mind, without any trace of personality or ego-consciousness, and similarly Schopenhauer's "Will" is without an ego. Modern psychologists, too, regard the unconscious as an egoless function below the threshold of consciousness. Unlike the philosophers, they tend to derive its subliminal functions from the conscious mind. Janet thinks that there is a certain weakness of consciousness which is unable to hold all the psychic processes together. Freud, on the other hand, favours the idea of conscious factors that suppress certain incompatible tendencies. Much can be said for both theories, since there are numerous cases where a weakness of consciousness actually causes certain contents to fall below the threshold, or where disagreeable contents are repressed. It is obvious that such careful observers as Janet and Freud would not have constructed theories deriving the unconscious mainly from conscious sources had they been able to discover traces of an independent personality or of an autonomous will in the manifestations of the unconscious.

If it were true that the unconscious consists of nothing but contents accidentally deprived of consciousness but otherwise indistinguishable from the conscious material, then one could identify the ego more or less with the totality of the psyche. But actually the situation is not quite so simple. Both theories are based mainly on observations in the field of neurosis. Neither Janet nor Freud had any specifically psychiatric experience. If they had, they would surely have been struck by the fact that the unconscious displays contents that are utterly different from conscious ones, so strange, indeed, that nobody can understand them, neither the patient himself nor his doctors. The patient is inundated by a flood of thoughts that are as strange to him as they are to a normal person. That is why we call him "crazy": we cannot understand his ideas. We understand something only if we have the necessary premises for doing so. But here the premises are just as remote from our consciousness as they were from the mind of the patient before he went mad. Otherwise he would never have become insane.

There is, in fact, no field directly known to us from which we could derive certain pathological ideas. It is not a question of more or less normal contents that became unconscious just by accident. They are, on the contrary, products whose nature is at first completely baffling. They differ in every respect from neurotic material, which cannot be said to be at all bizarre. The material of a neurosis is understandable in human terms, but that of a psychosis is not.*

*By this I mean only certain cases of schizophrenia, such as the famous Schreber case (*Memoirs of My Nervous Illness*) or the case published by Nelken ("Analytische Beobachtungen über Phantasien eines Schizophrenen," 1912).

This peculiar psychotic material cannot be derived from the conscious mind, because the latter lacks the premises which would help to explain the strangeness of the ideas. Neurotic contents can be integrated without appreciable injury to the ego, but psychotic ideas cannot. They remain inaccessible, and ego-consciousness is more or less swamped by them. They even show a distinct tendency to draw the ego into their "system."

Such cases indicate that under certain conditions the unconscious is capable of taking over the role of the ego. The consequence of this exchange is insanity and confusion, because the unconscious is not a second personality with organized and centralized functions but in all probability a decentralized congeries of psychic processes. However, nothing produced by the human mind lies absolutely outside the psychic realm. Even the craziest idea must correspond to something in the psyche. We cannot suppose that certain minds contain elements that do not exist at all in other minds. Nor can we assume that the unconscious is capable of becoming autonomous only in certain people, namely in those predisposed to insanity. It is very much more likely that the tendency to autonomy is a more or less general peculiarity of the unconscious. Mental disorder is, in a sense, only one outstanding example of a hidden but none the less general condition. This tendency to autonomy shows itself above all in affective states, including those of normal people. When in a state of violent affect one says or does things which exceed the ordinary. Not much is needed: love and hate, joy and grief, are often enough to make the ego and the unconscious change places. Very strange ideas indeed can take possession of otherwise healthy people on such occasions. Groups, communities, and even whole nations can be seized in this way by psychic epidemics.

The autonomy of the unconscious therefore begins where emotions are generated. Emotions are instinctive, involuntary reactions which upset the rational order of consciousness by their elemental outbursts. Affects are not "made" or wilfully produced; they simply happen. In a state of affect a trait of character sometimes appears which is strange even to the person concerned, or hidden contents may irrupt involuntarily. The more violent an affect the closer it comes to the pathological, to a condition in which the ego-consciousness is thrust aside by autonomous contents that were unconscious before. So long as the unconscious is in a dormant condition, it seems as if there were absolutely nothing in this hidden region. Hence we are continually surprised when something unknown suddenly appears "from nowhere." Afterwards, of course, the psychologist comes along and shows that things had to happen as they did for this or that reason. But who could have said so beforehand?

We call the unconscious "nothing," and yet it is a reality *in potentia*. The thought we shall think, the deed we shall do, even the fate we shall lament tomorrow, all lie unconscious in our today. The unknown in us which the affect uncovers was always there and sooner or later would have presented itself to consciousness. Hence we must always reckon with the presence of things not yet discovered. These, as I have said, may be unknown quirks of character. But possibilities of future development may also come to light in this way, perhaps in just such an outburst of affect which sometimes radically alters the whole situation. The unconscious has a Janus-face: on one side its contents point back to a preconscious, prehistoric world of instinct, while on the other side it potentially anticipates the future – precisely because of the instinctive readiness for action of the factors that determine man's fate. If we had complete knowledge of the ground plan lying dormant in an individual from the beginning, his fate would be in large measure predictable.

Now, to the extent that unconscious tendencies – be they backward-looking images or forward-looking anticipations – appear in dreams, dreams have been regarded, in all previous ages, less as historical regressions than as anticipations of the future, and rightly so. For everything that will be happens on the basis of what has been, and of what – consciously or unconsciously – still exists as a memory-trace. In so far as no man is born totally new, but continually repeats the stage of development last reached by the species, he contains unconsciously, as an *a priori* datum, the entire psychic structure developed both upwards and downwards by his ancestors in the course of the ages. That is what gives the unconscious its characteristic "historical" aspect, but it is at the same time the *sine qua non* for shaping the future. For this reason it is often very difficult to decide whether an autonomous manifestation of the unconscious should be interpreted as an *effect*

(and therefore historical) or as an *aim* (and therefore teleological and anticipatory). The conscious mind thinks as a rule without regard to ancestral preconditions and without taking into account the influence this *a priori* factor has on the shaping of the individual's fate. Whereas we think in periods of years, the unconscious thinks and lives in terms of millennia. So when something happens that seems to us an unexampled novelty, it is generally a very old story indeed. We still forget, like children, what happened yesterday. We are still living in a wonderful new world where man thinks himself astonishingly new and "modern." This is unmistakable proof of the youthfulness of human consciousness, which has not yet grown aware of its historical antecedents.

As a matter of fact, the "normal" person convinces me far more of the autonomy of the unconscious than does the insane person. Psychiatric theory can always take refuge behind real or alleged organic disorders of the brain and thus detract from the importance of the unconscious. But such a view is no longer applicable when it comes to normal humanity. What one sees happening in the world is not just a "shadowy vestige of activities that were once conscious," but the expression of a living psychic condition that still exists and always will exist. Were that not so, one might well be astonished. But it is precisely those who give least credence to the autonomy of the unconscious who are the most surprised by it. Because of its youthfulness and vulnerability, our consciousness tends to make light of the unconscious. This is understandable enough, for a young man should not let himself be overawed by the authority of his parents if he wants to start something on his own account. Historically as well as individually, our consciousness has developed out of the darkness and somnolence of primordial unconsciousness. There were psychic processes and functions long before any ego-consciousness existed. "Thinking" existed long before man was able to say: "I am conscious of thinking."

The primitive "perils of the soul" consist mainly of dangers to consciousness. Fascination, bewitchment, "loss of soul," possession, etc. are obviously phenomena of the dissociation and suppression of consciousness caused by unconscious contents. Even civilized man is not yet entirely free of the darkness of primeval times. The unconscious is the mother of consciousness. Where there is a mother there is also a father, yet he seems to be unknown. Consciousness, in the pride of its youth, may deny its father, but it cannot deny its mother. That would be too unnatural, for one can see in every child how hesitantly and slowly its ego-consciousness evolves out of a fragmentary consciousness lasting for single moments only, and how these islands gradually emerge from the total darkness of mere instinctuality.

Consciousness grows out of an unconscious psyche which is older than it, and which goes on functioning together with it or even in spite of it. Although there are numerous cases of conscious contents becoming unconscious again (through being repressed, for instance), the unconscious as a whole is far from being a mere remnant of consciousness. Or are the psychic functions of animals remnants of consciousness?

As I have said, there is little hope of our finding in the unconscious an order equivalent to that of the ego. It certainly does not look as if we were likely to discover an unconscious ego-personality, something in the nature of a Pythagorean "counter-earth." Nevertheless, we cannot overlook the fact that, just as consciousness arises from the unconscious, the ego-centre, too, crystallizes out of a dark depth in which it was somehow contained *in potentia.* Just as a human mother can only produce a human child, whose deepest nature lay hidden during its potential existence within her, so we are practically compelled to believe that the unconscious cannot be an entirely chaotic accumulation of instincts and images. There must be something to hold it together and give expression to the whole. Its centre cannot possibly be the ego, since the ego was born out of it into consciousness and turns its back on the unconscious, seeking to shut it out as much as possible. Or can it be that the unconscious loses its centre with the birth of the ego? In that case we would expect the ego to be far superior to the unconscious in influence and importance. The unconscious would then follow meekly in the footsteps of the conscious, and that would be just what we wish.

Unfortunately, the facts show the exact opposite: consciousness succumbs all too easily to unconscious influences, and these are often truer and wiser than our conscious thinking. Also, it frequently happens that unconscious motives overrule our conscious decisions, especially in matters of vital importance. Indeed, the fate of the individual is largely dependent on unconscious factors. Careful investigation shows how very much our conscious decisions depend on the undisturbed functioning of memory. But memory often suffers from the disturbing interference of unconscious contents. Moreover, it functions as a rule automatically. Ordinarily it uses the bridges of association, but often in such an extraordinary way that another thorough investigation of the whole process of memory-reproduction is needed in order to find out how certain memories managed to reach consciousness at all. And sometimes these bridges cannot be found. In such cases it is impossible to dismiss the hypothesis of the spontaneous activity of the unconscious. Another example is intuition, which is chiefly dependent on unconscious processes of a very complex nature. Because of this peculiarity, I have defined intuition as "perception via the unconscious."

Normally the unconscious collaborates with the conscious without friction or disturbance, so that one is not even aware of its existence. But when an individual or a social group deviates too far from their instinctual foundations, they then experience the full impact of unconscious forces. The collaboration of the unconscious is intelligent and purposive, and even when it acts in opposition to consciousness its expression is still compensatory in an intelligent way, as if it were trying to restore the lost balance.

There are dreams and visions of such an impressive character that some people refuse to admit that they could have originated in an unconscious psyche. They prefer to assume that such phenomena derive from a sort of "superconsciousness." Such people make a distinction between a quasi-physiological or instinctive unconscious and a psychic sphere or layer "above" consciousness, which they style the "superconscious." As a matter of fact, this psyche, which in Indian philosophy is called the "higher" consciousness, corresponds to what we in the West call the "unconscious." Certain dreams, visions, and mystical experiences do, however, suggest the existence of a consciousness in the unconscious. But, if we assume a consciousness in the unconscious, we are at once faced with the difficulty that no consciousness can exist without a subject, that is, an ego to which the contents are related. Consciousness needs a centre, an ego to which something is conscious. We know of no other kind of consciousness, nor can we imagine a consciousness without an ego. There can be no consciousness when there is no one to say: "*I* am conscious."

It is unprofitable to speculate about things we cannot know. I therefore refrain from making assertions that go beyond the bounds of science. It was never possible for me to discover in the unconscious anything like a personality comparable with the ego. But although a "second ego" cannot be discovered (except in the rare cases of dual personality), the manifestations of the unconscious do at least show *traces of personalities*. A simple example is the dream, where a number of real or imaginary people represent the dream-thoughts. In nearly all the important types of dissociation, the manifestations of the unconscious assume a strikingly personal form. Careful examination of the behaviour and mental content of these personifications, however, reveals their fragmentary character. They seem to represent complexes that have split off from a greater whole, and are the very reverse of a personal centre of the unconscious.

I have always been greatly impressed by the character of dissociated fragments as personalities. Hence I have often asked myself whether we are not justified in assuming that, if such fragments have personality, the whole from which they were broken off must have personality to an even higher degree. The inference seemed logical, since it does not depend on whether the fragments are large or small. Why, then, should not the whole have personality too? *Personality need not imply consciousness. It can just as easily be dormant or dreaming.*

The general aspect of unconscious manifestations is in the main chaotic and irrational, despite certain symptoms of intelligence and purposiveness. The unconscious produces dreams, visions, fantasies, emotions, grotesque ideas, and so forth. This is exactly what we would expect a dreaming personality to do. It seems to be a personality that was never awake and was never conscious of the life it had lived and of its own continuity. The only question is whether the hypothesis of a dormant and hidden personality is possible or not. It may be that all of the personality to be found in the unconscious is contained in the fragmentary personifications mentioned before. Since this is very possible, all my conjectures would be in vain – unless there were evidence of much less fragmentary and more complete personalities, even though they are hidden.

I am convinced that such evidence exists. Unfortunately, the material to prove this belongs to the subtleties of psychological analysis. It is therefore not exactly easy to give the reader a simple and convincing idea of it.

I shall begin with a brief statement: in the unconscious of every man there is hidden a feminine personality, and in that of every woman a masculine personality.

It is a well-known fact that sex is determined by a majority of male or female genes, as the case may be. But the minority of genes belonging to the other sex does not simply disappear. A man therefore has in him a feminine side, an unconscious feminine figure – a fact of which he is generally quite unaware. I may take it as known that I have called this figure the "anima," and its counterpart in a woman the "animus." In order not to repeat myself, I must refer the reader to the literature.* This figure frequently appears in dreams, where one can observe all the attributes I have mentioned in earlier publications.

Another, no less important and clearly defined figure is the "shadow." Like the anima, it appears either in projection on suitable persons, or personified as such in dreams. The shadow coincides with the "personal" unconscious (which corresponds to Freud's conception of the unconscious). Again like the anima, this figure has often been portrayed by poets and writers. I would mention the Faust-Mephistopheles relationship and E. T. A. Hoffmann's tale *The Devil's Elixir* as two especially typical descriptions. The shadow personifies everything that the subject refuses to acknowledge about himself and yet is always thrusting itself upon him directly or indirectly – for instance, inferior traits of character and other incompatible tendencies.

The fact that the unconscious spontaneously personifies certain affectively toned contents in dreams is the reason why I have taken over these personifications in my terminology and formulated them as names.

*Psychological Types, Def. "soul" (CW 6); "The Relations between the Ego and the Unconscious," Part II, ch. 2 (CW 7); Psychology and Alchemy, Part II (CW 12). Cf. also "Concerning the Archetypes . . ." (CW 9i).

Besides these figures there are still a few others, less frequent and less striking, which have likewise undergone poetic as well as mythological formulation. I would mention, for instance, the figure of the hero* and of the wise old man,† to name only two of the best known.

All these figures irrupt autonomously into consciousness as soon as it gets into a pathological state. With regard to the anima, I would particularly like to draw attention to the case described by Nelken.** Now the remarkable thing is that these figures show the most striking connections with the poetic, religious, or mythological formulations, though these connections are in no way factual. That is to say, they are spontaneous products of analogy. One such case even led to the charge of plagiarism: the French writer Benoît gave a description of the anima and her classic myth in his book *L'Atlantide*, which is an exact parallel of Rider Haggard's *She*. The lawsuit proved unsuccessful; Benoît had never heard of *She*. (It might, in the last analysis, have been an instance of cryptomnesic deception, which is often extremely difficult to rule out.) The distinctly "historical" aspect of the anima and her condensation with the figures of the sister, wife, mother, and daughter, plus the associated incest motif, can be found in Goethe ("You were in times gone by my wife or sister"), as well as in the anima figure of the *regina* and *femina alba* in alchemy. The English alchemist Eirenaeus Philalethes ("lover of truth"), writing about 1645, remarks that the "Queen" was the King's "sister, mother, or wife."†† The same idea can be found, ornately elaborated, in Nelken's patient and in a whole series of cases observed by me, where I was able to rule out with certainty any possibility of literary influence. For the rest, the anima complex is one of the oldest features of Latin alchemy.

When one studies the archetypal personalities and their behaviour with the help of the dreams, fantasies, and delusions of patients,*** one is profoundly impressed by their manifold and unmistakable connections with mythological ideas completely

---

Symbols of Transformation, Part II (CW 5).
†Cf. "The Phenomenology of the Spirit in Fairytales" (CW 9 i).
**See note [page 214] above.
††*Ripley Reviv'd; or, An Exposition upon Sir George Ripley's Hermetico-Poetical Works* (1678), trans. into German in 1741 and possibly known to Goethe.
***For an example of the method, see *Psychology and Alchemy*, Part II (CW 12).

unknown to the layman. They form a species of singular beings whom one would like to endow with ego-consciousness; indeed, they almost seem capable of it. And yet this idea is not borne out by the facts. There is nothing in their behaviour to suggest that they have an ego-consciousness as we know it. They show, on the contrary, all the marks of fragmentary personalities. They are masklike, wraithlike, without problems, lacking self-reflection, with no conflicts, no doubts, no sufferings; like gods, perhaps, who have no philosophy, such as the Brahma-gods of the *Samyutta-nikāya*, whose erroneous views needed correction by the Buddha. Unlike other contents, they always remain strangers in the world of consciousness, unwelcome intruders saturating the atmosphere with uncanny forebodings or even with the fear of madness.

If we examine their content, i.e., the fantasy material constituting their phenomenology, we find countless archaic and "historical" associations and images of an archetypal nature.* This peculiar fact permits us to draw conclusions about the "localization" of anima and animus in the psychic structure. They evidently live and function in the deeper layers of the unconscious, especially in that phylogenetic substratum which I have called the collective unconscious. This localization explains a good deal of their strangeness: they bring into our ephemeral consciousness an unknown psychic life belonging to a remote past. It is the mind of our unknown ancestors, their way of thinking and feeling, their way of experiencing life and the world, gods and men. The existence of these archaic strata is presumably the source of man's belief in reincarnations and in memories of "previous existences." Just as the human body is a museum, so to speak, of its phylogenetic history, so too is the psyche. We have no reason to suppose that the specific structure of the psyche is the only thing in the world that has no history outside its individual manifestations. Even the conscious mind cannot be denied a history reaching back at least five thousand years. It is only our ego-consciousness that has forever a new beginning and an early

*In my *Symbols of Transformation*, I have described the case of a young woman with a "hero-story," i.e., an animus fantasy that yielded a rich harvest of mythological material. Rider Haggard, Benoît, and Goethe (in *Faust*) have all stressed the historical character of the anima.

end. The unconscious psyche is not only immensely old, it is also capable of growing into an equally remote future. It moulds the human species and is just as much a part of it as the human body, which, though ephemeral in the individual, is collectively of immense age.

The anima and animus live in a world quite different from the world outside – in a world where the pulse of time beats infinitely slowly, where the birth and death of individuals count for little. No wonder their nature is strange, so strange that their irruption into consciousness often amounts to a psychosis. They undoubtedly belong to the material that comes to light in schizophrenia.

What I have said about the collective unconscious may give you a more or less adequate idea of what I mean by this term. If we now turn back to the problem of individuation, we shall see ourselves faced with a rather extraordinary task: the psyche consists of two incongruous halves which together should form a whole. One is inclined to think that ego-consciousness is capable of assimilating the unconscious, at least one hopes that such a solution is possible. But unfortunately the unconscious really is unconscious; in other words, it is unknown. And how can you assimilate something unknown? Even if you can form a fairly complete picture of the anima and animus, this does not mean that you have plumbed the depths of the unconscious. One hopes to control the unconscious, but the past masters in the art of self-control, the yogis, attain perfection in *samādhi*, a state of ecstasy, which so far as we know is equivalent to a state of unconsciousness. It makes no difference whether they call our unconscious a "universal consciousness"; the fact remains that in their case the unconscious has swallowed up ego-consciousness. They do not realize that a "universal consciousness" is a contradiction in terms, since exclusion, selection, and discrimination are the root and essence of everything that lays claim to the name "consciousness." "Universal consciousness" is logically identical with unconsciousness. It is nevertheless true that a correct application of the methods described in the Pāli Canon or in the *Yoga-sūtra* induces a remarkable extension of consciousness. But, with increasing extension, the contents of consciousness lose in clarity of detail. In the end, consciousness becomes all-embracing, but nebulous; an infinite number of things merge into an indefinite whole, a state in which subject and object are almost completely identical. This is all very beautiful, but scarcely to be recommended anywhere north of the Tropic of Cancer.

For this reason we must look for a different solution. We believe in ego-consciousness and in what we call reality. The realities of a northern climate are somehow so convincing that we feel very much better off when we do not forget them. For us it makes sense to concern ourselves with reality. Our European ego-consciousness is therefore inclined to swallow up the unconscious, and if this should not prove feasible we try to suppress it. But if we understand anything of the unconscious, we know that it cannot be swallowed. We also know that it is dangerous to suppress it, because the unconscious is life and this life turns against us if suppressed, as happens in neurosis.

Conscious and unconscious do not make a whole when one of them is suppressed and injured by the other. If they must contend, let it at least be a fair fight with equal rights on both sides. Both are aspects of life. Consciousness should defend its reason and protect itself, and the chaotic life of the unconscious should be given the chance of having its way too – as much of it as we can stand. This means open conflict and open collaboration at once. That, evidently, is the way human life should be. It is the old game of hammer and anvil: between them the patient iron is forged into an indestructible whole, an "individual."

This, roughly, is what I mean by the individuation process. As the name shows, it is a process or course of development arising out of the conflict between the two fundamental psychic facts. I have described the problems of this conflict, at least in their essentials, in my essay "The Relations between the Ego and the Unconscious." A special chapter, however, is the *symbolism* of the process, which is of the utmost importance for understanding the final stages of the encounter between conscious and unconscious, in practice as well as in theory. My investigations during these last years have been devoted mainly to this theme. It turned out, to my own great astonishment, that the symbol formation has the closest affinities with alchemical ideas, and especially with the conceptions of the "uniting symbol," which yield highly significant parallels. Naturally these are processes which have no meaning in the initial stages of psychological treatment. On the other hand, more difficult cases, such as cases of unresolved transference, develop these symbols. Knowledge of them is of inestimable importance in treating cases of this kind, especially when dealing with cultured patients.

How the harmonizing of conscious and unconscious data is to be undertaken cannot be indicated in the form of a recipe. It is an irrational life-process which expresses itself in definite symbols. It may be the task of the analyst to stand by this process with all the help he can give. In this case, knowledge of the symbols is indispensable, for it is in them that the union of conscious and unconscious contents is consummated. Out of this union emerge new situations and new conscious attitudes. I have therefore called the union of opposites the "transcendent function." This rounding out of the personality into a whole may well be the goal of any psychotherapy that claims to be more than a mere cure of symptoms.

In his commentary on The Secret of the Golden Flower,* *the ancient Taoist text which first aroused Jung's interest in alchemy, Jung points out that the process of individuation is a path followed by the few rather than by the many.*

From "**Commentary on *The Secret of the Golden Flower*"** CW 13, pars. 16–18

It would also be a great mistake to suppose that this is the path every neurotic must travel, or that it is the solution at every stage of the neurotic problem. It is appropriate only in those cases where consciousness has reached an abnormal degree of development and has diverged too far from the unconscious. This is the *sine qua non* of the process. Nothing would be more wrong than to open this way to neurotics who are ill on account of an excessive predominance of the unconscious. For the same reason, this way of development has scarcely any meaning before the middle of life

---

Richard Wilhelm and C. G. Jung, The Secret of the Golden Flower: a Chinese Book of Life, *tr. Cary F. Baynes, London and New York: new edition, 1962.*

(normally between the ages of thirty-five and forty), and if entered upon too soon can be decidedly injurious.

As I have said, the essential reason which prompted me to look for a new way was the fact that the fundamental problem of the patient seemed to me insoluble unless violence was done to one or the other side of his nature. I had always worked with the temperamental conviction that at bottom there are no insoluble problems, and experience justified me in so far as I have often seen patients simply outgrow a problem that had destroyed others. This "outgrowing," as I formerly called it, proved on further investigation to be a new level of consciousness. Some higher or wider interest appeared on the patient's horizon, and through this broadening of his outlook the insoluble problem lost its urgency. It was not solved logically in its own terms, but faded out when confronted with a new and stronger life urge. It was not repressed and made unconscious, but merely appeared in a different light, and so really did become different. What, on a lower level, had led to the wildest conflicts and to panicky outbursts of emotion, from the higher level of personality now looked like a storm in the valley seen from the mountain top. This does not mean that the storm is robbed of its reality, but instead of being in it one is above it. But since, in a psychic sense, we are both valley and mountain, it might seem a vain illusion to deem oneself beyond what is human. One certainly does feel the affect and is shaken and tormented by it, yet at the same time one is aware of a higher consciousness looking on which prevents one from becoming identical with the affect, a consciousness which regards the affect as an object, and can say, "I *know* that I suffer." What our text says of indolence, "Indolence of which a man is conscious, and indolence of which he is unconscious, are a thousand miles apart," holds true in the highest degree of affect.

Now and then it happened in my practice that a patient grew beyond himself because of unknown potentialities, and this became an experience of prime importance to me. In the meantime, I had learned that all the greatest and most important problems of life are fundamentally insoluble. They must be so, for they express the necessary polarity inherent in every self-regulating system. They can never be solved, but only outgrown. I therefore asked myself whether this outgrowing, this possibility of further psychic development, was not the normal thing, and whether getting stuck in a conflict was pathological. Everyone must possess that higher level, at least in embryonic form, and must under favourable circumstances be able to develop this potentiality. When I examined the course of development in patients who quietly, and as if unconsciously, outgrew themselves, I saw that their fates had something in common. The new thing came to them from obscure possibilities either outside or inside themselves; they accepted it and grew with its help. It seemed to me typical that some took the new thing from outside themselves, others from inside; or rather, that it grew into some persons from without, and into others from within. But the new thing never came exclusively either from within or from without. If it came from outside, it became a profound inner experience; if it came from inside, it became an outer happening. In no case was it conjured into existence intentionally or by conscious willing, but rather seemed to be borne along on the stream of time.

Part 7. Integration, Wholeness, and the Self

The goal toward which the individuation process is tending is "Wholeness" or "Integration": a condition in which all the different elements of the psyche, both conscious and unconscious, are welded together. The person who achieves this goal possesses "an attitude that is beyond the reach of emotional entanglements and violent shocks – a consciousness detached from the world." (CW 13, par. 68)

Individuation, in Jung's view, is a spiritual journey; and the person embarking upon it, although he might not subscribe to any recognized creed, was nonetheless pursuing a religious quest.

By paying careful attention to the unconscious, as manifested in dream and fantasy, the individual comes to change his attitude from one in which ego and will are paramount to one in which he acknowledges that he is guided by an integrating factor which is not of his own making.

This integrating factor, expressed by the emergence of quaternity or mandala symbols, is named the Self; an archetype which not only signifies union between the opposites within the psyche, but "is a God-image, or at least cannot be distinguished from one." (CW 9 ii, par. 42) Jung states:

> Unity and totality stand at the highest point on the scale of objective values because their symbols can no longer be distinguished from the *imago Dei*. Hence all statements about the God-image apply also to the empirical symbols of totality. [CW 9 ii, par. 42]

If we turn to Jung's autobiography, we find that, as he began to emerge from his period of "confrontation with the unconscious," he went through a period of drawing mandalas.

From **"Confrontation with the Unconscious"**   MDR, pp. 186–9/195–7

It was only towards the end of the First World War that I gradually began to emerge from the darkness. Two events contributed to this. The first was that I broke with the woman who was determined to convince me that my fantasies had artistic value; the second and principal event was that I began to understand mandala drawings. This happened in 1918–19. I had painted the first mandala in 1916 after writing the *Septem Sermones*: naturally I had not, then, understood it.

In 1918–19 I was in Château d'Oex as Commandant de la Région Anglaise des Internés de Guerre. While I was there I sketched every morning in a notebook a small circular drawing, a mandala, which seemed to correspond to my inner situation at the time. With the help of these drawings I could observe my psychic transformations from day to day. One day, for example, I received a letter from that aesthetic lady in which she again stubbornly maintained that the fantasies arising from my unconscious had artistic value and should be considered art. The letter got on my nerves. It was far from stupid and therefore dangerously persuasive. The modern artist, after all, seeks to create art out of the unconscious. The utilitarianism and self-importance concealed behind this thesis touched a doubt in myself, namely, my uncertainty as to whether the fantasies I was producing were really spontaneous and natural, and not ultimately my own arbitrary inventions. I was by no means free from the bigotry and hubris of consciousness which wants to believe that any half-way decent inspiration is due to one's own merit, whereas inferior reactions come merely by chance, or even derive from alien sources. Out of this irritation and disharmony within myself there proceeded, the following day, a changed mandala: part of the periphery had burst open and the symmetry was destroyed.

Only gradually did I discover what the mandala really is: "Formation, Transformation, Eternal Mind's eternal recreation."* And that is the self, the wholeness of the personality, which if all goes well is harmonious, but which cannot tolerate self-deceptions.

*Goethe, *Faust*, Part Two, trans. by Philip Wayne (Penguin Classics, 1959), p. 79.

1. *Jung's first painting of a mandala, 1916*

2. *Mandala painting by Jung, 1927*

3. *Mandala painting by Jung, 1928*

My mandalas were cryptograms concerning the state of the self which were presented to me anew each day. In them I saw the self – that is, my whole being – actively at work. To be sure, at first I could only dimly understand them; but they seemed to me highly significant, and I guarded them like precious pearls. I had the distinct feeling that they were something central, and in time I acquired through them a living conception of the self. The self, I thought, was like the monad which I am, and which is my world. The mandala represents this monad, and corresponds to the microcosmic nature of the psyche.

I no longer know how many mandalas I drew at this time. There were a great many. While I was working on them, the question arose repeatedly: What is this process leading to? Where is its goal? From my own experience, I knew by now that I could not presume to choose a goal which would seem trustworthy to me. It had been proved to me that I had to abandon the idea of the superordinate position of the ego. After all, I had been brought up short when I had attempted to maintain it. I had wanted to go on with the scientific analysis of myths which I had begun in *Symbols of Transformation*. That was still my goal – but I must not think of that! I was being compelled to go through this process of the unconscious. I had to let myself be carried along by the current, without a notion of where it would lead me. When I began drawing the mandalas, however, I saw that everything, all the paths I had been following, all the steps I had taken, were leading back to a single point – namely, to the mid-point. It became increasingly plain to me that the mandala is the centre. It is the exponent of all paths. It is the path to the centre, to individuation.

During those years, between 1918 and 1920, I began to understand that the goal of psychic development is the self. There is no linear evolution; there is only a circumambulation of the self. Uniform development exists, at most, only at the beginning; later, everything points towards the centre. This insight gave me stability, and gradually my inner peace returned. I knew that in finding the mandala as an expression of the self I had attained what was for me the ultimate. Perhaps someone else knows more, but not I.

Some years later (in 1927) I obtained confirmation of my ideas about the centre and the self by way of a dream. I represented its essence in a mandala which I called "Window on Eternity." The picture is reproduced in *The Secret of the Golden Flower* (Fig. 3). A year later I painted a second picture, likewise a mandala, with a golden castle in the centre. When it was finished, I asked myself, "Why is this so Chinese?" I was impressed by the form and choice of colours, which seemed to me Chinese, although there was nothing outwardly Chinese about it. Yet that was how it affected me. It was a strange coincidence that shortly afterwards I received a letter from Richard Wilhelm enclosing the manuscript of a Taoist-alchemical treatise entitled *The Secret of the Golden Flower*, with a request that I write a commentary on it. I devoured the manuscript at once, for the text gave me undreamed-of confirmation of my ideas about the mandala and the circumambulation of the centre. That was the first event which broke through my isolation. I became aware of an affinity; I could establish ties with something and someone.

In remembrance of this coincidence, this "synchronicity," I wrote underneath the picture which had made so Chinese an impression upon me: "In 1928, when I was painting this picture, showing the golden, well-fortified castle, Richard Wilhelm in Frankfurt sent me the thousand-year-old Chinese text on the yellow castle, the germ of the immortal body."

"Mandalas" CW 9 i, pars. 713–18

The Sanskrit word *mandala* means "circle" in the ordinary sense of the word. In the sphere of religious practices and in psychology it denotes circular images, which are drawn, painted, modelled, or danced. Plastic structures of this kind are to be found, for instance, in Tibetan Buddhism, and as dance figures these circular patterns occur also in Dervish monasteries. As psychological phenomena they appear spontaneously in dreams, in certain states of conflict, and in cases of schizophrenia. Very frequently they contain a quaternity or a multiple of four, in the form of a cross, a star, a square, an octagon, etc. In alchemy we encounter this motif in the form of the *quadratura circuli*.

In Tibetan Buddhism the figure has the significance of a ritual instrument (*yantra*), whose purpose is to assist meditation and concentration. Its meaning in alchemy is somewhat similar, inasmuch as it represents the synthesis of the four elements which are forever tending to fall apart. Its spontaneous occurrence in modern individuals enables psychological research to make a closer investigation into its functional meaning. As a rule a mandala occurs in conditions of psychic dissociation or disorientation, for instance in the case of children between the ages of eight and eleven whose parents are about to be divorced, or in adults who, as the result of a neurosis and its treatment, are confronted with the problem of opposites in human nature and are consequently disoriented; or again in schizophrenics whose view of the world has become confused, owing to the invasion of incomprehensible contents from the unconscious. In such cases it is easy to see how the severe pattern imposed by a circular image of this kind compensates the disorder and confusion of the psychic state – namely, through the construction of a central point to which everything is related, or by a concentric arrangement of the disordered multiplicity and of contradictory and irreconcilable elements. This is evidently an *attempt at self-healing* on the part of Nature, which does not spring from conscious reflection but from an instinctive impulse. Here, as comparative research has shown, a fundamental schema is made use of, an archetype which, so to speak, occurs everywhere and by no means owes its individual existence to tradition, any more than the instincts would need to be transmitted in that way. Instincts are given in the case of every newborn individual and belong to the inalienable stock of those qualities which characterize a species. What psychology designates as archetype is really a particular, frequently occurring, formal aspect of instinct, and is just as much an *a priori* factor as the latter. Therefore, despite external differences, we find a fundamental conformity in mandalas regardless of their origin in time and space.

The "squaring of the circle" is one of the many archetypal motifs which form the basic patterns of our dreams and fantasies. But it is distinguished by the fact that it is one of the most important of them from the functional point of view. Indeed, it could even be called the *archetype of wholeness*. Because of this significance, the "quaternity of the One" is the schema for all images of God, as depicted in the visions of Ezekiel, Daniel, and Enoch, and as the representation of Horus with his four sons also shows. The latter suggests an interesting differentiation, inasmuch as there are occasionally representations in which three of the sons have animals' heads and only one a human head, in keeping with the Old Testament visions as well as with the emblems of the seraphim which were transferred to the evangelists, and – last but not least – with the nature of the Gospels themselves: three of which are synoptic and one "Gnostic." Here I must add that, ever since the opening of Plato's *Timaeus* ("One, two, three . . . but where, my dear Socrates, is the fourth?") and right up to the Cabiri scene in *Faust*, the motif of four as three and one was the ever-recurring preoccupation of alchemy.

The profound significance of the quaternity with its singular process of differentiation extending over the centuries, and now manifest in the latest development of the Christian symbol,* may explain why *Du* chose just the archetype of wholeness as an example of symbol formation. For, just as this symbol claims a central position in the historical documents, individually too it has an outstanding significance. As is to be expected, individual mandalas display an enormous variety. The overwhelming majority are characterized by the circle and the quaternity. In a few, however, the three or the five predominates, for which there are usually special reasons.

Whereas ritual mandalas always display a definite style and a limited number of typical motifs as their content, individual mandalas make use of a well-nigh unlimited wealth of motifs and symbolic allusions, from which it can easily be seen that they are endeavouring to express either the totality of the individual in his inner or outer experience of the world, or its essential point of reference. Their object is the *self* in contradistinction to the *ego*, which is only the point of reference for consciousness, whereas the self comprises the totality of the psyche altogether, i.e., conscious *and* unconscious. It is therefore not unusual for individual mandalas to display a division into a light and a dark half, together with their typical symbols. An historical example of this kind is Jakob Böhme's mandala, in his treatise *Forty Questions concerning the Soul*. It is at the same time an image of God and is designated

*[Proclamation of the dogma of the Assumption of the Virgin, in 1950.]

as such. This is not a matter of chance, for Indian philosophy, which developed the idea of the self, Atman or Purusha, to the highest degree, makes no distinction in principle between the human essence and the divine. Correspondingly, in the Western mandala, the *scintilla* or soul-spark, the innermost divine essence of man, is characterized by symbols which can just as well express a God-image, namely the image of Deity unfolding in the world, in nature, and in man.

The fact that images of this kind have under certain circumstances a considerable therapeutic effect on their authors is empirically proved and also readily understandable, in that they often represent very bold attempts to see and put together apparently irreconcilable opposites and bridge over apparently hopeless splits. Even the mere attempt in this direction usually has a healing effect, but only when it is done spontaneously. Nothing can be expected from an artificial repetition or a deliberate imitation of such images.

As we saw earlier, Jung regarded the individuation process as a kind of religious quest. Jung thought that a religious attitude was natural to man, and that modern man who found himself unable to subscribe to one or other of the orthodox faiths was at risk of substituting something inferior like the worship of the State. "When the god is not acknowledged, egomania develops, and out of this mania comes sickness." (CW 13, par. 55) Above the door of his house, Jung had carved a sentence attributed to the Delphic Oracle (translated into Latin):"Vocatus atque non vocatus, deus aderit," that is, "Invoked or not invoked, the god will be present."

> It is not a matter of indifference whether one calls something a "mania" or a "god." To serve a mania is detestable and undignified, but to serve a god is full of meaning and promise because it is an act of submission to a higher, invisible, and spiritual being. [CW 13, par. 55]

In the lectures which he gave at Yale in 1937, Jung defines what he means by "religion."

(margin note, handwritten, vertical) Need for status quo

From *Psychology and Religion*, CW 11, pars. 6–9

In speaking of religion I must make clear from the start what I mean by that term. Religion, as the Latin word denotes, is a careful and scrupulous observation of what Rudolf Otto* aptly termed the *numinosum*, that is, a dynamic agency or effect not caused by an arbitrary act of will. On the contrary, it seizes and controls the human subject, who is always rather its victim than its creator. The *numinosum* – whatever its cause may be – is an experience of the subject independent of his will. At all events, religious teaching as well as the *consensus gentium* always and everywhere explain this experience as being due to a cause external to the individual. The *numinosum* is either a quality belonging to a visible object or the influence of an invisible presence that causes a peculiar alteration of consciousness. This is, at any rate, the general rule.

There are, however, certain exceptions when it comes to the question of religious practice or ritual. A great many ritualistic performances are carried out for the sole purpose of producing at will the effect of the *numinosum* by means of certain devices of a magical nature, such as invocation, incantation, sacrifice, meditation and other yoga practices, self-inflicted tortures of various descriptions, and so forth. But a religious belief in an external and objective divine cause is always prior to any such performance. The Catholic Church, for instance, administers the sacraments for the purpose of bestowing their spiritual blessings upon the believer; but since this act would amount to enforcing the presence of divine grace by an indubitably magical procedure, it is logically argued that nobody can compel divine grace to be present in the sacramental act, but that it is nevertheless inevitably present since the sacrament is a divine institution which God would not have caused to be if he had not intended to lend it his support.†

Religion appears to me to be a peculiar attitude of mind which could be formulated in accordance with the original use of the word

**The Idea of the Holy*, tr. John W. Harvey, Oxford: fourth impression 1926.
†*Gratia adiuvans* and *gratia sanctificans* are the effects of the *sacramentum ex opere operato*. The sacrament owes its undoubted efficacy to the fact that it is directly instituted by Christ himself. The Church is powerless to connect the rite with grace in such a way that the sacramental act would produce the presence and effect of grace. Consequently the rite performed by the priest is not a *causa instrumentalis*, but merely a *causa ministerialis*.

religio, which means a careful consideration and observation of certain dynamic factors that are conceived as "powers": spirits, daemons, gods, laws, ideas, ideals, or whatever name man has given to such factors in his world as he has found powerful, dangerous, or helpful enough to be taken into careful consideration, or grand, beautiful, and meaningful enough to be devoutly worshipped and loved. In colloquial speech one often says of somebody who is enthusiastically interested in a certain pursuit that he is almost "religiously devoted" to his cause; William James, for instance, remarks that a scientist often has no creed, but his "temper is devout."*

I want to make clear that by the term "religion"† I do not mean a creed. It is, however, true that every creed is originally based on the one hand upon πίστις, that is to say, trust or loyalty, the experience of the *numinosum* and on the other hand upon faith and confidence in a certain experience of a numinous nature and in the change of consciousness that ensues. The conversion of Paul is a striking example of this. We might say, then, that the term "religion" designates the attitude peculiar to a consciousness which has been changed by experience of the *numinosum*.

In part 2 of Psychology and Alchemy Jung described a series of dreams dreamed by a young scientist who had no religious belief at the level of consciousness, but who was compelled by his experience in analysis to adopt a religious attitude. The series of dreams discussed ended with a mandala in the shape of a "world clock," to which Jung refers in the following passage.

From *Psychology and Religion*, CW 11, pars. 138–49

If we allow ourselves to draw conclusions from modern mandalas we should ask people, first, whether they worship stars, suns, flowers, and snakes. They will deny this, and at the same

---

*"But our esteem for facts has not neutralized in us all religiousness. It is itself almost religious. Our scientific temper is devout." *Pragmatism*, London: Longmans, 1907, p. 14.

†"Religion is that which gives reverence and worship to some higher nature [which is called divine]." Cicero, *De inventione rhetorica*, II, 53, 161. For "testimony given under the sanction of religion on the faith of an oath" cf. Cicero, *Pro Coelio*, 55.

time they will assert that the globes, stars, crosses, and the like are symbols for a *centre in themselves*. And if asked what they mean by this centre, they will begin to stammer and to refer to this or that experience which may turn out to be something very similar to the confession of my patient, who found that the vision of his world clock had left him with a wonderful feeling of perfect harmony. Others will confess that a similar vision came to them in a moment of extreme pain or profound despair. To others again it is the memory of a sublime dream or of a moment when long and fruitless struggles came to an end and a reign of peace began. If you sum up what people tell you about their experiences, you can formulate it this way: They came to themselves, they could accept themselves, they were able to become reconciled to themselves, and thus were reconciled to adverse circumstances and events. This is almost like what used to be expressed by saying: He has made his peace with God, he has sacrificed his own will, he has submitted himself to the will of God.

A modern mandala is an involuntary confession of a peculiar mental condition. There is no deity in the mandala, nor is there any submission or reconciliation to a deity. The place of the deity seems to be taken by the wholeness of man.*

When one speaks of man, everybody means his own ego-personality – that is, his personality so far as he is conscious of it – and when one speaks of others one assumes that they have a very similar personality. But since modern research has acquainted us with the fact that individual consciousness is based on and surrounded by an indefinitely extended unconscious psyche, we must needs revise our somewhat old-fashioned prejudice that man is nothing but his consciousness. This naïve assumption must be confronted at once with the critical question: *Whose* consciousness? The fact is, it would be a difficult task to reconcile the picture I have of myself with the one which other people have of me. Who is right? And who is the real individual? If we go further and consider the fact that man is also what neither he himself nor other people know of him – an unknown something which can yet be proved to exist – the problem of identity becomes more difficult

*For the psychology of the mandala, see my commentary on *The Secret of the Golden Flower*.

still. Indeed, it is quite impossible to define the extent and the ultimate character of psychic existence. When we now speak of man we mean the indefinable whole of him, an ineffable totality, which can only be formulated symbolically. I have chosen the term "self" to designate the totality of man, the sum total of his conscious and unconscious contents.* I have chosen this term in accordance with Eastern philosophy, which for centuries has occupied itself with the problems that arise when even the gods cease to incarnate. The philosophy of the Upanishads corresponds to a psychology that long ago recognized the relativity of the gods.† This is not to be confused with a stupid error like atheism. The world is as it ever has been, but our consciousness undergoes peculiar changes. First, in remote times (which can still be observed among primitives living today), the main body of psychic life was apparently in human and in nonhuman objects: it was projected, as we should say now.** Consciousness can hardly exist in a state of complete projection. At most it would be a heap of emotions. Through the withdrawal of projections, conscious knowledge slowly developed. Science, curiously enough, began with the discovery of astronomical laws, and hence with the withdrawal, so to speak, of the most distant projections. This was the first stage in the despiritualization of the world. One step followed another: already in antiquity the gods were withdrawn from mountains and rivers, from trees and animals. Modern science has subtilized its projections to an almost unrecognizable degree, but our ordinary life still swarms with them. You can find them spread out in the newspapers, in books, rumours, and ordinary social gossip. All gaps in our actual knowledge are still filled out with projections. We are still so sure we know what other people think or what their true character is. We are convinced that certain people have all the bad qualities we do not know in ourselves or that they practise all those vices which could, of course, never be our own. We must still be exceedingly careful not to project our own shadows too shamelessly; we are still swamped with projected illusions. If you imagine someone who is brave

*See *Psychological Types*, Def. 51 (CW 6).
†Concerning the concept of the "relativity of God," see *Psychological Types* (CW 6), pars. 412ff.
**This fact accounts for the theory of animism.

enough to withdraw all these projections, then you get an
individual who is conscious of a considerable shadow. Such a man
has saddled himself with new problems and conflicts. He has
become a serious problem to himself, as he is now unable to say
that *they* do this or that, *they* are wrong, and *they* must be fought
against. He lives in the "House of the Gathering." Such a man
knows that whatever is wrong in the world is in himself, and if he
only learns to deal with his own shadow he has done something real
for the world. He has succeeded in shouldering at least an
infinitesimal part of the gigantic, unsolved social problems of our
day. These problems are mostly so difficult because they are
poisoned by mutual projections. How can anyone see straight
when he does not even see himself and the darkness he
unconsciously carries with him into all his dealings?

Modern psychological development leads to a much better
understanding as to what man really consists of. The gods at first
lived in superhuman power and beauty on the top of snow-clad
mountains or in the darkness of caves, woods, and seas. Later on
they drew together into one god, and then that god became man.
But in our day even the God-man seems to have descended from
his throne and to be dissolving himself in the common man. That
is probably why his seat is empty. Instead, the common man
suffers from a hybris of consciousness that borders on the
pathological. This psychic condition in the individual corresponds
by and large to the hypertrophy and totalitarian pretensions of the
idealized State. In the same way that the State has caught the
individual, the individual imagines that he has caught the psyche
and holds her in the hollow of his hand. He is even making a science
of her in the absurd supposition that the intellect, which is but a
part and a function of the psyche, is sufficient to comprehend the
much greater whole. In reality the psyche is the mother and the
maker, the subject and even the possibility of consciousness itself.
It reaches so far beyond the boundaries of consciousness that the
latter could easily be compared to an island in the ocean. Whereas
the island is small and narrow, the ocean is immensely wide and
deep and contains a life infinitely surpassing, in kind and degree,
anything known on the island – so that if it is a question of space,
it does not matter whether the gods are "inside" or "outside." It
might be objected that there is no proof that consciousness is

nothing more than an island in the ocean. Certainly it is impossible to prove this, since the known range of consciousness is confronted with the unknown extension of the unconscious, of which we only know that it exists and by the very fact of its existence exerts a limiting influence on consciousness and its freedom. Wherever unconsciousness reigns, there is bondage and possession. The immensity of the ocean is simply a comparison; it expresses in allegorical form the capacity of the unconscious to limit and threaten consciousness. Empirical psychology loved, until recently, to explain the "unconscious" as mere absence of consciousness – the term itself indicates as much – just as shadow is an absence of light. Today accurate observation of unconscious processes has recognized, with all other ages before us, that the unconscious possesses a creative autonomy such as a mere shadow could never be endowed with. When Carus, von Hartmann and, in a sense, Schopenhauer equated the unconscious with the world-creating principle, they were only summing up all those teachings of the past which, grounded in inner experience, saw the mysterious agent personified as the gods. It suits our hypertrophied and hybristic modern consciousness not to be mindful of the dangerous autonomy of the unconscious and to treat it negatively as an absence of consciousness. The hypothesis of invisible gods or daemons would be, psychologically, a far more appropriate formulation, even though it would be an anthropomorphic projection. But since the development of consciousness requires the withdrawal of all the projections we can lay our hands on, it is not possible to maintain any non-psychological doctrine about the gods. If the historical process of world despiritualization continues as hitherto, then everything of a divine or daemonic character outside us must return to the psyche, to the inside of the unknown man, whence it apparently originated.

The materialistic error was probably unavoidable at first. Since the throne of God could not be discovered among the galactic systems, the inference was that God had never existed. The second unavoidable error is psychologism: if God is anything, he must be an illusion derived from certain motives – from will to power, for instance, or from repressed sexuality. These arguments are not new. Much the same thing was said by the Christian missionaries who overthrew the idols of heathen gods. But whereas the early missionaries were conscious of serving a new God by combating the old ones, modern iconoclasts are unconscious of the one in whose name they are destroying old values. Nietzsche thought himself quite conscious and responsible when he smashed the old tablets, yet he felt a peculiar need to back himself up with a revivified Zarathustra, a sort of alter ego, with whom he often identifies himself in his great tragedy *Thus Spake Zarathustra*. Nietzsche was no atheist, but his God was dead. The result of this demise was a split in himself, and he felt compelled to call the other self "Zarathustra" or, at times, "Dionysus." In his fatal illness he signed his letters "Zagreus," the dismembered god of the Thracians. The tragedy of *Zarathustra* is that, because his God died, Nietzsche himself became a god; and this happened because he was no atheist. He was of too positive a nature to tolerate the urban neurosis of atheism. It seems dangerous for such a man to assert that "God is dead": he instantly becomes the victim of inflation.* Far from being a negation, God is actually the strongest and most effective "position" the psyche can reach, in exactly the same sense in which Paul speaks of people "whose God is their belly" (Phil. 3:19). The strongest and therefore the decisive factor in any individual psyche compels the same belief or fear, submission or devotion which a God would demand from man. Anything despotic and inescapable is in this sense "God," and it becomes absolute unless, by an ethical decision freely chosen, one succeeds in building up against this natural phenomenon a position that is equally strong and invincible. If this psychic position proves to be absolutely effective, it surely deserves to be named a "God," and what is more, a spiritual God, since it sprang from the freedom of ethical decision and therefore from the mind. Man is free to decide whether "God" shall be a "spirit" or a natural phenomenon like the craving of a morphine addict, and hence whether "God" shall act as a beneficent or a destructive force.

However indubitable and clearly understandable these psychic events or decisions may be, they are very apt to lead people to the false, unpsychological conclusion that it rests with them to decide whether they will *create* a "God" for themselves or not. There is

---

*Concerning the concept "inflation," see "The Relations between the Ego and the Unconscious" (CW 7), pars. 227ff.

no question of that, since each of us is equipped with a psychic disposition that limits our freedom in high degree and makes it practically illusory. Not only is "freedom of the will" an incalculable problem philosophically, it is also a misnomer in the practical sense, for we seldom find anybody who is not influenced and indeed dominated by desires, habits, impulses, prejudices, resentments, and by every conceivable kind of complex. All these natural facts function exactly like an Olympus full of deities who want to be propitiated, served, feared and worshipped, not only by the individual owner of this assorted pantheon, but by everybody in his vicinity. Bondage and possession are synonymous. Always, therefore, there is something in the psyche that takes possession and limits or suppresses our moral freedom. In order to hide this undeniable but exceedingly unpleasant fact from ourselves and at the same time pay lip-service to freedom, we have got accustomed to saying apotropaically, "*I have* such and such a desire or habit or feeling of resentment," instead of the more veracious "Such and such a desire or habit or feeling of resentment *has me*." The latter formulation would certainly rob us even of the illusion of freedom. But I ask myself whether this would not be better in the end than fuddling ourselves with words. The truth is that we do not enjoy masterless freedom; we are continually threatened by psychic factors which, in the guise of "natural phenomena," may take possession of us at any moment. The withdrawal of metaphysical projections leaves us almost defenceless in the face of this happening, for we immediately identify with every impulse instead of giving it the name of the "other," which would at least hold it at arm's length and prevent it from storming the citadel of the ego. "Principalities and powers" are always with us; we have no need to create them even if we could. It is merely incumbent on us to *choose* the master we wish to serve, so that his service shall be our safeguard against being mastered by the "other" whom we have not chosen. We do not *create* "God," we *choose* him.

Though our choice characterizes and defines "God," it is always man-made, and the definition it gives is therefore finite and imperfect. (Even the idea of perfection does not posit perfection.) The definition is an image, but this image does not raise the unknown fact it designates into the realm of intelligibility, otherwise we would be entitled to say that we had created a God. The "master" we choose is not identical with the image we project of him in time and space. He goes on working as before, like an unknown quantity in the depths of the psyche. We do not even know the nature of the simplest thought, let alone the ultimate principles of the psyche. Also, we have no control over its inner life. But because this inner life is intrinsically free and not subject to our will and intentions, it may easily happen that the living thing chosen and defined by us will drop out of its setting, the man-made image, even against our will. Then, perhaps, we could say with Nietzsche, "God is dead." Yet it would be truer to say, "He has put off our image, and where shall we find him again?" The interregnum is full of danger, for the natural facts will raise their claim in the form of various -isms, which are productive of nothing but anarchy and destruction because inflation and man's hybris between them have elected to make the ego, in all its ridiculous paltriness, lord of the universe. That was the case with Nietzsche, the uncomprehended portent of a whole epoch.

The individual ego is much too small, its brain is much too feeble, to incorporate all the projections withdrawn from the world. Ego and brain burst asunder in the effort; the psychiatrist calls it schizophrenia. When Nietzsche said "God is dead," he uttered a truth which is valid for the greater part of Europe. People were influenced by it not because he said so, but because it stated a widespread psychological fact. The consequences were not long delayed: after the fog of -isms, the catastrophe. Nobody thought of drawing the slightest conclusions from Nietzsche's pronouncement. Yet it has, for some ears, the same eerie sound as that ancient cry which came echoing over the sea to mark the end of the nature gods: "Great Pan is dead."

The life of Christ is understood by the Church on the one hand as an historical, and on the other hand as an eternally existing, mystery. This is especially evident in the sacrifice of the Mass. From a psychological standpoint this view can be translated as follows: Christ lived a concrete, personal, and unique life which, in all essential features, had at the same time an archetypal character. This character can be recognized from the numerous connections of the biographical details with worldwide myth-motifs. These undeniable connections are the main reason why it is so difficult for researchers into the life of Jesus to construct from the gospel reports on individual life divested of myth. In the gospels themselves factual reports, legends, and myths are woven into a whole. This is precisely what constitutes the meaning of the gospels, and they would immediately lose their character of wholeness if one tried to separate the individual from the archetypal with a critical scalpel. The life of Christ is no exception in that not a few of the great figures of history have realized, more or less clearly, the archetype of the hero's life with its characteristic changes of fortune. But the ordinary man, too, unconsciously lives archetypal forms, and if these are no longer valued it is only because of the prevailing psychological ignorance. Indeed, even the fleeting phenomena of dreams often reveal distinctly archetypal patterns. At bottom, all psychic events are so deeply grounded in the archetype and are so much interwoven with it that in every case considerable critical effort is needed to separate the unique from the typical with any certainty. Ultimately, every individual life is at the same time the eternal life of the species. The individual is continuously "historical" because strictly time-bound; the relation of the type to time, on the other hand, is irrelevant. Since the life of Christ is archetypal to a high degree, it represents to just that degree the life of the archetype. But since the archetype is the unconscious precondition of every human life, its life, when revealed, also reveals the hidden, unconscious ground-life of every individual. That is to say, <u>what happens in the life of Christ happens always and everywhere</u>. In the Christian archetype all lives of this kind are prefigured and are expressed over and over again or once and for all. And in it, too, the question that concerns us here of God's death is anticipated in perfect form. Christ himself is the <u>typical dying and self-transforming God.</u>

The psychological situation from which we started is tantamount to "Why seek ye the living among the dead? He is not here" (Luke 24:5f.). But where shall we find the risen Christ?

I do not expect any believing Christian to pursue these thoughts of mine any further, for they will probably seem to him absurd. I am not, however, addressing myself to the happy possessors of faith, but to those many people for whom the light has gone out, the mystery has faded, and God is dead. For most of them there is no going back, and one does not know either whether going back is always the better way. To gain an understanding of religious matters, probably all that is left us today is the psychological approach. That is why I take these thought-forms that have become historically fixed, try to melt them down again and pour them into moulds of immediate experience. It is certainly a difficult undertaking to discover connecting links between dogma and immediate experience of psychological archetypes, but a study of the natural symbols of the unconscious gives us the necessary raw material.

God's death, or his disappearance, is by no means only a Christian symbol. The search which follows the death is still repeated today after the death of a Dalai Lama, and in antiquity it was celebrated in the annual search for the Kore. Such a wide distribution argues in favour of the universal occurrence of this typical psychic process: the highest value, which gives life and meaning, has got lost. This is a typical experience that has been repeated many times, and its expression therefore occupies a central place in the Christian mystery. The death or loss must always repeat itself: Christ always dies, and always he is born; for the psychic life of the archetype is timeless in comparison with our individual time-boundness. According to what laws now one and now another aspect of the archetype enters into active manifestation, I do not know. I only know – and here I am expressing what countless other people know – that the present is a time of God's death and disappearance. The myth says he was not to be found where his body was laid. "Body" means the outward, visible form, the erstwhile but ephemeral setting for the highest value. The myth further says that the value rose again in a miraculous manner, transformed. It appears as a miracle, for, when a value disappears, it always seems to be lost irretrievably. So it is quite unexpected that it should come back. The three days' descent into hell during death describes the sinking of the vanished value into the unconscious, where, by conquering the power of darkness, it establishes a new order, and then rises up to heaven again, that is, attains supreme clarity of consciousness. The fact that only a few people see the Risen One means that no small difficulties stand in the way of finding and recognizing the transformed value.

Jung describes his search for historical parallels to the process of individuation which he was observing both in himself and in his patients.

From "The Work"   MDR, pp. 192–3/200–1; 195–7/204–6

As my life entered its second half, I was already embarked on the confrontation with the contents of the unconscious. My work on this was an extremely long-drawn-out affair, and it was only after some twenty years of it that I reached some degree of understanding of my fantasies.

First I had to find evidence for the historical prefiguration of my inner experiences. That is to say, I had to ask myself, "Where have my particular premises already occurred in history?" If I had not succeeded in finding such evidence, I would never have been able to substantiate my ideas. Therefore, my encounter with alchemy was decisive for me, as it provided me with the historical basis which I had hitherto lacked.

Analytical psychology is fundamentally a natural science, but it is subject far more than any other science to the personal bias of the observer. The psychologist must depend therefore in the highest degree upon historical and literary parallels if he wishes to exclude at least the crudest errors in judgment. Between 1918 and 1926 I had seriously studied the Gnostic writers, for they too had been confronted with the primal world of the unconscious and had dealt with its contents, with images that were obviously contaminated with the world of instinct. Just how they understood these images remains difficult to say, in view of the paucity of the accounts – which, moreover, mostly stem from their opponents, the Church Fathers. It seems to me highly unlikely that they had a psychological conception of them. But the Gnostics were too remote for me to establish any link with them in regard to the questions that were confronting me. As far as I could see, the tradition that might have connected Gnosis with the present seemed to have been severed, and for a long time it proved impossible to find any bridge that led from Gnosticism – or neo-Platonism – to the contemporary world. But when I began to understand alchemy I realized that it represented the historical link with Gnosticism, and that a continuity therefore existed between past and present. Grounded in the natural philosophy of the Middle Ages, alchemy formed the bridge on the one hand into the past, to Gnosticism, and on the other into the future, to the modern psychology of the unconscious.

. . . .

Light on the nature of alchemy began to come to me only after I had read the text of the *Golden Flower*, that specimen of Chinese alchemy which Richard Wilhelm sent me in 1928. I was stirred by the desire to become more closely acquainted with the alchemical texts. I commissioned a Munich bookseller to notify me of any alchemical books that might fall into his hands. Soon afterwards I received the first of them, the *Artis Auriferae Volumina Duo* (1593), a comprehensive collection of Latin treatises among which are a number of the "classics" of alchemy.

I let this book lie almost untouched for nearly two years. Occasionally I would look at the pictures, and each time I would think, "Good Lord, what nonsense! This stuff is impossible to understand." But it persistently intrigued me, and I made up my mind to go into it more thoroughly. The next winter I began, and soon found it provocative and exciting. To be sure, the texts still seemed to me blatant nonsense, but here and there would be passages that seemed significant to me, and occasionally I even found a few sentences which I thought I could understand. Finally I realized that the alchemists were talking in symbols – those old acquaintances of mine. "Why, this is fantastic," I thought. "I simply must learn to decipher all this." By now I was completely fascinated, and buried myself in the texts as often as I had the time. One night, while I was studying them, I suddenly recalled the dream that I was caught in the seventeenth century. At last I grasped its meaning. "So that's it! Now I am condemned to study alchemy from the very beginning."

It was a long while before I found my way about in the labyrinth of alchemical thought processes, for no Ariadne had put a thread into my hand. Reading the sixteenth-century text, "*Rosarium Philosophorum*," I noticed that certain strange expressions and turns of phrase were frequently repeated. For example, "*solve et coagula*," "*unum vas*," "*lapis*," "*prima materia*," "*Mercurius*," etc. I saw that these expressions were used again and again in a particular sense, but I could not make out what that sense was. I therefore decided to start a lexicon of key phrases with cross references. In the course of time I assembled several thousand such key phrases and words, and had volumes filled with excerpts. I worked along philological lines, as if I were trying to solve the riddle of an unknown language. In this way the alchemical mode of expression gradually yielded up its meaning. It was a task that kept me absorbed for more than a decade.

I had very soon seen that analytical psychology coincided in a most curious way with alchemy. The experiences of the alchemists were, in a sense, my experiences, and their world was my world. This was, of course, a momentous discovery: I had stumbled upon the historical counterpart of my psychology of the unconscious. The possibility of a comparison with alchemy, and the uninterrupted intellectual chain back to Gnosticism, gave substance to my psychology. When I pored over these old texts everything fell into place: the fantasy-images, the empirical material I had gathered in my practice, and the conclusions I had drawn from it. I now began to understand what these psychic contents meant when seen in historical perspective. My understanding of their typical character, which had already begun with my investigation of myths, was deepened. The primordial images and the nature of the archetype took a central place in my researches, and it became clear to me that without history there can be no psychology, and certainly no psychology of the unconscious. A psychology of consciousness can, to be sure, content itself with material drawn from personal life, but as soon as we wish to explain a neurosis we require an anamnesis which reaches deeper than the knowledge of consciousness. And when in the course of treatment unusual decisions are called for, dreams occur that need more than personal memories for their interpretation.

I regard my work on alchemy as a sign of my inner relationship to Goethe. Goethe's secret was that he was in the grip of that process of archetypal transformation which has gone on through the centuries. He regarded his *Faust* as an *opus magnum* or *divinum*. He called it his "main business," and his whole life was enacted within the framework of this drama. Thus, what was alive and active within him was a living substance, a suprapersonal process, the great dream of the *mundus archetypus* (archetypal world).

I myself am haunted by the same dream, and from my eleventh year I have been launched upon a single enterprise which is my "main business." My life has been permeated and held together by one idea and one goal: namely, to penetrate into the secret of the personality. Everything can be explained from this central point, and all my works relate to this one theme.

Jung's introduction to Psychology and Alchemy *is a clear summary of his views on the connection between alchemy and analytical psychology.*

"Introduction to the Religious and Psychological Problems of Alchemy" *Psychology and Alchemy*, CW 12, pars. 1–43

For the reader familiar with analytical psychology, there is no need of any introductory remarks to the subject of the following study. But for the reader whose interest is not professional and who comes to this book unprepared, some kind of preface will probably be necessary. The concepts of alchemy and the individuation process are matters that seem to lie very far apart, so that the imagination finds it impossible at first to conceive of any bridge between them. To this reader I owe an explanation, more particularly as I have had one or two experiences since the publication of my recent lectures which lead me to infer a certain bewilderment in my critics.

What I now have to put forward as regards the nature of the human psyche is based first and foremost on my observations of people. It has been objected that these observations deal with experiences that are either unknown or barely accessible. It is a remarkable fact, which we come across again and again, that absolutely everybody, even the most unqualified layman, thinks he knows all about psychology as though the psyche were something that enjoyed the most universal understanding. But anyone who really knows the human psyche will agree with me when I say that it is one of the darkest and most mysterious regions of our experience. There is no end to what can be learned in this field. Hardly a day passes in my practice but I come across something new and unexpected. True enough, my experiences are not commonplaces lying on the surface of life. They are, however, within easy reach of every psychotherapist working in this particular field. It is therefore rather absurd, to say the least, that ignorance of the experiences I have to offer should be twisted into an accusation against me. I do not hold myself responsible for the shortcomings in the lay public's knowledge of psychology.

There is in the analytical process, that is to say in the dialectical discussion between the conscious mind and the unconscious, a development or an advance towards some goal or end, the perplexing nature of which has engaged my attention for many years. Psychological treatment may come to an *end* at any stage in the development without one's always or necessarily having the feeling that a *goal* has also been reached. Typical and temporary terminations may occur (1) after receiving a piece of good advice; (2) after making a fairly complete but nevertheless adequate confession; (3) after having recognized some hitherto unconscious but essential psychic content whose realization gives a new impetus to one's life and activity; (4) after a hard-won separation from the childhood psyche; (5) after having worked out a new and rational mode of adaptation to perhaps difficult or unusual circumstances and surroundings; (6) after the disappearance of painful symptoms; (7) after some positive turn of fortune such as an examination, engagement, marriage, divorce, change of profession, etc.; (8) after having found one's way back to the church or creed to which one previously belonged, or after a conversion; and finally, (9) after having begun to build up a practical philosophy of life (a "philosophy" in the classical sense of the word).

Although the list could admit of many more modifications and additions, it ought to define by and large the main situations in which the analytical or psychotherapeutic process reaches a temporary or sometimes even a definitive end. Experience shows, however, that there is a relatively large number of patients for whom the outward termination of work with the doctor is far from denoting the end of the analytical process. It is rather the case that the dialectical discussion with the unconscious still continues, and follows much the same course as it does with those who have not given up their work with the doctor. Occasionally one meets such patients again after several years and hears the often highly remarkable account of their subsequent development. It was experiences of this kind which first confirmed me in my belief that there is in the psyche a process that seeks its own goal independently of external factors, and which freed me from the worrying feeling that I myself might be the sole cause of an unreal – and perhaps unnatural – process in the psyche of the patient. This apprehension was not altogether misplaced inasmuch as no amount of argument based on any of the nine categories mentioned above – not even a religious conversion or the most startling removal of neurotic symptoms – can persuade certain patients to give up their analytical work. It was these cases that finally convinced me that the treatment of neurosis opens up a problem which goes far beyond purely medical considerations and to which medical knowledge alone cannot hope to do justice.

Although the early days of analysis now lie nearly half a century behind us, with their pseudo-biological interpretations and their depreciation of the whole process of psychic development, memories die hard and people are still very fond of describing a lengthy analysis as "running away from life," "unresolved transference," "auto-eroticism" – and by other equally unpleasant epithets. But since there are two sides to everything, it is legitimate to condemn this so-called "hanging on" as negative to life only if it can be shown that it really does contain nothing positive. The very understandable impatience felt by the doctor does not prove anything in itself. Only through infinitely patient research has the new science succeeded in building up a profounder knowledge of the nature of the psyche, and if there have been certain unexpected therapeutic results, these are due to the self-sacrificing perseverance of the doctor. Unjustifiably negative judgments are easily come by and at times harmful; moreover they arouse the suspicion of being a mere cloak for ignorance if not an attempt to evade the responsibility of a thorough-going analysis. For since the analytical work must inevitably lead sooner or later to a fundamental discussion between "I" and "You" and "You" and "I" on a plane stripped of all human pretences, it is very likely, indeed it is almost certain, that not only the patient but the doctor as well will find the situation "getting under his skin." Nobody can meddle with fire or poison without being affected in some vulnerable spot; for the true physician does not stand outside his work but is always in the thick of it.

This "hanging on," as it is called, may be something undesired by both parties, something incomprehensible and even unendurable, without necessarily being negative to life. On the contrary, it can easily be a positive "hanging on," which, although it constitutes an apparently insurmountable obstacle, represents just for that reason a unique situation that demands the maximum effort and therefore enlists the energies of the whole man. In fact, one could say that while the patient is unconsciously and unswervingly seeking the solution to some ultimately insoluble problem, the art and technique of the doctor are doing their best to help him towards it. "Ars totum requirit hominem!" exclaims an old alchemist. It is just this *homo totus* whom we seek. The labours of the doctor as well as the quest of the patient are directed towards that hidden and as yet unmanifest "whole" man, who is at once the greater and the future man. But the right way to wholeness is made up, unfortunately, of fateful detours and wrong turnings. It is a *longissima via*, not straight but snakelike, a path that unites the opposites in the manner of the guiding caduceus, a path whose labyrinthine twists and turns are not lacking in terrors. It is on this *longissima via* that we meet with those experiences which are said to be "inaccessible." Their inaccessibility really consists in the fact that they cost us an enormous amount of effort: they demand the very thing we most fear, namely the "wholeness" which we talk about so glibly and which lends itself to endless theorizing, though in actual life we give it the widest possible berth.* It is infinitely more popular to go in for "compartment psychology," where the left-hand pigeon-hole does not know what is in the right.

I am afraid that we cannot hold the unconsciousness and impotence of the individual entirely responsible for this state of affairs: it is due also to the general psychological education of the

---

*It is worth noting that a Protestant theologian, writing on homiletics, had the courage to demand wholeness of the preacher from the ethical point of view. He substantiates his argument by referring to my psychology. See Händler, *Die Predigt*, Berlin, 1941.

European. Not only is this education the proper concern of the ruling religions, it belongs to their very nature – for religion excels all rationalistic systems in that it alone relates to the outer and inner man in equal degree. We can accuse Christianity of arrested development if we are determined to excuse our own shortcomings; but I do not wish to make the mistake of blaming religion for something that is due mainly to human incompetence. I am speaking therefore not of the deepest and best understanding of Christianity but of the superficialities and disastrous misunderstandings that are plain for all to see. The demand made by the *imitatio Christi* – that we should follow the ideal and seek to become like it – ought logically to have the result of developing and exalting the inner man. In actual fact, however, the ideal has been turned by superficial and formalistically-minded believers into an external object of worship, and it is precisely this veneration for the object that prevents it from reaching down into the depths of the psyche and giving the latter a wholeness in keeping with the ideal. Accordingly the divine mediator stands outside as an image, while man remains fragmentary and untouched in the deepest part of him. Christ can indeed be imitated even to the point of stigmatization without the imitator coming anywhere near the ideal or its meaning. For it is not a question of an imitation that leaves a man unchanged and makes him into a mere artifact, but of realizing the ideal on one's own account – *Deo concedente* – in one's own individual life. We must not forget, however, that even a mistaken imitation may sometimes involve a tremendous moral effort which has all the merits of a total surrender to some supreme value, even though the real goal may never be reached and the value is represented externally. It is conceivable that by virtue of this total effort a man may even catch a fleeting glimpse of his wholeness, accompanied by the feeling of grace that always characterizes this experience.

The mistaken idea of a merely outward *imitatio Christi* is further exacerbated by a typically European prejudice which distinguishes the Western attitude from the Eastern. Western man is held in thrall by the "ten thousand things"; he sees only particulars, he is ego-bound and thing-bound, and unaware of the deep root of all being. Eastern man, on the other hand, experiences the world of particulars and even his own ego, like a dream; he is rooted essentially in the "Ground," which attracts him so powerfully that his relations with the world are relativized to a degree that is often incomprehensible to us. The Western attitude, with its emphasis on the object, tends to fix the ideal – Christ – in its outward aspect and thus to rob it of its mysterious relation to the inner man. It is this prejudice, for instance, which impels the Protestant interpreters of the Bible to interpret ἐντὸς ὑμῶν (referring to the Kingdom of God) as "among you" instead of "within you." I do not mean to say anything about the validity of the Western attitude: we are sufficiently convinced of its rightness. But if we try to come to a real understanding of Eastern man – as the psychologist must – we find it hard to rid ourselves of certain misgivings. Anyone who can square it with his conscience is free to decide this question as he pleases, though he may be unconsciously setting himself up as an *arbiter mundi*. I for my part prefer the precious gift of doubt, for the reason that it does not violate the virginity of things beyond our ken.

Christ the ideal took upon himself the sins of the world. But if the ideal is wholly outside then the sins of the individual are also outside, and consequently he is more of a fragment than ever, since superficial misunderstanding conveniently enables him, quite literally, to "cast his sins upon Christ" and thus to evade his deepest responsibilities – which is contrary to the spirit of Christianity. Such formalism and laxity were not only one of the prime causes of the Reformation, they are also present within the body of Protestantism. If the supreme value (Christ) and the supreme negation (sin) are outside, then the soul is void: its highest and lowest are missing. The Eastern attitude (more particularly the Indian) is the other way about: everything, highest and lowest, is in the (transcendental) Subject. Accordingly the significance of the Atman, the Self, is heightened beyond all bounds. But with Western man the value of the self sinks to zero. Hence the universal depreciation of the soul in the West. Whoever speaks of the reality of the soul or psyche is accused of "psychologism." Psychology is spoken of as if it were "only" psychology and nothing else. The notion that there can be psychic factors which correspond to divine figures is regarded as a devaluation of the latter. It smacks of blasphemy to think that a religious experience is a psychic process;

for, so it is argued, a religious experience "is not *only* psychological." Anything psychic is *only* Nature and therefore, people think, nothing religious can come out of it. At the same time such critics never hesitate to derive all religions – with the exception of their own – from the nature of the psyche. It is a telling fact that two theological reviewers of my book *Psychology and Religion* – one of them Catholic, the other Protestant – assiduously overlooked my demonstration of the psychic origin of religious phenomena.

Faced with this situation, we must really ask: How do we know so much about the psyche that we can say "only" psychic? For this is how Western man, whose soul is evidently "of little worth," speaks and thinks. If much were in his soul he would speak of it with reverence. But since he does not do so we can only conclude that there is nothing of value in it. Not that this is necessarily so always and everywhere, but only with people who put nothing into their souls and have "all God outside." (A little more Meister Eckhart would be a very good thing sometimes!)

An exclusively religious projection may rob the soul of its values so that through sheer inanition it becomes incapable of further development and gets stuck in an unconscious state. At the same time it falls victim to the delusion that the cause of all misfortune lies outside, and people no longer stop to ask themselves how far it is their own doing. So insignificant does the soul seem that it is regarded as hardly capable of evil, much less of good. But if the soul no longer has any part to play, religious life congeals into externals and formalities. However we may picture the relationship between God and soul, one thing is certain: that the soul cannot be "nothing but."* On the contrary it has the dignity of an entity endowed with consciousness of a relationship to Deity. Even if it were only the relationship of a drop of water to the sea, that sea would not exist but for the multitude of drops. The immortality of the soul insisted upon by dogma exalts it above the transitoriness of mortal man and causes it to partake of some supernatural quality. It thus infinitely surpasses the perishable, conscious individual in significance, so that logically the Christian is

---

*[The term "nothing but" (*nichts als*), which occurs frequently in Jung to denote the habit of explaining something unknown by reducing it to something apparently known and thereby devaluing it, is borrowed from William James, *Pragmatism*, p. 16: "What is higher is explained by what is lower and treated for ever as a case of 'nothing but' – nothing but something else of a quite inferior sort."]

forbidden to regard the soul as a "nothing but."* As the eye to the sun, so the soul corresponds to God. Since our conscious mind does not comprehend the soul it is ridiculous to speak of the things of the soul in a patronizing or depreciatory manner. Even the believing Christian does not know God's hidden ways and must leave him to decide whether he will work on man from outside or from within, through the soul. So the believer should not boggle at the fact that there are *somnia a Deo missa* (dreams sent by God) and illuminations of the soul which cannot be traced back to any external causes. It would be blasphemy to assert that God can manifest himself everywhere save only in the human soul. Indeed the very intimacy of the relationship between God and the soul precludes from the start any devaluation of the latter.† It would be going perhaps too far to speak of an affinity; but at all events the soul must contain in itself the faculty of relationship to God, i.e., a correspondence, otherwise a connection could never come about.** *This correspondence is, in psychological terms, the archetype of the God-image.*

Every archetype is capable of endless development and differentiation. It is therefore possible for it to be more developed or less. In an outward form of religion where all the emphasis is on the outward figure (hence where we are dealing with a more or less complete projection), the archetype is identical with externalized ideas but remains unconscious as a psychic factor. When an unconscious content is replaced by a projected image to that extent, it is cut off from all participation in and influence on the conscious mind. Hence it largely forfeits its own life, because prevented from exerting the formative influence on consciousness natural to it; what is more, it remains in its original form – unchanged, for nothing changes in the unconscious. At a certain point it even develops a tendency to regress to lower and more archaic levels. It may easily happen, therefore, that a Christian who

---

*The dogma that man is formed in the likeness of God weighs heavily in the scales in any assessment of man – not to mention the Incarnation.
†The fact that the devil too can take possession of the soul does not diminish its significance in the least.
**It is therefore psychologically quite unthinkable for God to be simply the "wholly other," for a "wholly other" could never be one of the soul's deepest and closest intimacies – which is precisely what God is. The only statements that have psychological validity concerning the God-image are either paradoxes or antinomies.

believes in all the sacred figures is still undeveloped and unchanged in his inmost soul because he has "all God outside" and does not experience him in the soul. His deciding motives, his ruling interests and impulses, do not spring from the sphere of Christianity but from the unconscious and undeveloped psyche, which is as pagan and archaic as ever. Not the individual alone but the sum total of individual lives in a nation proves the truth of this contention. The great events of our world as planned and executed by man do not breathe the spirit of Christianity but rather of unadorned paganism. These things originate in a psychic condition that has remained archaic and has not been even remotely touched by Christianity. The Church assumes, not altogether without reason, that the fact of *semel credidisse* (having once believed) leaves certain traces behind it; but of these traces nothing is to be seen in the broad march of events. Christian civilization has proved hollow to a terrifying degree: it is all veneer, but the inner man has remained untouched and therefore unchanged. His soul is out of key with his external beliefs; in his soul the Christian has not kept pace with external developments. Yes, everything is to be found outside – in image and in word, in Church and Bible – but never inside. Inside reign the archaic gods, supreme as of old; that is to say the inner correspondence with the outer God-image is undeveloped for lack of psychological culture and has therefore got stuck in heathenism. Christian education has done all that is humanly possible, but it has not been enough. Too few people have experienced the divine image as the innermost possession of their own souls. Christ only meets them from without, never from within the soul; that is why dark paganism still reigns there, a paganism which, now in a form so blatant that it can no longer be denied and now in all too threadbare disguise, is swamping the world of so-called Christian civilization.

With the methods employed hitherto we have not succeeded in Christianizing the soul to the point where even the most elementary demands of Christian ethics can exert any decisive influence on the main concerns of the Christian European. The Christian missionary may preach the gospel to the poor naked heathen, but the spiritual heathen who populate Europe have as yet heard nothing of Christianity. Christianity must indeed begin again from the very beginning if it is to meet its high educative task.

So long as religion is only faith and outward form, and the religious function is not experienced in our own souls, nothing of any importance has happened. It has yet to be understood that the *mysterium magnum* is not only an actuality but is first and foremost rooted in the human psyche. The man who does not know this from his own experience may be a most learned theologian, but he has no idea of religion and still less of education.

Yet when I point out that the soul possesses by nature a religious function,* and when I stipulate that it is the prime task of all education (of adults) to convey the archetype of the God-image, or its emanations and effects, to the conscious mind, then it is precisely the theologian who seizes me by the arm and accuses me of "psychologism." But were it not a fact of experience that supreme values reside in the soul (quite apart from the ἀντίμιμον πνεῦμα who is also there), psychology would not interest me in the least, for the soul would then be nothing but a miserable vapour. I know, however, from hundredfold experience that it is nothing of the sort, but on the contrary contains the equivalents of everything that has been formulated in dogma and a good deal more, which is just what enables it to be an eye destined to behold the light. This requires limitless range and unfathomable depth of vision. I have been accused of "deifying the soul." Not I but God himself has deified it! *I* did not attribute a religious function to the soul, I merely produced the facts which prove that the soul is *naturaliter religiosa*, i.e., possesses a religious function. I did not invent or insinuate this function, it produces itself of its own accord without being prompted thereto by any opinions or suggestions of mine. With a truly tragic delusion these theologians fail to see that it is not a matter of proving the existence of the light, but of blind people who do not know that their eyes could see. It is high time we realized that it is pointless to praise the light and preach it if nobody can see it. It is much more needful to teach people the art of seeing. For it is obvious that far too many people are incapable of establishing a connection between the sacred figures and their own psyche: they cannot see to what extent the equivalent images are lying dormant in their own unconscious. In order to facilitate this inner vision we must first clear the way for the faculty of

*Tertullian, *Apologeticus*, xvii: "Anima naturaliter christiana."

seeing. How this is to be done without psychology, that is, without making contact with the psyche, is frankly beyond my comprehension.*

Another equally serious misunderstanding lies in imputing to psychology the wish to be a new and possibly heretical doctrine. If a blind man can gradually be helped to see it is not to be expected that he will at once discern new truths with an eagle eye. One must be glad if he sees anything at all, and if he begins to understand what he sees. Psychology is concerned with the act of seeing and not with the construction of new religious truths, when even the existing teachings have not yet been perceived and understood. In religious matters it is a well-known fact that we cannot understand a thing until we have experienced it inwardly, for it is in the inward experience that the connection between the psyche and the outward image or creed is first revealed as a relationship or correspondence like that of *sponsus* and *sponsa*. Accordingly when I say as a psychologist that God is an archetype, I mean by that the "type" in the psyche. The word "type" is, as we know, derived from τύπος, "blow" or "imprint"; thus an archetype presupposes an imprinter. Psychology as the science of the soul has to confine itself to its subject and guard against overstepping its proper boundaries by metaphysical assertions or other professions of faith. Should it set up a God, even as a hypothetical cause, it would have implicitly claimed the possibility of proving God, thus exceeding its competence in an absolutely illegitimate way. Science can only be science; there are no "scientific" professions of faith and similar *contradictiones in adiecto*. We simply do not know the ultimate derivation of the archetype any more than we know the origin of the psyche. The competence of psychology as an empirical science only goes so far as to establish, on the basis of comparative research, whether for instance the imprint found in the psyche can or cannot reasonably be termed a "God-image." Nothing positive or negative has thereby been asserted about the possible existence of God, any more than the archetype of the "hero" posits the actual existence of a hero.

Now if my psychological researches have demonstrated the

*Since it is a question here of human effort, I leave aside acts of grace which are beyond man's control.

existence of certain psychic types and their correspondence with well-known religious ideas, then we have opened up a possible approach to those experienceable contents which manifestly and undeniably form the empirical foundations of all religious experience. The religious-minded man is free to accept whatever metaphysical explanations he pleases about the origin of these images; not so the intellect, which must keep strictly to the principles of scientific interpretation and avoid trespassing beyond the bounds of what can be known. Nobody can prevent the believer from accepting God, Purusha, the Atman, or Tao as the Prime Cause and thus putting an end to the fundamental disquiet of man. The scientist is a scrupulous worker; he cannot take heaven by storm. Should he allow himself to be seduced into such an extravagance he would be sawing off the branch on which he sits.

The fact is that with the knowledge and actual experience of these inner images a way is opened for reason and feeling to gain access to those other images which the teachings of religion offer to mankind. Psychology thus does just the opposite of what it is accused of: it provides possible approaches to a better understanding of these things, it opens people's eyes to the real meaning of dogmas, and, far from destroying, it throws open an empty house to new inhabitants. I can corroborate this from countless experiences: people belonging to creeds of all imaginable kinds, who had played the apostate or cooled off in their faith, have found a new approach to their old truths, not a few Catholics among them. Even a Parsee found the way back to the Zoroastrian fire-temple, which should bear witness to the objectivity of my point of view.

But this objectivity is just what my psychology is most blamed for: it is said not to decide in favour of this or that religious doctrine. Without prejudice to my own subjective convictions I should like to raise the question: Is it not thinkable that when one refrains from setting oneself up as an *arbiter mundi* and, deliberately renouncing all subjectivism, cherishes on the contrary the belief, for instance, that God has expressed himself in many languages and appeared in divers forms and that all these statements are *true* – is it not thinkable, I say, that this too is a decision? The objection raised, more particularly by Christians, that it is impossible for contradictory statements to be true, must permit itself to be politely asked: Does one equal three? How can three be one? Can a mother be a virgin? And so on. Has it not yet been observed that all religious statements contain logical contradictions and assertions that are impossible in principle, that this is in fact the very essence of religious assertion? As witness to this we have Tertullian's avowal: "And the Son of God is dead, which is worthy of belief because it is absurd. And when buried He rose again, which is certain because it is impossible."* If Christianity demands faith in such contradictions it does not seem to me that it can very well condemn those who assert a few paradoxes more. Oddly enough the paradox is one of our most valuable spiritual possessions, while uniformity of meaning is a sign of weakness. Hence a religion becomes inwardly impoverished when it loses or waters down its paradoxes; but their multiplication enriches because only the paradox comes anywhere near to comprehending the fulness of life. Non-ambiguity and non-contradiction are one-sided and thus unsuited to express the incomprehensible.

Not everyone possesses the spiritual strength of a Tertullian. It is evident not only that he had the strength to sustain paradoxes but that they actually afforded him the highest degree of religious certainty. The inordinate number of spiritual weaklings makes paradoxes dangerous. So long as the paradox remains unexamined and is taken for granted as a customary part of life, it is harmless enough. But when it occurs to an insufficiently cultivated mind (always, as we know, the most sure of itself) to make the paradoxical nature of some tenet of faith the object of its lucubrations, as earnest as they are impotent, it is not long before such a one will break out into iconoclastic and scornful laughter, pointing to the manifest absurdity of the mystery. Things have gone rapidly downhill since the Age of Enlightenment, for, once this petty reasoning mind, which cannot endure any paradoxes, is awakened, no sermon on earth can keep it down. A new task then arises: to lift this still undeveloped mind step by step to a higher level and to increase the number of persons who have at least some inkling of the scope of paradoxical truth. If this is not possible, then it must be admitted that the spiritual approaches to

*Tertullian, *De carne Christi*, 5.

Christianity are as good as blocked. We simply do not understand any more what is meant by the paradoxes contained in dogma; and the more external our understanding of them becomes the more we are affronted by their irrationality, until finally they become completely obsolete, curious relics of the past. The man who is stricken in this way cannot estimate the extent of his spiritual loss, because he has never experienced the sacred images as his inmost possession and has never realized their kinship with his own psychic structure. But it is just this indispensable knowledge that the psychology of the unconscious can give him, and its scientific objectivity is of the greatest value here. Were psychology bound to a creed it would not and could not allow the unconscious of the individual that free play which is the basic condition for the production of archetypes. It is precisely the spontaneity of archetypal contents that convinces, whereas any prejudiced intervention is a bar to genuine experience. If the theologian really believes in the almighty power of God on the one hand and in the validity of dogma on the other, why then does he not trust God to speak in the soul? Why this fear of psychology? Or is, in complete contradiction to dogma, the soul itself a hell from which only demons gibber? Even if this were really so it would not be any the less convincing; for as we all know the horrified perception of the reality of evil has led to at least as many conversions as the experience of good.

The archetypes of the unconscious can be shown empirically to be the equivalents of religious dogmas. In the hermeneutic language of the Fathers the Church possesses a rich store of analogies with the individual and spontaneous products to be found in psychology. What the unconscious expresses is far from being merely arbitrary or opinionated; it is something that happens to be "just-so," as is the case with every other natural being. It stands to reason that the expressions of the unconscious are natural and not formulated dogmatically; they are exactly like the patristic allegories which draw the whole of nature into the orbit of their amplifications. If these present us with some astonishing *allegoriae Christi*, we find much the same sort of thing in the psychology of the unconscious. The only difference is that the patristic allegory *ad Christum spectat* – refers to Christ – whereas the psychic archetype is simply itself and can therefore be interpreted according to time, place, and milieu. In the West the archetype is filled out with the dogmatic figure of Christ; in the East, with Purusha, the Atman, Hiranyagarbha, the Buddha, and so on. The religious point of view, understandably enough, puts the accent on the imprinter, whereas scientific psychology emphasizes the *typos*, the imprint – the only thing it can understand. The religious point of view understands the imprint as the working of an imprinter; the scientific point of view understands it as the symbol of an unknown and incomprehensible content. Since the *typos* is less definite and more variegated than any of the figures postulated by religion, psychology is compelled by its empirical material to express the *typos* by means of a terminology not bound by time, place, or milieu. If, for example, the *typos* agreed in every detail with the dogmatic figure of Christ, and if it contained no determinant that went beyond that figure, we would be bound to regard the *typos* as at least a faithful copy of the dogmatic figure, and to name it accordingly. The *typos* would then coincide with Christ. But as experience shows, this is not the case, seeing that the unconscious, like the allegories employed by the Church Fathers, produces countless other determinants that are not explicitly contained in the dogmatic formula; that is to say, non-Christian figures such as those mentioned above are included in the *typos*. But neither do these figures comply with the indeterminate nature of the archetype. It is altogether inconceivable that there could be any definite figure capable of expressing archetypal indefiniteness. For this reason I have found myself obliged to give the corresponding archetype the psychological name of the "self" – a term on the one hand definite enough to convey the essence of human wholeness and on the other hand indefinite enough to express the indescribable and indeterminable nature of this wholeness. The paradoxical qualities of the term are a reflection of the fact that wholeness consists partly of the conscious man and partly of the unconscious man. But we cannot define the latter or indicate his boundaries. Hence in its scientific usage the term "self" refers neither to Christ nor to the Buddha but to the totality of the figures that are its equivalent, and each of these figures is a symbol of the self. This mode of expression is an intellectual necessity in scientific psychology and in no sense denotes a transcendental prejudice. On the contrary, as we have said before, this objective attitude enables one man to decide in favour of the determinant Christ, another in favour of the Buddha, and so on. Those who are irritated by this objectivity should reflect that science is quite impossible without it. Consequently by denying psychology the right to objectivity they are making an untimely attempt to extinguish the life-light of a science. Even if such a preposterous attempt were to succeed, it would only widen the already catastrophic gulf between the secular mind on the one hand and Church and religion on the other.

It is quite understandable for a science to concentrate more or less exclusively on its subject – indeed, that is its absolute *raison d'être*. Since the concept of the self is of central interest in psychology, the latter naturally thinks along lines diametrically opposed to theology: for psychology the religious figures point to the self, whereas for theology the self points to its – theology's – own central figure. In other words, theology might possibly take the psychological self as an allegory of Christ. This opposition is, no doubt, very irritating, but unfortunately inevitable, unless psychology is to be denied the right to exist at all. I therefore plead for tolerance. Nor is this very hard for psychology since as a science it makes no totalitarian claims.

The Christ-symbol is of the greatest importance for psychology in so far as it is perhaps the most highly developed and differentiated symbol of the self, apart from the figure of the Buddha. We can see this from the scope and substance of all the pronouncements that have been made about Christ: they agree with the psychological phenomenology of the self in unusually high degree, although they do not include all aspects of this archetype. The almost limitless range of the self might be deemed a disadvantage as compared with the definiteness of a religious figure, but it is by no means the task of science to pass value judgments. Not only is the self indefinite but – paradoxically enough – it also includes the quality of definiteness and even of uniqueness. This is probably one of the reasons why precisely those religions founded by historical personages have become world religions, such as Christianity, Buddhism, and Islam. The inclusion in a religion of a unique human personality – especially when conjoined to an indeterminable divine nature – is consistent with the absolute individuality of the self, which combines uniqueness with eternity and the individual with the universal. The self is a union of opposites *par excellence*, and this is where it differs essentially from the Christ-symbol. The androgyny of Christ is the utmost concession the Church has made to the problem of opposites. The opposition between light and good on the one hand and darkness and evil on the other is left in a state of open conflict, since Christ simply represents good, and his counterpart the devil, evil. This opposition is the real world problem, which at present is still unsolved. The self, however, is absolutely paradoxical in that it represents in every respect thesis and antithesis, and at the same time synthesis. (Psychological proofs of this assertion abound, though it is impossible for me to quote them here *in extenso*. I would refer the knowledgeable reader to the symbolism of the mandala.)

Once the exploration of the unconscious has led the conscious mind to an experience of the archetype, the individual is confronted with the abysmal contradictions of human nature, and this confrontation in turn leads to the possibility of a direct experience of light and darkness, of Christ and the devil. For better or worse there is only a bare possibility of this, and not a guarantee; for experiences of this kind cannot of necessity be induced by any human means. There are factors to be considered which are not under our control. Experience of the opposites has nothing whatever to do with intellectual insight or with empathy. It is more what we would call fate. Such an experience can convince one person of the truth of Christ, another of the truth of the Buddha, to the exclusion of all other evidence.

Without the experience of the opposites there is no experience of wholeness and hence no inner approach to the sacred figures. For this reason Christianity rightly insists on sinfulness and original sin, with the obvious intent of opening up the abyss of universal opposition in every individual – at least from the outside. But this method is bound to break down in the case of a moderately alert intellect: dogma is then simply no longer believed and on top of that is thought absurd. Such an intellect is merely one-sided and sticks at the *ineptia mysterii*. It is miles from Tertullian's antinomies; in fact, it is quite incapable of enduring the suffering such a tension involves. Cases are not unknown where the rigorous exercises and proselytizings of the Catholics, and a certain type of Protestant education that is always sniffing out sin, have brought about psychic damage that leads not to the Kingdom of Heaven but to the consulting room of the doctor. Although insight into the problem of opposites is absolutely imperative, there are very few people who can stand it in practice – a fact which has not escaped the notice of the confessional. By way of a reaction to this we have the palliative of "moral probabilism," a doctrine that has suffered frequent attack from all quarters because it tries to mitigate the crushing effect of sin.* Whatever one may think of this phenomenon one thing is certain: that apart from anything else it holds within it a large humanity and an understanding of human weakness which compensate for the world's unbearable antinomies. The tremendous paradox implicit in the insistence on original sin on the one hand and the concession made by probabilism on the other is, for the psychologist, a necessary consequence of the Christian problem of opposites outlined above – for in the self good and evil are indeed closer than identical twins! The reality of evil and its incompatibility with good cleave the opposites asunder and lead inexorably to the crucifixion and suspension of everything that lives. Since "the soul is by nature Christian" this result is bound to come as infallibly as it did in the

*Otto Zöckler ("Probabilismus," in Albert Hauck, ed., *Realencyklopädie für protestantische Theologie und Kirche*, Leipzig, 1896–1913 (24 vols.), p. 67) defines it as follows: "Probabilism is the name generally given to that way of thinking which is content to answer scientific questions with a greater or lesser degree of probability. The moral probabilism with which alone we are concerned here consists in the principle that acts of ethical self-determination are to be guided not by conscience but according to what is probably right, i.e., according to whatever has been recommended by any representative or doctrinal authority." The Jesuit probabilist Escobar (d. 1669) was, for instance, of the opinion that if the penitent should plead a probable opinion as the motive of his action, the father confessor would be obliged to absolve him even if he were not of the same opinion. Escobar quotes a number of Jesuit authorities on the question of how often one is bound to love God in a lifetime. According to one opinion, loving God shortly before death is sufficient; another says once a year or once every three or four years. He himself comes to the conclusion that it is sufficient to love God once at the first awakening of reason, then once every five years, and finally once in the hour of death. In his opinion the large number of different moral doctrines forms one of the main proofs of God's kindly providence, "because they make the yoke of Christ so light" (Zöckler, p. 68).

life of Jesus: we all have to be "crucified with Christ," i.e., suspended in a moral suffering equivalent to veritable crucifixion. In practice this is only possible up to a point, and apart from that is so unbearable and inimical to life that the ordinary human being can afford to get into such a state only occasionally, in fact as seldom as possible. For how could he remain ordinary in face of such suffering! A more or less probabilistic attitude to the problem of evil is therefore unavoidable. Hence the truth about the self – the unfathomable union of good and evil – comes out concretely in the paradox that although sin is the gravest and most pernicious thing there is, it is still not so serious that it cannot be disposed of with "probabilist" arguments. Nor is this necessarily a lax or frivolous proceeding but simply a practical necessity of life. The confessional proceeds like life itself, which successfully struggles against being engulfed in an irreconcilable contradiction. Note that at the same time the conflict remains in full force, as is once more consistent with the antinomial character of the self, which is itself both conflict and unity.

Christianity has made the antinomy of good and evil into a world problem and, by formulating the conflict dogmatically, raised it to an absolute principle. Into this as yet unresolved conflict the Christian is cast as a protagonist of good, a fellow player in the world drama. Understood in its deepest sense, being Christ's follower involves a suffering that is unendurable to the great majority of mankind. Consequently the example of Christ is in reality followed either with reservation or not at all, and the pastoral practice of the Church even finds itself obliged to "lighten the yoke of Christ." This means a pretty considerable reduction in the severity and harshness of the conflict and hence, in practice, a relativism of good and evil. Good is equivalent to the unconditional imitation of Christ and evil is its hindrance. Man's moral weakness and sloth are what chiefly hinder the imitation, and it is to these that probabilism extends a practical understanding which may sometimes, perhaps, come nearer to Christian tolerance, mildness, and love of one's neighbour than the attitude of those who see in probabilism a mere laxity. Although one must concede a number of cardinal Christian virtues to the probabilist endeavour, one must still not overlook the fact that it obviates much of the suffering involved in the imitation of Christ and that the conflict of good and evil is thus robbed of its harshness and toned down to tolerable proportions. This brings about an approach to the psychic archetype of the self, where even these opposites seem to be united – though, as I say, it differs from the Christian symbolism, which leaves the conflict open. For the latter there is a rift running through the world: light wars against night and the upper against the lower. The two are not one, as they are in the psychic archetype. But, even though religious dogma may condemn the idea of two being one, religious practice does, as we have seen, allow the natural psychological symbol of the self at one with itself an approximate means of expression. On the other hand, dogma insists that three are one, while denying that four are one. Since olden times, not only in the West but also in China, uneven numbers have been regarded as masculine and even numbers as feminine. The Trinity is therefore a decidedly masculine deity, of which the androgyny of Christ and the special position and veneration accorded to the Mother of God are not the real equivalent.

With this statement, which may strike the reader as peculiar, we come to one of the central axioms of alchemy, namely the saying of Maria Prophetissa: "One becomes two, two becomes three, and out of the third comes the one as the fourth." As the reader has already seen from its title, this book is concerned with the psychological significance of alchemy and thus with a problem which, with very few exceptions, has so far eluded scientific research. Until quite recently science was interested only in the part that alchemy played in the history of chemistry, concerning itself very little with the part it played in the history of philosophy and religion. The importance of alchemy for the historical development of chemistry is obvious, but its cultural importance is still so little known that it seems almost impossible to say in a few words wherein that consisted. In this introduction, therefore, I have attempted to outline the religious and psychological problems which are germane to the theme of alchemy. The point is that alchemy is rather like an undercurrent to the Christianity that ruled on the surface. It is to this surface as the dream is to consciousness, and just as the dream compensates the conflicts of the conscious mind, so alchemy endeavours to fill in the gaps left open by the Christian tension of opposites. Perhaps the most pregnant expression of this is the axiom of Maria Prophetissa quoted above, which runs like a *leitmotiv* throughout almost the whole of the lifetime of alchemy, extending over more than seventeen centuries. In this aphorism the even numbers which signify the feminine principle, earth, the regions under the earth, and evil itself are interpolated between the uneven numbers of the Christian dogma. They are personified by the *serpens mercurii*, the dragon that creates and destroys itself and represents the *prima materia*. This fundamental idea of alchemy points back to the םוהת (Tehom),* to Tiamat with her dragon attribute, and thus to the primordial matriarchal world which, in the theomachy of the Marduk myth, was overthrown by the masculine world of the father. The historical shift in the world's consciousness towards the masculine is compensated at first by the chthonic femininity of the unconscious. In certain pre-Christian religions the differentiation of the masculine principle had taken the form of the father-son specification, a change which was to be of the utmost importance for Christianity. Were the unconscious merely complementary, this shift of consciousness would have been accompanied by the production of a mother and daughter, for which the necessary material lay ready to hand in the myth of Demeter and Persephone. But, as alchemy shows, the unconscious chose rather the Cybele-Attis type in the form of the *prima materia* and the *filius macrocosmi*, thus proving that it is not complementary but compensatory. This goes to show that the unconscious does not simply act *contrary* to the conscious mind but *modifies* it more in the manner of an opponent or partner. The son type does not call up a daughter as a complementary image from the depths of the "chthonic" unconscious – it calls up another son. This remarkable fact would seem to be connected with the incarnation in our earthly human nature of a purely spiritual God, brought about by the Holy Ghost impregnating the womb of the Blessed Virgin. Thus the higher, the spiritual, the masculine inclines to the lower, the earthly, the feminine; and accordingly, the mother, who was anterior to the world of the father, accommodates herself to the

*Cf. Genesis 1:2.

masculine principle and, with the aid of the human spirit (alchemy or "the philosophy"), produces a son – not the antithesis of Christ but rather his chthonic counterpart, not a divine man but a fabulous being conforming to the nature of the primordial mother. And just as the redemption of man the microcosm is the task of the "upper" son, so the "lower" son has the function of a *salvator macrocosmi*.

This, in brief, is the drama that was played out in the obscurities of alchemy. It is superfluous to remark that these two sons were never united, except perhaps in the mind and innermost experience of a few particularly gifted alchemists. But it is not very difficult to see the "purpose" of this drama: in the Incarnation it looked as though the masculine principle of the father-world were approximating to the feminine principle of the mother-world, with the result that the latter felt impelled to approximate in turn to the father-world. What it evidently amounted to was an attempt to bridge the gulf separating the two worlds as compensation for the open conflict between them.

I hope the reader will not be offended if my exposition sounds like a Gnostic myth. We are moving in those psychological regions where, as a matter of fact, Gnosis is rooted. The message of the Christian symbol is Gnosis, and the compensation effected by the unconscious is Gnosis in even higher degree. Myth is the primordial language natural to these psychic processes, and no intellectual formulation comes anywhere near the richness and expressiveness of mythical imagery. Such processes are concerned with the primordial images, and these are best and most succinctly reproduced by figurative language.

The process described above displays all the characteristic features of psychological compensation. We know that the mask of the unconscious is not rigid – it reflects the face we turn towards it. Hostility lends it a threatening aspect, friendliness softens its features. It is not a question of mere optical reflection but of an autonomous answer which reveals the self-sufficing nature of that which answers. Thus the *filius philosophorum* is not just the reflected image, in unsuitable material, of the son of God; on the contrary, this son of Tiamat reflects the features of the primordial maternal figure. Although he is decidedly hermaphroditic he has a masculine name – a sign that the chthonic underworld, having been rejected by the spirit and identified with evil, has a tendency to compromise. There is no mistaking the fact that he is a concession to the spiritual and masculine principle, even though he carries in himself the weight of the earth and the whole fabulous nature of primordial animality.

This answer of the mother-world shows that the gulf between it and the father-world is not unbridgeable, seeing that the unconscious holds the seed of the unity of both. The essence of the conscious mind is discrimination; it must, if it is to be aware of things, separate the opposites, and it does this *contra naturam*. In nature the opposites seek one another – *les extrêmes se touchent* – and so it is in the unconscious, and particularly in the archetype of unity, the self. Here, as in the deity, the opposites cancel out. But as soon as the unconscious begins to manifest itself they split asunder, as at the Creation; for every act of dawning consciousness is a creative act, and it is from this psychological experience that all our cosmogonic symbols are derived.

Alchemy is pre-eminently concerned with the seed of unity which lies hidden in the chaos of Tiamat and forms the counterpart to the divine unity. Like this, the seed of unity has a trinitarian character in Christian alchemy and a triadic character in pagan alchemy. According to other authorities it corresponds to the unity of the four elements and is therefore a quaternity. The overwhelming majority of modern psychological findings speaks in favour of the latter view. The few cases I have observed which produced the number three were marked by a systematic deficiency in consciousness, that is to say, by an unconsciousness of the "inferior function." The number three is not a natural expression of wholeness, since four represents the minimum number of determinants in a whole judgment. It must nevertheless be stressed that side by side with the distinct leanings of alchemy (and of the unconscious) towards quaternity there is always a vacillation between three and four which comes out over and over again. Even in the axiom of Maria Prophetissa the quaternity is muffled and alembicated. In alchemy there are three as well as four *regimina* or procedures, three as well as four colours. There are always four elements, but often three of them are grouped together, with the fourth in a special position – sometimes earth, sometimes fire.

Mercurius* is of course *quadratus*, but he is also a three-headed snake or simply a triunity. This uncertainty has a duplex character – in other words, the central ideas are ternary as well as quaternary. The psychologist cannot but mention the fact that a similar puzzle exists in the psychology of the unconscious: the least differentiated or "inferior" function is so much contaminated with the collective unconscious that, on becoming conscious, it brings up among others the archetype of the self as well – τὸ ἕν τέταρτον, as Maria Prophetissa says. Four signifies the feminine, motherly, physical; three the masculine, fatherly, spiritual. Thus the uncertainty as to three or four amounts to a wavering between the spiritual and the physical – a striking example of how every human truth is a last truth but one.

I began my introduction with human wholeness as the goal to which the psychotherapeutic process ultimately leads. This question is inextricably bound up with one's philosophical or religious assumptions. Even when, as frequently happens, the patient believes himself to be quite unprejudiced in this respect, the assumptions underlying his thought, mode of life, morale, and language are historically conditioned down to the last detail, a fact of which he is often kept unconscious by lack of education combined with lack of self-criticism. The analysis of his situation will therefore lead sooner or later to a clarification of his general spiritual background going far beyond his personal determinants, and this brings up the problems I have attempted to sketch in the preceding pages. This phase of the process is marked by the production of symbols of unity, the so-called mandalas, which occur either in dreams or in the form of concrete visual impressions, often as the most obvious compensation of the contradictions and conflicts of the conscious situation. It would

---

*In alchemical writings the word "Mercurius" is used with a very wide range of meaning, to denote not only the chemical element mercury or quicksilver, Mercury (Hermes) the god, and Mercury the planet, but also – and primarily – the secret "transforming substance" which is at the same time the "spirit" indwelling in all living creatures. These different connotations will become apparent in the course of the book. It would be misleading to use the English "Mercury" and "mercury," because there are innumerable passages where neither word does justice to the wealth of implications. It has therefore been decided to retain the Latin "Mercurius" as in the German text, and to use the personal pronoun (since "Mercurius" is personified), the word "quicksilver" being employed only where the chemical element (Hg) is plainly meant.

hardly be correct to say that the gaping "rift" in the Christian order of things is responsible for this, since it is easy to show that Christian symbolism is particularly concerned with healing, or attempting to heal, this very wound. It would be more correct to take the open conflict as a symptom of the psychic situation of Western man, and to deplore his inability to assimilate the whole range of the Christian symbol. As a doctor I cannot demand anything of my patients in this respect, also I lack the Church's means of grace. Consequently I am faced with the task of taking the only path open to me: the archetypal images – which in a certain sense correspond to the dogmatic images – must be brought into consciousness. At the same time I must leave my patient to decide in accordance with his assumptions, his spiritual maturity, his education, origins, and temperament, so far as this is possible without serious conflicts. As a doctor it is my task to help the patient to cope with life. I cannot presume to pass judgment on his final decisions, because I know from experience that all coercion – be it suggestion, insinuation, or any other method of persuasion – ultimately proves to be nothing but an obstacle to the highest and most decisive experience of all, which is to be alone with his own self, or whatever else one chooses to call the objectivity of the psyche. The patient must be alone if he is to find out what it is that supports him when he can no longer support himself. Only this experience can give him an indestructible foundation.

I would be only too delighted to leave this anything but easy task to the theologian, were it not that it is just from the theologian that many of my patients come. They ought to have hung on to the community of the Church, but they were shed like dry leaves from the great tree and now find themselves "hanging on" to the treatment. Something in them clings, often with the strength of despair, as if they or the thing they cling to would drop off into the void the moment they relaxed their hold. They are seeking firm ground on which to stand. Since no outward support is of any use to them they must finally discover it in themselves – admittedly the most unlikely place from the rational point of view, but an altogether possible one from the point of view of the unconscious. We can see this from the archetype of the "lowly origin of the redeemer."

The way to the goal seems chaotic and interminable at first, and only gradually do the signs increase that it is leading anywhere. The way is not straight but appears to go round in circles. More accurate knowledge has proved it to go in spirals: the dream-motifs always return after certain intervals to definite forms, whose characteristic it is to define a centre. And as a matter of fact the whole process revolves about a central point or some arrangement round a centre, which may in certain circumstances appear even in the initial dreams. As manifestations of unconscious processes the dreams rotate or circumambulate round the centre, drawing closer to it as the amplifications increase in distinctness and in scope. Owing to the diversity of the symbolical material it is difficult at first to perceive any kind of order at all. Nor should it be taken for granted that dream sequences are subject to any governing principle. But, as I say, the process of development proves on closer inspection to be cyclic or spiral. We might draw a parallel between such spiral courses and the processes of growth in plants; in fact the plant motif (tree, flower, etc.) frequently recurs in these dreams and fantasies and is also spontaneously drawn or painted.* In alchemy the tree is the symbol of Hermetic philosophy.

The first of the following two studies – that which composes Part II – deals with a series of dreams which contain numerous symbols of the centre or goal. The development of these symbols is almost the equivalent of a healing process. The centre or goal thus signifies *salvation* in the proper sense of the word. The justification for such a terminology comes from the dreams themselves, for these contain so many references to religious phenomena that I was able to use some of them as the subject of my book *Psychology and Religion*. It seems to me beyond all doubt that these processes are concerned with the religion-creating archetypes. Whatever else religion may be, those psychic ingredients of it which are empirically verifiable undoubtedly consist of unconscious manifestations of this kind. People have dwelt far too long on the fundamentally sterile question of whether the assertions of faith are true or not. Quite apart from the impossibility of ever proving or refuting the truth of a metaphysical assertion, the very existence of the assertion is a self-evident fact that needs no further proof, and when a *consensus*

*See the illustrations in Jung, "Concerning Mandala Symbolism" (CW 9 i).

gentium allies itself thereto the validity of the statement is proved to just that extent. The only thing about it that we can verify is the psychological phenomenon, which is incommensurable with the category of objective rightness or truth. No phenomenon can ever be disposed of by rational criticism, and in religious life we have to deal with phenomena and facts and not with arguable hypotheses.

During the process of treatment the dialectical discussion leads logically to a meeting between the patient and his shadow, that dark half of the psyche which we invariably get rid of by means of projection: either by burdening our neighbours – in a wider or narrower sense – with all the faults which we obviously have ourselves, or by casting our sins upon a divine mediator with the aid of *contritio* or the milder *attritio*.* We know of course that without sin there is no repentance and without repentance no redeeming grace, also that without original sin the redemption of the world could never have come about; but we assiduously avoid investigating whether in this very power of evil God might not have placed some special purpose which it is most important for us to know. One often feels driven to some such view when, like the psychotherapist, one has to deal with people who are confronted with their blackest shadow.† At any rate the doctor cannot afford to point, with a gesture of facile moral superiority, to the tablets of the law and say, "Thou shalt not." He has to examine things objectively and weigh up possibilities, for he knows, less from religious training and education than from instinct and experience, that there is something very like a *felix culpa*. He knows that one can miss not only one's happiness but also one's final guilt, without which a man will never reach his wholeness. Wholeness is in fact

---

*Contritio is "perfect" repentance; *attritio* "imperfect" repentance (*contritio imperfecta*, to which category *contritio naturalis* belongs). The former regards sin as the opposite of the highest good; the latter reprehends it not only on account of its wicked and hideous nature but also from fear of punishment.

†A religious terminology comes naturally, as the only adequate one in the circumstances, when we are faced with the tragic fate that is the unavoidable concomitant of wholeness. "My fate" means a daemonic will to precisely that fate – a will not necessarily coincident with my own (the ego will). When it is opposed to the ego, it is difficult not to feel a certain "power" in it, whether divine or infernal. The man who submits to his fate calls it the will of God; the man who puts up a hopeless and exhausting fight is more apt to see the devil in it. In either event this terminology is not only universally understood but meaningful as well.

a charisma which one can manufacture neither by art nor by cunning; one can only grow into it and endure whatever its advent may bring. No doubt it is a great nuisance that mankind is not uniform but compounded of individuals whose psychic structure spreads them over a span of at least ten thousand years. Hence there is absolutely no truth that does not spell salvation to one person and damnation to another. All universalisms get stuck in this terrible dilemma. Earlier on I spoke of Jesuit probabilism: this gives a better idea than anything else of the tremendous catholic task of the Church. Even the best-intentioned people have been horrified by probabilism, but, when brought face to face with the realities of life, many of them have found their horror evaporating or their laughter dying on their lips. The doctor too must weigh and ponder, not whether a thing is for or against the Church but whether it is for or against life and health. On paper the moral code looks clear and neat enough; but the same document written on the "living tables of the heart" is often a sorry tatter, particularly in the mouths of those who talk the loudest. We are told on every side that evil is evil and that there can be no hesitation in condemning it, but that does not prevent evil from being the most problematical thing in the individual's life and the one which demands the deepest reflection. What above all deserves our keenest attention is the question "Exactly *who* is the doer?" For the answer to this question ultimately decides the value of the deed. It is true that society attaches greater importance at first to what is done, because it is immediately obvious; but in the long run the right deed in the hands of the wrong man will also have a disastrous effect. No one who is far-sighted will allow himself to be hoodwinked by the right deed of the wrong man, any more than by the wrong deed of the right man. Hence the psychotherapist must fix his eye not on what is done but on how it is done, because therein is decided the whole character of the doer. Evil needs to be pondered just as much as good, for good and evil are ultimately nothing but ideal extensions and abstractions of doing, and both belong to the chiaroscuro of life. In the last resort there is no good that cannot produce evil and no evil that cannot produce good.

The encounter with the dark half of the personality, or "shadow," comes about of its own accord in any moderately thorough treatment. This problem is as important as that of sin in the Church. The open conflict is unavoidable and painful. I have often been asked, "And what do you *do* about it?" I do nothing; there is nothing I can do except wait, with a certain trust in God, until, out of a conflict borne with patience and fortitude, there emerges the solution destined – although I cannot foresee it – for that particular person. Not that I am passive or inactive meanwhile: I help the patient to understand all the things that the unconscious produces during the conflict. The reader may believe me that these are no ordinary products. On the contrary, they are among the most significant things that have ever engaged my attention. Nor is the patient inactive; he must do the right thing, and do it with all his might, in order to prevent the pressure of evil from becoming too powerful in him. He needs "justification by works," for "justification by faith" alone has remained an empty sound for him as for so many others. Faith can sometimes be a substitute for lack of experience. In these cases what is needed is real work. Christ espoused the sinner and did not condemn him. The true follower of Christ will do the same, and, since one should do unto others as one would do unto oneself, one will also take the part of the sinner who is oneself. And as little as we would accuse Christ of fraternizing with evil, so little should we reproach ourselves that to love the sinner who is oneself is to make a pact with the devil. Love makes a man better, hate makes him worse – even when that man is oneself. The danger in this point of view is the same as in the imitation of Christ; but the Pharisee in us will never allow himself to be caught talking to publicans and whores. I must emphasize of course that psychology invented neither Christianity nor the imitation of Christ. I wish everybody could be freed from the burden of their sins by the Church. But he to whom she cannot render this service must bend very low in the imitation of Christ in order to take the burden of his cross upon him. The ancients could get along with the Greek wisdom of the ages: *Μηδὲν ἄγαν, τῷ καιρῷ πάντα πρόσεστι καλά* (Exaggerate nothing, all good lies in right measure). But what an abyss still separates us from reason!

Apart from the moral difficulty there is another danger which is not inconsiderable and may lead to complications, particularly with individuals who are pathologically inclined. This is the fact that the contents of the personal unconscious (i.e., the shadow) are indistinguishably merged with the archetypal contents of the collective unconscious and drag the latter with them when the shadow is brought into consciousness. This may exert an uncanny influence on the conscious mind; for activated archetypes have a disagreeable effect even – or I should perhaps say, particularly – on the most cold-blooded rationalist. He is afraid that the lowest form of conviction, namely superstition, is, as he thinks, forcing itself on him. But superstition in the truest sense only appears in such people if they are pathological, not if they can keep their balance. It then takes the form of the fear of "going mad" – for everything that the modern mind cannot define it regards as insane. It must be admitted that the archetypal contents of the collective unconscious can often assume grotesque and horrible forms in dreams and fantasies, so that even the most hard-boiled rationalist is not immune from shattering nightmares and haunting fears. The psychological elucidation of these images, which cannot be passed over in silence or blindly ignored, leads logically into the depths of religious phenomenology. The history of religion in its widest sense (including therefore mythology, folklore, and primitive psychology) is a treasure-house of archetypal forms from which the doctor can draw helpful parallels and enlightening comparisons for the purpose of calming and clarifying a consciousness that is all at sea. It is absolutely necessary to supply these fantastic images that rise up so strange and threatening before the mind's eye with some kind of context so as to make them more intelligible. Experience has shown that the best way to do this is by means of comparative mythological material.

Part II of this volume gives a large number of such examples. The reader will be particularly struck by the numerous connections between individual dream symbolism and medieval alchemy. This is not, as one might suppose, a prerogative of the case in question, but a general fact which only struck me some ten years ago when first I began to come to grips with the ideas and symbolism of alchemy.

Part III contains an introduction to the symbolism of alchemy in relation to Christianity and Gnosticism. As a bare introduction it is naturally far from being a complete exposition of this complicated and obscure subject – indeed, most of it is concerned only with the *lapis*-Christ parallel. True, this parallel gives rise to a comparison between the aims of the *opus alchymicum* and the central ideas of Christianity, for both are of the utmost importance in understanding and interpreting the images that appear in dreams and in assessing their psychological effect. This has considerable bearing on the practice of psychotherapy, because more often than not it is precisely the more intelligent and cultured patients who, finding a return to the Church impossible, come up against archetypal material and thus set the doctor problems which can no longer be mastered by a narrowly personalistic psychology. Nor is a mere knowledge of the psychic structure of a neurosis by any means sufficient; for once the process has reached the sphere of the collective unconscious we are dealing with healthy material, i.e., with the universal basis of the individually varied psyche. Our understanding of these deeper layers of the psyche is helped not only by a knowledge of primitive psychology and mythology, but to an even greater extent by some familiarity with the history of our modern consciousness and the stages immediately preceding it. On the one hand it is a child of the Church; on the other, of science, in whose beginnings very much lies hid that the Church was unable to accept – that is to say, remnants of the classical spirit and the classical feeling for nature which could not be exterminated and eventually found refuge in the natural philosophy of the Middle Ages. As the "spiritus metallorum" and the astrological components of destiny the old gods of the planets lasted out many a Christian century.* Whereas in the Church the increasing differentiation of ritual and dogma alienated consciousness from its natural roots in the unconscious, alchemy and astrology were ceaselessly engaged in preserving the bridge to nature, i.e., to the unconscious psyche, from decay. Astrology led the conscious mind back again and again to the knowledge of Heimarmene, that is, the dependence of character and destiny on certain moments in time; and alchemy afforded numerous "hooks" for the projection of those archetypes which could not be fitted smoothly into the Christian process. It is true that alchemy always stood on the verge of heresy and that certain decrees leave no doubt as to the Church's attitude towards it, but on the other hand it was effectively

---

*Paracelsus still speaks of the "gods" enthroned in the *mysterium magnum* (*Philosophia ad Athenienses*), and so does the 18th-cent. treatise of Abraham Eleazar, *Uraltes chymisches Werk*, which was influenced by Paracelsus.

protected by the obscurity of its symbolism, which could always be explained as harmless allegory. For many alchemists the allegorical aspect undoubtedly occupied the foreground to such an extent that they were firmly convinced that their sole concern was with chemical substances. But there were always a few for whom laboratory work was primarily a matter of symbols and their psychic effect. As the texts show, they were quite conscious of this, to the point of condemning the naïve goldmakers as liars, frauds, and dupes. Their own standpoint they proclaimed with propositions like "Aurum nostrum non est aurum vulgi." Although their labours over the retort were a serious effort to elicit the secrets of chemical transformation, it was at the same time – and often in overwhelming degree – the reflection of a parallel psychic process which could be projected all the more easily into the unknown chemistry of matter since that process is an unconscious phenomenon of nature, just like the mysterious alteration of substances. What the symbolism of alchemy expresses is the whole problem of the evolution of personality described above, the so-called individuation process.

Whereas the Church's great buttress is the imitation of Christ, the alchemist, without realizing it and certainly without wanting it, easily fell victim, in the loneliness and obscure problems of his work, to the promptings and unconscious assumptions of his own mind, since, unlike the Christians, he had no clear and unmistakable models on which to rely. The authors he studied provided him with symbols whose meaning he thought he understood in his own way; but in reality they touched and stimulated his unconscious. Ironical towards themselves, the alchemists coined the phrase "obscurum per obscurius." But with this method of explaining the obscure by the more obscure they only sank themselves deeper in the very process from which the Church was struggling to redeem them. While the dogmas of the Church offered analogies to the alchemical process, these analogies, in strict contrast to alchemy, had become detached from the world of nature through their connection with the historical figure of the Redeemer. The alchemical four in one, the philosophical gold, the *lapis angularis*, the *aqua divina*, became, in the Church, the four-armed cross on which the Only-Begotten had sacrificed himself once in history and at the same time for all eternity. The alchemists ran counter to the

Church in preferring to seek through knowledge rather than to find through faith, though as medieval people they never thought of themselves as anything but good Christians. Paracelsus is a classical example in this respect. But in reality they were in much the same position as modern man, who prefers immediate personal experience to belief in traditional ideas, or rather has it forced upon him. Dogma is not arbitrarily invented nor is it a unique miracle, although it is often described as miraculous with the obvious intent of lifting it out of its natural context. The central ideas of Christianity are rooted in Gnostic philosophy, which, in accordance with psychological laws, simply *had* to grow up at a time when the classical religions had become obsolete. It was founded on the perception of symbols thrown up by the unconscious individuation process which always sets in when the collective dominants of human life fall into decay. At such a time there is bound to be a considerable number of individuals who are possessed by archetypes of a numinous nature that force their way to the surface in order to form new dominants. This state of possession shows itself almost without exception in the fact that the possessed identify themselves with the archetypal contents of their unconscious, and, because they do not realize that the role which is being thrust upon them is the effect of new contents still to be understood, they exemplify these concretely in their own lives, thus becoming prophets and reformers. In so far as the archetypal content of the Christian drama was able to give satisfying expression to the uneasy and clamorous unconscious of the many, the *consensus omnium* raised this drama to a universally binding truth – not of course by an act of judgment, but by the irrational fact of possession, which is far more effective. Thus Jesus became the tutelary image or amulet against the archetypal powers that threatened to possess everyone. The glad tidings announced: "It has happened, but it will not happen to you inasmuch as you believe in Jesus Christ, the Son of God!" Yet it could and it can and it will happen to everyone in whom the Christian dominant has decayed. For this reason there have always been people who, not satisfied with the dominants of conscious life, set forth – under cover and by devious paths, to their destruction or salvation – to seek direct experience of the eternal roots, and, following the lure of the restless unconscious psyche, find themselves in the wilderness where, like Jesus, they come up against the son of darkness, the ἀντίμιμον πνεῦμα. Thus an old alchemist – and he a cleric! – prays: "Horridas nostrae mentis purga tenebras, accende lumen sensibus!" (Purge the horrible darknesses of our mind, light a light for our senses!) The author of this sentence must have been undergoing the experience of the *nigredo*, the first stage of the work, which was felt as "melancholia" in alchemy and corresponds to the encounter with the shadow in psychology.

When, therefore, modern psychotherapy once more meets with the activated archetypes of the collective unconscious, it is merely the repetition of a phenomenon that has often been observed in moments of great religious crisis, although it can also occur in individuals for whom the ruling ideas have lost their meaning. An example of this is the *descensus ad inferos* depicted in *Faust*, which, consciously or unconsciously, is an *opus alchymicum*.

The problem of opposites called up by the shadow plays a great – indeed, the decisive – role in alchemy, since it leads in the ultimate phase of the work to the union of opposites in the archetypal form of the *hierosgamos* or "chymical wedding." Here the supreme opposites, male and female (as in the Chinese *yang* and *yin*), are melted into a unity purified of all opposition and therefore incorruptible. The prerequisite for this, of course, is that the artifex should not identify himself with the figures in the work but should leave them in their objective, impersonal state. So long as the alchemist was working in his laboratory he was in a favourable position, psychologically speaking, for he had no opportunity to identify himself with the archetypes as they appeared, since they were all projected immediately into the chemical substances. The disadvantage of this situation was that the alchemist was forced to represent the incorruptible substance as a chemical product – an impossible undertaking which led to the downfall of alchemy, its place in the laboratory being taken by chemistry. But the psychic part of the work did not disappear. It captured new interpreters, as we can see from the example of *Faust*, and also from the signal connection between our modern psychology of the unconscious and alchemical symbolism.

Jung returned to the subject of the union of opposites in his last work of book length, Mysterium Coniunctionis, *completed in his eightieth year.*

From "**The Conjunction**" *Mysterium Coniunctionis*, CW 14, pars. 654–68

THE ALCHEMICAL VIEW OF THE UNION OF OPPOSITES

Herbert Silberer rightly called the coniunctio the "central idea" of the alchemical procedure.* This author correctly recognized that alchemy was, in the main, symbolical, whereas the historian of alchemy, Eduard von Lippmann, a chemist, did not mention the term "coniunctio" even in his index.† Anyone who has but a slight acquaintance with the literature knows that the adepts were ultimately concerned with a union of the substances – by whatever names these may have been called. By means of this union they hoped to attain the goal of the work: the production of the gold or a symbolical equivalent of it. Although the coniunctio is unquestionably the primordial image of what we today would call chemical combination, it is hardly possible to prove beyond a doubt that the adept thought as concretely as the modern chemist. Even when he spoke of a union of the "natures," or of an "amalgam" of iron and copper, or of a compound of sulphur and mercury, he meant it at the same time as a symbol: iron was Mars and copper was Venus, and their fusion was at the same time a love-affair. The union of the "natures" which "embrace one another" was not physical and concrete, for they were "celestial natures" which multiplied "by the command of God."** When "red lead" was roasted with gold it produced a "spirit," that is, the compound became "spiritual,"†† and from the "red spirit" proceeded the "principle of the world."*** The combination of sulphur and mercury was followed by the "bath" and "death."††† By the combination of copper and the *aqua permanens*, which was usually quicksilver, we think only of an amalgam. But for the

Problems of Mysticism and Its Symbolism, New York, 1917, p. 121.
†*Entstehung und Ausbreitung der Alchemie*, Berlin, 1919–54 (3 vols.).
**Turba Philosophorum* (ed. Ruska), Berlin, 1941, p. 119.
††Ibid., p. 127.
***Ibid.
†††P. 126.

alchemists it meant a secret, "philosophical" sea, since for them the *aqua permanens* was primarily a symbol or a philosophical postulate which they hoped to discover – or believed they had discovered – in the various "fluids." The substances they sought to combine in reality always had – on account of their unknown nature – a numinous quality which tended towards phantasmal personification. They were substances which, like living organisms, "fertilized one another and thereby produced the living being [ζῷον] sought by the Philosophers."* The substances seemed to them hermaphroditic, and the conjunction they strove for was a philosophical operation, namely the union of form and matter. This inherent duality explains the duplications that so often occur, e.g., two sulphurs, two quicksilvers, *Venus alba et rubea, aurum nostrum* and *aurum vulgi*.

It is therefore not surprising that the adepts, as we have seen in the previous chapters, piled up vast numbers of synonyms to express the mysterious nature of the substances – an occupation which, though it must seem utterly futile to the chemist, affords the psychologist a welcome explanation concerning the nature of the projected contents. Like all numinous contents, they have a tendency to self-amplification, that is to say they form the nuclei for an aggregation of synonyms. These synonyms represent the elements to be united as a pair of opposites; for instance as man and woman, god and goddess, son and mother, red and white, active and passive, body and spirit, and so on. The opposites are usually derived from the quaternio of elements, as we can see very clearly from the anonymous treatise "De sulphure," which says:

Thus the fire began to work upon the air and brought forth Sulphur. Then the air began to work upon the water and brought forth Mercurius. The water began to work upon the earth and brought forth Salt. But the earth, having nothing to work upon, brought forth nothing, so the product remained within it. Therefore only three principles were produced, and the earth became the nurse and matrix of the others.

From these three principles were produced male and female, the

*Berthelot, *Collections des anciens alchemistes grecs*, III, xl 2, Paris, 1887–8.

male obviously from Sulphur and Mercurius, and the female from Mercurius and Salt. Together they bring forth the "incorruptible One," the *quinta essentia*, "and thus quadrangle will answer to quadrangle."*

The synthesis of the incorruptible One or quintessence follows the Axiom of Maria, the earth representing the "fourth." The separation of the hostile elements corresponds to the initial state of chaos and darkness. From the successive unions arise an active principle (sulphur) and a passive (salt), as well as a mediating, ambivalent principle, Mercurius. This classical alchemical trinity then produces the relationship of male to female as the supreme and essential opposition. Fire comes at the beginning and is acted on by nothing, and earth at the end acts on nothing. Between fire and earth there is no interaction; hence the four elements do not constitute a circle, i.e., a totality. This is produced only by the synthesis of male and female. Thus the square at the beginning corresponds to the quaternio of elements united in the *quinta essentia* at the end – "quadrangle will answer to quadrangle."

The alchemical description of the beginning corresponds psychologically to a primitive consciousness which is constantly liable to break up into individual affective processes – to fall apart, as it were, in four directions. As the four elements represent the whole physical world, their falling apart means dissolution into the constituents of the world, that is, into a purely inorganic and hence unconscious state. Conversely, the combination of the elements and the final synthesis of male and female is an achievement of the art and a product of conscious endeavour. The result of the synthesis was consequently conceived by the adept as self-knowledge,† which, like the knowledge of God, is needed for the preparation of the Philosophers' Stone. Piety is needed for the work, and this is nothing but knowledge of oneself. This thought occurs not only in late alchemy but also in Greek tradition, as in the Alexandrian treatise of Krates (transmitted by the Arabs), where it is said that a perfect knowledge of the soul enables the adept to understand the many different names which the Philosophers have given to the arcane substance. The "Liber

---

*Arthur Edward Waite, *The Hermetic Museum Restored and Enlarged*, London, 1893; reprinted 1953, pp. 142ff.
†See *Aion* (CW 9 ii), pars. 250ff.

quartorum" emphasizes that there must be self-observation in the work as well as of events in due time. It is evident from this that the chemical process of the coniunctio was at the same time a psychic synthesis. Sometimes it seems as if self-knowledge brought about the union, sometimes as if the chemical process were the efficient cause. The latter alternative is decidedly the more frequent: the coniunctio takes place in the retort or, more indefinitely, in the "natural vessel" or matrix. The vessel is also called the grave, and the union a "shared death." This state is named the "eclipse of the sun."

The coniunctio does not always take the form of a direct union, since it needs – or occurs in – a medium: "Only through a medium can the transition take place," and, "Mercurius is the medium of conjunction." Mercurius is the soul (anima), which is the "mediator between body and spirit." The same is true of the synonyms for Mercurius, the green lion and the *aqua permanens* or spiritual water, which are likewise media of conjunction. The "Consilium coniugii" mentions as a connective agent the sweet smell or "smoky vapour," recalling Basilides' idea of the sweet smell of the Holy Ghost. Obviously this refers to the "spiritual" nature of Mercurius, just as the spiritual water, also called *aqua aëris* (aerial water or air-water), is a life principle and the "marriage maker" between man and woman. A common synonym for the water is the "sea," as the place where the chymical marriage is celebrated. The "Tractatus Micreris" mentions as further synonyms the "Nile of Egypt," the "Sea of the Indians," and the "Meridian Sea." The "marvels" of this sea are that it mitigates and unites the opposites. An essential feature of the royal marriage is therefore the sea-journey, as described by Christian Rosencreutz. This alchemical motif was taken up by Goethe in *Faust II*, where it underlies the meaning of the Aegean Festival. The archetypal content of this festival has been elaborated by Kerényi in a brilliant amplificatory interpretation. The bands of nereids on Roman sarcophagi reveal the "epithalamic and the sepulchral element," for "basic to the antique mysteries ... is the identity of marriage and death on the one hand, and of birth and the eternal resurgence of life from death on the other."[*]

*Karl Kerényi, *Das Aegaeische Fest*, Zurich, 1941, p. 55.

Mercurius, however, is not just the medium of conjunction but also that which is to be united, since he is the essence or "seminal matter" of both man and woman. *Mercurius masculinus* and *Mercurius foemineus* are united in and through *Mercurius menstrualis*, which is the "aqua." Dorn gives the "philosophical" explanation of this in his "Physica Trismegisti": In the beginning God created *one* world (*unus mundus*). This he divided into two – heaven and earth. "Beneath this spiritual and corporeal binarius lieth hid a third thing, which is the bond of holy matrimony. This same is the medium enduring until now in all things, partaking of both their extremes, without which it cannot be at all, nor they without this medium be what they are, one thing out of three." The division into two was necessary in order to bring the "one" world out of the state of potentiality into reality. Reality consists of a multiplicity of things. But one is not a number; the first number is two, and with it multiplicity and reality begin.

It is apparent from this explanation that the desperately evasive and universal Mercurius – that Proteus twinkling in a myriad shapes and colours – is none other than the "unus mundus," the original, non-differentiated unity of the world or of Being; the ἀγνωσία of the Gnostics, the primordial unconsciousness. The Mercurius of the alchemists is a personification and concretization of what we today would call the collective unconscious. While the concept of the *unus mundus* is a metaphysical speculation, the unconscious can be indirectly experienced via its manifestations. Though in itself an hypothesis, it has at least as great a probability as the hypothesis of the atom. It is clear from the empirical material at our disposal today that the contents of the unconscious, unlike conscious contents, are mutually contaminated to such a degree that they cannot be distinguished from one another and can therefore easily take one another's place, as can be seen most clearly in dreams. The indistinguishableness of its contents gives one the impression that everything is connected with everything else and therefore, despite their multifarious modes of manifestation, that they are at bottom a unity. The only comparatively clear contents consist of motifs or types round which the individual associations congregate. As the history of the human mind shows, these archetypes are of great stability and so distinct that they allow themselves to be personified and named, even though their boundaries are blurred or cut across those of other archetypes, so that certain of their qualities can be interchanged. In particular, mandala symbolism shows a marked tendency to concentrate all the archetypes on a common centre, comparable to the relationship of all conscious contents to the ego. The analogy is so striking that a layman unfamiliar with this symbolism is easily misled into thinking that the mandala is an artificial product of the conscious mind. Naturally mandalas can be imitated, but this does not prove that all mandalas are imitations. They are produced spontaneously, without external influence, even by children and adults who have never come into contact with any such ideas.* One might perhaps regard the mandala as a reflection of the egocentric nature of consciousness, though this view would be justified only if it could be proved that the unconscious is a secondary phenomenon. But the unconscious is undoubtedly older and more original than consciousness, and for this reason one could just as well call the egocentrism of consciousness a reflection or imitation of the "self"-centrism of the unconscious.

The mandala symbolizes, by its central point, the ultimate unity of all archetypes as well as of the multiplicity of the phenomenal world, and is therefore the empirical equivalent of the metaphysical concept of a *unus mundus*. The alchemical equivalent is the lapis and its synonyms, in particular the Microcosm.†

Dorn's explanation is illuminating in that it affords us a deep insight into the alchemical *mysterium coniunctionis*. If this is nothing less than a restoration of the original state of the cosmos and the divine unconsciousness of the world, we can understand the extraordinary fascination emanating from this mystery. It is the Western equivalent of the fundamental principle of classical Chinese philosophy, namely the union of *yang* and *yin* in *tao*, and at the same time a premonition of that "tertium quid" which, on the basis of psychological experience on the one hand and of Rhine's experiments on the other, I have called "synchronicity."** If mandala symbolism is the psychological equivalent of the *unus mundus*, then synchronicity is its parapsychological equivalent. Though synchronistic phenomena occur in time and space they

*See "Concerning Mandala Symbolism" (CW 9i), par. 645.
†Cf. *Psychology and Alchemy* (CW 12), par. 426 and n. 2, fig. 195.
**Cf. my "Synchronicity: An Acausal Connecting Principle" (CW 8).

manifest a remarkable independence of both these indispensable determinants of physical existence and hence do not conform to the law of causality. The causalism that underlies our scientific view of the world breaks everything down into individual processes which it punctiliously tries to isolate from all other parallel processes. This tendency is absolutely necessary if we are to gain reliable knowledge of the world, but philosophically it has the disadvantage of breaking up, or obscuring, the universal interrelationship of events so that a recognition of the greater relationship, i.e., of the unity of the world, becomes more and more difficult. Everything that happens, however, happens in the same "one world" and is a part of it. For this reason events must possess an *a priori* aspect of unity, though it is difficult to establish this by the statistical method. So far as we can see at present, Rhine seems to have successfully demonstrated this unity by his extrasensory-perception experiments (ESP).* Independence of time and space brings about a concurrence or meaningful coincidence of events not causally connected with one another – phenomena which till now were summed under the purely descriptive concepts of telepathy, clairvoyance, and precognition. These concepts naturally have no explanatory value as each of them represents an X which cannot be distinguished from the X of the other. The characteristic feature of all these phenomena, including Rhine's psychokinetic effect and other synchronistic occurrences, is *meaningful coincidence*, and as such I have defined the synchronistic principle. This principle suggests that there is an inter-connection or unity of causally unrelated events, and thus postulates a unitary aspect of being which can very well be described as the *unus mundus*.

Mercurius usually stands for the arcane substance, whose synonyms are the panacea and the "spagyric medicine." Dorn identifies the latter with the "balsam" of Paracelsus, which is a close analogy of the μύϱον of the Basilidians. In the *De vita longa* of Paracelsus, balsam as an *elixir vitae* is associated with the term "gamonymus," which might be rendered "having the name of matrimony." Dorn thinks that the balsam, which "stands higher

*Cf. his *New Frontiers of the Mind*, London, 1937, and *The Reach of the Mind*, New York, 1947; London, 1948. The relevant phenomena are discussed in "Synchronicity," pars. 833ff.

than nature," is to be found in the human body and is a kind of aetheric substance. He says it is the best medicament not only for the body but also for the mind (*mens*). Though it is a corporeal substance, as a combination of the spirit and soul of the spagyric medicine it is essentially spiritual.

> We conclude that meditative philosophy consists in the over-coming of the body by mental union [*unio mentalis*]. This first union does not as yet make the wise man, but only the mental disciple of wisdom. The second union of the mind with the body shows forth the wise man, hoping for and expecting that blessed third union with the first unity [i.e., the *unus mundus*, the latent unity of the world]. May Almighty God grant that all men be made such, and may He be one in All.

* * *

It is significant for the whole of alchemy that in Dorn's view a mental union was not the culminating point but merely the first stage of the procedure. The second stage is reached when the mental union, that is, the unity of spirit and soul, is conjoined with the body. But a consummation of the *mysterium coniunctionis* can be expected only when the unity of spirit, soul, and body is made one with the original *unus mundus*. This third stage of the coniunctio was depicted* after the manner of an Assumption and Coronation of Mary, in which the Mother of God represents the body. The Assumption is really a wedding feast, the Christian version of the hierosgamos, whose originally incestuous nature played a great role in alchemy. The traditional incest always indicated that the supreme union of opposites expressed a combination of things which are related but of unlike nature.† This may begin with a purely intra-psychic *unio mentalis* of intellect or reason with Eros, representing feeling. Such an interior operation means a great deal, since it brings a considerable increase of self-knowledge as well as of personal maturity, but its reality is

*Cf. *Psychology and Alchemy* (CW 12), fig. 232.
†See "Psychology of the Transference" (CW 16), pars. 419ff. The incest symbolism is due to the intrusion of endogamous libido. The primitive "cross-cousin-marriage" was superseded by a pure exogamy which left the endogamous demands unsatisfied. It is these demands that come to the fore in incest symbolism.

merely potential and is validated only by a union with the physical world of the body. The alchemists therefore pictured the *unio mentalis* as Father and Son and their union as the dove (the "spiration" common to both), but the world of the body they represented by the feminine or passive principle, namely Mary. Thus, for more than a thousand years, they prepared the ground for the dogma of the Assumption. It is true that the far-reaching implications of a marriage of the fatherly spiritual principle with the principle of matter, or maternal corporeality, are not to be seen from the dogma at first glance. Nevertheless, it does bridge over a gulf that seems unfathomable: the apparently irremediable separation of spirit from nature and the body. Alchemy throws a bright light on the background of the dogma, for the new article of faith expresses in symbolical form exactly what the adepts recognized as being the secret of their coniunctio. The correspondence is indeed so great that the old Masters could legitimately have declared that the new dogma has written the Hermetic secret in the skies. As against this it will be said that the alchemists smuggled the mystic or theological marriage into their obscure procedures. This is contradicted by the fact that the alchymical marriage is not only older than the corresponding formulation in the liturgy and of the Church Fathers but is based on classical and pre-Christian tradition. The alchemical tradition cannot be brought into relationship with the Apocalyptic marriage of the Lamb. The highly differentiated symbolism of the latter (lamb and city) is itself an offshoot of the archetypal hierosgamos, just as this is the source for the alchemical idea of the coniunctio.

The adepts strove to realize their speculative ideas in the form of a chemical substance which they thought was endowed with all kinds of magical powers. This is the literal meaning of their uniting the *unio mentalis* with the body. For us it is certainly not easy to include moral and philosophical reflections in this amalgamation, as the alchemists obviously did. For one thing we know too much about the real nature of chemical combination, and for another we have a much too abstract conception of the mind to be able to understand how a "truth" can be hidden in matter or what an effective "balsam" must be like. Owing to medieval ignorance both of chemistry and of psychology, and the lack of any epistemological criticism, the two concepts could easily mix, so that things that for us have no recognizable connection with one another could enter into mutual relationship.

The dogma of the Assumption and the alchemical *mysterium coniunctionis* express the same fundamental thought even though in very different symbolism. Just as the Church insists on the literal taking up of the physical body into heaven, so the alchemists believed in the possibility, or even in the actual existence, of their stone or of the philosophical gold. In both cases belief was a substitute for the missing empirical reality. Even though alchemy was essentially more materialistic in its procedures than the dogma, both of them remain at the second, anticipatory stage of the coniunctio, the union of the *unio mentalis* with the body. Even Dorn did not venture to assert that he or any other adept had perfected the third stage in his lifetime. Naturally there were as many swindlers and dupes as ever who claimed to possess the lapis or golden tincture, or to be able to make it. But the more honest alchemists readily admitted that they had not yet plumbed the final secret.

One should not be put off by the physical impossibilities of dogma or of the coniunctio, for they are symbols in regard to which the allurements of rationalism are entirely out of place and miss the mark. If symbols mean anything at all, they are tendencies which pursue a definite but not yet recognizable goal and consequently can express themselves only in analogies. In this uncertain situation one must be content to leave things as they are, and give up trying to know anything beyond the symbol. In the case of dogma such a renunciation is reinforced by the fear of possibly violating the sanctity of a religious idea, and in the case of alchemy it was until very recently considered not worth while to rack one's brains over medieval absurdities. Today, armed with psychological understanding, we are in a position to penetrate into the meaning of even the most abstruse alchemical symbols, and there is no justifiable reason why we should not apply the same method to dogma. Nobody, after all, can deny that it consists of ideas which are born of man's imagining and thinking. The question of how far this thinking may be inspired by the Holy Ghost is not affected at all, let alone decided, by psychological investigation, nor is the possibility of a metaphysical background denied. Psychology cannot advance any argument either for or against the objective validity of any metaphysical view. I have repeated this statement in various places in order to give the lie to the obstinate and grotesque notion that a psychological explanation must necessarily be either psychologism or its opposite, namely a metaphysical assertion. The psychic is a phenomenal world in itself, which can be reduced neither to the brain nor to metaphysics.

I have just said that symbols are tendencies whose goal is as yet unknown.* We may assume that the same fundamental rules obtain in the history of the human mind as in the psychology of the individual. In psychotherapy it often happens that, long before they reach consciousness, certain unconscious tendencies betray their presence by symbols, occurring mostly in dreams but also in waking fantasies and symbolic actions. Often we have the impression that the unconscious is trying to enter consciousness by means of all sorts of allusions and analogies, or that it is making more or less playful attempts to attract attention to itself. One can observe these phenomena very easily in a dream-series. The series I discussed in *Psychology and Alchemy* offers a good example.† Ideas develop from seeds, and we do not know what ideas will develop from what seeds in the course of history. The Assumption of the Virgin, for instance, is vouched for neither in Scripture nor in the tradition of the first five centuries of the Christian Church. For a long time it was officially denied even, but, with the connivance of the whole medieval and modern Church, it gradually developed as a "pious opinion" and gained so much power and influence that it finally succeeded in thrusting aside the necessity for scriptural proof and for a tradition going back to primitive times, and in attaining definition in spite of the fact that the content of the dogma is not even definable.** The papal declaration made a reality of what had long been condoned. This irrevocable step beyond the confines of historical Christianity is the strongest proof of the autonomy of archetypal images.

---

*This does not contradict the statement that symbols are the best possible formulation of an idea whose referent is not clearly known. Such an idea is always based on a tendency to represent its referent in its own way.
†Another example is the series of mandalas in "A Study of the Process of Individuation" (CW 9 i).
**Further material in F. Heiler, *Das neue Mariendogma im Lichte der Geschichte*, Munich and Basel, 1951.

Part 8. Self and Opposites: God and the Problem of Evil

If wholeness or integration consists in the union of opposites, symbolized by the emergence of quaternities and mandalas, it follows that the most obvious pair of opposites, good and evil, are to be found in the self. Yet the self, as we have seen, "is a God-image, or at least cannot be distinguished from one." (CW 9 ii, par. 42) The conventional Christian view of God is dualistic, in that God is entirely good (the doctrine of the Summum Bonum), while evil is contained in Satan. Jung points out that an earlier Christian belief was monotheistic. "Clement of Rome taught that God rules the world with a right and a left hand, the right being Christ, the left Satan."* (CW 11, pp. 357–8, prefatory note to Answer to Job) *All his life, Jung wrestled with the problem of the origin of evil. In his discussion of Christ as a manifestation of the self, Jung writes:*

From "**Christ, a Symbol of the Self**" *Aion*, CW 9 ii, pars. 79–98

Just as we have to remember the gods of antiquity in order to appreciate the psychological value of the anima/animus archetype, so Christ is our nearest analogy of the self and its meaning. It is naturally not a question of a collective value artificially manufactured or arbitrarily awarded, but of one that is effective and present *per se*, and that makes its effectiveness felt whether the subject is conscious of it or not. Yet, although the attributes of

---

**Naturally enough, theologians could not accept this view of the Deity. For discussion of the* privatio boni, *see Jung's correspondence with Fr Victor White, a Dominican priest who was a professor of theology at Blackfriars, Oxford. See especially C. G. Jung,* Letters, *vol. 2, pp. 58 and 71. Their disagreement led to an estrangement between the two men. See also Victor White's* God and the Unconscious, *pp. 75–6, n. 1.*

Christ (consubstantiality with the Father, co-eternity, filiation, parthenogenesis, crucifixion, Lamb sacrificed between opposites, One divided into Many, etc.) undoubtedly mark him out as an embodiment of the self, looked at from the psychological angle he corresponds to only one half of the archetype. The other half appears in the Antichrist. The latter is just as much a manifestation of the self, except that he consists of its dark aspect. Both are Christian symbols, and they have the same meaning as the image of the Saviour crucified between two thieves. This great symbol tells us that the progressive development and differentiation of consciousness leads to an ever more menacing awareness of the conflict and involves nothing less than a crucifixion of the ego, its agonizing suspension between irreconcilable opposites.* Naturally there can be no question on a total extinction of the ego, for then the focus of consciousness would be destroyed, and the result would be complete unconsciousness. The relative abolition

---

*"Oportuit autem ut alter illorum extremorum isque optimus appellaretur Dei filius propter suam excellentiam; alter vero ipsi *ex diametro oppositus* mali daemonis, Satanae diabolique filius diceretur" (But it is fitting that one of these two extremes, and that the best, should be called the Son of God because of his excellence, and the other, *diametrically opposed* to him, the son of the evil demon, of Satan and the devil) (Origen, *Contra Celsum*, VI, 45; trans. by Chadwick). The opposites even condition one another: "Ubi quid malum est ... ibi necessario bonum esse malo contrarium... Alterum ex altero sequitur: proinde aut utrumque tollendum est negandumque bona et mala esse; aut admisso altero maximeque malo, bonum quoque admissum oportet." (Where there is evil ... there must needs be good contrary to the evil... The one follows from the other; hence we must either do away with both, and deny that good and evil exist, or if we admit the one, and particularly evil, we must also admit the good.) (*Contra Celsum*, II, 51; trans. by Chadwick.) In contrast to this clear, logical statement Origen cannot help asserting elsewhere that the "Powers, Thrones, and Principalities" down to the evil spirits and impure demons "do not have it – the contrary virtue – substantially" ("non substantialiter id habeant scl. virtus adversaria"), and that they were not created evil but chose the condition of wickedness ("malitiae gradus") of their own free will. (*De principiis*, I, VIII, 4.) Origen is already committed, at least by implication, to the definition of God as the Summum Bonum, and hence betrays the inclination to deprive evil of substance. He comes very close to the Augustinian conception of the *privatio boni* when he says: "Certum namque est malum esse bono carere" (For it is certain that to be evil means to be deprived of good). But this sentence is immediately preceded by the following: "Recedere autem a bono, non aliud est quam effici in malo" (To turn aside from good is nothing other than to be perfected in evil) (*De principiis*, II, IX, 2). This shows clearly that an increase in the one means a diminution of the other, so that good and evil represent equivalent halves of an opposition.

of the ego affects only those supreme and ultimate decisions which confront us in situations where there are insoluble conflicts of duty. This means, in other words, that in such cases the ego is a suffering bystander who decides nothing but must submit to a decision and surrender unconditionally. The "genius" of man, the higher and more spacious part of him whose extent no one knows, has the final word. It is therefore well to examine carefully the psychological aspects of the individuation process in the light of Christian tradition, which can describe it for us with an exactness and impressiveness far surpassing our feeble attempts, even though the Christian image of the self – Christ – lacks the shadow that properly belongs to it.

The reason for this, as already indicated, is the doctrine of the Summum Bonum. Irenaeus says very rightly, in refuting the Gnostics, that exception must be taken to the "light of their Father," because it "could not illuminate and fill even those things which were within it," namely the shadow and the void. It seemed to him scandalous and reprehensible to suppose that within the pleroma of light there could be a "dark and formless void." For the Christian neither God nor Christ could be a paradox; they had to have a single meaning, and this holds true to the present day. No one knew, and apparently (with a few commendable exceptions) no one knows even now, that the hybris of the speculative intellect had already emboldened the ancients to propound a philosophical definition of God that more or less obliged him to be the Summum Bonum. A Protestant theologian has even had the temerity to assert that "God *can* only be good." Yahweh could certainly have taught him a thing or two in this respect, if he himself is unable to see his intellectual trespass against God's freedom and omnipotence. This forcible usurpation of the Summum Bonum naturally has its reasons, the origins of which lie far back in the past (though I cannot enter into this here). Nevertheless, it is the effective source of the concept of the *privatio boni*, which nullifies the reality of evil and can be found as early as Basil the Great (330–79) and Dionysius the Areopagite (2nd half of the 4th century), and is fully developed in Augustine.

The earliest authority of all for the later axiom "Omne bonum a Deo, omne malum ab homine" is Tatian (2nd century), who says: "Nothing evil was created by God; we ourselves have produced all wickedness." This view is also adopted by Theophilus of Antioch (2nd century) in his treatise *Ad Autolycum*.

Basil says:

> You must not look upon God as the author of the existence of evil, not consider that evil has any subsistence in itself [*ἰδίαν ὑπόστασιν τοῦ κακοῦ εἶναι*]. For evil does not subsist as a living being does, nor can we set before our eyes any substantial essence [*οὐσίαν ἐνυπόστατον*] thereof. For evil is the privation [*στέρησις*] of good ... And thus evil does not inhere in its own substance [*ἐν ἰδίᾳ ὑπάρξει*], but arises from the mutilation [*πηρώμασιν*] of the soul.* Neither is it uncreated, as the wicked say who set up evil for the equal of good ... nor is it created. For if all things are of God, how can evil arise from good?

Another passage sheds light on the logic of this statement. In the second homily of the *Hexaemeron* Basil says:

> It is equally impious to say that evil has its origin from God, because the contrary cannot proceed from the contrary. Life does not engender death, darkness is not the origin of light, sickness is not the maker of health ... Now if evil is neither uncreated nor created by God, whence comes its nature? That evil exists no one living in the world will deny. What shall we say, then? That evil is not a living and animated entity, but a condition [*διάθεσις*] of the soul opposed to virtue, proceeding from light-minded [*ῥαθύμοις*] persons on account of their falling away from good ... Each of us should acknowledge that he is the first author of the wickedness in him.

The perfectly natural fact that when you say "high" you immediately postulate "low" is here twisted into a causal relationship and reduced to absurdity, since it is sufficiently obvious that darkness produces no light and light produces no darkness. The idea of good and evil, however, is the premise for any moral judgment. They are a logically equivalent pair of opposites and,

---

*Basil thought that the darkness of the world came from the shadow cast by the body of heaven.

as such, the *sine qua non* of all acts of cognition. From the empirical standpoint we cannot say more than this. And from this standpoint we would have to assert that good and evil, being coexistent halves of a moral judgment, do not derive from one another but are always there together. Evil, like good, belongs to the category of human values, and we are the authors of moral value judgments, but only to a limited degree are we authors of the facts submitted to our moral judgment. These facts are called by one person good and by another evil. Only in capital cases is there anything like a *consensus generalis*. If we hold with Basil that man is the author of evil, we are saying in the same breath that he is also the author of good. But man is first and foremost the author merely of judgments; in relation to the facts judged, his responsibility is not so easy to determine. In order to do this, we would have to give a clear definition of the extent of his free will. The psychiatrist knows what a desperately difficult task this is.

For these reasons the psychologist shrinks from metaphysical assertions but must criticize the admittedly human foundations of the *privatio boni*. When therefore Basil asserts on the one hand that evil has no substance of its own but arises from a "mutilation of the soul," and if on the other hand he is convinced that evil really exists, then the relative reality of evil is grounded on a real "mutilation" of the soul which must have an equally real cause. If the soul was originally created good, then it has really been corrupted and by something that is real, even if this is nothing more than carelessness, indifference, and frivolity, which are the meaning of the word ῥαθυμία. When something – I must stress this with all possible emphasis – is traced back to a psychic condition or fact, it is very definitely not reduced to nothing and thereby nullified, but is shifted on to the plane of *psychic reality*, which is very much easier to establish empirically than, say, the reality of the devil in dogma, who according to the authentic sources was not invented by man at all but existed long before he did. If the devil fell away from God of his own free will, this proves firstly that evil was in the world before man, and therefore that man cannot be the sole author of it, and secondly that the devil already had a "mutilated" soul for which we must hold a real cause responsible. The basic flaw in Basil's argument is the *petitio principii* that lands him in insoluble contradictions: it is laid down from the start that the independent existence of evil must be denied even in face of the eternity of the devil as asserted by dogma. The historical reason for this was the threat presented by Manichaean dualism. This is especially clear in the treatise of Titus of Bostra (d. *c.* 370), entitled *Adversus Manichaeos*, where he states in refutation of the Manichaeans that, so far as substance is concerned, there is no such thing as evil.

John Chrysostom (*c.* 344–407) uses, instead of στέρησις (privatio), the expression ἐκτροπὴ τοῦ καλοῦ (deviation, or turning away, from good). He says: "Evil is nothing other than a turning away from good, and therefore evil is secondary in relation to good."

Dionysius the Areopagite gives a detailed explanation of evil in the fourth chapter of *De divinis nominibus*. Evil, he says, cannot come from good, because if it came from good it would not be evil. But since everything that exists comes from good, everything is in some way good, but "evil does not exist at all" (τὸ δε κακὸν οὔτε ὄν ἐστιν).

Evil in its nature is neither a thing nor does it bring anything forth.

Evil does not exist at all and is neither good nor productive of good [οὐκ ἔστι καθόλου τὸ κακὸν οὔτε ἀγαθὸν οὔτε ἀγαθοποιόν].

All things which are, by the very fact that they are, are good and come from good; but in so far as they are deprived of good, they are neither good nor do they exist.

That which has no existence is not altogether evil, for the absolutely non-existent will be nothing, unless it be thought of as subsisting in the good superessentially [κατὰ τὸ ὑπερούσιον]. Good, then, as absolutely existing and as absolutely non-existing, will stand in the foremost and highest place [πολλῷ πρότερον ὑπεριδρύμενον], while evil is neither in that which exists nor in that which does not exist [τὸ δὲ κακὸν οὔτε ἐν τοῖς οὖσιν, οὔτε ἐν τοῖς μὴ οὖσιν].

These quotations show with what emphasis the reality of evil was denied by the Church Fathers. As already mentioned, this hangs together with the Church's attitude to Manichaean dualism, as can plainly be seen in St. Augustine. In his polemic against the Manichaeans and Marcionites he makes the following declaration:

For this reason all things are good, since some things are better than others and the goodness of the less good adds to the glory of the better... Those things we call evil, then, are defects in good things, and quite incapable of existing in their own right outside good things... But those very defects testify to the natural goodness of things. For what is evil by reason of a defect must obviously be good of its own nature. For a defect is something contrary to nature, something which damages the nature of a thing – and it can do so only by diminishing that thing's goodness. *Evil therefore is nothing but the privation of good.* And thus it can have no existence anywhere except in some good thing... So there can be things which are good without any evil in them, such as God himself, and the higher celestial beings; but there can be no evil things without good. For if evils cause no damage to anything, they are not evils; if they do damage something, they diminish its goodness; and if they damage it still more, it is because it still has some goodness which they diminish; and if they swallow it up altogether, nothing of its nature is left to be damaged. And so there will be no evil by which it can be damaged, since there is then no nature left whose goodness any damage can diminish.*

The *Liber Sententiarum ex Augustino* says (CLXXVI): "Evil is not a substance,† for as it has not God for its author, it does not exist; and so the defect of corruption is nothing else than the desire

---

*Although the *Dialogus Quaestionum LXV* is not an authentic writing of Augustine's, it reflects his standpoint very clearly. (Question XVI: Since God created all things good and there is nothing which was not created by him, whence arises evil? Answer: Evil is not a natural thing, it is rather the name given to the privation of good. Thus there can be good without evil, but there cannot be evil without good, nor can there be evil where there is no good... Therefore, when we call a thing good, we praise its inherent nature; when we call a thing evil, we blame not its nature, but some defect in it contrary to its nature, which is good.)
†"Iniquity has no substance" (CCXXVIII). "There is a nature in which there is no evil – in which, indeed, there can be no evil. But it is impossible for a nature to exist in which there is no good" (CLX).

or act of a misdirected will."* Augustine agrees with this when he says: "The steel is not evil; but the man who uses the steel for a criminal purpose, he is evil."†

These quotations clearly exemplify the standpoint of Dionysius and Augustine: evil has no substance or existence in itself, since it is merely a diminution of good, which alone has substance. Evil is a *vitium*, a bad use of things as a result of erroneous decisions of the will (blindness due to evil desire, etc.). Thomas Aquinas, the great theoretician of the Church, says with reference to the above quotation from Dionysius:

> One opposite is known through the other, as darkness is known through light. Hence also what evil is must be known from the nature of good. Now we have said above that good is everything appetible; and thus, since every nature desires its own being and its own perfection, it must necessarily be said that the being and perfection of every created thing is essentially good. Hence it cannot be that evil signifies a being, or any form or nature. Therefore it must be that by the name of evil is signified the absence of good.**
>
> Evil is not a being, whereas good is a being.††
>
> That every agent works for an end clearly follows from the fact that every agent tends to something definite. Now that to which an agent tends definitely must needs be befitting to that agent, since the latter would not tend to it save on account of some fittingness thereto. But that which is befitting to a thing is good for it. Therefore every agent works for a good.***

St. Thomas himself recalls the saying of Aristotle that "the thing is the whiter, the less it is mixed with black,"††† without mentioning, however, that the reverse proposition: "the thing is

---

Augustini Opera omnia, Maurist edn., X, Part 2, Paris, 1835–9, cols. 2561–2618.
†*Sermones supposititii*, Sermo I, 3, Maurist edn., V, col. 2287.
**Summa theologica*, I, q. 48, ad 1 (trans. by the Fathers of the English Dominican Province, London, 1911–22, II, p. 264).
††Ibid., I, q. 48, ad 3 (trans., p. 268).
***"... Quod autem conveniens est illi bonum. Ergo omne agens agit propter bonum" (*Summa contra Gentiles*, III, ch. 3, trans. by the English Dominican Fathers, London, 1924–9, vol. III, p. 7).
†††*Summa theologica*, I, q. 48, ad 2 (trans., II, p. 266, citing Aristotle's *Topics*, iii, 4).

the blacker, the less it is mixed with white," not only has the same validity as the first but is also its logical equivalent. He might also have mentioned that not only darkness is known through light, but that, conversely, light is known through darkness.

As only that which works is real, so, according to St. Thomas, only good is real in the sense of "existing." His argument, however, introduces a good that is tantamount to "convenient, sufficient, appropriate, suitable." One ought therefore to translate "omne agens agit propter bonum" as: "Every agent works for the sake of what suits it." That's what the devil does too, as we all know. He too has an "appetite" and strives after perfection – not in good but in evil. Even so, one could hardly conclude from this that his striving is "essentially good."

Obviously evil can be represented as a diminution of good, but with this kind of logic one could just as well say: The temperature of the Arctic winter, which freezes our noses and ears, is relatively speaking only a little below the heat prevailing at the equator. For the Arctic temperature seldom falls much lower than 230° C. above absolute zero. All things on earth are "warm" in the sense that nowhere is absolute zero even approximately reached. Similarly, all things are more or less "good," and just as cold is nothing but a diminution of warmth, so evil is nothing but a diminution of good. The *privatio boni* argument remains a euphemistic *petitio principii* no matter whether evil is regarded as a lesser good or as an effect of the finiteness and limitedness of created things. The false conclusion necessarily follows from the premise "Deus = Summum Bonum," since it is unthinkable that the perfect good could ever have created evil. It merely created the good and the less good (which last is simply called "worse" by laymen). Just as we freeze miserably despite a temperature of 230° above absolute zero, so there are people and things that, although created by God, are good only to the minimal and bad to the maximal degree.

It is probably from this tendency to deny any reality to evil that we get the axiom "Omne bonum a Deo, omne malum ab homine." This is a contradiction of the truth that he who created the heat is also responsible for the cold ("the goodness of the less good"). We can certainly hand it to Augustine that all natures are good, yet just not good enough to prevent their badness from being equally obvious.

*

One could hardly call the things that have happened, and still happen, in the concentration camps of the dictator states an "accidental lack of perfection" – it would sound like mockery.

Psychology does not know what good and evil are in themselves; it knows them only as judgments about relationships. "Good" is what seems suitable, acceptable, or valuable from a certain point of view; evil is its opposite. If the things we call good are "really" good, then there must be evil things that are "real" too. It is evident that psychology is concerned with a more or less subjective judgment, i.e., with a psychic antithesis that cannot be avoided in naming value relationships: "good" denotes something that is not bad, and "bad" something that is not good. There are things which from a certain point of view are extremely evil, that is to say dangerous. There are also things in human nature which are very dangerous and which therefore seem proportionately evil to anyone standing in their line of fire. It is pointless to gloss over these evil things, because that only lulls one into a sense of false security. Human nature is capable of an infinite amount of evil, and the evil deeds are as real as the good ones so far as human experience goes and so far as the psyche judges and differentiates between them. Only unconsciousness makes no difference between good and evil. Inside the psychological realm one honestly does not know which of them predominates in the world. We hope, merely, that good does – i.e., what seems suitable to us. No one could possibly say what the general good might be. No amount of insight into the relativity and fallibility of our moral judgment can deliver us from these defects, and those who deem themselves beyond good and evil are usually the worst tormentors of mankind, because they are twisted with the pain and fear of their own sickness.

Today as never before it is important that human beings should not overlook the danger of the evil lurking within them. It is unfortunately only too real, which is why psychology must insist on the reality of evil and must reject any definition that regards it as insignificant or actually non-existent. Psychology is an empirical science and deals with realities. As a psychologist, therefore, I have neither the inclination nor the competence to mix myself up with metaphysics. Only, I have to get polemical when metaphysics encroaches on experience and interprets it in a way that is not justified empirically. My criticism of the *privatio boni* holds only so far as psychological experience goes. From the scientific point of view the *privatio boni*, as must be apparent to everyone, is founded on a *petitio principii*, where what invariably comes out at the end is what you put in at the beginning. Arguments of this kind have no power of conviction. But the fact that such arguments are not only used but are undoubtedly believed is something that cannot be disposed of so easily. It proves that there is a tendency, existing right from the start, to give priority to "good," and to do so with all the means in our power, whether suitable or unsuitable. So if Christian metaphysics clings to the *privatio boni*, it is giving expression to the tendency always to increase the good and diminish the bad. The *privatio boni* may therefore be a metaphysical truth. I presume to no judgment on this matter. I must only insist that in our field of experience white and black, light and dark, good and bad, are equivalent opposites which always predicate one another.

Jung continues his examination of the problem of evil in Answer to Job: *a controversial work which shocked some theologians. While he was writing it, Jung himself referred to the book as "pure poison." Jung states that his concern is*

> with the way in which a modern man with a Christian education and background comes to terms with the divine darkness which is unveiled in the Book of Job, and what effect it has on him . . . I hope to act as a voice for many who feel the same way as I do, and to give expression to the shattering emotion which the unvarnished spectacle of divine savagery and ruthlessness produces in us. [CW 11, par. 561]

Jung conceives that Job, by confronting God with his own capriciousness and ruthless cruelty, brings about a change in God's behaviour. "Job stands morally higher than Yahweh. In this respect the creature has surpassed the creator." (CW 11, par. 640) It is for this reason, Jung affirms, that God decides to become man in Christ. *

See also Alan Watts, Myth and Ritual in Christianity, *London: Thames and Hudson, 1953, ch. 2, "God and Satan."*

From *Answer to Job*, CW 11, pars. 579–608

The Book of Job places this pious and faithful man, so heavily afflicted by the Lord, on a brightly lit stage where he presents his case to the eyes and ears of the world. It is amazing to see how easily Yahweh, quite without reason, had let himself be influenced by one of his sons, by a *doubting thought*,* and made unsure of Job's faithfulness. With his touchiness and suspiciousness the mere possibility of doubt was enough to infuriate him and induce that peculiar double-faced behaviour of which he had already given proof in the Garden of Eden, when he pointed out the tree to the First Parents and at the same time forbade them to eat of it. In this way he precipitated the Fall, which he apparently never intended. Similarly, his faithful servant Job is now to be exposed to a rigorous moral test, quite gratuitously and to no purpose, although Yahweh is convinced of Job's faithfulness and constancy, and could moreover have assured himself beyond all doubt on this point had he taken counsel with his own omniscience. Why, then, is the experiment made at all, and a bet with the unscrupulous slanderer settled, without a stake, on the back of a powerless creature? It is indeed no edifying spectacle to see how quickly Yahweh abandons his faithful servant to the evil spirit and lets him fall without compunction or pity into the abyss of physical and moral suffering. From the human point of view Yahweh's behaviour is so revolting that one has to ask oneself whether there is not a deeper motive hidden behind it. Has Yahweh some secret resistance against Job? That would explain his yielding to Satan. But what does man possess that God does not have? Because of his littleness, puniness, and defencelessness against the Almighty, he possesses, as we have already suggested, a somewhat keener consciousness based on self-reflection: he must, in order to survive, always be mindful of his impotence. God has no need of this circumspection, for nowhere does he come up against an insuperable obstacle that would force him to hesitate and hence make him reflect on himself. Could a suspicion have grown up in God that man possesses an infinitely small yet more concentrated light than he, Yahweh,

---

*Satan is presumably one of God's eyes which "go to and fro in the earth and walk up and down in it" (Job 1:7). In Persian tradition, Ahriman proceeded from one of Ormuzd's doubting thoughts.

possesses? A jealousy of that kind might perhaps explain his behaviour. It would be quite explicable if some such dim, barely understood deviation from the definition of a mere "creature" had aroused his divine suspicions. Too often already these human beings had not behaved in the prescribed manner. Even his trusty servant Job might have something up his sleeve ... Hence Yahweh's surprising readiness to listen to Satan's insinuations against his better judgment.

Without further ado Job is robbed of his herds, his servants are slaughtered, his sons and daughters are killed by a whirlwind, and he himself is smitten with sickness and brought to the brink of the grave. To rob him of peace altogether, his wife and his old friends are let loose against him, all of whom say the wrong things. His justified complaint finds no hearing with the judge who is so much praised for his justice. Job's right is refused in order that Satan be not disturbed in his play.

One must bear in mind here the dark deeds that follow one another in quick succession: robbery, murder, bodily injury with premeditation, and denial of a fair trial. This is further exacerbated by the fact that Yahweh displays no compunction, remorse, or compassion, but only ruthlessness and brutality. The plea of unconsciousness is invalid, seeing that he flagrantly violates at least three of the commandments he himself gave out on Mount Sinai.

Job's friends do everything in their power to contribute to his moral torments, and instead of giving him, whom God has perfidiously abandoned, their warm-hearted support, they moralize in an all too human manner, that is, in the stupidest fashion imaginable, and "fill him with wrinkles." They thus deny him even the last comfort of sympathetic participation and human understanding, so that one cannot altogether suppress the suspicion of connivance in high places.

Why Job's torments and the divine wager should suddenly come to an end is not quite clear. So long as Job does not actually die, the pointless suffering could be continued indefinitely. We must, however, keep an eye on the background of all these events: it is just possible that something in this background will gradually begin to take shape as a compensation for Job's undeserved suffering – something to which Yahweh, even if he had only a faint inkling of it, could hardly remain indifferent. Without Yahweh's knowledge and contrary to his intentions, the tormented though guiltless Job had secretly been lifted up to a superior knowledge of God which God himself did not possess. Had Yahweh consulted his omniscience, Job would not have had the advantage of him. But then, so many other things would not have happened either.

Job realizes God's inner antinomy, and in the light of this realization his knowledge attains a divine numinosity. The possibility of this development lies, one must suppose, in man's "godlikeness," which one should certainly not look for in human morphology. Yahweh himself had guarded against this error by expressly forbidding the making of images. Job, by his insistence on bringing his case before God, even without hope of a hearing, had stood his ground and thus created the very obstacle that forced God to reveal his true nature. With this dramatic climax Yahweh abruptly breaks off his cruel game of cat and mouse. But if anyone should expect that his wrath will now be turned against the slanderer, he will be severely disappointed. Yahweh does not think of bringing this mischief-making son of his to account, nor does it ever occur to him to give Job at least the moral satisfaction of explaining his behaviour. Instead, he comes riding along on the tempest of his almightiness and thunders reproaches at the half-crushed human worm:

> Who is this that darkens counsel
> by words without insight?*

In view of the subsequent words of Yahweh, one must really ask oneself: *Who* is darkening *what* counsel? The only dark thing here is how Yahweh ever came to make a bet with Satan. It is certainly not Job who has darkened anything and least of all a counsel, for there was never any talk of this nor will there be in what follows. The bet does not contain any "counsel" so far as one can see – unless, of course, it was Yahweh himself who egged Satan on for the ultimate purpose of exalting Job. Naturally this development was foreseen in omniscience, and it may be that the word "counsel" refers to this eternal and absolute knowledge. If so, Yahweh's

*Job 38:2 (Zürcher Bibel).

attitude seems the more illogical and incomprehensible, as he could then have enlightened Job on this point – which, in view of the wrong done to him, would have been only fair and equitable. I must therefore regard this possibility as improbable.

Whose words are without insight? Presumably Yahweh is not referring to the words of Job's friends, but is rebuking Job. But what is Job's guilt? The only thing he can be blamed for is his incurable optimism in believing that he can appeal to divine justice. In this he is mistaken, as Yahweh's subsequent words prove. God does not want to be just; he merely flaunts might over right. Job could not get that into his head, because he looked upon God as a moral being. He had never doubted God's might, but had hoped for right as well. He had, however, already taken back this error when he recognized God's contradictory nature, and by so doing he assigned a place to God's justice and goodness. So one can hardly speak of lack of insight.

The answer to Yahweh's conundrum is therefore: it is Yahweh himself who darkens his own counsel and who has no insight. He turns the tables on Job and blames him for what he himself does: man is not permitted to have an opinion about him, and, in particular, is to have no insight which he himself does not possess. For seventy-one verses he proclaims his world-creating power to his miserable victim, who sits in ashes and scratches his sores with potsherds, and who by now has had more than enough of superhuman violence. Job has absolutely no need of being impressed by further exhibitions of this power. Yahweh, in his omniscience, could have known just how incongruous his attempts at intimidation were in such a situation. He could easily have seen that Job believes in his omnipotence as much as ever and has never doubted it or wavered in his loyalty. Altogether, he pays so little attention to Job's real situation that one suspects him of having an ulterior motive which is more important to him: Job is no more than the outward occasion for an inward process of dialectic in God. His thunderings at Job so completely miss the point that one cannot help but see how much he is occupied with himself. The tremendous emphasis he lays on his omnipotence and greatness makes no sense in relation to Job, who certainly needs no more convincing, but only becomes intelligible when aimed at a listener *who doubts it*. This "doubting thought" is Satan, who after completing his evil handiwork has returned to the paternal bosom in order to continue his subversive activity there. Yahweh must have seen that Job's loyalty was unshakable and that Satan had lost his bet. He must also have realized that, in accepting this bet, he had done everything possible to drive his faithful servant to disloyalty, even to the extent of perpetrating a whole series of crimes. Yet it is not remorse and certainly not moral horror that rises to his consciousness, but an obscure intimation of something that questions his omnipotence. He is particularly sensitive on this point, because "might" is the great argument. But omniscience knows that might excuses nothing. The said intimation refers, of course, to the extremely uncomfortable fact that Yahweh had let himself be bamboozled by Satan. This weakness of his does not reach full consciousness, since Satan is treated with remarkable tolerance and consideration. Evidently Satan's intrigue is deliberately overlooked at Job's expense.

Luckily enough, Job had noticed during this harangue that everything else had been mentioned except his right. He has understood that it is at present impossible to argue the question of right, as it is only too obvious that Yahweh has no interest whatever in Job's cause but is far more preoccupied with his own affairs. Satan, that is to say, has somehow to disappear, and this can best be done by casting suspicion on Job as a man of subversive opinions. The problem is thus switched on to another track, and the episode with Satan remains unmentioned and unconscious. To the spectator it is not quite clear why Job is treated to this almighty exhibition of thunder and lightning, but the performance as such is sufficiently magnificent and impressive to convince not only a larger audience but above all Yahweh himself of his unassailable power. Whether Job realizes what violence Yahweh is doing to his own omniscience by behaving like this we do not know, but his silence and submission leave a number of possibilities open. Job has no alternative but formally to revoke his demand for justice, and he therefore answers in the words quoted at the beginning: "I lay my hand on my mouth."

He betrays not the slightest trace of mental reservation – in fact, his answer leaves us in no doubt that he has succumbed completely and without question to the tremendous force of the divine demonstration. The most exacting tyrant should have been satisfied with this, and could be quite sure that his servant – from terror alone, to say nothing of his undoubted loyalty – would not dare to nourish a single improper thought for a very long time to come.

Strangely enough, Yahweh does not notice anything of the kind. He does not see Job and his situation at all. It is rather as if he had another powerful opponent in the place of Job, one who was better worth challenging. This is clear from his twice-repeated taunt:

> Gird up your loins like a man;
>   I will question you, and you shall declare to me.*

One would have to choose positively grotesque examples to illustrate the disproportion between the two antagonists. Yahweh sees something in Job which we would not ascribe to him but to God, that is, an equal power which causes him to bring out his whole power apparatus and parade it before his opponent. Yahweh projects on to Job a sceptic's face which is hateful to him because it is his own, and which gazes at him with an uncanny and critical eye. He is afraid of it, for only in face of something frightening does one let off a cannonade of references to one's power, cleverness, courage, invincibility, etc. What has all that to do with Job? Is it worth the lion's while to terrify a mouse?

Yahweh cannot rest satisfied with the first victorious round. Job has long since been knocked out, but the great antagonist whose phantom is projected on to the pitiable sufferer still stands menacingly upright. Therefore Yahweh raises his arm again:

> Will you even put me in the wrong?
>   Will you condemn me that you may be justified?
> Have you an arm like God,
>   and can you thunder with a voice like his?†

Man, abandoned without protection and stripped of his rights, and whose nothingness is thrown in his face at every opportunity, evidently appears to be so dangerous to Yahweh that he must be

*Job 38:3 and 40:7.
†40:8–9.

battered down with the heaviest artillery. What irritates Yahweh can be seen from his challenge to the ostensible Job:

> Look on every one that is proud, and bring him low;
>   and tread down the wicked where they stand.
> Hide them in the dust together;
>   bind their faces in the hidden place.
> Then will I also acknowledge to you
>   that your own right hand can give you victory.*

Job is challenged as though he himself were a god. But in the contemporary metaphysics there was no *deuteros theos*, no other god except Satan, who owns Yahweh's ear and is able to influence him. He is the only one who can pull the wool over his eyes, beguile him, and put him up to a massive violation of his own penal code. A formidable opponent indeed, and, because of his close kinship, so compromising that he must be concealed with the utmost discretion – even to the point of God's hiding him from his own consciousness in his own bosom! In his stead God must set up his miserable servant as the bugbear whom he has to fight, in the hope that by banishing the dreaded countenance to "the hidden place" he will be able to maintain himself in a state of unconsciousness.

The stage-managing of this imaginary duel, the speechifying, and the impressive performance given by the prehistoric menagerie would not be sufficiently explained if we tried to reduce them to the purely negative factor of Yahweh's fear of becoming conscious and of the relativization which this entails. The conflict becomes acute for Yahweh as a result of a new factor, which is, however, not hidden from omniscience – though in this case the existing knowledge is not accompanied by any conclusion. The new factor is something that has never occurred before in the history of the world, the unheard-of fact that, without knowing it or wanting it, a mortal man is raised by his moral behaviour above the stars in heaven, from which position of advantage

---

*40:12–14 ("in the hidden place" is Revised Standard Version alternative reading for "in the world below").

he can behold the back of Yahweh, the abysmal world of "shards."*

Does Job know what he has seen? If he does, he is astute or canny enough not to betray it. But his words speak volumes:

> I know that thou canst do all things,
> and that no purpose of thine can be thwarted.†

Truly, Yahweh can do all things and permits himself all things without batting an eyelid. With brazen countenance he can project his shadow side and remain unconscious at man's expense. He can boast of his superior power and enact laws which mean less than air to him. Murder and manslaughter are mere bagatelles, and if the mood takes him he can play the feudal grand seigneur and generously recompense his bondslave for the havoc wrought in his wheat-fields. "So you have lost your sons and daughters? No harm done, I will give you new and better ones."

Job continues (no doubt with downcast eyes and in a low voice):

> "Who is this that hides counsel without insight?"
> Therefore I have uttered what I did not understand,
> things too wonderful for me, which I did not know.
> "Hear, and I will speak;
> I will question you, and you declare to me."
> I had heard of thee by the hearing of the ear,
> but now my eye sees thee;
> therefore I abhor myself,
> and repent in dust and ashes.**

Shrewdly, Job takes up Yahweh's aggressive words and prostrates himself at his feet as if he were indeed the defeated antagonist. Guileless as Job's speech sounds, it could just as well be equivocal. He has learnt his lesson well and experienced "wonderful things" which are none too easily grasped. Before, he had known Yahweh "by the hearing of the ear," but now he has

---

*This is an allusion to an idea found in the later cabalistic philosophy.
†42:2.
**42:3–6 (modified).

got a taste of his reality, more so even than David – an incisive lesson that had better not be forgotten. Formerly he was naïve, dreaming perhaps of a "good" God, or of a benevolent ruler and just judge. He had imagined that a "covenant" was a legal matter and that anyone who was party to a contract could insist on his rights as agreed; that God would be faithful and true or at least just, and, as one could assume from the Ten Commandments, would have some recognition of ethical values or at least feel committed to his own legal standpoint. But, to his horror, he has discovered that Yahweh is not human but, in certain respects, less than human, that he is just what Yahweh himself says of Leviathan (the crocodile):

> He beholds everything that is high:
> He is king over all proud beasts.*

Unconsciousness has an animal nature. Like all old gods Yahweh has his animal symbolism with its unmistakable borrowings from the much older theriomorphic gods of Egypt, especially Horus and his four sons. Of the four animals of Yahweh only one has a human face. That is probably Satan, the godfather of man as a spiritual being. Ezekiel's vision attributes three-fourths animal nature and only one-fourth human nature to the animal deity, while the upper deity, the one above the "sapphire throne," merely had the "likeness" of a man.† This symbolism explains Yahweh's behaviour, which, from the human point of view, is so intolerable: it is the behaviour of an unconscious being who cannot be judged morally. Yahweh is a *phenomenon* and, as Job says, "not a man."**

One could, without too much difficulty, impute such a meaning

*Job 41:25 (Zürcher Bibel); cf. 41:34 (Authorized and Revised Standard Version).
†Ezekiel 1:26.
**The naïve assumption that the creator of the world is a conscious being must be regarded as a disastrous prejudice which later gave rise to the most incredible dislocations of logic. For example, the nonsensical doctrine of the *privatio boni* would never have been necessary had one not had to assume in advance that it is impossible for the consciousness of a good God to produce evil deeds. Divine unconsciousness and lack of reflection, on the other hand, enable us to form a conception of God which puts his actions beyond moral judgment and allows no conflict to arise between goodness and beastliness.

to Job's speech. Be that as it may, Yahweh calmed down at last. The therapeutic measure of unresisting acceptance had proved its value yet again. Nevertheless, Yahweh is still somewhat nervous of Job's friends – they "have not spoken of me what is right."* The projection of his doubt-complex extends – comically enough, one must say – to these respectable and slightly pedantic old gentlemen, as though God-knows-what depended on what they thought. But the fact that men should think at all, and especially about him, is maddeningly disquieting and ought somehow to be stopped. It is far too much like the sort of thing his vagrant son is always springing on him, thus hitting him in his weakest spot. How often already has he bitterly regretted his unconsidered outbursts!

One can hardly avoid the impression that Omniscience is gradually drawing near to a realization, and is threatened with an insight that seems to be hedged about with fears of self-destruction. Fortunately, Job's final declaration is so formulated that one can assume with some certainty that, for the protagonists, the incident is closed for good and all.

We, the commenting chorus on this great tragedy, which has never at any time lost its vitality, do not feel quite like that. For our modern sensibilities it is by no means apparent that with Job's profound obeisance to the majesty of the divine presence, and his prudent silence, a real answer has been given to the question raised by the Satanic prank of a wager with God. Job has not so much answered as reacted in an adjusted way. In so doing he displayed remarkable self-discipline, but an unequivocal answer has still to be given.

To take the most obvious thing, what about the moral wrong Job has suffered? Is man so worthless in God's eyes that not even a *tort moral* can be inflicted on him? That contradicts the fact that man is desired by Yahweh and that it obviously matters to him whether men speak "right" of him or not. He needs Job's loyalty, and it means so much to him that he shrinks at nothing in carrying out his test. This attitude attaches an almost divine importance to man, for what else is there in the whole wide world that could mean anything to one who has everything? Yahweh's divided attitude,

*Job 42:7.

which on the one hand tramples on human life and happiness without regard, and on the other hand must have man for a partner, puts the latter in an impossible position. At one moment Yahweh behaves as irrationally as a cataclysm; the next moment he wants to be loved, honoured, worshipped, and praised as just. He reacts irritably to every word that has the faintest suggestion of criticism, while he himself does not care a straw for his own moral code if his actions happen to run counter to its statutes.

One can submit to such a God only with fear and trembling, and can try indirectly to propitiate the despot with unctuous praises and ostentatious obedience. But a relationship of trust seems completely out of the question to our modern way of thinking. Nor can moral satisfaction be expected from an unconscious nature god of this kind. Nevertheless, Job got his satisfaction, without Yahweh's intending it and possibly without himself knowing it, as the poet would have it appear. Yahweh's allocutions have the unthinking yet none the less transparent purpose of showing Job the brutal power of the demiurge: "This is I, the creator of all the ungovernable, ruthless forces of Nature, which are not subject to any ethical laws. I, too, am an amoral force of Nature, a purely phenomenal personality that cannot see its own back."

This is, or at any rate could be, a moral satisfaction of the first order for Job, because through this declaration man, in spite of his impotence, is set up as a judge over God himself. We do not know whether Job realizes this, but we do know from the numerous commentaries on Job that all succeeding ages have overlooked the fact that a kind of Moira or Dike rules over Yahweh, causing him to give himself away so blatantly. Anyone can see how he unwittingly raises Job by humiliating him in the dust. By so doing he pronounces judgment on himself and gives man the moral satisfaction whose absence we found so painful in the Book of Job.

The poet of this drama showed a masterly discretion in ringing down the curtain at the very moment when his hero gave unqualified recognition to the ἀπόφασις μεγάλη of the Demiurge by prostrating himself at the feet of His Divine Majesty. No other impression was permitted to remain. An unusual scandal was blowing up in the realm of metaphysics, with supposedly devastating consequences, and nobody was ready with a saving formula which would rescue the monotheistic conception of God from disaster. Even in those days the critical intellect of a Greek could easily have seized on this new addition to Yahweh's biography and used it in his disfavour (as indeed happened, though very much later) so as to mete out to him the fate that had already overtaken the Greek gods. But a relativization of God was utterly unthinkable at that time, and remained so for the next two thousand years.

The unconscious mind of man sees correctly even when conscious reason is blind and impotent. The drama has been consummated for all eternity: Yahweh's dual nature has been revealed, and somebody or something has seen and registered this fact. Such a revelation, whether it reached man's consciousness or not, could not fail to have far-reaching consequences.

The bodily assumption of Mary into heaven was defined as a dogma of the Catholic faith by Pope Pius XII in November 1950. Jung, who had examined the doctrine of the Trinity ("A Psychological Approach to the Dogma of the Trinity," CW 11, pars. 172–295) believed this to be "the most important religious event since the Reformation." For the new dogma adds a fourth figure to the Trinity, converting it into a quaternity. (See also Part 7 above, prayer 287-97.)

From *Answer to Job* CW 11, pars. 748–57

The promulgation of the new dogma of the Assumption of the Virgin Mary could, in itself, have been sufficient reason for examining the psychological background. It was interesting to note that, among the many articles published in the Catholic and Protestant press on the declaration of the dogma, there was not one, so far as I could see, which laid anything like the proper emphasis on what was undoubtedly the most powerful motive: namely, the popular movement and the psychological need behind it. Essentially, the writers of the articles were satisfied with learned considerations, dogmatic and historical, which have no bearing on the living religious process. But anyone who has followed with attention the visions of Mary which have been increasing in number over the last few decades, and has taken their psychological significance into account, might have known what was brewing. The fact, especially, that it was largely children who had the visions might have given pause for thought, for in such cases the collective unconscious is always at work. Incidentally, the Pope himself is rumoured to have had several visions of the Mother of God on the occasion of the declaration. One could have known for a long time that there was a deep longing in the masses for an intercessor and mediatrix who would at last take her place alongside the Holy Trinity and be received as the "Queen of Heaven and Bride at the heavenly court." For more than a thousand years it had been taken for granted that the Mother of God dwelt there, and we know from the Old Testament that Sophia was with God before the creation. From the ancient Egyptian theology of the divine Pharaohs we know that God wants to become man by means of a human mother, and it was recognized even in prehistoric times that the primordial divine being is both male and female. But such a truth eventuates in time only when it is solemnly proclaimed or rediscovered. It is psychologically significant for our day that in the year 1950 the heavenly bride was united with the bridegroom. In order to interpret this event, one has to consider not only the arguments adduced by the Papal Bull, but the prefigurations in the apocalyptic marriage of the Lamb and in the Old Testament anamnesis of Sophia. The nuptial union in the *thalamus* (bridal-chamber) signifies the *hieros gamos*, and this in turn is the first step towards incarnation, towards the birth of the saviour who, since antiquity, was thought of as the *filius solis et lunae*, the *filius sapientiae*, and the equivalent of Christ. When, therefore, a longing for the exaltation of the Mother of God passes through the people, this tendency, if thought to its logical conclusion, means the desire for the birth of a saviour, a peacemaker, a "mediator pacem faciens inter inimicos."* Although he is already born in the pleroma, his birth in time can only be accomplished when it is perceived, recognized, and declared by man.

The motive and content of the popular movement which contributed to the Pope's decision solemnly to declare the new

---

*"A mediator making peace between enemies."

dogma consist not in the birth of a new god, but in the continuing incarnation of God which began with Christ. Arguments based on historical criticism will never do justice to the new dogma; on the contrary, they are as lamentably wide of the mark as are the unqualified fears to which the English archbishops have given expression. In the first place, the declaration of the dogma has changed nothing in principle in the Catholic ideology as it has existed for more than a thousand years; and in the second place, the failure to understand that God has eternally wanted to become man, and for that purpose continually incarnates through the Holy Ghost in the temporal sphere, is an alarming symptom and can only mean that the Protestant standpoint has lost ground by not understanding the signs of the times and by ignoring the continued operation of the Holy Ghost. It is obviously out of touch with the tremendous archetypal happenings in the psyche of the individual and the masses, and with the symbols which are intended to compensate the truly apocalyptic world situation today.* It seems to have succumbed to a species of rationalistic historicism and to have lost any understanding of the Holy Ghost who works in the hidden places of the soul. It can therefore neither understand nor admit a further revelation of the divine drama.

This circumstance has given me, a layman in things theological, cause to put forward my views on these dark matters. My attempt is based on the psychological experience I have harvested during the course of a long life. I do not underestimate the psyche in any respect whatsoever, nor do I imagine for a moment that psychic happenings vanish into thin air by being explained. Psychologism represents a still primitive mode of magical thinking, with the help of which one hopes to conjure the reality of the soul out of existence, after the manner of the "Proktophantasmist" in *Faust*:

---

*The papal rejection of psychological symbolism may be explained by the fact that the Pope is primarily concerned with the reality of metaphysical happenings. Owing to the undervaluation of the psyche that everywhere prevails, every attempt at adequate psychological understanding is immediately suspected of psychologism. It is understandable that dogma must be protected from this danger. If, in physics, one seeks to explain the nature of light, nobody expects that as a result there will be no light. But in the case of psychology everybody believes that what it explains is explained away. However, I cannot expect that my particular deviationist point of view could be known in any competent quarter.

Are you still here? Nay, it's a thing unheard.
Vanish at once! We've said the enlightening word.

One would be very ill advised to identify me with such a childish standpoint. However, I have been asked so often whether I believe in the existence of God or not that I am somewhat concerned lest I be taken for an adherent of "psychologism" far more commonly than I suspect. What most people overlook or seem unable to understand is the fact that I regard the psyche as *real*. They believe only in physical facts, and must consequently come to the conclusion that either the uranium itself or the laboratory equipment created the atom bomb. That is no less absurd than the assumption that a non-real psyche is responsible for it. God is an obvious psychic and non-physical fact, i.e., a fact that can be established psychically but not physically. Equally, these people have still not got it into their heads that the psychology of religion falls into two categories, which must be sharply distinguished from one another: firstly, the psychology of the religious person, and secondly, the psychology of religion proper, i.e., of religious contents.

It is chiefly my experiences in the latter field which have given me the courage to enter into the discussion of the religious question and especially into the pros and cons of the dogma of the Assumption – which, by the way, I consider to be the most important religious event since the Reformation. It is a *petra scandali* for the unpsychological mind: how can such an unfounded assertion as the bodily reception of the Virgin into heaven be put forward as worthy of belief? But the method which the Pope uses in order to demonstrate the truth of the dogma makes sense to the psychological mind, because it bases itself firstly on the necessary prefigurations, and secondly on a tradition of religious assertions reaching back for more than a thousand years. Clearly, the material evidence for the existence of this psychic phenomenon is more than sufficient. It does not matter at all that a physically impossible fact is asserted, because all religious assertions are physical impossibilities. If they were not so, they would, as I said earlier, necessarily be treated in the text-books of natural science. But religious statements without exception have to do with the reality of the *psyche* and not with the reality of *physis*. What outrages the

Protestant standpoint in particular is the boundless approximation of the Deipara to the Godhead and, in consequence, the endangered supremacy of Christ, from which Protestantism will not budge. In sticking to this point it has obviously failed to consider that its hymnology is full of references to the "heavenly bridegroom," who is now suddenly supposed not to have a bride with equal rights. Or has, perchance, the "bridegroom," in true psychologistic manner, been understood as a mere metaphor?

The logical consistency of the papal declaration cannot be surpassed, and it leaves Protestantism with the odium of being nothing but a *man's religion* which allows no metaphysical representation of woman. In this respect it is similar to Mithraism, and Mithraism found this prejudice very much to its detriment. Protestantism has obviously not given sufficient attention to the signs of the times which point to the equality of women. But this equality requires to be metaphysically anchored in the figure of a "divine" woman, the bride of Christ. Just as the person of Christ cannot be replaced by an organization, so the bride cannot be replaced by the Church. The feminine, like the masculine, demands an equally personal representation.

The dogmatizing of the Assumption does not, however, according to the dogmatic view, mean that Mary has attained the status of a goddess, although, as mistress of heaven (as opposed to the prince of the sublunary aerial realm, Satan) and mediatrix, she is functionally on a par with Christ, the king and mediator. At any rate her position satisfies the need of the archetype. The new dogma expresses a renewed hope for the fulfilment of that yearning for peace which stirs deep down in the soul, and for a resolution of the threatening tension between the opposites. Everyone shares this tension and everyone experiences it in his individual form of unrest, the more so the less he sees any possibility of getting rid of it by rational means. It is no wonder, therefore, that the hope, indeed the expectation of divine intervention arises in the collective unconscious and at the same time in the masses. The papal declaration has given comforting expression to this yearning. How could Protestantism so completely miss the point? This lack of understanding can only be explained by the fact that the dogmatic symbols and hermeneutic allegories have lost their meaning for Protestant rationalism. This is also true, in some measure, of the opposition to the new dogma within the Catholic Church itself, or rather to the dogmatization of the old doctrine. Naturally, a certain degree of rationalism is better suited to Protestantism than it is to the Catholic outlook. The latter gives the archetypal symbolisms the necessary freedom and space in which to develop over the centuries while at the same time insisting on their original form, unperturbed by intellectual difficulties and the objections of rationalists. In this way the Catholic Church demonstrates her maternal character, because she allows the tree growing out of her matrix to develop according to its own laws. Protestantism, in contrast, is committed to the paternal spirit. Not only did it develop, at the outset, from an encounter with the worldly spirit of the times, but it continues this dialectic with the spiritual currents of every age; for the pneuma, in keeping with its original wind nature, is flexible, ever in living motion, comparable now to water, now to fire. It can desert its original haunts, can even go astray and get lost, if it succumbs too much to the spirit of the age. In order to fulfil its task, the Protestant spirit must be full of unrest and occasionally troublesome; it must even be revolutionary, so as to make sure that tradition has an influence on the change of contemporary values. The shocks it sustains during this encounter modify and at the same time enliven the tradition, which in its slow progress through the centuries would, without these disturbances, finally arrive at complete petrifaction and thus lose its effect. By merely criticizing and opposing certain developments within the Catholic Church, Protestantism would gain only a miserable bit of vitality, unless, mindful of the fact that Christianity consists of two separate camps, or rather, is a disunited brother-sister pair, it remembers that besides defending its own existence it must acknowledge Catholicism's right to exist too. A brother who for theological reasons wanted to cut the thread of his elder sister's life would rightly be called inhuman – to say nothing of Christian charity – and the converse is also true. Nothing is achieved by merely negative criticism. It is justified only to the degree that it is creative. Therefore it would seem profitable to me if, for example, Protestantism admitted that it is shocked by the new dogma not only because it throws a distressing light on the gulf between brother and sister, but because, for fundamental reasons, a situation has developed within Christianity which removes it further than ever from the sphere of worldly understanding. Protestantism knows, or could know, how much it owes its very existence to the Catholic Church. How much or how little does the Protestant still possess if he can no longer criticize or protest? In view of the intellectual *skandalon* which the new dogma represents, he should remind himself of his Christian responsibility – "Am I my brother's (or in this case, my sister's) keeper?" – and examine in all seriousness the reasons, explicit or otherwise, that decided the declaration of the new dogma. In so doing, he should guard against casting cheap aspersions and would do well to assume that there is more in it than papal arbitrariness. It would be desirable for the Protestant to understand that the new dogma has placed upon him a new responsibility towards the worldly spirit of our age, for he cannot simply deny his problematical sister before the eyes of the world. He must, even if he finds her antipathetic, be fair to her if he does not want to lose his self-respect. For instance, this is a favourable opportunity for him to ask himself, for a change, what is the meaning not only of the new dogma but of all more or less dogmatic assertions over and above their literal concretism. Considering the arbitrary and protean state of his own dogmas, and the precarious, schism-riven condition of his Church, he cannot afford to remain rigid and impervious to the spirit of the age. And since, moreover, in accordance with his obligations to the spirit, he is more concerned to come to terms with the world and its ideas than with God, it would seem clearly indicated that, on the occasion of the entry of the Mother of God into the heavenly bridal-chamber, he should bend to the great task of reinterpreting all the Christian traditions. If it is a question of truths which are anchored deep in the soul – and no one with the slightest insight can doubt this fact – then the solution of this task must be possible. For this we need the freedom of the spirit, which, as we know, is assured only in Protestantism. The dogma of the Assumption is a slap in the face for the historical and rationalistic view of the world, and would remain so for all time if one were to insist obstinately on the arguments of reason and history. This is a case, if ever there was one, where psychological understanding is needed, because the mythologem coming to light is so obvious that we must be deliberately blinding ourselves if we cannot see its symbolic nature and interpret it in symbolic terms.

The dogmatization of the *Assumptio Mariae* points to the *hieros gamos* in the pleroma, and this in turn implies, as we have said, the future birth of the divine child, who, in accordance with the divine trend towards incarnation, will choose as his birthplace the empirical man. The metaphysical process is known to the psychology of the unconscious as the individuation process. In so far as this process, as a rule, runs its course unconsciously as it has from time immemorial, it means no more than that the acorn becomes an oak, the calf a cow, and the child an adult. But if the individuation process is made conscious, consciousness must confront the unconscious and a balance between the opposites must be found. As this is not possible through logic, one is dependent on *symbols* which make the irrational union of opposites possible. They are produced spontaneously by the unconscious and are amplified by the conscious mind. The central symbols of this process describe the self, which is man's totality, consisting on the one hand of that which is conscious to him, and on the other hand of the contents of the unconscious. The self is the τέλειος ἄνθρωπος, the whole man, whose symbols are the divine child and its synonyms. This is only a very summary sketch of the process, but it can be observed at any time in modern man, or one can read about it in the documents of Hermetic philosophy from the Middle Ages. The parallelism between the symbols is astonishing to anyone who knows both the psychology of the unconscious and alchemy.

The difference between the "natural" individuation process, which runs its course unconsciously, and the one which is consciously realized, is tremendous. In the first case consciousness nowhere intervenes; the end remains as dark as the beginning. In the second case so much darkness comes to light that the personality is permeated with light, and consciousness necessarily gains in scope and insight. The encounter between conscious and unconscious has to ensure that the light which shines in the darkness is not only comprehended by the darkness, but comprehends it. The *filius solis et lunae* is the possibility as well as the symbol of the union of opposites. It is the alpha and omega of the process, the mediator and intermedius. "It has a thousand names," say the alchemists, meaning that the source from which the individuation process rises and the goal towards which it aims is nameless, ineffable.

It is only through the psyche that we can establish that God acts upon us, but we are unable to distinguish whether these actions emanate from God or from the unconscious. We cannot tell whether God and the unconscious are two different entities. Both are border-line concepts for transcendental contents. But empirically it can be established, with a sufficient degree of probability, that there is in the unconscious an archetype of wholeness which manifests itself spontaneously in dreams, etc., and a tendency, independent of the conscious will, to relate other archetypes to this centre. Consequently, it does not seem improbable that the archetype of wholeness occupies as such a central position which approximates it to the God-image. The similarity is further borne out by the peculiar fact that the archetype produces a symbolism which has always characterized and expressed the Deity. These facts make possible a certain qualification of our above thesis concerning the indistinguishableness of God and the unconscious. Strictly speaking, the God-image does not coincide with the unconscious as such, but with a special content of it, namely the archetype of the self. It is this archetype from which we can no longer distinguish the God-image empirically. We can arbitrarily postulate a difference between these two entities, but that does not help us at all. On the contrary, it only helps us to separate man from God, and prevents God from becoming man. Faith is certainly right when it impresses on man's mind and heart how infinitely far away and inaccessible God is; but it also teaches his nearness, his immediate presence, and it is just this nearness which has to be empirically real if it is not to lose all significance. Only that which acts upon me do I recognize as real and actual. But that which has no effect upon me might as well not exist. The religious need longs for wholeness, and therefore lays hold of the images of wholeness offered by the unconscious, which, independently of the conscious mind, rise up from the depths of our psychic nature.

Part 9. "*Unus Mundus*" and Synchronicity

Jung, in common with other thinkers at different periods of history, believed in an ultimate unity of all existence. Using the terminology of medieval philosophy, he referred to this as the unus mundus. *This unity is outside the human categories of time and space, and beyond our separation of reality into physical and mental. In* Psychology and Alchemy *Jung writes of*

> actualizing those contents of the unconscious which are outside nature, i.e. not a datum of our empirical world, and therefore an *a priori* of archetypal character. The place or the medium of realization is neither mind nor matter, but that intermediate realm of subtle reality which can adequately be expressed only by the symbol. [CW 12, par. 400]

If our categories of physical and mental are artificial, "objective" events and states of mind may be interrelated. Jung certainly believed that archetypes manifested themselves, at least occasionally, in physical events and in states of mind at the same time. *He named this phenomenon* synchronicity.

From "**Flying Saucers: a Modern Myth of Things Seen in the Skies**" CW 10, pars. 779–80

Thus it is a fact of singular importance that number also characterizes the "personal" nature of the mediating figure, that it appears as a mediator. From the psychological standpoint, and having regard to the limits set to all scientific knowledge, I have called the mediating or "uniting" symbol which necessarily proceeds from a sufficiently great tension of opposites the "self." I chose this term in order to make clear that I am concerned primarily with the formulation of empirical facts and not with dubious incursions into metaphysics. There I would trespass upon all manner of religious convictions. Living in the West, I would have to say Christ instead of "self," in the Near East it would be Khidr, in the Far East atman or Tao or the Buddha, in the Far West maybe a hare or Mondamin, and in cabalism it would be Tifereth. Our world has shrunk, and it is dawning on us that humanity is *one*, with *one* psyche. Humility is a not inconsiderable virtue which should prompt Christians, for the sake of charity – the greatest of all virtues – to set a good example and acknowledge that though there is only *one* truth it speaks in many tongues, and that if we still cannot see this it is simply due to lack of understanding. No one is so godlike that he alone knows the true word. All of us gaze into that "dark glass" in which the dark myth takes shape, adumbrating the invisible truth. In this glass the eyes of the spirit glimpse an image which we call the self, fully conscious of the fact that it is an anthropomorphic image which we have merely named but not explained. By "self" we mean psychic wholeness, but what realities underlie this concept we do not know, because psychic contents cannot be observed in their unconscious state, and moreover the psyche cannot know itself. The conscious can know the unconscious only so far as it has become conscious. We have only a very hazy idea of the changes an unconscious content undergoes in the process of becoming conscious, but no certain knowledge. The concept of psychic wholeness necessarily implies an element of transcendence on account of the existence of unconscious components. Transcendence in this sense is not equivalent to a metaphysical postulate or hypostasis; it claims to be no more than a borderline concept, to quote Kant.

That there is something beyond the borderline, beyond the frontiers of knowledge, is shown by the archetypes and, most clearly of all, by numbers, which this side of the border are quantities but on the other side are autonomous psychic entities, capable of making qualitative statements which manifest themselves in *a priori* patterns of order. These patterns include not only causally explicable phenomena like dream-symbols and such, but remarkable relativizations of time and space which simply cannot be explained causally. They are the parapsychological phenomena which I have summed up under the term "synchronicity" and which have been statistically investigated by Rhine. The positive results of his experiments elevate these phenomena to the rank of undeniable facts. This brings us a little nearer to understanding the mystery of psychophysical parallelism, for we now know that a factor exists which mediates between the apparent incommensurability of body and psyche, giving matter a kind of "psychic" faculty and the psyche a kind of "materiality," by means of which the one can work on the other. That the body can work on the psyche seems to be a truism, but strictly speaking all we know is that any bodily defect or illness also expresses itself psychically. Naturally this assumption only holds good if, contrary to the popular materialistic view, the psyche is credited with an existence of its own. But materialism in its turn cannot explain how chemical changes can produce a psyche. Both views, the materialistic as well as the spiritualistic, are metaphysical prejudices. It accords better with experience to suppose that living matter has a psychic aspect, and the psyche a physical aspect. If we give due consideration to the facts of parapsychology, then the hypothesis of the psychic aspect must be extended beyond the sphere of biochemical processes to matter in general. In that case all reality would be grounded on an as yet unknown substrate possessing material and at the same time psychic qualities. In view of the trend of modern theoretical physics, this assumption should arouse fewer resistances than before. It would also do away with the awkward hypothesis of psychophysical parallelism, and afford us an opportunity to construct a new world model closer to the idea of the *unus mundus*. The "acausal" correspondences between mutually independent psychic and physical events, i.e., synchronistic phenomena, and in particular psychokinesis, would then become more understandable, for every physical event would involve a psychic one and vice versa. Such reflections are not idle speculations; they are forced on us in any serious psychological investigation of the Ufo phenomenon.

Jung's collaboration with the physicist Wolfgang Pauli (The Interpretation of Nature and the Psyche, *London and New York, 1955) led to the recognition of a shared problem. Jung repeatedly emphasized*

*the fact that, in psychology, the observer could not be separated from
what he observed, and that making the contents of the unconscious
conscious altered the way in which each functioned. Modern physicists,
trying to observe the behaviour of minute particles, found that their
observations altered the behaviour of the particles. As Pauli writes: "In
microphysics, however, the natural laws are of such a kind that every
bit of knowledge gained from a measurement must be paid for by the
loss of other, complementary items of knowledge." ("The Influence of
Archetypal Ideas on Kepler's Theories," p. 211) Both physicist and
psychologist, therefore, are up against the problem of defining an
objective order of nature. Pauli also points out that scientific laws and
theories are not derived entirely from the observation of the external
world, but that "intuition and the direction of attention play a
considerable role in the development of the concepts and ideas." (ibid.,
p. 151) Pauli writes: "It seems most satisfactory to introduce at this
point the postulate of a cosmic order independent of our choice and
distinct from the world of phenomena." (ibid., p. 152)*

From "**The Conjunction**" *Mysterium Coniunctionis*, CW 14, pars.
767–80

If Dorn, then, saw the consummation of the mysterium
coniunctionis in the union of the alchemically produced *caelum*
with the *unus mundus*, he expressly meant not a fusion of the
individual with his environment, or even his adaptation to it, but
a *unio mystica* with the potential world. Such a view indeed seems
to us "mystical," if we misuse this word in its pejorative modern
sense. It is not, however, a question of thoughtlessly used words
but of a view which can be translated from medieval language into
modern concepts. Undoubtedly the idea of the *unus mundus* is
founded on the assumption that the multiplicity of the empirical
world rests on an underlying unity, and that not two or more
fundamentally different worlds exist side by side or are mingled
with one another. Rather, everything divided and different
belongs to one and the same world, which is not the world of sense
but a postulate whose probability is vouched for by the fact that
until now no one has been able to discover a world in which the
known laws of nature are invalid. That even the psychic world,

which is so extraordinarily different from the physical world, does not have its roots outside the one cosmos is evident from the undeniable fact that causal connections exist between the psyche and the body which point to their underlying unitary nature.

All that *is* is not encompassed by our knowledge, so that we are not in a position to make any statements about its total nature. Microphysics is feeling its way into the unknown side of matter, just as complex psychology is pushing forward into the unknown side of the psyche. Both lines of investigation have yielded findings which can be conceived only by means of antinomies, and both have developed concepts which display remarkable analogies. If this trend should become more pronounced in the future, the hypothesis of the unity of their subject-matters would gain in probability. Of course there is little or no hope that the unitary Being can ever be conceived, since our powers of thought and language permit only of antinomian statements. But this much we do know beyond all doubt, that empirical reality has a transcendental background – a fact which, as Sir James Jeans has shown, can be expressed by Plato's parable of the cave. The common background of microphysics and depth-psychology is as much physical as psychic and therefore neither, but rather a third thing, a neutral nature which can at most be grasped in hints since in essence it is transcendental.

The background of our empirical world thus appears to be in fact a *unus mundus*. This is at least a probable hypothesis which satisfies the fundamental tenet of scientific theory: "Explanatory principles are not to be multiplied beyond the necessary." The transcendental psychophysical background corresponds to a "potential world" in so far as all those conditions which determine the form of empirical phenomena are inherent in it. This obviously holds good as much for physics as for psychology, or, to be more precise, for macrophysics as much as for the psychology of consciousness.

A further extract illustrating Jung's collaboration with Pauli may help to clarify his conception.

From "**On the Nature of the Psyche**" CW 8, pars. 439–40

The application of statistical laws to processes of atomic magnitude in physics has a noteworthy correspondence in psychology, so far as psychology investigates the bases of consciousness by pursuing the conscious processes until they lose themselves in darkness and unintelligibility, and nothing more can be seen but effects which have an *organizing* influence on the contents of consciousness.* Investigation of these effects yields the singular fact that they proceed from an unconscious, i.e., objective, reality which behaves at the same time like a subjective one – in other words, like a consciousness. Hence the reality underlying the unconscious effects includes the observing subject and is therefore constituted in a way that we cannot conceive. It is, at one and the same time, absolute subjectivity and universal truth, for in principle it can be shown to be present everywhere, which certainly cannot be said of conscious contents of a personalistic nature. The elusiveness, capriciousness, haziness, and uniqueness that the lay mind always associates with the idea of the psyche applies only to consciousness, and not to the absolute

*It may interest the reader to hear the opinion of a physicist on this point. Professor Pauli, who was good enough to glance through the ms. of this supplement, writes: "As a matter of fact the physicist would expect a psychological correspondence at this point, because the epistemological situation with regard to the concepts 'conscious' and 'unconscious' seems to offer a pretty close analogy to the undermentioned 'complementarity' situation in physics. On the one hand the unconscious can only be inferred indirectly from its (organizing) effects on conscious contents. On the other hand every 'observation of the unconscious,' i.e., every conscious realization of unconscious contents, has an uncontrollable reactive effect on these same contents (which as we know precludes in principle the possibility of 'exhausting' the unconscious by making it conscious). Thus the physicist will conclude *per analogiam* that this uncontrollable reactive effect of the observing subject on the unconscious limits the objective character of the latter's reality and lends it at the same time a certain subjectivity. Although the *position* of the 'cut' between conscious and unconscious is (at least up to a point) left to the free choice of the 'psychological experimenter,' the *existence* of this 'cut' remains an unavoidable necessity. Accordingly, from the standpoint of the psychologist, the 'observed system' would consist not of physical objects only, but would also include the unconscious, while consciousness would be assigned the role of 'observing medium.' It is undeniable that the development of 'microphysics' has brought the way in which nature is described in this science very much closer to that of the newer psychology: but whereas the former, on account of the basic 'complementarity' situation, is faced with the impossibility of eliminating the effects of the observer by determinable correctives, and has therefore to abandon in principle any objective understanding of physical phenomena, the latter can supplement the purely subjective psychology of consciousness by postulating the existence of an unconscious that possesses a large measure of objective reality."

unconscious. The qualitatively rather than quantitatively definable units with which the unconscious works, namely the archetypes, therefore have a nature that *cannot with certainty be designated as psychic.*

Although I have been led by purely psychological considerations to doubt the exclusively psychic nature of the archetypes, psychology sees itself obliged to revise its "only psychic" assumptions in the light of the physical findings too. Physics has demonstrated, as plainly as could be wished, that in the realm of atomic magnitudes an observer is postulated in objective reality, and that only on this condition is a satisfactory scheme of explanation possible. This means that a subjective element attaches to the physicist's world picture, and secondly that a connection necessarily exists between the psyche to be explained and the objective space-time continuum. Since the physical continuum is inconceivable it follows that we can form no picture of its psychic aspect either, which also necessarily exists. Nevertheless, the relative or partial identity of psyche and physical continuum is of the greatest importance theoretically, because it brings with it a tremendous simplification by bridging over the seeming incommensurability between the physical world and the psychic, not of course in any concrete way, but from the physical side by means of mathematical equations, and from the psychological side by means of empirically derived postulates – archetypes – whose content, if any, cannot be represented to the mind. Archetypes, so far as we can observe and experience them at all, manifest themselves only through their ability to *organize* images and ideas, and this is always an unconscious process which cannot be detected until afterwards. By assimilating ideational material whose provenance in the phenomenal world is not to be contested, they become visible and *psychic.* Therefore they are recognized at first only as psychic entities and are conceived as such, with the same right with which we base the physical phenomena of immediate perception on Euclidean space. Only when it comes to explaining psychic phenomena of a minimal degree of clarity are we driven to assume that archetypes must have a nonpsychic aspect. Grounds for such a conclusion are supplied by the phenomena of synchronicity, which are associated with the activity of unconscious operators and have hitherto been regarded, or repudiated, as "telepathy," etc.* Scepticism should, however, be levelled only at incorrect theories and not at facts which exist in their own right. No unbiased observer can deny them. Resistance to the recognition of such facts rests principally on the repugnance people feel for an allegedly supernatural faculty tacked on to the psyche, like "clairvoyance." The very diverse and confusing aspects of these phenomena are, so far as I can see at present, completely explicable on the assumption of a psychically relative space-time continuum. As soon as a psychic content crosses the threshold of consciousness, the synchronistic marginal phenomena disappear, time and space resume their accustomed sway, and consciousness is once more isolated in its subjectivity. We have here one of those instances which can best be understood in terms of the physicist's idea of "complementarity." When an unconscious content passes over into consciousness its synchronistic manifestation ceases; conversely, synchronistic phenomena can be evoked by putting the subject into an unconscious state (trance). The same relationship of complementarity can be observed just as easily in all those extremely common medical cases in which certain clinical symptoms disappear when the corresponding unconscious contents are made conscious. We also know that a number of psychosomatic phenomena which are otherwise outside the control of the will can be induced by hypnosis, that is, by this same restriction of consciousness. Professor Pauli formulates the physical side of the complementarity relationship here expressed, as follows: "It rests with the free choice of the experimenter (or observer) to decide ... which insights he will gain and which he will lose; or, to put it in popular language, whether he will measure A and ruin B or ruin A and measure B. It does *not* rest with him, however, to gain only insights and not lose any." This is particularly true of the relation between the physical standpoint and the psychological. Physics determines quantities and their relation to one another; psychology determines qualities without being able to measure quantities. Despite that, both sciences arrive at ideas which come significantly close to one another. The parallelism of psychological and physical explanations has already

*The physicist Pascual Jordan ("Positivistische Bemerkungen über die parapsychischen Erscheinungen," *Zentralblatt für Psychotherapie*, IX, Leipzig, 1956, 14 ff.) has already used the idea of relative space to explain telepathic phenomena.

been pointed out by C. A. Meier in his essay "Moderne Physik – Moderne Psychologie."* He says: "Both sciences have, in the course of many years of independent work, amassed observations and systems of thought to match them. Both sciences have come up against certain barriers which ... display similar basic characteristics. The object to be investigated, and the human investigator with his organs of sense and knowledge and their extensions (measuring instruments and procedures), are indissolubly bound together. That is complementarity in physics as well as in psychology." Between physics and psychology there is in fact "a genuine and authentic relationship of complementarity."

In his long essay "Synchronicity: an Acausal Connecting Principle," Jung gives examples of what he means by synchronous events.

From "**Synchronicity: an Acausal Connecting Principle**" CW 8, pars. 843–5

The problem of synchronicity has puzzled me for a long time, ever since the middle twenties,† when I was investigating the phenomena of the collective unconscious and kept on coming across connections which I simply could not explain as chance groupings or "runs." What I found were "coincidences" which were connected so meaningfully that their "chance" concurrence would represent a degree of improbability that would have to be expressed by an astronomical figure. By way of example, I shall mention an incident from my own observation. A young woman I was treating had, at a critical moment, a dream in which she was given a golden scarab. While she was telling me this dream I sat

*Die Kulturelle Bedeutung der komplexen Psychologie, Berlin, 1935.
†Even before that time certain doubts had arisen in me as to the unlimited applicability of the causal principle in psychology. In the foreword to the 1st edn. of Collected Papers on Analytical Psychology, I had written (p. ix): "Causality is only one principle and psychology essentially cannot be exhausted by causal methods only, because the mind [= psyche] lives by aims as well." Psychic finality rests on a "pre-existent" meaning which becomes problematical only when it is an unconscious arrangement. In that case we have to suppose a "knowledge" prior to all consciousness. Hans Driesch comes to the same conclusion (Die "Seele" als elementarer Naturfaktor, Leipzig, 1903, pp. 8off.).

with my back to the closed window. Suddenly I heard a noise behind me, like a gentle tapping. I turned round and saw a flying insect knocking against the window-pane from outside. I opened the window and caught the creature in the air as it flew in. It was the nearest analogy to a golden scarab that one finds in our latitudes, a scarabaeid beetle, the common rose-chafer (*Cetonia aurata*), which contrary to its usual habits had evidently felt an urge to get into a dark room at this particular moment. I must admit that nothing like it ever happened to me before or since, and that the dream of the patient has remained unique in my experience.

I should like to mention another case that is typical of a certain category of events. The wife of one of my patients, a man in his fifties, once told me in conversation that, at the deaths of her mother and her grandmother, a number of birds gathered outside the windows of the death-chamber. I had heard similar stories from other people. When her husband's treatment was nearing its end, his neurosis having been cleared up, he developed some apparently quite innocuous symptoms which seemed to me, however, to be those of heart-disease. I sent him along to a specialist, who after examining him told me in writing that he could find no cause for anxiety. On the way back from this consultation (with the medical report in his pocket) my patient collapsed in the street. As he was brought home dying, his wife was already in a great state of anxiety because, soon after her husband had gone to the doctor, a whole flock of birds alighted on their house. She naturally remembered the similar incidents that had happened at the death of her own relatives, and feared the worst.

Although I was personally acquainted with the people concerned and know very well that the facts here reported are true, I do not imagine for a moment that this will induce anybody who is determined to regard such things as pure "chance" to change his mind. My sole object in relating these two incidents is simply to give some indication of how meaningful coincidences usually present themselves in practical life. The meaningful connection is obvious enough in the first case in view of the approximate identity of the chief objects (the scarab and the beetle); but in the second case the death and the flock of birds seem to be incommensurable with one another. If one considers, however, that in the Babylonian Hades the souls wore a "feather dress," and that in ancient Egypt the *ba*, or soul, was thought of as a bird,★ it is not too far-fetched to suppose that there may be some archetypal symbolism at work. Had such an incident occurred in a dream, that interpretation would be justified by the comparative psychological material. There also seems to be an archetypal foundation to the first case. It was an extraordinarily difficult case to treat, and up to the time of the dream little or no progress had been made. I should explain that the main reason for this was my patient's animus, which was steeped in Cartesian philosophy and clung so rigidly to its own idea of reality that the efforts of three doctors – I was the third – had not been able to weaken it. Evidently something quite irrational was needed which was beyond my powers to produce. The dream alone was enough to disturb ever so slightly the rationalistic attitude of my patient. But when the "scarab" came flying in through the window in actual fact, her natural being could burst through the armour of her animus possession and the process of transformation could at last begin to move. Any essential change of attitude signifies a psychic renewal which is usually accompanied by symbols of rebirth in the patient's dreams and fantasies. The scarab is a classic example of a rebirth symbol. The ancient Egyptian Book of What Is in the Netherworld describes how the dead sun-god changes himself at the tenth station into Khepri, the scarab, and then, at the twelfth station, mounts the barge which carries the rejuvenated sun-god into the morning sky. The only difficulty here is that with educated people cryptomnesia often cannot be ruled out with certainty (although my patient did not happen to know this symbol). But this does not alter the fact that the psychologist is continually coming up against cases where the emergence of symbolic parallels† cannot be explained without the hypothesis of the collective unconscious.

Jung took over from Gnostic theology the term "pleroma," which is defined in the OED as "the abode of God and of the totality of the Divine powers and emanations." In the Septem Sermones ad

---

★In Homer the souls of the dead "twitter."

†Naturally these can only be verified when the doctor himself has the necessary knowledge of symbology.

Mortuos, *written during the period of mental stress which Jung experienced during the First World War, he writes:*

> A thing that is infinite and eternal hath no qualities, since it hath all qualities. This nothingness or fullness we name the PLEROMA. Therein both thinking and being cease, since the eternal and infinite possess no qualities. In it no being is, for he then would be distinct from the pleroma, and would possess qualities which would distinguish him as something distinct from the pleroma. In the pleroma there is nothing and everything. It is quite fruitless to think about the pleroma, for this would mean self-dissolution. [*Sermo* I]

The opposites are contained in the pleroma, but because they are equally balanced, they are void. Although the opposites are manifested in individuals, they are not balanced and void. The individual's task is to pursue his own distinctiveness, and this involves him in distinguishing himself from the opposites.

> We labour to attain to the good and beautiful, yet at the same time we also lay hold of the evil and ugly, since in the pleroma these are one with the good and the beautiful. When, however, we remain true to our own nature, which is distinctiveness, we distinguish ourselves from the good and the beautiful, and, therefore, at the same time, from the evil and the ugly. And thus we fall not into the pleroma, namely into nothingness and dissolution. [*Sermo* I]

In Answer to Job, *Jung writes:*

> In the pleromatic or (as the Tibetans call it) Bardo state, there is a perfect interplay of cosmic forces, but with the Creation – that is, with the division of the world into distinct processes in space and time – events begin to rub and jostle one another. [CW 11, par. 620]

This preamble may help to clarify Jung's view as to the autonomy of archetypes.

From *Answer to Job*, CW 11, pars. 629–31

Although the birth of Christ is an event that occurred but once in history, it has always existed in eternity. For the layman in these matters, the identity of a nontemporal, eternal event with a unique historical occurrence is something that is extremely difficult to conceive. He must, however, accustom himself to the idea that "time" is a relative concept and needs to be complemented by that of the "simultaneous" existence, in the Bardo or pleroma, of all historical processes. What exists in the pleroma as an eternal process appears in time as an aperiodic sequence, that is to say, it is repeated many times in an irregular pattern. To take but one example: Yahweh had one good son and one who was a failure. Cain and Abel, Jacob and Esau, correspond to this prototype, and so, in all ages and in all parts of the world, does the motif of the hostile brothers, which in innumerable modern variants still causes dissension in families and keeps the psychotherapist busy. Just as many examples, no less instructive, could be found for the two women prefigured in eternity. When these things occur as modern variants, therefore, they should not be regarded merely as personal episodes, moods, or chance idiosyncrasies in people, but as fragments of the pleromatic process itself, which, broken up into individual events occurring in time, is an essential component or aspect of the divine drama.

When Yahweh created the world from his *prima materia*, the "Void," he could not help breathing his own mystery into the Creation which is himself in every part, as every reasonable theology has long been convinced. From this comes the belief that it is possible to know God from his Creation. When I say that he could not help doing this, I do not imply any limitation of his omnipotence; on the contrary, it is an acknowledgment that all possibilities are contained in him, and that there are in consequence no other possibilities than those which express him.

All the world is God's, and God is in all the world from the very beginning. Why, then, the *tour de force* of the Incarnation? one asks oneself, astonished. God is in everything already, and yet there must be something missing if a sort of second entrance into Creation has now to be staged with so much care and circumspection. Since Creation is universal, reaching to the remotest stellar galaxies, and since it has also made organic life infinitely variable and capable of endless differentiation, we can hardly see where the defect lies. The fact that Satan has everywhere intruded his corrupting influence is no doubt regrettable for many reasons, but it makes no difference in principle. It is not easy to give an answer to this question. One would like to say that Christ had to appear in order to deliver mankind from evil. But when one considers that evil was originally slipped into the scheme of things by Satan, and still is, then it would seem much simpler if Yahweh would, for once, call this "practical joker" severely to account, get rid of his pernicious influence, and thus eliminate the root of all evil. He would then not need the elaborate arrangement of a special Incarnation with all the unforeseeable consequences which this entails. One should make clear to oneself what it means when God becomes man. It means nothing less than a world-shaking transformation of God. It means more or less what Creation meant in the beginning, namely an objectivation of God. At the time of the Creation he revealed himself in Nature; now he wants to be more specific and become man. It must be admitted, however, that there was a tendency in this direction right from the start. For, when those other human beings, who had evidently been created before Adam, appeared on the scene along with the higher mammals, Yahweh created on the following day, by a special act of creation, a man who was the image of God. This was the first prefiguration of his becoming man. He took Adam's descendants, especially the people of Israel, into his personal possession, and from time to time he filled this people's prophets with his spirit. All these things were preparatory events and symptoms of a tendency within God to become man. But in omniscience there had existed from all eternity a knowledge of the human nature of God or of the divine nature of man. That is why, long before Genesis was written, we find corresponding testimonies in the ancient Egyptian records. These intimations and prefigurations of the Incarnation must strike one as either completely incomprehensible or superfluous, since all creation *ex nihilo* is God's and consists of nothing but God, with the result that man, like the rest of creation, is simply God become concrete. Prefigurations, however, are not in themselves creative events, but are only stages in the process of becoming conscious. It was only quite late that we realized (or rather, are beginning to realize) that God is Reality itself and therefore – last but not least – man. This realization is a millennial process.

Jung's conception of "the millennial process" referred to in the last extract may help us to understand why he believed that a profound change was about to take place in man's conception of himself and the universe. Traditionally, the reign of Christ ended with the first millennium, to be succeeded by the reign of Antichrist. This is now nearing its end, coinciding with the entry of the vernal equinox into Aquarius, and the end of the aeon of Pisces.

From "**Flying Saucers: a Modern Myth of Things Seen in the Skies**" CW 10, pars. 589–90

It is difficult to form a correct estimate of the significance of contemporary events, and the danger that our judgment will remain caught in subjectivity is great. So I am fully aware of the risk I am taking in proposing to communicate my views concerning certain contemporary events, which seem to me important, to those who are patient enough to hear me. I refer to those reports reaching us from all corners of the earth, rumours of round objects that flash through the troposphere and stratosphere and go by the name of Flying Saucers, *soucoupes*, disks, and "Ufos" (Unidentified Flying Objects). These rumours, or the possible physical existence of such objects, seem to me so significant that I feel myself compelled, as once before* when events of fateful consequence were brewing for Europe, to sound a note of warning. I know that, just as before, my voice is much too weak to reach the ear of the multitude. It is not presumption that drives me, but my conscience as a psychiatrist that bids me fulfil my duty and prepare those few who will hear me for coming events which are in accord with the end of an era. As we know from ancient Egyptian history, they are manifestations of psychic changes which always appear at the end of one Platonic month and at the beginning of another. Apparently they are changes in the constellation of

*"Wotan" (CW 10), pars. 371–99.

psychic dominants, of the archetypes, or "gods" as they used to be called, which bring about, or accompany, long-lasting transformations of the collective psyche. This transformation started in the historical era and left its traces first in the passing of the aeon of Taurus into that of Aries, and then of Aries into Pisces, whose beginning coincides with the rise of Christianity. We are now nearing that great change which may be expected when the spring-point enters Aquarius.

It would be frivolous of me to try to conceal from the reader that such reflections are not only exceedingly unpopular but even come perilously close to those turbid fantasies which becloud the minds of world-reformers and other interpreters of "signs and portents." But I must take this risk, even if it means putting my hard-won reputation for truthfulness, reliability, and capacity for scientific judgment in jeopardy. I can assure my readers that I do not do this with a light heart. I am, to be quite frank, concerned for all those who are caught unprepared by the events in question and disconcerted by their incomprehensible nature. Since, so far as I know, no one has yet felt moved to examine and set forth the possible psychic consequences of this foreseeable astrological change, I deem it my duty to do what I can in this respect. I undertake this thankless task in the expectation that my chisel will make no impression on the hard stone it encounters.

In a letter to Father Victor White, Jung refers to the same approaching change.

From **Letters**, vol. 2, pp. 167–8

[BOLLINGEN, 10 APRIL 1954]

The symbolic history of the Christ's life shows, as the essential teleological tendency, the crucifixion, viz. the union of Christ with the symbol of the tree. It is no longer a matter of an impossible reconciliation of Good and Evil, but of man with his vegetative (=unconscious) life. In the case of the Christian symbol the tree however is dead and man upon the Cross is going to die, i.e., the solution of the problem takes place after death. That is so as far as Christian truth goes. But it is possible that the Christian symbolism expresses man's mental condition in the aeon of Pisces, as the ram and the bull gods do for the ages of Aries and Taurus. In this case the post-mortal solution would be symbolic of an entirely new psychological status, viz. that of Aquarius, which is certainly a oneness, presumably that of the Anthropos, the realization of Christ's allusion: *"Dii estis."*★ This is a formidable secret and difficult to understand, because it means that man will be essentially God and God man. The signs pointing in this direction consist in the fact that the cosmic power of self-destruction is given into the hands of man and that man inherits the dual nature of the Father. He will [mis]understand it and he will be tempted to ruin the universal life of the earth by radioactivity. Materialism and atheism, the negation of God, are indirect means to attain this goal. Through the negation of God one becomes deified, i.e., god-almighty-like, and then one knows what is good for mankind. That is how destruction begins. The intellectual schoolmasters in the Kremlin are a classic example. The danger of following the same path is very great indeed. It begins with the lie, i.e., the projection of the shadow.

There is need of people knowing about their shadow, because there must be somebody who does not project. They ought to be in a visible position where they would be expected to project and unexpectedly they do not project! They can thus set a visible example which would not be seen if they were invisible.

★"Ye are gods." John 10:34.

Part 10. Man and His Future

Throughout his long life, Jung commented on the state of society as well as pursuing his investigations into the psychology of the unconscious. A late work, published in 1957, once again affirms Jung's belief in the importance of the individual, and suggests that individual self-knowledge and the capacity for human relationships which this brings is the only power strong enough to resist the collective dominance of the State. "The Undiscovered Self" seems an appropriate essay with which to end this selection from the works of C. G. Jung.

"The Undiscovered Self (Present and Future)" CW 10, pars. 488–588

1. THE PLIGHT OF THE INDIVIDUAL IN MODERN SOCIETY

What will the future bring? From time immemorial this question has occupied men's minds, though not always to the same degree. Historically, it is chiefly in times of physical, political, economic, and spiritual distress that men's eyes turn with anxious hope to the future, and when anticipations, utopias, and apocalyptic visions multiply. One thinks, for instance, of the chiliastic expectations of the Augustan age at the beginning of the Christian era, or of the spiritual changes in the West which accompanied the end of the first millennium. Today, as the end of the second millennium draws near, we are again living in an age filled with apocalyptic images of universal destruction. What is the significance of that split, symbolized by the "Iron Curtain," which divides humanity into two halves? What will become of our civilization, and of man himself, if the hydrogen bombs begin to go off, or if the spiritual and moral darkness of State absolutism should spread over Europe?

We have no reason to take this threat lightly. Everywhere in the West there are subversive minorities who, sheltered by our humanitarianism and our sense of justice, hold the incendiary torches ready, with nothing to stop the spread of their ideas except the critical reason of a single, fairly intelligent, mentally stable stratum of the population. One should not overestimate the thickness of this stratum. It varies from country to country in accordance with national temperament. Also, it is regionally dependent on public education and is subject to the influence of acutely disturbing factors of a political and economic nature. Taking plebiscites as a criterion, one could on an optimistic estimate put its upper limit at about forty per cent of the electorate. A rather more pessimistic view would not be unjustified either, since the gift of reason and critical reflection is not one of man's outstanding peculiarities, and even where it exists it proves to be wavering and inconstant, the more so, as a rule, the bigger the political groups are. The mass crushes out the insight and reflection that are still possible with the individual, and this necessarily leads to doctrinaire and authoritarian tyranny if ever the constitutional State should succumb to a fit of weakness.

Rational argument can be conducted with some prospect of success only so long as the emotionality of a given situation does not exceed a certain critical degree. If the affective temperature rises above this level, the possibility of reason's having any effect ceases and its place is taken by slogans and chimerical wish-fantasies. That is to say, a sort of collective possession results which rapidly develops into a psychic epidemic. Under these conditions all those elements whose existence is merely tolerated as asocial under the rule of reason come to the top. Such individuals are by no means rare curiosities to be met with only in prisons and lunatic asylums. For every manifest case of insanity there are, in my estimation, at least ten latent cases who seldom get to the point of breaking out openly but whose views and behaviour, for all their appearance of normality, are influenced unconsciously by patho-logical and perverse factors. There are, of course, no medical statistics on the frequency of latent psychoses – for understandable reasons. But even if their number should amount to less than ten times that of the manifest psychoses and of manifest criminality, the relatively small percentage of the population figures they represent is more than compensated for by the peculiar dangerousness of these people. Their mental state is that of a collectively excited group ruled by affective judgments and wish-fantasies. In a milieu of this kind they are the adapted ones, and consequently they feel quite at home in it. They know from their own experience the language of these conditions, and they know how to handle them. Their chimerical ideas, sustained by fanatical resentment, appeal to the collective irrationality and find fruitful soil there; they express all those motives and resentments which lurk in more normal people under the cloak of reason and insight. They are, therefore, despite their small number in comparison with the population as a whole, dangerous as sources of infection precisely because the so-called normal person possesses only a limited degree of self-knowledge.

Most people confuse "self-knowledge" with knowledge of their conscious ego-personalities. Anyone who has any ego-consciousness at all takes it for granted that he knows himself. But the ego knows only its own contents, not the unconscious and its contents. People measure their self-knowledge by what the average person in their social environment knows of himself, but not by the real psychic facts which are for the most part hidden from them. In this respect the psyche behaves like the body, of whose physiological and anatomical structure the average person knows very little too. Although he lives in it and with it, most of it is totally unknown to the layman, and special scientific knowledge is needed to acquaint consciousness with what is known of the body, not to speak of all that is *not* known, which also exists.

What is commonly called "self-knowledge" is therefore a very limited knowledge, most of it dependent on social factors, of what goes on in the human psyche. Hence one is always coming up against the prejudice that such and such a thing does not happen "with us" or "in our family" or among our friends and acquaintances. On the other hand, one meets with equally illusory assumptions about the alleged presence of qualities which merely serve to cover up the true facts of the case.

In this broad belt of unconsciousness, which is immune to conscious criticism and control, we stand defenceless, open to all kinds of influences and psychic infections. As with all dangers, we can guard against the risk of psychic infection only when we know what is attacking us, and how, where and when the attack will come. Since self-knowledge is a matter of getting to know the individual facts, theories are of very little help. For the more a theory lays claim to universal validity, the less capable it is of doing justice to the individual facts. Any theory based on experience is necessarily *statistical*; it formulates an *ideal average* which abolishes all exceptions at either end of the scale and replaces them by an abstract mean. This mean is quite valid, though it need not necessarily occur in reality. Despite this it figures in the theory as an unassailable fundamental fact. The exceptions at either extreme, though equally factual, do not appear in the final result at all, since they cancel each other out. If, for instance, I determine the weight of each stone in a bed of pebbles and get an average weight of five ounces, this tells me very little about the real nature of the pebbles. Anyone who thought, on the basis of these findings, that he could pick up a pebble of five ounces at the first try would be in for a serious disappointment. Indeed, it might well happen that however long he searched he would not find a single pebble weighing exactly five ounces.

The statistical method shows the facts in the light of the ideal average but does not give us a picture of their empirical reality. While reflecting an indisputable aspect of reality, it can falsify the actual truth in a most misleading way. This is particularly true of theories which are based on statistics. The distinctive thing about real facts, however, is their individuality. Not to put too fine a point on it, one could say that the real picture consists of nothing but exceptions to the rule, and that, in consequence, absolute reality has predominantly the character of *irregularity*.

These considerations must be borne in mind whenever there is talk of a theory serving as a guide to self-knowledge. There is and can be no self-knowledge based on theoretical assumptions, for the object of this knowledge is an individual – a relative exception and an irregular phenomenon. Hence it is not the universal and the regular that characterize the individual, but rather the unique. He is not to be understood as a recurrent unit but as something unique and singular which in the last analysis can be neither known nor compared with anything else. At the same time man, as member of a species, can and must be described as a statistical unit; otherwise nothing general could be said about him. For this purpose he has to be regarded as a comparative unit. This results in a universally valid anthropology or psychology, as the case may be, with an abstract picture of man as an average unit from which all individual features have been removed. But it is precisely these features which are of paramount importance for *understanding* man. If I want to understand an individual human being, I must lay aside all scientific knowledge of the average man and discard all theories in order to adopt a completely new and unprejudiced attitude. I can only approach the task of *understanding* with a free and open mind, whereas *knowledge* of man, or insight into human character, presupposes all sorts of knowledge about mankind in general.

Now whether it is a question of understanding a fellow human being or of self-knowledge, I must in both cases leave all theoretical assumptions behind me. Since scientific knowledge not only enjoys universal esteem but, in the eyes of modern man, counts as the only intellectual and spiritual authority, understanding the individual obliges me to commit the *lèse majesté*, so to speak, of turning a blind eye to scientific knowledge. This is a sacrifice not lightly made, for the scientific attitude cannot rid itself so easily of its sense of responsibility. And if the psychologist happens to be a doctor who wants not only to classify his patient scientifically but also to understand him as a human being, he is threatened with a conflict of duties between the two diametrically opposed and mutually exclusive attitudes of knowledge on the one hand and understanding on the other. This conflict cannot be solved by an either/or but only by a kind of two-way thinking: doing one thing while not losing sight of the other.

In view of the fact that, in principle, the positive advantages of *knowledge* work specifically to the disadvantage of *understanding*, the judgment resulting therefrom is likely to be something of a paradox. Judged scientifically, the individual is nothing but a unit which repeats itself *ad infinitum* and could just as well be designated with a letter of the alphabet. For understanding, on the other hand, it is just the unique individual human being who, when stripped of all those conformities and regularities so dear to the heart of the scientist, is the supreme and only real object of investigation. The doctor, above all, should be aware of this contradiction. On the one hand, he is equipped with the statistical truths of his scientific training, and on the other, he is faced with the task of treating a sick person who, especially in the case of psychic suffering, requires *individual understanding*. The more schematic the treatment is, the more resistances it – quite rightly – calls up in the patient, and the more the cure is jeopardized. The psychotherapist sees himself compelled, willy-nilly, to regard the individuality of a patient as an essential fact in the picture and to arrange his methods of treatment accordingly. Today, over the whole field of medicine, it is recognized that the task of the doctor consists in treating the sick person, not an abstract illness.

This illustration from the realm of medicine is only a special instance of the problem of education and training in general. Scientific education is based in the main on statistical truths and abstract knowledge and therefore imparts an unrealistic, rational picture of the world, in which the individual, as a merely marginal phenomenon, plays no role. The individual, however, as an irrational datum, is the true and authentic carrier of reality, the *concrete* man as opposed to the unreal ideal or "normal" man to whom the scientific statements refer. What is more, most of the natural sciences try to represent the results of their investigations as though these had come into existence without man's intervention, in such a way that the collaboration of the psyche – an indispensable factor – remains invisible. (An exception to this is modern physics, which recognizes that the observed is not independent of the observer.) So, in this respect as well, science conveys a picture of the world from which a real human psyche appears to be excluded – the very antithesis of the "humanities."

Under the influence of scientific assumptions, not only the psyche but the individual man and, indeed, all individual events whatsoever suffer a levelling down and a process of blurring that distorts the picture of reality into a conceptual average. We ought not to underestimate the psychological effect of the statistical world-picture: it thrusts aside the individual in favour of anonymous units that pile up into mass formations. Instead of the concrete individual, you have the names of organizations and, at the highest point, the abstract idea of the State as the principle of political reality. The moral responsibility of the individual is then inevitably replaced by the policy of the State (*raison d'état*). Instead of moral and mental differentiation of the individual, you have public welfare and the raising of the living standard. The goal and meaning of individual life (which is the only *real* life) no longer lie in individual development but in the policy of the State, which is thrust upon the individual from outside and consists in the execution of an abstract idea which ultimately tends to attract all life to itself. The individual is increasingly deprived of the moral decision as to how he should live his own life, and instead is ruled, fed, clothed, and educated as a social unit, accommodated in the appropriate housing unit, and amused in accordance with the standards that give pleasure and satisfaction to the masses. The rulers, in their turn, are just as much social units as the ruled, and are distinguished only by the fact that they are specialized mouthpieces of the State doctrine. They do not need to be personalities capable of judgment, but thoroughgoing specialists who are unusable outside their line of business. State policy decides what shall be taught and studied.

The seemingly omnipotent State doctrine is for its part manipulated in the name of State policy by those occupying the highest positions in the government, where all the power is concentrated. Whoever, by election or caprice, gets into one of these positions is subject to no higher authority; he is the State policy itself and within the limits of the situation can proceed at his own discretion. With Louis XIV he can say, "L'état c'est moi." He is thus the only individual or, at any rate, one of the few individuals who could make use of their individuality if only they knew how to differentiate themselves from the State doctrine. They are more likely, however, to be the slaves of their own fictions. Such one-sidedness is always compensated psychologically by unconscious subversive tendencies. Slavery and rebellion are inseparable correlates. Hence, rivalry for power and exaggerated distrust pervade the entire organism from top to bottom. Furthermore, in order to compensate for its chaotic formlessness, a mass always produces a "Leader," who infallibly becomes the victim of his own inflated ego-consciousness, as numerous examples in history show.

This development becomes logically unavoidable the moment the individual combines with the mass and thus renders himself obsolete. Apart from the agglomeration of huge masses in which the individual disappears anyway, one of the chief factors responsible for psychological mass-mindedness is scientific rationalism, which robs the individual of his foundations and his dignity. As a social unit he has lost his individuality and become a mere abstract number in the bureau of statistics. He can only play the role of an interchangeable unit of infinitesimal importance. Looked at rationally and from outside, that is exactly what he is, and from this point of view it seems positively absurd to go on talking about the value or meaning of the individual. Indeed, one can hardly imagine how one ever came to endow individual human life with so much dignity when the truth to the contrary is as plain as the palm of your hand.

Seen from this standpoint, the individual really is of diminishing importance and anyone who wished to dispute this would soon find himself at a loss for arguments. The fact that the individual feels himself or the members of his family or the esteemed friends in his circle to be important merely underlines the slightly comic subjectivity of his feeling. For what are the few compared with ten thousand or a hundred thousand, let alone a million? This recalls the argument of a thoughtful friend with whom I once got caught up in a huge crowd of people. Suddenly he exclaimed, "Here you have the most convincing reason for not believing in immortality: all *that lot* wants to be immortal!"

The bigger the crowd the more negligible the individual becomes. But if the individual, overwhelmed by the sense of his own puniness and impotence, should feel that his life has lost its meaning – which, after all, is not identical with public welfare and higher standards of living – then he is already on the road to State slavery and, without knowing or wanting it, has become its proselyte. The man who looks only outside and quails before the big battalions has nothing with which to combat the evidence of his senses and his reason. But that is just what is happening today: we are all fascinated and overawed by statistical truths and large numbers and are daily apprised of the nullity and futility of the individual personality, since it is not represented and personified by any mass organization. Conversely, those personages who strut about on the world stage and whose voices are heard far and wide seem, to the uncritical public, to be borne along on some mass movement or on the tide of public opinion and for this reason are either applauded or execrated. Since mass suggestion plays the predominant role here, it remains a moot point whether their message is their own, for which they are personally responsible, or whether they merely function as a megaphone for collective opinion.

Under these circumstances it is small wonder that individual judgment grows increasingly uncertain of itself and that responsibility is collectivized as much as possible, i.e., is shuffled off by the individual and delegated to a corporate body. In this way the individual becomes more and more a function of society, which in its turn usurps the function of the real life carrier, whereas, in actual fact, society is nothing more than an abstract idea like the State. Both are hypostatized, that is, have become autonomous. The State in particular is turned into a quasi-animate personality from whom everything is expected. In reality it is only a camouflage for those individuals who know how to manipulate it. Thus the constitutional State drifts into the situation of a primitive form of society – the communism of a primitive tribe where everybody is subject to the autocratic rule of a chief or an oligarchy.

2. RELIGION AS THE COUNTERBALANCE TO MASS-MINDEDNESS

In order to free the fiction of the sovereign State – in other words, the whims of the chieftains who manipulate it – from every wholesome restriction, all socio-political movements tending in this direction invariably try to cut the ground from under *religion*. For, in order to turn the individual into a function of the State, his dependence on anything else must be taken from him. Religion means dependence on and submission to the irrational facts of experience. These do not refer directly to social and physical conditions; they concern far more the individual's psychic attitude.

But it is possible to have an attitude to the external conditions of life only when there is a point of reference outside them. Religion gives, or claims to give, such a standpoint, thereby enabling the individual to exercise his judgment and his power of decision. It builds up a reserve, as it were, against the obvious and inevitable force of circumstances to which everyone is exposed who lives only in the outer world and has no other ground under his feet except the pavement. If statistical reality is the only one, then that is the sole authority. There is then only *one* condition, and since no contrary condition exists, judgment and decision are not only superfluous but impossible. Then the individual is bound to be a function of statistics and hence a function of the State or whatever the abstract principle of order may be called.

Religion, however, teaches another authority opposed to that of the "world." The doctrine of the individual's dependence on God makes just as high a claim upon him as the world does. It may even happen that the absoluteness of this claim estranges him from the world in the same way as he is estranged from himself when he succumbs to the collective mentality. He can forfeit his judgment and power of decision in the former case (for the sake of religious doctrine) quite as much as in the latter. This is the goal which religion openly aspires to unless it compromises with the State. When it does so, I prefer to call it not "religion" but a "creed." A creed gives expression to a definite collective belief, whereas the word *religion* expresses a subjective relationship to certain metaphysical, extramundane factors. A creed is a confession of faith intended chiefly for the world at large and is thus an intramundane affair, while the meaning and purpose of religion lie in the relationship of the individual to God (Christianity, Judaism, Islam) or to the path of salvation and liberation (Buddhism). From this basic fact all ethics is derived, which without the individual's responsibility before God can be called nothing more than conventional morality.

Since they are compromises with mundane reality, the creeds have accordingly seen themselves obliged to undertake a progressive codification of their views, doctrines, and customs, and in so doing have externalized themselves to such an extent that the authentic religious element in them – the living relationship to and direct confrontation with their extramundane point of reference – has been thrust into the background. The denominational standpoint measures the worth and importance of the subjective religious relationship by the yardstick of traditional doctrine, and where this is not so frequent, as in Protestantism, one immediately hears talk of pietism, sectarianism, eccentricity, and so forth, as soon as anyone claims to be guided by God's will. A creed coincides with the established Church or, at any rate, forms a public institution whose members include not only true believers but vast numbers of people who can only be described as "indifferent" in matters of religion and who belong to it simply by force of habit. Here the difference between a creed and a religion becomes palpable.

To be the adherent of a creed, therefore, is not always a religious matter but more often a social one and, as such, it does nothing to give the individual any foundation. For this he has to depend exclusively on his relation to an authority which is not of this world. The criterion here is not lip service to a creed but the psychological fact that the life of the individual is not determined solely by the ego and its opinions or by social factors, but quite as much, if not more, by a transcendent authority. It is not ethical principles, however lofty, or creeds, however orthodox, that lay the foundations for the freedom and autonomy of the individual, but simply and solely the empirical awareness, the incontrovertible experience of an intensely personal, reciprocal relationship between man and an extramundane authority which acts as a counterpoise to the "world" and its "reason."

This formulation will not please either the mass man or the collective believer. For the former the policy of the State is the supreme principle of thought and action. Indeed, this was the purpose for which he was enlightened, and accordingly the mass man grants the individual a right to exist only in so far as he is a function of the State. The believer, on the other hand, while admitting that the State has a moral and factual claim on him, confesses to the belief that not only man but the State that rules him is subject to the overlordship of "God," and that, in case of doubt, the supreme decision will be made by God and not by the State. Since I do not presume to any metaphysical judgments, I must leave it an open question whether the "world," i.e., the phenomenal world of man, and hence nature in general, is the "opposite" of God or not. I can only point to the fact that the psychological opposition between these two realms of experience is not only vouched for in the New Testament but is still exemplified very plainly today in the negative attitude of the dictator States to religion and of the Church to atheism and materialism.

Just as man, as a social being, cannot in the long run exist without a tie to the community, so the individual will never find the real justification for his existence and his own spiritual and moral autonomy anywhere except in an extramundane principle capable of relativizing the overpowering influence of external factors. The individual who is not anchored in God can offer no resistance on his own resources to the physical and moral blandishments of the world. For this he needs the evidence of inner, transcendent experience which alone can protect him from the otherwise inevitable submersion in the mass. Merely intellectual or even moral insight into the stultification and moral irresponsibility of the mass man is a negative recognition only and amounts to not much more than a wavering on the road to the atomization of the individual. It lacks the driving force of religious conviction, since it is merely rational. The dictator State has one great advantage over bourgeois reason: along with the individual it swallows up his religious forces. The State takes the place of God; that is why, seen from this angle, the socialist dictatorships are religions and State slavery is a form of worship. But the religious function cannot be dislocated and falsified in this way without giving rise to secret doubts, which are immediately repressed so as to avoid conflict with the prevailing trend towards mass-mindedness. The result, as always in such cases, is overcompensation in the form of *fanaticism*, which in its turn is used as a weapon for stamping out the least flicker of opposition. Free opinion is stifled and moral decision ruthlessly suppressed, on the plea that the end justifies the means, even the vilest. The policy of the State is exalted to a creed, the leader or party boss becomes a demigod beyond good and evil, and his votaries are honoured as heroes, martyrs, apostles, missionaries. There is only *one* truth and beside it no other. It is sacrosanct and above criticism. Anyone who thinks differently is a heretic, who, as we know from history, is threatened with all manner of unpleasant things. Only the party boss, who holds the political power in his hands, can interpret the State doctrine authentically, and he does so just as suits him.

When, through mass rule, the individual becomes social unit No. so-and-so and the State is elevated to the supreme principle, it is only to be expected that the religious function too will be sucked into the maelstrom. Religion, as the careful observation and taking account of certain invisible and uncontrollable factors, is an *instinctive* attitude peculiar to man, and its manifestations can be followed all through human history. Its evident purpose is to maintain the psychic balance, for the natural man has an equally natural "knowledge" of the fact that his conscious functions may at any time be thwarted by uncontrollable happenings coming from inside as well as from outside. For this reason he has always taken care that any difficult decision likely to have consequences for himself and others shall be rendered safe by suitable measures of a religious nature. Offerings are made to the invisible powers, formidable blessings are pronounced, and all kinds of solemn rites are performed. Everywhere and at all times there have been *rites d'entrée et de sortie* whose efficacy is impugned as magic and superstition by rationalists incapable of psychological insight. But magic has above all a psychological effect whose importance should not be underestimated. The performance of a "magical" action gives the person concerned a feeling of security which is absolutely essential for carrying out a decision, because a decision is inevitably somewhat one-sided and is therefore rightly felt to be a risk. Even a dictator thinks it necessary not only to accompany his acts of State with threats but to stage them with all manner of solemnities. Brass bands, flags, banners, parades, and monster demonstrations are no different in principle from ecclesiastical processions, cannonades, and fireworks to scare off demons. Only, the suggestive parade of State power engenders a collective feeling of security which, unlike religious demonstrations, gives the individual no protection against his inner demonism. Hence he will cling all the more to the power of the State, i.e., to the mass, thus delivering himself up to it psychically as well as morally and putting the finishing touch to his social depotentiation. The State, like the Church, demands enthusiasm, self-sacrifice, and love, and if religion requires or presupposes the "fear of God," then the dictator State takes good care to provide the necessary terror.

When the rationalist directs the main force of his attack against the miraculous effect of the rite as asserted by tradition, he has in reality completely missed the mark. The essential point, the *psychological* effect, is overlooked, although both parties make use

of it for directly opposite purposes. A similar situation prevails
with regard to their respective conceptions of the goal. The goals
of religion – deliverance from evil, reconciliation with God,
rewards in the hereafter, and so on – turn into worldly promises
about freedom from care for one's daily bread, the just distribution
of material goods, universal prosperity in the future, and shorter
working hours. That the fulfilment of these promises is as far off
as Paradise only furnishes yet another analogy and underlines the
fact that the masses have been converted from an extramundane
goal to a purely worldly belief, which is extolled with exactly the
same religious fervour and exclusiveness that the creeds display in
the other direction.

In order not to repeat myself unnecessarily, I shall not
enumerate all the parallels between worldly and otherworldly
beliefs, but shall content myself with emphasizing the fact that a
natural function which has existed from the beginning, like the
religious function, cannot be disposed of with rationalistic and
so-called enlightened criticism. You can, of course, represent the
doctrinal contents of the creeds as impossible and subject them to
ridicule, but such methods miss the point and do not affect the
religious function which forms the basis of the creeds. Religion,
in the sense of conscientious regard for the irrational factors of the
psyche and individual fate, reappears – evilly distorted – in the
deification of the State and the dictator: *Naturam expellas furca
tamen usque recurret* (You can throw out Nature with a pitchfork,
but she'll always turn up again). The leaders and dictators, having
weighed up the situation correctly, are therefore doing their best
to gloss over the all too obvious parallel with the deification of
Caesar and to hide their real power behind the fiction of the State,
though this, of course, alters nothing.*

As I have already pointed out, the dictator State, besides robbing
the individual of his rights, has also cut the ground from under his
feet psychically by depriving him of the metaphysical foundations
of his existence. The ethical decision of the individual human being
no longer counts – what alone matters is the blind movement of
the masses, and the *lie* thus becomes the operative principle of

*Since this essay was written, in the spring of 1956, there has been a noticeable
reaction in the U.S.S.R. to this objectionable state of affairs.

political action. The State has drawn the logical conclusions from this, as the existence of many millions of State slaves completely deprived of all rights mutely testifies.

Both the dictator State and denominational religion lay quite particular emphasis on the idea of *community*. This is the basic ideal of "communism," and it is thrust down the throats of the people so much that it has the exact opposite of the desired effect: it inspires divisive mistrust. The Church, which is no less emphatic, appears on its side as a communal ideal, and where the Church is notoriously weak, as in Protestantism, the hope of or belief in a "communal experience" makes up for the painful lack of cohesion. As can easily be seen, "community" is an indispensable aid in the organization of masses and is therefore a two-edged weapon. Just as the addition of however many zeros will never make a unit, so the value of a community depends on the spiritual and moral stature of the individuals composing it. For this reason one cannot expect from the community any effect that would outweigh the suggestive influence of the environment – that is, a real and fundamental change in individuals, whether for good or for bad. Such changes can come only from the personal encounter between man and man, but not from communistic or Christian baptisms *en masse*, which do not touch the inner man. How superficial the effect of communal propaganda actually is can be seen from recent events in Eastern Europe.* The communal ideal reckons without its host, overlooking the individual human being, who in the end will assert his claims.

3. THE POSITION OF THE WEST ON THE QUESTION OF RELIGION

Confronting this development in the twentieth century of our Christian era, the Western world stands with its heritage of Roman law, the treasures of Judaeo-Christian ethics grounded on metaphysics, and its ideal of the inalienable rights of man. Anxiously it asks itself the question: How can this development be brought to a standstill or put into reverse? It is useless to pillory the socialist dictatorship as utopian and to condemn its economic principles as

*Added in January 1957.

unreasonable, because, in the first place, the criticizing West has only itself to talk to, its arguments being heard only on this side of the Iron Curtain, and, in the second place, any economic principles you like can be put into practice so long as you are prepared to accept the sacrifices they entail. You can carry through any social and economic reforms you please if, like Stalin, you let three million peasants starve to death and have a few million unpaid labourers at your disposal. A State of this kind has no social or economic crises to fear. So long as its power is intact – that is to say, so long as there is a well-disciplined and well-fed police army in the offing – it can maintain its existence for an indefinitely long period and can go on increasing its power to an indefinite extent. Thanks to its excess birth-rate, it can multiply the number of its unpaid workers almost at will in order to compete with its rivals, regardless of the world market, which is to a large measure dependent on wages. A real danger can come to it only from outside, through the threat of military attack. But this risk grows less every year, firstly because the war potential of the dictator States is steadily increasing, and secondly because the West cannot afford to arouse latent Russian or Chinese nationalism and chauvinism by an attack which would have exactly the opposite effect to the one intended.

So far as one can see, only one possibility remains, and that is a break-down of power from within, which must, however, be left to follow its own inner development. Any support from outside at present would have little effect, in view of the existing security measures and the danger of nationalistic reactions. The absolute State has an army of fanatical missionaries to do its bidding in matters of foreign policy, and these in their turn can count on a fifth column who are guaranteed asylum under the laws and constitutions of the Western States. In addition the communes of believers, very strong in places, considerably weaken Western governments' powers of decision, whereas the West has no opportunity to exert a similar influence on the other side, though we are probably not wrong in surmising that there is a certain amount of opposition among the masses in the East. There are always upright and truth-loving people to whom lying and tyranny are hateful, but one cannot judge whether they exert any decisive influence on the masses under the police régimes.*

In view of this uncomfortable situation the question is heard again and again in the West: What can we do to counter this threat from the East? Even though the West has considerable industrial power and a sizable defence potential at its command, we cannot rest content with this, for we know that even the biggest armaments and the heaviest industry coupled with a relatively high living standard are not enough to check the psychic infection spread by religious fanaticism.

The West has unfortunately not yet woken up to the fact that our appeal to idealism and reason and other desirable virtues, delivered with so much enthusiasm, is mere bombination in the void. It is a puff of wind swept away in the storm of religious faith, however twisted this faith may appear to us. We are faced, not with a situation that can be overcome by rational or moral arguments, but with an unleashing of emotional forces and ideas engendered by the spirit of the times; and these, as we know from experience, are not much influenced by rational reflection and still less by moral exhortation. It has been correctly realized in many quarters that the alexipharmic, the antidote, should in this case be an equally potent faith of a different and non-materialistic kind, and that the religious attitude grounded upon it would be the only effective defence against the danger of psychic infection. Unhappily, the little word "should," which never fails to appear in this connection, points to a certain weakness, if not the absence, of this desideratum. Not only does the West lack a uniform faith that could block the progress of a fanatical ideology, but, as the father of Marxist philosophy, it makes use of exactly the same intellectual assumptions, the same arguments and aims. Although the Churches in the West enjoy full freedom, they are not less full or empty than in the East. Yet they exercise no noticeable influence on the broad course of politics. The disadvantage of a creed as a public institution is that it serves two masters: on the one hand, it derives its existence from the relationship of man to God, and on the other hand, it owes a duty to the State, i.e., to the world,

*Recent events in Poland and Hungary have shown that this opposition is more considerable than could have been foreseen.

in which connection it can appeal to the saying "Render unto Caesar..." and various other admonitions in the New Testament.

In early times and until comparatively recently there was, therefore, talk of "powers ordained by God" (Romans 13:1). Today this conception is antiquated. The Churches stand for traditional and collective convictions which in the case of many of their adherents are no longer based on their own inner experience but on *unreflecting belief*, which is notoriously apt to disappear as soon as one begins thinking about it. The content of belief then comes into collision with knowledge, and it often turns out that the irrationality of the former is no match for the ratiocinations of the latter. Belief is no adequate substitute for inner experience, and where this is absent even a strong faith which came miraculously as a gift of grace may depart equally miraculously. People call faith the true religious experience, but they do not stop to consider that actually it is a secondary phenomenon arising from the fact that something happened to us in the first place which instilled πίστις into us – that is, trust and loyalty. This experience has a definite content that can be interpreted in terms of one or other of the denominational creeds. But the more this is so, the more the possibilities of these conflicts with knowledge mount up, which in themselves are quite pointless. That is to say, the standpoint of the creeds is archaic; they are full of impressive mythological symbolism which, if taken literally, comes into insufferable conflict with knowledge. But if, for instance, the statement that Christ rose from the dead is to be understood not literally but symbolically, then it is capable of various interpretations that do not conflict with knowledge and do not impair the meaning of the statement. The objection that understanding it symbolically puts an end to the Christian's hope of immortality is invalid, because long before the coming of Christianity mankind believed in a life after death and therefore had no need of the Easter event as a guarantee of immortality. The danger that a mythology understood too literally, and as taught by the Church, will suddenly be repudiated lock, stock and barrel is today greater than ever. Is it not time that the Christian mythology, instead of being wiped out, was understood symbolically for once?

It is still too early to say what might be the consequences of a

general recognition of the fatal parallelism between the State
religion of the Marxists and the State religion of the Church. The
absolutist claim of a *Civitas Dei* that is represented by man bears
an unfortunate resemblance to the "divinity" of the State, and the
moral conclusion drawn by Ignatius Loyola from the authority of
the Church ("the end sanctifies the means") anticipates the lie as
a political instrument in an exceedingly dangerous way. Both
demand unqualified submission to faith and thus curtail man's
freedom, the one his freedom before God and the other his freedom
before the State, thereby digging the grave for the individual. The
fragile existence of this – so far as we know – unique carrier of life
is threatened on both sides, despite their respective promises of
spiritual and material idylls to come – and how many of us can in
the long run fight against the proverbial wisdom of "a bird in the
hand is worth two in the bush"? Besides which, the West cherishes
the same "scientific" and rationalistic *Weltanschauung* with its
statistical levelling-down tendency and materialistic aims as the
State religion of the Eastern bloc, as I have explained above.

What, then, has the West, with its political and denominational
schisms, to offer to modern man in his need? Nothing, unfortunately, except a variety of paths all leading to one goal which is
practically indistinguishable from the Marxist ideal. It requires no
special effort of understanding to see where the Communist
ideology gets the certainty of its belief that time is on its side, and
that the world is ripe for conversion. The facts speak a language
that is all too plain in this respect. It will not help us in the West
to shut our eyes to this and not recognize our fatal vulnerability.
Anyone who has once learned to submit absolutely to a collective
belief and to renounce his eternal right to freedom and the equally
eternal duty of individual responsibility will persist in this attitude,
and will be able to march with the same credulity and the same lack
of criticism in the reverse direction, if another and manifestly
"better" belief is foisted upon his alleged idealism. What happened
not so long ago to a civilized European nation? We accuse the
Germans of having forgotten it all again already, but the truth is
that we don't know for certain whether something similar might
not happen elsewhere. It would not be surprising if it did and if
another civilized nation succumbed to the infection of a uniform
and one-sided idea. We permit ourselves the question: which

countries have the biggest Communist parties? America, which – *O quae mutatio rerum!* – forms the real political backbone of Western Europe, seems to be immune because of the outspoken counterposition she has adopted, but in point of fact she is perhaps even more vulnerable than Europe, since her educational system is the most influenced by the scientific *Weltanschauung* with its statistical truths, and her mixed population finds it difficult to strike roots in a soil that is practically without history. The historical and humanistic type of education so sorely needed in such circumstances leads, on the contrary, a Cinderella existence. Though Europe possesses this latter requirement, she uses it to her own undoing in the form of nationalistic egoisms and paralysing scepticism. Common to both is the materialistic and collectivist goal, and both lack the very thing that expresses and grips the whole man, namely, an idea which puts the individual human being in the centre as the measure of all things.

This idea alone is enough to arouse the most violent doubts and resistances on all sides, and one could almost go so far as to assert that the valuelessness of the individual in comparison with large numbers is the one belief that meets with universal and unanimous assent. To be sure, we all say that this is the century of the common man, that he is the lord of the earth, the air, and the water, and that on his decision hangs the historical fate of the nations. This proud picture of human grandeur is unfortunately an illusion and is counterbalanced by a reality that is very different. In this reality man is the slave and victim of the machines that have conquered space and time for him; he is intimidated and endangered by the might of the military technology which is supposed to safeguard his physical existence; his spiritual and moral freedom, though guaranteed within limits in one half of his world, is threatened with chaotic disorientation, and in the other half is abolished altogether. Finally, to add comedy to tragedy, this lord of the elements, this universal arbiter, hugs to his bosom notions which stamp his dignity as worthless and turn his autonomy into an absurdity. All his achievements and possessions do not make him bigger; on the contrary, they diminish him, as the fate of the factory-worker under the rule of a "just" distribution of goods clearly demonstrates. He pays for his share of the factory with the loss of personal property, he exchanges his freedom of movement for the doubtful pleasure of being tied to his place of employment, he forfeits all means of improving his position if he jibs against being ground down by exhausting piece-work, and if he shows any signs of intelligence, political precepts are thrust down his throat – with a bit of technical knowledge thrown in, if he is lucky. However, a roof over one's head and a daily feed for the useful animal are not to be sneezed at when the bare necessities of life may be cut off from one day to the next.

4. THE INDIVIDUAL'S UNDERSTANDING OF HIMSELF

It is astounding that man, the instigator, inventor and vehicle of all these developments, the originator of all judgments and decisions and the planner of the future, must make himself such a *quantité négligeable*. The contradiction, the paradoxical evaluation of humanity by man himself, is in truth a matter for wonder, and one can only explain it as springing from an extraordinary uncertainty of judgment – in other words, man is an enigma to himself. This is understandable, seeing that he lacks the means of comparison necessary for self-knowledge. He knows how to distinguish himself from the other animals in point of anatomy and physiology, but as a conscious, reflecting being, gifted with speech, he lacks all criteria for self-judgment. He is on this planet a unique phenomenon which he cannot compare with anything else. The possibility of comparison and hence of self-knowledge would arise only if he could establish relations with quasi-human mammals inhabiting other stars.

Until then man must continue to resemble a hermit who knows that in respect of comparative anatomy he has affinities with the anthropoids but, to judge by appearances, is extraordinarily different from his cousins in respect of his psyche. It is just in this most important characteristic of his species that he cannot know himself and therefore remains a mystery to himself. The differing degrees of self-knowledge within his own species are of little significance compared with the possibilities which would be opened out by an encounter with a creature of similar structure but different origin. Our psyche, which is primarily responsible for all the historical changes wrought by the hand of man on the face of this planet, remains an insoluble puzzle and an incomprehensible wonder, an object of abiding perplexity – a feature it shares with all Nature's secrets. In regard to the latter we still have hope of making more discoveries and finding answers to the most difficult questions. But in regard to the psyche and psychology there seems to be a curious hesitancy. Not only is it the youngest of the empirical sciences, but it has great difficulty in getting anywhere near its proper object.

In the same way that our picture of the world had to be freed by Copernicus from the prejudice of geocentricity, the most strenuous efforts of a well-nigh revolutionary nature were needed to free psychology, first from the spell of mythological ideas, and then from the prejudice that the psyche is, on the one hand, a mere epiphenomenon of a biochemical process in the brain and, on the other hand, a purely personal matter. The connection with the brain does not in itself prove that the psyche is an epiphenomenon, a secondary function causally dependent on biochemical processes in the physical substrate. Nevertheless, we know only too well how much the psychic function can be disturbed by verifiable processes in the brain, and this fact is so impressive that the subsidiary nature of the psyche seems an almost unavoidable inference. The phenomena of parapsychology, however, warn us to be careful, for they point to a relativization of space and time through psychic factors which casts doubt on our naïve and overhasty explanation in terms of psychophysical parallelism. For the sake of this explanation people deny the findings of parapsychology outright, either for philosophical reasons or from intellectual laziness. This can hardly be considered a scientifically responsible attitude, even though it is a popular way out of a quite extraordinary intellectual difficulty. To assess the psychic phenomenon, we have to take account of all the other phenomena that go with it, and accordingly we can no longer practise any psychology that ignores the existence of the unconscious or of parapsychology.

The structure and physiology of the brain furnish no explanation of the psychic process. The psyche has a peculiar nature which cannot be reduced to anything else. Like physiology, it presents a relatively self-contained field of experience, to which we must attribute a quite special importance because it includes one of the two indispensable conditions for existence as such, namely, the phenomenon of consciousness. Without consciousness there would, practically speaking, be no world, for the world exists for us only in so far as it is consciously reflected by a psyche. *Consciousness is a precondition of being.* Thus the psyche is endowed with the dignity of a cosmic principle, which philosophically and in fact gives it a position co-equal with the principle of physical being. The carrier of this consciousness is the individual, who does not produce the psyche of his own volition but is, on the contrary, preformed by it and nourished by the gradual awakening of consciousness during childhood. If therefore the psyche is of overriding empirical importance, so also is the individual, who is the only immediate manifestation of the psyche.

This fact must be expressly emphasized for two reasons. Firstly, the individual psyche, just because of its individuality, is an exception to the statistical rule and is therefore robbed of one of its main characteristics when subjected to the levelling influence of statistical evaluation. Secondly, the Churches grant it validity only in so far as it acknowledges their dogmas – in other words, when it submits to a collective category. In both cases the will to individuality is regarded as egotistic obstinacy. Science devalues this as subjectivism, and the Churches condemn it morally as heresy and spiritual pride. As to the latter charge, it should not be forgotten that, unlike other religions, Christianity holds up before us a symbol whose content is the individual way of life of a man, the Son of Man, and that it even regards this individuation process as the incarnation and revelation of God himself. Hence the development of man into a self acquires a significance whose full implications have hardly begun to be appreciated, because too much attention to externals blocks the way to immediate inner experience. Were not the autonomy of the individual the secret longing of many people it would scarcely be able to survive the collective suppression either morally or spiritually.

All these obstacles make it more difficult to arrive at a correct appreciation of the human psyche, but they count for very little beside one other remarkable fact that deserves mentioning. This is the common psychiatric experience that the devaluation of the psyche and other resistances to psychological enlightenment are based in large measure on fear – on panic fear of the discoveries that might be made in the realm of the unconscious. These fears are found not only among persons who are frightened by the picture Freud painted of the unconscious; they also troubled the originator of psychoanalysis himself, who confessed to me that it was necessary to make a dogma of his sexual theory because this was the sole bulwark of reason against a possible "eruption of the black flood of occultism." In these words Freud was expressing his conviction that the unconscious still harboured many things that might lend themselves to "occult" interpretation, as is in fact the case. These "archaic vestiges," or archetypal forms grounded on the instincts and giving expression to them, have a numinous quality that sometimes arouses fear. They are ineradicable, for they represent the ultimate foundations of the psyche itself. They cannot be grasped intellectually, and when one has destroyed one manifestation of them, they reappear in altered form. It is this fear of the unconscious psyche which not only impedes self-knowledge but is the gravest obstacle to a wider understanding and knowledge of psychology. Often the fear is so great that one dares not admit it even to oneself. This is a question which every religious person should consider very seriously; he might get an illuminating answer.

A scientifically oriented psychology is bound to proceed abstractly; that is, it removes itself just sufficiently far from its object not to lose sight of it altogether. That is why the findings of laboratory psychology are, for all practical purposes, often so remarkably unenlightening and devoid of interest. The more the individual object dominates the field of vision, the more practical, detailed, and alive will be the knowledge derived from it. This means that the objects of investigation, too, become more and more complicated and that the uncertainty of the individual factors grows in proportion to their number, thus increasing the possibility of error. Understandably enough, academic psychology is scared of this risk and prefers to avoid complex situations by asking ever simpler questions, which it can do with impunity. It has full freedom in the choice of questions it will put to Nature.

Medical psychology, on the other hand, is very far from being in this more or less enviable position. Here the object puts the question and not the experimenter. The analyst is confronted with facts which are not of his choosing and which he probably never *would* choose if he were a free agent. It is the sickness or the patient himself that puts the crucial questions – in other words, Nature experiments with the doctor in expecting an answer from him. The uniqueness of the individual and of his situation stares the analyst in the face and demands an answer. His duty as a physician forces him to cope with a situation swarming with uncertainty factors. At first he will apply principles based on general experience, but he will soon realize that principles of this kind do not adequately express the facts and fail to meet the nature of the case. The deeper his understanding penetrates, the more the general principles lose their meaning. But these principles are the foundation of objective knowledge and the yardstick by which it is measured. With the growth of what both patient and doctor feel to be "understanding," the situation becomes increasingly subjectivized. What was an advantage to begin with threatens to turn into a dangerous disadvantage. Subjectivation (in technical terms, transference and countertransference) creates isolation from the environment, a social limitation which neither party wishes for but which invariably sets in when understanding predominates and is no longer balanced by knowledge. As understanding deepens, the further removed it becomes from knowledge. An ideal understanding would ultimately result in each party's unthinkingly going along with the other's experience – a state of uncritical passivity coupled with the most complete subjectivity and lack of social responsibility. Understanding carried to such lengths is in any case impossible, for it would require the virtual identification of two different individuals. Sooner or later the relationship reaches a point where one partner feels he is being forced to sacrifice his own individuality so that it may be assimilated by that of the other. This inevitable consequence breaks the understanding, for understanding also presupposes the integral preservation of the individuality of both partners. It is therefore advisable to carry understanding only to the point where the balance between understanding and knowledge is reached, for understanding at all costs is injurious to both partners.

This problem arises whenever complex, individual situations have to be known and understood. It is the specific task of the medical psychologist to provide just this knowledge and understanding. It would also be the task of the "director of conscience" zealous in the cure of souls, were it not that his office inevitably obliges him to apply the yardstick of his denominational bias at the critical moment. As a result, the individual's right to exist as such is cut short by a collective prejudice and often curtailed in the most sensitive area. The only time this does not happen is when the dogmatic symbol, for instance the model life of Christ, is understood concretely and felt by the individual to be adequate. How far this is the case today I would prefer to leave to the judgment of others. At all events, the analyst very often has to treat patients to whom denominational limitations mean little or nothing. His profession therefore compels him to have as few preconceptions as possible. Similarly, while respecting metaphysical (i.e., non-verifiable) convictions and assertions, he will take care not to credit them with universal validity. This caution is called for because the individual traits of the patient's personality ought not to be twisted out of shape by arbitrary interventions from outside. The analyst must leave this to environmental influences, to the patient's own inner development, and – in the widest sense – to fate with its wise or unwise decrees.

Many people will perhaps find this heightened caution exaggerated. In view of the fact, however, that there is in any case such a multitude of reciprocal influences at work in the dialectical process between two individuals, even if it is conducted with the most tactful reserve, the responsible analyst will refrain from adding unnecessarily to the collective factors to which his patient has already succumbed. Moreover, he knows very well that the preaching of even the worthiest precepts only provokes the patient into open hostility or secret resistance and thus needlessly endangers the aim of the treatment. The psychic situation of the individual is so menaced nowadays by advertising, propaganda, and other more or less well-meant advice and suggestions that for once in his life the patient might be offered a relationship that does not repeat the nauseating "you should," "you must" and similar confessions of impotence. Against the onslaught from outside no less than against its repercussions in the psyche of the individual the analyst sees himself obliged to play the role of counsel for the defence. Fear that anarchic instincts will thereby be let loose is a possibility that is greatly exaggerated, seeing that obvious safeguards exist within and without. Above all, there is the natural cowardice of most men to be reckoned with, not to mention morality, good taste and – last but not least – the penal code. This fear is nothing compared with the enormous effort it usually costs people to help the first stirrings of individuality into consciousness, let alone put them into effect. And where these individual impulses have broken through too boldly and unthinkingly, the analyst must protect them from the patient's own clumsy recourse to shortsightedness, ruthlessness, and cynicism.

As the dialectical discussion proceeds, a point is reached when an evaluation of these individual impulses becomes necessary. By that time the patient should have acquired enough certainty of judgment to enable him to act on his own insight and decision and not from the mere wish to copy convention – even if he happens to agree with collective opinion. Unless he stands firmly on his own feet, the so-called objective values profit him nothing, since they then only serve as a substitute for character and so help to suppress his individuality. Naturally, society has an indisputable right to protect itself against arrant subjectivisms, but, in so far as society is itself composed of de-individualized human beings, it is completely at the mercy of ruthless individualists. Let it band together into groups and organizations as much as it likes – it is just this banding together and the resultant extinction of the individual personality that makes it succumb so readily to a dictator. A million zeros joined together do not, unfortunately, add up to one. Ultimately everything depends on the quality of the individual, but our fatally shortsighted age thinks only in terms of large numbers and mass organizations, though one would think that the world had seen more than enough of what a well-disciplined mob can do in the hands of a single madman. Unfortunately, this realization does not seem to have penetrated very far – and our blindness is extremely dangerous. People go on blithely organizing and believing in the sovereign remedy of mass action, without the least consciousness of the fact that the most powerful organizations can be maintained only by the greatest ruthlessness of their leaders and the cheapest of slogans.

Curiously enough, the Churches too want to avail themselves of mass action in order to cast out the devil with Beelzebub – the very Churches whose care is the salvation of the *individual* soul. They do not appear to have heard of the elementary axiom of mass psychology that the individual becomes morally and spiritually inferior in the mass, and for this reason they do not bother themselves overmuch with their real task of helping the individual to achieve a *metanoia*, a rebirth of the spirit – *Deo concedente*. It is, unfortunately, only too clear that if the individual is not truly regenerated in spirit, society cannot be either, for society is the sum total of individuals in need of redemption. I can therefore see it only as a delusion when the Churches try – as they apparently do – to rope the individual into some social organization and reduce him to a condition of diminished responsibility, instead of raising him out of the torpid, mindless mass and making clear to him that *he* is the one important factor and that the salvation of the world consists in the salvation of the individual soul. It is true that mass meetings parade these ideas before him and seek to impress them on his mind by dint of mass suggestion, with the melancholy result that once the intoxication has worn off the mass man promptly succumbs to another even more obvious and still louder slogan. His individual relation to God would be an effective shield against these pernicious influences. Did Christ, perchance, call his disciples to him at a mass meeting? Did the feeding of the five thousand bring him any followers who did not afterwards cry with the rest, "Crucify him!" when even the rock named Peter showed signs of wavering? And are not Jesus and Paul prototypes of those who, trusting their inner experience, have gone their individual ways in defiance of the world?

This argument should certainly not cause us to overlook the reality of the situation confronting the Church. When the Church tries to give shape to the amorphous mass by uniting individuals into a community of believers and to hold such an organization together with the help of suggestion, it is not only performing a great *social* service, but it also secures for the individual the inestimable boon of a meaningful form of life. These, however, are gifts which as a rule only confirm certain tendencies and do not change them. As experience unfortunately shows, the inner man remains unchanged however much community he has. His environment cannot give him as a gift something which he can win for himself only with effort and suffering. On the contrary, a favourable environment merely strengthens the dangerous tendency to expect everything from outside – even that metamorphosis which external reality cannot provide. By this I mean a far-reaching change of the inner man, which is all the more urgent in view of the mass phenomena of today and the still greater problems of overpopulation looming in the future. It is time we asked ourselves exactly what we are lumping together in mass organizations and what constitutes the nature of the individual human being, i.e., of the real man and not the statistical man. This is hardly possible except by a new process of self-reflection.

All mass movements, as one might expect, slip with the greatest ease down an inclined plane made up of large numbers. Where the many are, there is security; what the many believe must of course be true; what the many want must be worth striving for, and necessary, and therefore good. In the clamour of the many resides the power to snatch wish-fulfilments by force; sweetest of all, however, is that gentle and painless slipping back into the kingdom of childhood, into the paradise of parental care, into happy-go-luckiness and irresponsibility. All the thinking and looking after are done from the top; to all questions there is an answer, and for all needs the necessary provision is made. The infantile dream-state of the mass man is so unrealistic that he never thinks to ask who is paying for this paradise. The balancing of accounts is left to a higher political or social authority, which welcomes the task, for its power is thereby increased; and the more power it has, the weaker and more helpless the individual becomes.

Whenever social conditions of this type develop on a large scale, the road to tyranny lies open and the freedom of the individual turns into spiritual and physical slavery. Since every tyranny is *ipso facto* immoral and ruthless, it has much more freedom in the choice of its methods than an institution which still takes account of the individual. Should such an institution come into conflict with the organized State, it is soon made aware of the very real disadvantage of its morality and therefore feels compelled to avail itself of the same methods as its opponent. In this way the evil spreads almost of necessity, even when direct infection might be avoided. The danger of infection is greater when decisive importance is attached to large numbers and to statistical values, as is everywhere the case in our Western world. The suffocating power of the masses is paraded before our eyes in one form or another every day in the newspapers, and the insignificance of the individual is rubbed into him so thoroughly that he loses all hope of making himself heard. The outworn ideals of *liberté, égalité, fraternité* help him not at all, as he can direct this appeal only to his executioners, the spokesmen of the masses.

Resistance to the organized mass can be effected only by the man who is as well organized in his individuality as the mass itself. I fully realize that this proposition must sound well-nigh unintelligible to the man of today. The helpful medieval view that man is a microcosm, a reflection of the great cosmos in miniature, has long since dropped away from him, although the very existence of his world-embracing and world-conditioning psyche might have taught him better. Not only is the image of the macrocosm imprinted upon his psychic nature, but he also creates this image for himself on an ever-widening scale. He bears this cosmic "correspondence" within him by virtue of his reflecting consciousness on the one hand, and, on the other, thanks to the hereditary, archetypal nature of his instincts, which bind him to his environment. But his instincts not only attach him to the macrocosm, they also, in a sense, tear him apart, because his desires pull him in different directions. In this way he falls into continual conflict with himself and only very rarely succeeds in giving his life an undivided goal – for which, as a rule, he must pay very dearly by repressing other sides of his nature. One often has to ask oneself whether this kind of single-mindedness is worth forcing at all, seeing that the natural state of the human psyche consists in a jostling together of its components and in their contradictory behaviour – that is, in a certain degree of dissociation. The Buddhist name for this is attachment to the "ten thousand things." Such a condition cries out for order and synthesis.

Just as the chaotic movements of the crowd, all ending in mutual frustration, are impelled in a definite direction by a dictatorial will, so the individual in his dissociated state needs a directing and ordering principle. Ego-consciousness would like to let its own will play this role, but overlooks the existence of powerful unconscious factors which thwart its intentions. If it wants to reach the goal of synthesis, it must first get to know the nature of these factors. It must *experience* them, or else it must possess a numinous *symbol* that expresses them and leads to their synthesis. A religious symbol that comprehended and visibly represented what is seeking expression in modern man might possibly do this; but our conception of the Christian symbol to date has certainly not been able to do so. On the contrary, that frightful world split runs right through the domains of the "Christian" white man, and our Christian outlook on life has proved powerless to prevent the recrudescence of an archaic social order like Communism.

This is not to say that Christianity is finished. I am, on the contrary, convinced that it is not Christianity, but our conception and interpretation of it, that has become antiquated in face of the present world situation. The Christian symbol is a living thing that carries in itself the seeds of further development. It can go on developing; it depends only on us, whether we can make up our minds to meditate again, and more thoroughly, on the Christian premises. This requires a very different attitude towards the individual, towards the microcosm of the self, from the one we have adopted hitherto. That is why nobody knows what ways of approach are open to man, what inner experiences he could still pass through and what psychic facts underlie the religious myth. Over all this hangs so universal a darkness that no one can see why he should be interested or to what end he should commit himself. Before this problem we stand helpless.

This is not surprising, since practically all the trump cards are in the hands of our opponents. They can appeal to the big battalions and their crushing power. Politics, science, and technology stand ranged on their side. The imposing arguments of science represent the highest degree of intellectual certainty yet achieved by the mind of man. So at least it seems to the man of today, who has received hundred-fold enlightenment concerning the backwardness and darkness of past ages and their superstitions. That his teachers have themselves gone seriously astray by making false comparisons between incommensurable factors never enters his head. All the more so as the intellectual *élite* to whom he puts his questions are almost unanimously agreed that what science regards as impossible today was impossible at all other times as well. Above all, the facts of faith, which might give him the chance of an extramundane standpoint, are treated in the same context as the facts of science. Thus, when the individual questions the Churches and their spokesmen, to whom is entrusted the cure of souls, he is informed that to belong to a church – a decidedly worldly institution – is more or less *de rigueur*; that the facts of faith which have become questionable for him were concrete historical events; that certain ritual actions produce miraculous effects; and that the sufferings of Christ have vicariously saved him from sin and its consequences (i.e., eternal damnation). If, with the limited means at his disposal, he begins to reflect on these things, he will have to confess that he does not understand them at all and that only two possibilities remain open to him: either to believe implicitly, or to reject such statements because they are flatly incomprehensible.

Whereas the man of today can easily think about and understand all the "truths" dished out to him by the State, his understanding of religion is made considerably more difficult owing to the lack of explanations. ("Do you understand what you are reading?" And he said, "How can I, unless someone guides me?" Acts 8:30.) If, despite this, he has still not discarded all his religious convictions, this is because the religious impulse rests on an instinctive basis and is therefore a specifically human function. You can take away a man's gods, but only to give him others in return. The leaders of the mass State could not help being deified, and wherever crudities of this kind have not yet been put over by force, obsessive factors arise in their stead, charged with demonic energy – money, work, political influence, and so forth. When any natural human function gets lost, i.e., is denied conscious and intentional expression, a general disturbance results. Hence, it is quite natural that with the triumph of the Goddess of Reason a general neuroticizing of modern man should set in, a dissociation of personality analogous to the splitting of the world today by the Iron Curtain. This boundary line bristling with barbed wire runs through the psyche of modern man, no matter on which side he lives. And just as the typical neurotic is unconscious of his *shadow side*, so the normal individual, like the neurotic, sees his shadow in his neighbour or in the man beyond the great divide. It has even become a political and social duty to apostrophize the capitalism of the one and the communism of the other as the very devil, so as to fascinate the outward eye and prevent it from looking within. But just as the neurotic, despite unconsciousness of his other side, has a dim premonition that all is not well with his psychic economy, so Western man has developed an instinctive interest in his psyche and in "psychology."

Thus it is that the psychiatrist is summoned willy-nilly to appear on the world stage, and questions are addressed to him which primarily concern the most intimate and hidden life of the individual, but which in the last analysis are the direct effects of the *Zeitgeist*. Because of its personal symptomatology this material is usually considered to be "neurotic" – and rightly so, since it is made up of infantile fantasies which ill accord with the contents of an adult psyche and are therefore repressed by our moral judgment, in so far as they reach consciousness at all. Most fantasies of this kind do not, in the nature of things, come to consciousness in any form, and it is very improbable, to say the least of it, that they were ever conscious and were consciously repressed. Rather, they seem to have been present from the beginning or, at any rate, to have arisen unconsciously and to have persisted in that state until the psychologist's intervention enabled them to cross the threshold of consciousness. The activation of unconscious fantasies is a process that occurs when consciousness finds itself in a situation of distress. Were that not so, the fantasies would be produced normally and would then bring no neurotic disturbances in their train. In reality, fantasies of this kind belong to the world of childhood and give rise to disturbances only when prematurely strengthened by abnormal conditions of conscious life. This is particularly likely to happen when unfavourable influences emanate from the parents, poisoning the atmosphere and producing conflicts which upset the psychic balance of the child.

When a neurosis breaks out in an adult, the fantasy world of childhood reappears, and one is tempted to explain the onset of the neurosis causally, as due to the presence of infantile fantasies. But that does not explain why the fantasies did not develop any pathological effects during the interim period. These effects develop only when the individual is faced with a situation which he cannot overcome by conscious means. The resultant standstill in the development of personality opens a sluice for infantile fantasies, which, of course, are latent in everybody but do not display any activity so long as the conscious personality can continue on its way unimpeded. When the fantasies reach a certain level of intensity, they begin to break through into consciousness and create a conflict situation that becomes perceptible to the patient himself, splitting him into two personalities with different characters. The dissociation, however, had been prepared long before in the unconscious, when the energy flowing off from consciousness (because unused) reinforced the negative qualities of the unconscious and particularly the infantile traits of the personality.

Since the normal fantasies of a child are nothing other, at bottom, than the *imagination of the instincts*, and may thus be regarded as preliminary exercises in the use of future conscious activities, it follows that the fantasies of the neurotic, even though pathologically altered and perhaps perverted by the regression of energy, contain a core of normal instinct, the hallmark of which is adaptedness. A neurotic illness always implies an unadapted alteration and distortion of normal dynamisms and of the "imagination" proper to them. Instincts, however, are highly conservative and of extreme antiquity as regards both their dynamism and their form. Their form, when represented to the mind, appears as an *image* which expresses the nature of the instinctive impulse visually and concretely, like a picture. If we could look into the psyche of the yucca moth,★ for instance, we would find in it a pattern of ideas, of a numinous or fascinating character, which not only compels the moth to carry out its fertilizing activity on the yucca plant but helps it to "recognize" the total situation. Instinct is anything but a blind and indefinite impulse, since it proves to be attuned and adapted to a definite external situation. This latter circumstance gives it its specific and irreducible form. Just as instinct is original and hereditary, so, too, its form is age-old, that is to say, *archetypal*. It is even older and more conservative than the body's form.

These biological considerations naturally apply also to *Homo sapiens*, who still remains within the framework of general biology despite the possession of consciousness, will, and reason. The fact that our conscious activity is rooted in instinct and derives from it its dynamism as well as the basic features of its ideational forms has the same significance for human psychology as for all other members of the animal kingdom. Human knowledge consists essentially in the constant adaptation of the primordial patterns of

★This is a classic instance of the symbiosis of insect and plant.

ideas that were given us *a priori*. These need certain modifications, because, in their original form, they are suited to an archaic mode of life but not to the demands of a specifically differentiated environment. If the flow of instinctive dynamism into our life is to be maintained, as is absolutely necessary for our existence, then it is imperative that we should remould these archetypal forms into ideas which are adequate to the challenge of the present.

5. THE PHILOSOPHICAL AND THE PSYCHOLOGICAL APPROACH TO LIFE

Our ideas have, however, the unfortunate but inevitable tendency to lag behind the changes in the total situation. They can hardly do otherwise, because, so long as nothing changes in the world, they remain more or less adapted and therefore function in a satisfactory way. There is then no cogent reason why they should be changed and adapted anew. Only when conditions have altered so drastically that there is an unendurable rift between the outer situation and our ideas, now become antiquated, does the general problem of our *Weltanschauung*, or philosophy of life, arise, and with it the question of how the primordial images that maintain the flow of instinctive energy are to be reoriented or readapted. They cannot simply be replaced by a new rational configuration, for this would be moulded too much by the outward situation and not enough by man's biological needs. Moreover, not only would it build no bridge to the original man, but it would block the approach to him altogether. This is in keeping with the aims of Marxist education, which seeks, like God himself, to remake man, but in the image of the State.

Today, our basic convictions are becoming increasingly rationalistic. Our philosophy is no longer a way of life, as it was in antiquity; it has turned into an exclusively intellectual and academic exercise. Our denominational religions with their archaic rites and conceptions – justified enough in themselves – express a view of the world which caused no great difficulties in the Middle Ages but has become strange and unintelligible to modern man. Despite this conflict with the modern scientific outlook, a deep instinct bids him hang on to ideas which, if taken literally, leave out of account all the mental developments of the last five hundred years. The obvious purpose of this is to prevent him from falling into the abyss of nihilistic despair. But even when, as a rationalist, he feels impelled to criticize denominational religion as literalistic, narrow-minded, and obsolescent, he should never forget that it proclaims a doctrine whose symbols, although their interpretation may be disputed, nevertheless possess a life of their own by virtue of their archetypal character. Consequently, intellectual understanding is by no means indispensable in all cases, but is called for only when evaluation through feeling and intuition does not suffice, that is to say, in the case of people for whom the intellect carries the prime power of conviction.

Nothing is more characteristic and symptomatic in this respect than the gulf that has opened out between *faith* and *knowledge*. The contrast has become so enormous that one is obliged to speak of the incommensurability of these two categories and their way of looking at the world. And yet they are concerned with the same empirical world in which we live, for even the theologians tell us that faith is supported by facts that became historically perceptible in this known world of ours – namely that Christ was born as a real human being, worked many miracles and suffered his fate, died under Pontius Pilate, and rose up in the flesh after his death. Theology rejects any tendency to take the assertions of its earliest records as written myths and, accordingly, to understand them symbolically. Indeed, it is the theologians themselves who have recently made the attempt – no doubt as a concession to "knowledge" – to "demythologize" the object of their faith while drawing the line quite arbitrarily at the crucial points. But to the critical intellect it is only too obvious that myth is an integral component of all religions and therefore cannot be excluded from the assertions of faith without injuring them.

The rupture between faith and knowledge is a symptom of the *split consciousness* which is so characteristic of the mental disorder of our day. It is as if two different persons were making statements about the same thing, each from his own point of view, or as if one person in two different frames of mind were sketching a picture of his experience. If for "person" we substitute "modern society," it is evident that the latter is suffering from a mental dissociation, i.e., a neurotic disturbance. In view of this, it does not help matters at all if one party pulls obstinately to the right and the other to the left. This is what happens in every neurotic psyche, to its own deep distress, and it is just this distress that brings the patient to the analyst.

As I stated above in all brevity – while not neglecting to mention certain practical details whose omission might have perplexed the reader – the analyst has to establish a relationship with *both* halves of his patient's personality, because only from them can he put together a whole and complete man, and not merely from one half by suppression of the other half. But this suppression is just what the patient has been doing all along, for the modern *Weltanschauung* leaves him with no alternative. His individual situation is the same in principle as the collective situation. He is a social microcosm, reflecting on the smallest scale the qualities of society at large, or conversely the smallest social unit cumulatively producing the collective dissociation. The latter possibility is the more likely one, as the only direct and concrete carrier of life is the individual personality, while society and the State are conventional ideas and can claim reality only in so far as they are represented by a conglomeration of individuals.

Far too little attention has been paid to the fact that, for all our irreligiousness, the distinguishing mark of the Christian epoch, its highest achievement, has become the congenital vice of our age: *the supremacy of the word*, of the Logos, which stands for the central figure of our Christian faith. The word has literally become our god and so it has remained, even if we know of Christianity only from hearsay. Words like "Society" and "State" are so concretized that they are almost personified. In the opinion of the man in the street, the "State," far more than any king in history, is the inexhaustible giver of all good; the "State" is invoked, made responsible, grumbled at, and so on and so forth. Society is elevated to the rank of a supreme ethical principle; indeed, it is even credited with positively creative capacities. No one seems to notice that this worship of the word, which was necessary at a certain phase of man's mental development, has a perilous shadow side. That is to say, the moment the word, as a result of centuries of education, attains universal validity, it severs its original connection with the divine Person. There is then a personified Church, a personified State; belief in the word becomes credulity, and the word itself an infernal slogan capable of any deception. With credulity come propaganda and advertising to dupe the citizen with political jobbery and compromises, and the lie reaches proportions never known before in the history of the world.

Thus the word, originally announcing the unity of all men and their union in the figure of the one great Man, has in our day become a source of suspicion and distrust of all against all. Credulity is one of our worst enemies, but that is the makeshift the neurotic always resorts to in order to quell the doubter in his own breast or to conjure him out of existence. People think you have only to "tell" a person that he "ought" to do something in order to put him on the right track. But whether he can or will do it is another matter. The psychologist has come to see that nothing is achieved by telling, persuading, admonishing, giving good advice. He must acquaint himself with all the particulars and have an authentic knowledge of the psychic inventory of his patient. He has therefore to relate to the individuality of the sufferer and feel his way into all the nooks and crannies of his mind, to a degree that far exceeds the capacity of a teacher or even of a *directeur de conscience*. His scientific objectivity, which excludes nothing, enables him to see his patient not only as a human being but also as an anthropoid, who is bound to his body like an animal. His training directs his medical interest beyond the conscious personality to the world of unconscious instinct dominated by sexuality and the power drive (or self-assertion), which correspond to the twin moral concepts of Saint Augustine: *concupiscentia* and *superbia*. The clash between these two fundamental instincts (preservation of the species and self-preservation) is the source of numerous conflicts. They are, therefore, the chief object of moral judgment, whose purpose it is to prevent instinctual collisions as far as possible.

As I explained earlier, instinct has two main aspects: on the one hand, that of dynamism and compulsion, and on the other, specific meaning and intention. It is highly probable that all man's psychic functions have an instinctual foundation, as is obviously the case with animals. It is easy to see that in animals instinct functions as the *spiritus rector* of all behaviour. This observation lacks certainty only when the learning capacity begins to develop, for instance in the higher apes and in man. In animals, as a result of their learning capacity, instinct undergoes numerous modifications and differentiations, and in civilized man the instincts are so split up that only a few of the basic ones can be recognized with any certainty in their original form. The most important are the two fundamental instincts already mentioned and their derivatives, and these have been the exclusive concern of medical psychology so far. But in following up the ramifications of instinct investigators came upon configurations which could not with certainty be ascribed to either group. To take but one example: The discoverer of the power instinct raised the question whether an apparently indubitable expression of the sexual instinct might not be better explained as a "power arrangement," and Freud himself felt obliged to acknowledge the existence of "ego instincts" in addition to the overriding sexual instinct – a clear concession to the Adlerian standpoint. In view of this uncertainty, it is hardly surprising that in most cases neurotic symptoms can be explained, almost without contradiction, in terms of either theory. This perplexity does not mean that one or the other standpoint is erroneous or that both are. Rather, both are *relatively* valid and, unlike certain one-sided and dogmatic tendencies, admit the existence and competition of still other instincts. Although, as I have said, the question of human instinct is a far from simple matter, we shall probably not be wrong in assuming that the learning capacity, a quality almost exclusive to man, is based on the instinct for imitation found in animals. It is in the nature of this instinct to disturb other instinctive activities and eventually to modify them, as can be observed, for instance, in the songs of birds when they adopt other melodies.

Nothing estranges man more from the ground-plan of his instincts than his learning capacity, which turns out to be a genuine drive for progressive transformation of human modes of behaviour. It, more than anything else, is responsible for the altered conditions of his existence and the need for new adaptations which civilization brings. It is also the ultimate source of those numerous psychic disturbances and difficulties which are occasioned by man's progressive alienation from his instinctual foundation, i.e., by his uprootedness and identification with his conscious knowledge of himself, by his concern with consciousness at the expense of the unconscious. The result is that modern man knows himself only in so far as he can become conscious of himself – a capacity largely dependent on environmental conditions, knowledge and control of which necessitated or suggested certain modifications of his original instinctive tendencies. His consciousness therefore orients itself chiefly by observing and investigating the world around him, and it is to the latter's peculiarities that he must adapt his psychic and technical resources. This task is so exacting, and its fulfilment so profitable, that he forgets himself in the process, losing sight of his instinctual nature and putting his own conception of himself in place of his real being. In this way he slips imperceptibly into a purely conceptual world where the products of his conscious activity progressively take the place of reality.

Separation from his instinctual nature inevitably plunges civilized man into the conflict between conscious and unconscious, spirit and nature, knowledge and faith, a split that becomes pathological the moment his consciousness is no longer able to neglect or suppress his instinctual side. The accumulation of individuals who have got into this critical state starts off a mass movement purporting to be the champion of the suppressed. In accordance with the prevailing tendency of consciousness to seek the source of all ills in the outside world, the cry goes up for political and social changes which, it is supposed, would automatically solve the much deeper problem of split personality. Hence it is that whenever this demand is fulfilled, political and social conditions arise which bring the same ills back again in altered form. What then happens is a simple reversal: the underside comes to the top and the shadow takes the place of the light, and since the former is always anarchic and turbulent, the freedom of the "liberated" underdog must suffer Draconian curtailment. The devil is cast out with Beelzebub. All this is unavoidable, because the root of the evil is untouched and merely the counterposition has come to light.

The Communist revolution has debased man far lower than democratic collective psychology has done, because it robs him of his freedom not only in the social but in the moral and spiritual sphere. Aside from the political difficulties, this entailed a great psychological disadvantage for the West that had already made itself unpleasantly felt in the days of German Nazism: we can now point a finger at the shadow. He is clearly on the other side of the political frontier, while we are on the side of good and enjoy the possession of the right ideals. Did not a well-known statesman recently confess that he had "no imagination for evil"?* In the name of the multitude he was expressing the fact that Western man is in danger of losing his shadow altogether, of identifying himself with his fictive personality and the world with the abstract picture painted by scientific rationalism. His spiritual and moral opponent, who is just as real as he, no longer dwells in his own breast but beyond the geographical line of division, which no longer represents an outward political barrier but splits off the conscious from the unconscious man more and more menacingly. Thinking and feeling lose their inner polarity, and where religious orientation has grown ineffective, not even a god can check the sovereign sway of unleashed psychic functions.

Our rational philosophy does not bother itself with whether the other person in us, pejoratively described as the "shadow," is in sympathy with our conscious plans and intentions. Evidently it still does not know that we carry in ourselves a real shadow whose existence is grounded in our instinctual nature. No one can overlook either the dynamism or the imagery of the instincts without the gravest injury to himself. Violation or neglect of instinct has painful consequences of a physiological and psychological nature for whose treatment medical help, above all, is required.

For more than fifty years we have known, or could have known, that there is an unconscious counterbalance to consciousness. Medical psychology has furnished all the necessary empirical and experimental proofs of this. There is an unconscious psychic reality which demonstrably influences consciousness and its contents. All this is known, but no practical conclusions have been drawn from this fact. We still go on thinking and acting as before, as if we were *simplex* and not *duplex*. Accordingly, we imagine ourselves to be innocuous, reasonable, and humane. We do not think of distrusting our motives or of asking ourselves how the inner man feels about the things we do in the outside world. But actually it is frivolous, superficial, and unreasonable of us, as well as psychically unhygienic, to overlook the reaction and standpoint of the unconscious. One can regard one's stomach or heart as

---

*Since these words were written, the shadow has followed up this overbright picture hotfoot with the Charge of the Light Brigade to Suez.

unimportant and worthy of contempt, but that does not prevent overeating or overexertion from having consequences that affect the whole man. Yet we think that psychic mistakes and their consequences can be got rid of with mere words, for "psychic" means less than air to most people. All the same, nobody can deny that without the psyche there would be no world at all, and still less a human world. Virtually everything depends on the human psyche and its functions. It should be worthy of all the attention we can give it, especially today, when everyone admits that the weal or woe of the future will be decided neither by the threat of wild animals, nor by natural catastrophes, nor by the danger of world-wide epidemics, but simply and solely by the psychic changes in man. It needs only an almost imperceptible disturbance of equilibrium in a few of our rulers' heads to plunge the world into blood, fire, and radioactivity. The technical means necessary for this are present on both sides. And certain conscious deliberations, uncontrolled by any inner opponent, can be put into effect all too easily, as we have seen already from the example of one "Leader." The consciousness of modern man still clings so much to external objects that he makes them exclusively responsible, as if it were on them that the decision depended. That the psychic state of certain individuals could ever emancipate itself from the behaviour of objects is something that is considered far too little, although irrationalities of this sort are observed every day and can happen to everyone.

The forlorn state of consciousness in our world is due primarily to loss of instinct, and the reason for this lies in the development of the human mind over the past aeon. The more power man had over nature, the more his knowledge and skill went to his head, and the deeper became his contempt for the merely natural and accidental, for all irrational data – including the objective psyche, which is everything that consciousness is not. In contrast to the subjectivism of the conscious mind the unconscious is objective, manifesting itself mainly in the form of contrary feelings, fantasies, emotions, impulses, and dreams, none of which one makes oneself but which come upon one objectively. Even today psychology is still, for the most part, the science of conscious contents, measured as far as possible by collective standards. The individual psyche has become a mere accident, a marginal phenomenon, while the unconscious, which can manifest itself only in the real, "irrationally given" human being, has been ignored altogether. This was not the result of carelessness or of lack of knowledge, but of downright resistance to the mere possibility that there could be a second psychic authority besides the ego. It seems a positive menace to the ego that its monarchy could be doubted. The religious person, on the other hand, is accustomed to the thought of not being sole master in his own house. He believes that God, and not he himself, decides in the end. But how many of us would dare to let the will of God decide, and which of us would not feel embarrassed if he had to say how far the decision came from God himself?

The religious person, so far as one can judge, is directly influenced by the reaction of the unconscious. As a rule, he calls this the operation of *conscience*. But since the same psychic background produces reactions other than moral ones, the believer is measuring his conscience by the traditional ethical standard and thus by a collective value, in which endeavour he is assiduously supported by his Church. So long as the individual can hold fast to his traditional beliefs, and the circumstances of his time do not demand stronger emphasis on individual autonomy, he can rest content with the situation. But the situation is radically altered when the worldly-minded man who is oriented to external factors and has lost his religious beliefs appears *en masse*, as is the case today. The believer is then forced onto the defensive and must catechize himself on the foundation of his beliefs. He is no longer sustained by the tremendous suggestive power of the *consensus omnium* and is keenly aware of the weakening of the Church and the precariousness of its dogmatic assumptions. To counter this, the Church recommends more faith, as if this gift of grace depended on man's good will and pleasure. The seat of faith, however, is not consciousness but spontaneous religious experience, which brings the individual's faith into immediate relation with God.

Here each of us must ask: Have I any religious experience and immediate relation to God, and hence that certainty which will keep me, as an individual, from dissolving in the crowd?

6. SELF-KNOWLEDGE

To this question there is a positive answer only when the individual is willing to fulfil the demands of rigorous self-examination and self-knowledge. If he does this, he will not only discover some important truths about himself but will also have gained a psychological advantage: he will have succeeded in deeming himself worthy of serious attention and sympathetic interest. He will have set his hand, as it were, to a declaration of his own human dignity and taken the first step towards the foundations of his consciousness – that is, towards the unconscious, the only available source of religious experience. This is certainly not to say that what we call the unconscious is identical with God or is set up in his place. It is simply the medium from which religious experience seems to flow. As to what the further cause of such experience may be, the answer to this lies beyond the range of human knowledge. Knowledge of God is a transcendental problem.

The religious person enjoys a great advantage when it comes to answering the crucial question that hangs over our time like a threat: he has a clear idea of the way his subjective existence is grounded in his relation to "God." I put the word "God" in quotes in order to indicate that we are dealing with an anthropomorphic idea whose dynamism and symbolism are filtered through the medium of the unconscious psyche. Anyone who wants to can at least draw near to the source of such experiences, no matter whether he believes in God or not. Without this approach it is only in rare cases that we witness those miraculous conversions of which Paul's Damascus experience is the prototype. That religious experiences exist no longer needs proof. But it will always remain doubtful whether what metaphysics and theology call God and the gods is the real ground of these experiences. The question is idle, actually, and answers itself by reason of the subjectively overwhelming numinosity of the experience. Anyone who has had it is *seized* by it and therefore not in a position to indulge in fruitless metaphysical or epistemological speculations. Absolute certainty brings its own evidence and has no need of anthropomorphic proofs.

In view of the general ignorance of and bias against psychology it must be accounted a misfortune that the one experience which makes sense of individual existence should seem to have its origin in a medium that is certain to catch everybody's prejudices. Once more the doubt is heard: "What good can come out of Nazareth?" The unconscious, if not regarded outright as a sort of refuse bin underneath the conscious mind, is at any rate supposed to be of "merely animal nature." In reality, however, and by definition it is of uncertain extent and constitution, so that overvaluation or undervaluation of it is pointless and can be dismissed as mere prejudice. At all events, such judgments sound very queer in the mouths of Christians, whose Lord was himself born on the straw of a stable, among the domestic animals. It would have been more to the taste of the multitude if he had got himself born in a temple. In the same way, the worldly-minded mass man looks for the numinous experience in the mass meeting, which provides an infinitely more imposing background than the individual soul. Even Church Christians share this pernicious delusion.

Psychology's insistence on the importance of unconscious processes for religious experience is extremely unpopular, no less with the political Right than with the Left. For the former the deciding factor is the historical revelation that came to man from outside; to the latter this is sheer nonsense, and man has no religious function at all, except belief in the party doctrine, when suddenly the most intense faith is called for. On top of this, the various creeds assert quite different things, and each of them claims to possess the absolute truth. Yet today we live in a unitary world where distances are reckoned by hours and no longer by weeks and months. Exotic races have ceased to be peepshows in ethnological museums. They have become our neighbours, and what was yesterday the private concern of the ethnologist is today a political, social, and psychological problem. Already the ideological spheres begin to touch, to interpenetrate, and the time may not be far off when the question of mutual understanding will become acute. To make oneself understood is certainly impossible without far-reaching comprehension of the other's standpoint. The insight needed for this will have repercussions on both sides. History will undoubtedly pass over those who feel it is their vocation to resist this inevitable development, however desirable and psychologically necessary it may be to cling to what is essential and good in our own tradition. Despite all the differences, the unity of mankind will assert itself irresistibly. On this card Marxist doctrine has staked its life, while the West hopes to achieve its aim with technology and economic aid. Communism has not overlooked the enormous importance of the ideological element and the universality of basic principles. The coloured races share our ideological weakness and in this respect are just as vulnerable as we are.

The underestimation of the psychological factor is likely to take a bitter revenge. It is therefore high time we caught up with ourselves in this matter. For the present this must remain a pious wish, because self-knowledge, as well as being highly unpopular, seems to be an unpleasantly idealistic goal, reeks of morality, and is preoccupied with the psychological shadow, which is normally denied whenever possible or at least not spoken of. The task that faces our age is indeed almost insuperably difficult. It makes the highest demands on our responsibility if we are not to be guilty of another *trahison des clercs*. It addresses itself to those leading and influential personalities who have the necessary intelligence to understand the situation our world is in. One might expect them to consult their consciences. But since it is a matter not only of intellectual understanding but of moral conclusions, there is unfortunately no cause for optimism. Nature, as we know, is not so lavish with her boons that she joins to a high intelligence the gifts of the heart also. As a rule, where one is present the other is missing, and where one capacity is present in perfection it is generally at the cost of all the others. The discrepancy between intellect and feeling, which get in each other's way at the best of times, is a particularly painful chapter in the history of the human psyche.

There is no sense in formulating the task that our age has forced upon us as a moral demand. We can, at best, merely make the psychological world situation so clear that it can be seen even by the myopic, and give utterance to words and ideas which even the hard of hearing can hear. We may hope for men of understanding and men of good will, and must therefore not grow weary of reiterating those thoughts and insights which are needed. Finally, even the truth can spread and not only the popular lie.

With these words I should like to draw the reader's attention to the main difficulty he has to face. The horror which the dictator States have of late brought upon mankind is nothing less than the culmination of all those atrocities of which our ancestors made themselves guilty in the not so distant past. Quite apart from the barbarities and blood baths perpetrated by the Christian nations among themselves throughout European history, the European has also to answer for all the crimes he has committed against the coloured races during the process of colonization. In this respect the white man carries a very heavy burden indeed. It shows us a picture of the common human shadow that could hardly be painted in blacker colours. The evil that comes to light in man and that undoubtedly dwells within him is of gigantic proportions, so that for the Church to talk of original sin and to trace it back to Adam's relatively innocent slip-up with Eve is almost a euphemism. The case is far graver and is grossly underestimated.

Since it is universally believed that man *is* merely what his consciousness knows of itself, he regards himself as harmless and so adds stupidity to iniquity. He does not deny that terrible things have happened and still go on happening, but it is always "the others" who do them. And when such deeds belong to the recent or remote past, they quickly and conveniently sink into the sea of forgetfulness, and that state of chronic woolly-mindedness returns which we describe as "normality." In shocking contrast to this is the fact that nothing has finally disappeared and nothing has been made good. The evil, the guilt, the profound unease of conscience, the dark foreboding, are there before our eyes, if only we would see. Man has done these things; I am a man, who has his share of human nature; therefore I am guilty with the rest and bear unaltered and indelibly within me the capacity and the inclination to do them again at any time. Even if, juristically speaking, we were not accessories to the crime, we are always, thanks to our human nature, potential criminals. In reality we merely lacked a suitable opportunity to be drawn into the infernal mêlée. None of us stands outside humanity's black collective shadow. Whether the crime occurred many generations back or happens today, it remains the symptom of a disposition that is always and everywhere present – and one would therefore do well to possess some "imagination for evil," for only the fool can permanently disregard the conditions of his own nature. In fact, this negligence is the best means of making him an instrument of evil. Harmlessness and naïveté are as little helpful as it would be for a cholera patient and those in his vicinity to remain unconscious of the contagiousness of the disease. On the contrary, they lead to projection of the unrecognized evil into the "other." This strengthens the opponent's position in the most effective way, because the projection carries the *fear* which we involuntarily and secretly feel for our own evil over to the other side and considerably increases the formidableness of his threat. What is even worse, our lack of insight deprives us of the *capacity to deal with evil*. Here, of course, we come up against one of the main prejudices of the Christian tradition, and one that is a great stumbling block to our policies. We should, so we are told, eschew evil and, if possible, neither touch nor mention it. For evil is also the thing of ill omen, that which is tabooed and feared. This apotropaic attitude towards evil, and the apparent circumventing of it, flatter the primitive tendency in us to shut our eyes to evil and drive it over some frontier or other, like the Old Testament scapegoat, which was supposed to carry the evil into the wilderness.

But if one can no longer avoid the realization that evil, without man's ever having chosen it, is lodged in human nature itself, then it bestrides the psychological stage as the equal and opposite partner of good. This realization leads straight to a psychological dualism, already unconsciously prefigured in the political world schism and in the even more unconscious dissociation in modern man himself. The dualism does not come from this realization; rather, we are in a split condition to begin with. It would be an insufferable thought that we had to take personal responsibility for so much guiltiness. We therefore prefer to localize the evil in individual criminals or groups of criminals, while washing our hands in innocence and ignoring the general proclivity to evil. This sanctimoniousness cannot be kept up in the long run, because the evil, as experience shows, lies in man – unless, in accordance with the Christian view, one is willing to postulate a metaphysical principle of evil. The great advantage of this view is that it exonerates man's conscience of too heavy a responsibility and foists it off on the devil, in correct psychological appreciation of the fact that man is much more the victim of his psychic constitution than its inventor. Considering that the evil of our day puts everything that has ever agonized mankind in the deepest shade, one must ask oneself how it is that, for all our progress in the administration of justice, in medicine and in technology, for all our concern with life and health, monstrous engines of destruction have been invented which could easily exterminate the human race.

No one will maintain that the atomic physicists are a pack of criminals because it is to their efforts that we owe that peculiar flower of human ingenuity, the hydrogen bomb. The vast amount of intellectual work that went into the development of nuclear physics was put forth by men who dedicated themselves to their task with the greatest exertion and self-sacrifice, and whose moral achievement could therefore just as easily have earned them the merit of inventing something useful and beneficial to humanity. But even though the first step along the road to a momentous invention may be the outcome of a conscious decision, here, as everywhere, the spontaneous idea – the hunch or intuition – plays an important part. In other words, the unconscious collaborates too and often makes decisive contributions. So it is not the conscious effort alone that is responsible for the result; somewhere or other the unconscious, with its barely discernible goals and intentions, has its finger in the pie. If it puts a weapon in your hand, it is aiming at some kind of violence. Knowledge of the truth is the foremost goal of science, and if in pursuit of the longing for light we stumble upon an immense danger, then one has the impression more of fatality than of premeditation. It is not that present-day man is capable of greater evil than the man of antiquity or the primitive. He merely has incomparably more effective means with which to realize his propensity to evil. As his consciousness has broadened and differentiated, so his moral nature has lagged behind. That is the great problem before us today. *Reason alone no longer suffices.*

In theory, it lies within the power of reason to desist from experiments of such hellish scope as nuclear fission if only because of their dangerousness. But fear of the evil which one does not see in one's own bosom but always in somebody else's checks reason every time, although everyone knows that the use of this weapon means the certain end of our present human world. The fear of universal destruction may spare us the worst, yet the possibility of it will nevertheless hang over us like a dark cloud so long as no bridge is found across the world-wide psychic and political split – a bridge as certain as the existence of the hydrogen bomb. If only a world-wide consciousness could arise that all division and all fission are due to the splitting of opposites in the psyche, then we should know where to begin. But if even the smallest and most personal stirrings of the individual psyche – so insignificant in themselves – remain as unconscious and unrecognized as they have hitherto, they will go on accumulating and produce mass groupings and mass movements which cannot be subjected to reasonable control or manipulated to a good end. All direct efforts to do so are no more than shadow boxing, the most infatuated by illusion being the gladiators themselves.

The crux of the matter is man's own dualism, to which he knows no answer. This abyss has suddenly yawned open before him with the latest events in world history, after mankind had lived for many centuries in the comfortable belief that a unitary God had created man in his own image, as a little unity. Even today people are largely unconscious of the fact that every individual is a cell in the structure of various international organisms and is therefore causally implicated in their conflicts. He knows that as an individual being he is more or less meaningless and feels himself the victim of uncontrollable forces, but, on the other hand, he harbours within himself a dangerous shadow and adversary who is involved as an invisible helper in the dark machinations of the political monster. It is in the nature of political bodies always to see the evil in the opposite group, just as the individual has an ineradicable tendency to get rid of everything he does not know and does not want to know about himself by foisting it off on somebody else.

Nothing has a more divisive and alienating effect upon society than this moral complacency and lack of responsibility, and nothing promotes understanding and *rapprochement* more than the mutual withdrawal of projections. This necessary corrective demands self-criticism, for one cannot just tell the other person to withdraw them. He does not recognize them for what they are any more than one does oneself. We can recognize our prejudices and illusions only when, from a broader psychological knowledge of ourselves and others, we are prepared to doubt the absolute rightness of our assumptions and compare them carefully and conscientiously with the objective facts. Funnily enough, "self-criticism" is an idea much in vogue in Marxist countries, but there it is subordinated to ideological considerations and must serve the State, and not truth and justice in men's dealings with one another. The mass State has no intention of promoting mutual understanding and the relationship of man to man; it strives, rather, for atomization, for the psychic isolation of the individual. The more unrelated individuals are, the more consolidated the State becomes, and vice versa.

There can be no doubt that in the democracies too the distance between man and man is much greater than is conducive to public welfare, let alone beneficial to our psychic needs. True, all sorts of attempts are being made to level out glaring social contrasts by appealing to people's idealism, enthusiasm, and ethical conscience; but, characteristically, one forgets to apply the necessary self-criticism, to answer the question: *Who* is making the idealistic demand? Is it, perchance, someone who jumps over his own shadow in order to hurl himself avidly on some idealistic programme that offers him a welcome alibi? How much respectability and apparent morality is there, cloaking in deceptive colours a very different inner world of darkness? One would first like to be assured that the man who talks of ideals is himself ideal, so that his words and deeds *are* more than they *seem*. To be ideal is impossible, and remains therefore an unfulfilled postulate. Since we usually have keen noses in this respect, most of the idealisms that are preached and paraded before us sound rather hollow and become acceptable only when their opposite is also openly admitted. Without this counterweight the ideal exceeds our human capacity, becomes incredible because of its humourlessness, and degenerates into bluff, albeit a well-meant one. Bluff is an illegitimate way of overpowering and suppressing others and leads to no good.

Recognition of the shadow, on the other hand, leads to the modesty we need in order to acknowledge imperfection. And it is just this conscious recognition and consideration that are needed whenever a human relationship is to be established. A human relationship is not based on differentiation and perfection, for these only emphasize the differences or call forth the exact opposite; it is based, rather, on imperfection, on what is weak, helpless and in need of support – the very ground and motive for dependence. The perfect have no need of others, but weakness has, for it seeks support and does not confront its partner with anything that might force him into an inferior position and even humiliate him. This humiliation may happen only too easily when high idealism plays too prominent a role.

Reflections of this kind should not be taken as superfluous sentimentalities. The question of human relationship and of the inner cohesion of our society is an urgent one in view of the atomization of the pent-up mass man, whose personal relationships are undermined by general mistrust. Wherever justice is uncertain and police spying and terror are at work, human beings fall into isolation, which, of course, is the aim and purpose of the dictator State, since it is based on the greatest possible accumulation of depotentiated social units. To counter this danger, the free society needs a bond of an affective nature, a principle of a kind like *caritas*, the Christian love of your neighbour. But it is just this love for one's fellow man that suffers most of all from the lack of understanding wrought by projection. It would therefore be very much in the interest of the free society to give some thought to the question of human relationship from the psychological point of view, for in this resides its real cohesion and consequently its strength. Where love stops, power begins, and violence, and terror.

These reflections are not intended as an appeal to idealism, but only to promote a consciousness of the psychological situation. I do not know which is weaker: the idealism or the insight of the public. I only know that it needs time to bring about psychic changes that have any prospect of enduring. Insight that dawns slowly seems to me to have more lasting effects than a fitful idealism, which is unlikely to hold out for long.

7. THE MEANING OF SELF-KNOWLEDGE

What our age thinks of as the "shadow" and inferior part of the psyche contains more than something merely negative. The very fact that through self-knowledge, that is, by exploring our own souls, we come upon the instincts and their world of imagery should throw some light on the powers slumbering in the psyche, of which we are seldom aware so long as all goes well. They are potentialities of the greatest dynamism, and it depends entirely on the preparedness and attitude of the conscious mind whether the irruption of these forces, and the images and ideas associated with them, will tend towards construction or catastrophe. The psychologist seems to be the only person who knows from experience how precarious the psychic preparedness of modern man is, for he is the only one who sees himself compelled to seek out in man's own nature those helpful powers and ideas which over and over have enabled him to find the right way through darkness and danger. For this exacting work the psychologist requires all his patience; he may not rely on any traditional oughts and musts, leaving the other person to make all the effort and contenting himself with the easy role of adviser and admonisher. Everyone knows the futility of preaching about things that are desirable, yet the general helplessness in this situation is so great, and the need so dire, that one prefers to repeat the old mistake instead of racking one's brains over a subjective problem. Besides, it is always a question of treating one single individual only and not ten thousand, when the trouble one takes would ostensibly have more impressive results, though one knows well enough that nothing has happened at all unless the individual changes.

The effect on *all* individuals, which one would like to see realized, may not set in for hundreds of years, for the spiritual transformation of mankind follows the slow tread of the centuries and cannot be hurried or held up by any rational process of reflection, let alone brought to fruition in one generation. What does lie within our reach, however, is the change in individuals who have, or create for themselves, an opportunity to influence others of like mind. I do not mean by persuading or preaching – I am thinking, rather, of the well-known fact that anyone who has insight into his own actions, and has thus found access to the unconscious, involuntarily exercises an influence on his environment. The deepening and broadening of his consciousness produce the kind of effect which the primitives call "mana." It is an unintentional influence on the unconscious of others, a sort of unconscious prestige, and its effect lasts only so long as it is not disturbed by conscious intention.

Nor is the striving for self-knowledge altogether without

prospects of success, since there exists a factor which, though completely disregarded, meets our expectations halfway. This is the unconscious *Zeitgeist*. It compensates the attitude of the conscious mind and anticipates changes to come. An excellent example of this is modern art: though seeming to deal with aesthetic problems, it is really performing a work of psychological education on the public by breaking down and destroying their previous aesthetic views of what is beautiful in form and meaningful in content. The pleasingness of the artistic product is replaced by chill abstractions of the most subjective nature which brusquely slam the door on the naïve and romantic delight in the senses and on the obligatory love for the object. This tells us, in plain and universal language, that the prophetic spirit of art has turned away from the old object-relationship towards the – for the time being – dark chaos of subjectivisms. Certainly art, so far as we can judge of it, has not yet discovered in this darkness what it is that could hold all men together and give expression to their psychic wholeness. Since reflection seems to be needed for this purpose, it may be that such discoveries are reserved for other fields of endeavour.

Great art till now has always derived its fruitfulness from myth, from the unconscious process of symbolization which continues through the ages and, as the primordial manifestation of the human spirit, will continue to be the root of all creation in the future. The development of modern art with its seemingly nihilistic trend towards disintegration must be understood as the symptom and symbol of a mood of universal destruction and renewal that has set its mark on our age. This mood makes itself felt everywhere, politically, socially, and philosophically. We are living in what the Greeks called the καιρός – the right moment – for a 'metamorphosis of the gods," of the fundamental principles and symbols. This peculiarity of our time, which is certainly not of our conscious choosing, is the expression of the unconscious man within us who is changing. Coming generations will have to take account of this momentous transformation if humanity is not to destroy itself through the might of its own technology and science.

As at the beginning of the Christian era, so again today we are faced with the problem of the general moral backwardness which has failed to keep pace with our scientific, technical, and social progress. So much is at stake and so much depends on the psychological constitution of modern man. Is he capable of resisting the temptation to use his power for the purpose of staging a world conflagration? Is he conscious of the path he is treading, and what the conclusions are that must be drawn from the present world situation and his own psychic situation? Does he know that he is on the point of losing the life-preserving myth of the inner man which Christianity has treasured up for him? Does he realize what lies in store should this catastrophe ever befall him? Is he even capable of realizing that this would in fact be a catastrophe? And finally, does the individual know that *he* is the makeweight that tips the scales?

Happiness and contentment, equability of mind and meaningfulness of life – these can be experienced only by the individual and not by a State, which, on the one hand, is nothing but a convention agreed to by independent individuals and, on the other, continually threatens to paralyse and suppress the individual. The psychiatrist is one of those who know most about the conditions of the soul's welfare, upon which so infinitely much depends in the social sum. The social and political circumstances of the time are certainly of considerable significance, but their importance for the weal or woe of the individual has been boundlessly overestimated in so far as they are taken for the sole deciding factors. In this respect all our social goals commit the error of overlooking the psychology of the person for whom they are intended and – very often – of promoting only his illusions.

I hope, therefore, that a psychiatrist, who in the course of a long life has devoted himself to the causes and consequences of psychic disorders, may be permitted to express his opinion, in all the modesty enjoined upon him as an individual, about the questions raised by the world situation today. I am neither spurred on by excessive optimism nor in love with high ideals, but am merely concerned with the fate of the individual human being – that infinitesimal unit on whom a world depends, and in whom, if we read the meaning of the Christian message aright, even God seeks his goal.

Chronology of Jung's Life and Work

From *C. G. Jung: Word and Image*, ed. Aniela Jaffé, Bollingen Series XCVII: 2, Princeton University Press, 1979.

1875
26 July: born to Johann Paul Achilles Jung (1842–96), then parson at Kesswil (Canton Thurgau), and Emilie, née Preiswerk (1848–1923).

1879
The family moves to Klein-Hüningen, near Basel.

1884
Birth of sister Gertrud (d. 1935).

1896
Death of father.

1895–1900
Medical training (and qualification) at Basel University.

1900
Assistant Staff Physician under Eugen Bleuler at the Burghölzli, the insane asylum of Canton Zurich and psychiatric clinic of Zurich University.

1902
Senior Assistant Staff Physician at the Burghölzli.
MD dissertation (Zurich University): *Zur Psychologie und Pathologie sogenannter occulter Phänomene* ("On the Psychology and Pathology of So-called Occult Phenomena," CW 1).

1902–3
Winter semester with Pierre Janet at the Salpêtrière, in Paris, for the study of theoretical psychopathology.

1903
Marriage to Emma Rauschenbach, of Schaffhausen (1882–1955); one son and four daughters.

1903–5
Experimental researches on word associations, published in *Diagnostische Assoziationsstudien* (1906, 1909) (*Studies in Word-Association*, 1918; CW 2).

1905–9
Senior Staff Physician at the Burghölzli. Conducts policlinical courses on hypnotic therapy. Research on dementia praecox (schizophrenia).

1905–13
Lecturer (*Privatdozent*) on the medical faculty of Zurich University; lectures on psychoneuroses and psychology.

1906
April: correspondence with Freud begins.

1907
Über die Psychologie der Dementia Praecox (*The Psychology of Dementia Praecox*, 1909; CW 3).
March: first meeting with Freud, in Vienna.

1908
First International Psychoanalytic Congress, Salzburg.

1909
June: moves to his own house in Küsnacht/Zurich, and withdraws from the clinic to devote himself to private practice.
September: first visit to USA, with Freud and Ferenczi, on the occasion of the twentieth anniversary of Clark University, Worcester, Mass., where

Jung lectures on the association experiment and receives honorary degree of LL.D.

1909–13
Editor of *Jahrbuch für psychoanalytische und psychopathologische Forschungen*.

1910
Second International Psychoanalytic Congress, Nuremberg.

1910–14
First president of the International Psychoanalytic Association.

1911
Third International Psychoanalytic Congress, Weimar.

1912
Another visit to USA for series of lectures at Fordham University, New York, on "The Theory of Psychoanalysis" (CW 4).
"Neue Bahnen der Psychologie" ("New Paths in Psychology," later revised and expanded as "On the Psychology of the Unconscious"; both CW 7).
Wandlungen und Symbole der Libido (*Psychology of the Unconscious*, 1916; for revision, see 1952) leading to

1913
break with Freud.
Fourth International Psychoanalytic Congress, Munich.
Jung designates his psychology as "Analytical Psychology" (later also "Complex Psychology").
Resigns lectureship at Zurich University.

1914
Resigns as president of the International Psychoanalytic Association.

1913–19
Period of intense introversion: confrontation with the unconscious.

1916
"Septem Sermones ad Mortuos"; first mandala painting.
Collected Papers on Analytical Psychology.
First description of process of "active imagination" in "Die transzendente Funktion" (not pub. until 1957; in CW 8).
First use of terms "personal unconscious," "collective unconscious", "individuation," "animus/anima," "persona" in "La Structure de l'inconscient" (CW 7, App.).
Beginning of study of Gnostic writings.

1918
"Über das Unbewusste" ("The Role of the Unconscious," CW 10).

1918–19
Commandant of camp for interned British soldiers at Château d'Oex (Canton Vaud).
First use of term "archetype" in "Instinct and the Unconscious" (CW 8).

1920
Journey to Algeria and Tunisia.

1921
Psychologische Typen; first use of term "self" (*Psychological Types*, 1923; CW 6).

1922
Purchase of property in village of Bollingen.

1923
First Tower built in Bollingen.
Death of mother.
Richard Wilhelm's lecture on the *I Ching* at the Psychological Club, Zurich.

1924–5
December: trip to the USA.
January: visits the Pueblo Indians in New Mexico; also New Orleans and New York.

1925
First English seminar at the Psychological Club, Zurich.
Visits the Wembley Exhibition, London.

1925–6
Expedition to Kenya, Uganda, and the Nile; visit with the Elgonyi on Mount Elgon.

1928
Beginning of encounter with alchemy.
Two Essays on Analytical Psychology (CW 7).
Über die Energetik der Seele (various essays, now in CW 8).

1928–30
English seminars on "Dream Analysis" at the Psychological Club, Zurich.

1929
Publication, with Richard Wilhelm, of *Das Geheimnis der goldenen Blüte (The Secret of the Golden Flower*; Jung's contribution in CW 13).
Contributions to Analytical Psychology.

1930
Vice-president of General Medical Society for Psychotherapy, under Ernst Kretschmer as president.

1930–4
English seminars on "Interpretation of Visions" at the Psychological Club, Zurich.

1931
Seelenprobleme der Gegenwart (essays in CW 4, 6, 8, 10, 15, 16, 17).

1932
Awarded Literature Prize of the City of Zurich.

1933
First lectures at the Eidgenössische Technische Hochschule (ETH), Zurich (Swiss Federal Polytechnic), on "Modern Psychology."
Modern Man in Search of a Soul.
First Eranos lecture, on "A Study in the Process of Individuation" (CW 9 i).
Cruise to Egypt and Palestine.

1934
Founds International General Medical Society for Psychotherapy and becomes its first president.
Eranos lecture on "Archetypes of the Collective Unconscious" (CW 9 i).
Wirklichkeit der Seele (essays in CW 8, 10, 15, 16, 17).

1934–9
English seminars on "Psychological Aspects of Nietzsche's *Zarathustra*" at the Psychological Club, Zurich.

1934–9
Editor of *Zentralblatt für Psychotherapie und ihre Grenzgebiete* (Leipzig).

1935
Appointed titular professor at the ETH, Zurich.
Founds Schweizerische Gesellschaft für Praktische Psychologie.
Eranos lecture on "Dream Symbols of the Individuation Process" (expanded to Part II of *Psychology and Alchemy*, CW 12). Tavistock Lectures at the Institute of Medical Psychology, London (not published until 1968: *Analytical Psychology; Its Theory and Practice*; CW 18).

1936
Receives honorary doctoral degree from Harvard University.
Eranos lecture on "Ideas of Redemption in Alchemy" (expanded as Part III of *Psychology and Alchemy*); "Wotan" (CW 10).

1937
Terry Lectures on "Psychology and Religion" (CW 11) at Yale University, New Haven, Conn.
Eranos lecture on "The Visions of Zosimos" (CW 13).

1938
Invitation to India on the twenty-fifth anniversary of the Indian Science Congress, Calcutta; honorary doctorates from the universities of Calcutta, Benares and Allahabad.
International Congress for Psychotherapy at Oxford with Jung as President; he receives honorary doctorate of Oxford University.
Appointed Honorary Fellow of the Royal Society of Medicine, London.
Eranos lecture on "Psychological Aspects of the Mother Archetype" (CW 9 i).

1939
Eranos lecture on "Concerning Rebirth" (CW 9 i).

1940
Eranos lecture on "A Psychological Approach to the Dogma of the Trinity" (CW 11).

1941
Publication, together with Karl Kerényi, of *Einführung in das Wesen der Mythologie* (*Essays on a Science of Mythology*; Jung's contribution in CW 9 i).

Eranos lecture on "Transformation Symbolism in the Mass" (CW 11).

1942
Resigns appointment as professor at ETH.
Paracelsica (essays in CW 13, 15).
Eranos lecture on "The Spirit Mercurius" (CW 13).

1943
Honorary member of the Swiss Academy of Sciences.
Appointed to the chair of Medical Psychology at Basel University.

1944
Resigns Basel chair on account of critical illness.
Psychologie und Alchemie (CW 12).

1945
Honorary doctorate of Geneva University on the occasion of his seventieth birthday.
Eranos lecture on "The Psychology of the Spirit," expanded as "The Phenomenology of the Spirit in Fairytales" (CW 9 i).

1946
Eranos lecture on "The Spirit of Psychology" (expanded as "On the Nature of the Psyche," CW 8).
Die Psychologie der Übertragung ("The Psychology of the Transference," CW 16); *Aufsätze zur Zeitgeschichte* (*Essays on Contemporary Events*; in CW 10); *Psychologie und Erziehung* (CW 17).

1948
Symbolik des Geistes (essays in CW 9 i, 11, 13).
Eranos lecture "On the Self" (expanded to ch. IV of *Aion*, CW 9 ii).
Inauguration of the C. G. Jung Institute, Zurich.

1950
Gestaltungen des Unbewussten (essays in CW 9 i and 15).

1951
Aion (CW 9 ii).
Eranos lecture "On Synchronicity" (CW 8, App.).

1952
Publication, with W. Pauli, of *Naturerklärung und Psyche* (*The Interpretation of Nature and Psyche*; Jung's contribution "Synchronicity: an Acausal Connecting Principle," CW 8).
Symbole der Wandlung (*Symbols of Transformation*, CW 5: 4th, greatly revised edition of *Psychology of the Unconscious*).

Antwort auf Hiob ("Answer to Job," CW 11).
Another serious illness.

1953
Publication of the first volume of the American/British edition of the *Collected Works* (tr. by R. F. C. Hull): *Psychology and Alchemy* (CW 12).

1954
Von den Wurzeln des Bewusstseins (essays in CW 8, 9 i, 11, 13).

1955
Honorary doctorate of the ETH, Zurich, on the occasion of his eightieth birthday.
Death of his wife (27 November).

1955–6
Mysterium Coniunctionis (CW 14); the final work on the psychological significance of alchemy.

1957
Gegenwart und Zukunft ("The Undiscovered Self [Present and Future]," CW 10).
Starts work on *Memories, Dreams, Reflections* with the collaboration of Aniela Jaffé (pub. 1962).
BBC television interview with John Freeman.

1958
Ein moderner Mythus ("Flying Saucers: a Modern Myth," CW 10).
Publication of initial volume in Swiss edition of *Gesammelte Werke: Praxis der Psychotherapie* (Bd. 16).

1960
Honorary Citizen of Küsnacht on the occasion of his eighty-fifth birthday.

1961
Finishes his last work ten days before his death: "Approaching the Unconscious," in *Man and His Symbols* (1964).
Dies after short illness on 6 June in his house at Küsnacht.

Glossary

From MDR and *C. G. Jung: Word and Image*.

Alchemy. The older form of chemistry, which combined experimental chemistry in the modern sense with general, symbolic, intuitive, quasi-religious speculations about nature and man. Onto the unknown *materia* were projected many symbols which we now recognize as contents of the unconscious. The alchemist sought the "secret of God" in the unknown substance and thereby embarked on procedures and paths of exploration which resemble those of the modern-day psychology of the unconscious. This science, too, finds itself confronted with an unknown objective phenomenon – the unconscious.

The philosophical alchemy of the Middle Ages must be viewed in historical terms as a compensatory movement issuing from the unconscious in response to Christianity, for the subject of alchemical meditations and techniques – the realm of nature and *materia* – had been denied a place and any adequate evaluation within Christianity; it was seen rather as that which was to be overcome. Thus alchemy consists of dim, primitive mirrorings of Christian imagery and ideas, as Jung was able to show in *Psychology and Alchemy* (CW 12), using the analogy between the central concept of alchemy, the *lapis* or philosophers' stone, and Christ. The language of the alchemist employs symbolic images and paradoxes. Both correspond to the elusive nature of life and the unconscious psyche. Thus, for instance, it is stated that the stone is no stone (i.e., it is a spiritual or religious concept as well), or that the alchemical Mercurius, a spirit hidden in matter, is evasive, fugitive like the deer, for he is not to be grasped. "He has a thousand names," none of which expresses his entire being, just as no definition can capture entirely the nature of a psychic concept.

Amplification. Elaboration and clarification of a dream-image by means of *directed* association (*q.v.*) and of parallels from the humane science (symbology, mythology, mysticism, folklore, history of religion, ethnology, etc.).

Anima and Animus. Personification of the feminine nature of a man's unconscious and masculine nature of a woman's. This psychological bisexuality is a reflection of the biological fact that it is the larger number of male (or female) genes which is the decisive factor in the determination of sex. The smaller number of contrasexual genes seems to produce a corresponding contrasexual character, which usually remains unconscious. Anima and animus manifest themselves most typically in personified form as figures in dreams and fantasies ("dream-girl," "dream-lover"), or in the irrationalities of a man's *feeling* and a woman's *thinking*. As regulators of behaviour they are two of the most influential archetypes (*q.v.*).

C. G. Jung: "Every man carries with him the eternal image of woman, not the image of this or that particular woman, but a definitive feminine image. This image is fundamentally unconscious, an hereditary factor of primordial origin engraved in the living organic system of the man, an imprint or 'archetype' (*q.v.*) of all the ancestral experiences of the female, a deposit, as it were, of all the impressions ever made by woman ... Since this image is unconscious, it is always unconsciously projected upon the person of the beloved, and is one of the chief reasons for passionate attraction or aversion." (CW 17, par. 338.)

"In its primary 'unconscious' form the animus is a compound of spontaneous, unpremeditated opinions which exercise a powerful influence on the woman's emotional life, while the anima is similarly compounded of feelings which thereafter influence or distort the man's understanding ('she has turned his head'). Consequently the animus likes to project itself upon 'intellectuals' and all kinds of 'heroes,' including tenors, artists, sporting celebrities etc. The anima has a predilection for everything that is unconscious, dark, equivocal, and purposeless in woman, and also for her vanity, frigidity, helplessness, and so forth ..." (CW 16, par. 521.)

"No man can converse with an animus for five minutes without becoming the victim of his own anima. Anyone who still had enough sense of humour to listen objectively to the ensuing dialogue would be staggered by the vast number of commonplaces, misapplied truisms, clichés from newspapers and novels, shop-soiled platitudes of every description interspersed with vulgar abuse and brain-splitting lack of logic. It is a dialogue which, irrespective of its participants, is repeated millions and millions of times in all languages of the world and always remains essentially the same." (CW 9 ii, par. 29.)

"The natural function of the animus (as well as of the anima) is to remain in (their) place between individual consciousness and the collective unconscious (*q.v.*); exactly as the persona (*q.v.*) as a sort of stratum between the ego consciousness and the objects of the external world. The animus and the anima should function as a bridge, or a door, leading to the images of the collective unconscious, as the persona should be a sort of bridge into the world." (Unpublished seminar notes. *"Visions"* I.)

Archetype. C. G. Jung: "The concept of the archetype . . . is derived from the repeated observation that, for instance, the myths and fairy tales of world literature contain definite motifs which crop up everywhere. We meet these same motifs in the fantasies, dreams, deliria, and delusions of individuals living to-day. These typical images and associations are what I call archetypal ideas. The more vivid they are, the more they will be coloured by particularly strong feeling-tones (*q.v.*). . . . They impress, influence, and fascinate us. They have their origin in the archetype, which in itself is an irrepresentable, unconscious, pre-existent form that seems to be part of the inherited structure of the psyche and can therefore manifest itself spontaneously anywhere, at any time. Because of its instinctual nature, the archetype underlies the feeling-toned complexes (*q.v.*) and shares their autonomy." (CW 10, par. 847.)

"Again and again I encounter the mistaken notion that an archetype is determined in regard to its content, in other words, that it is a kind of unconscious idea (if such an expression be admissible). It is necessary to point out once more that archetypes are not determined as regards their content, but only as regards their form and then only to a very limited degree. A primordial image (*q.v.*) is determined as to its content only when it has become conscious and is therefore filled out with the material of conscious experience. Its form, however ... might perhaps be compared to the axial system of a crystal, which, as it were, performs the crystalline structure in the mother liquid, although it has no material existence of its own. This first appears according to the specific way in which the ions and molecules aggregate. The archetype in itself is empty and purely formal, nothing but a *facultas praeformandi*, a possibility of representation which is given *a priori*. The representations themselves are not inherited, only the forms, and in that respect they correspond in every way to the instincts, which are also determined in form only. The existence of the instincts can no more be proved than the existence of the archetypes, so long as they do not manifest themselves concretely." (CW 9 i, pars. 155ff.)

"It seems to me probable that the real nature of the archetype as such is not capable of being made conscious, that it is transcendent, on which account I call it psychoid" (*q.v.*). (CW 8, par. 417.)

Association. The linking of ideas, perceptions, etc. according to similarity, coexistence, opposition, and causal dependence. *Free association* in Freudian dream interpretation: spontaneous ideas occurring to the dreamer, which need not necessarily refer to the dream situation. *Directed or controlled association* in Jungian dream interpretation: spontaneous ideas which proceed from a given dream situation and constantly relate to it.

Association test. Methods for discovering complexes (*q.v.*) by measuring the reaction time and interpreting the answers to given stimulus words.

Complex-indicators: prolonged reaction time, faults, or the idiosyncratic quality of the answers when the stimulus words touch on complexes which the subject wishes to hide or is not conscious of.

Complex. C. G. Jung: "Complexes are psychic fragments which have split off owing to traumatic (*q.v.*) influences or certain incompatible tendencies. As the association experiments prove, complexes interfere with the intentions of the will and disturb the conscious performance: they produce disturbances of memory and blockages in the flow of association (*q.v.*); they appear and disappear according to their own laws; they can temporarily obsess consciousness, or influence speech and action in an unconscious way. In a word, complexes behave like independent beings, a fact especially evident in abnormal states of mind. In the voices heard by the insane they even take on a personal ego-character like that of the spirits who manifest themselves through automatic writing and similar techniques." (CW 8, par. 253.)

Consciousness. C. G. Jung: "When one reflects upon what consciousness really is, one is profoundly impressed by the extreme wonder of the fact that an event which takes place outside in the cosmos simultaneously produces an internal image, that it takes place, so to speak, inside as well, which is to say: becomes conscious." (*Basel Seminar*, privately printed, 1934, p. 1.)

"For indeed our consciousness does not create itself – it wells up from unknown depths. In childhood it awakens gradually, and all through life it wakes each morning out of the depths of sleep from an unconscious condition. It is like a child that is born daily out of the primordial womb of the unconscious." (CW 11, par. 935.)

Dream. C. G. Jung: "The dream is a little hidden door in the innermost and most secret recesses of the psyche, opening into that cosmic night which was psyche long before there was any ego consciousness, and which will remain psyche no matter how far our ego consciousness may extend . . . All consciousness separates; but in dreams we put on the likeness of that more universal, truer, more eternal man dwelling in the darkness of primordial night. There he is still the whole, and the whole is in him, indistinguishable from nature and bare of all egohood. Out of these all-uniting depths arises the dream, be it never so infantile, never so grotesque, never so immoral." (CW 10, par. 304.)

Extraversion. Attitude-type characterized by concentration of interest on the external object. See *Introversion.*

God-image. A term derived from the Church Fathers, according to whom the *imago Dei* is imprinted on the human soul. When such an image is spontaneously produced in dreams, fantasies, visions, etc. it is, from the psychological point of view, a symbol of the self (*q.v.*), of psychic wholeness.

C. G. Jung: "It is only through the psyche that we can establish that God acts upon us, but we are unable to distinguish whether God and the unconscious are two different entities. Both are border-line concepts for transcendental contents. But empirically it can be established, with a sufficient degree of probability, that there is in the unconscious an archetype of wholeness which manifests itself spontaneously in dreams, etc., and a tendency, independent of the conscious will, to relate other archetypes to this centre. Consequently, it does not seem improbable that the archetype produces a symbolism which has always characterized and expressed the Deity . . . The God-image does not coincide with the unconscious as such, but with a special content of it, namely the archetype of the self. It is this archetype from which we can no longer distinguish the God-image empirically." (CW 11, par. 757.)

"One can, then, explain the God-image . . . as a reflection of the self, or, conversely, explain the self as an *imago Dei* in man." (par. 282.)

Hierosgamos. Sacred or spiritual marriage, union of archetypal figures in the rebirth mysteries of antiquity and also in alchemy. Typical examples are the representation of Christ and the Church as bridegroom and bride (*sponsus et sponsa*) and the alchemical conjunction of sun and moon.

Individuation. C. G. Jung: "I use the term 'individuation' to denote the process by which a person becomes a psychological 'individual,' that is, a separate, indivisible unity or 'whole.'" (CW 9 i, par. 490.)

"Individuation means becoming a single, homogeneous being, and, in so far as 'in-dividuality' embraces our innermost, last, and incomparable uniqueness, it also implies becoming one's own self. We could therefore translate individuation as 'coming to selfhood' or 'self-realization.'" (CW 7, par. 266.)

"But again and again I note that the individuation process is confused with the coming of the ego into consciousness and that the ego is in consequence identified with the self, which naturally produces a hopeless conceptual muddle. Individuation is then nothing but ego-centredness and autoeroticism. But the self comprises infinitely more than a mere ego ... It is as much one's self, and all other selves, as the ego. Individuation does not shut one out from the world, but gathers the world to one's self." (CW 8, par. 432.)

Inflation. Expansion of the personality beyond its proper limits by identification with the persona (*q.v.*) or with an archetype (*q.v.*), or in pathological cases with a historical or religious figure. It produces an exaggerated sense of one's self-importance and is usually compensated by feelings of inferiority.

Introversion. Attitude-type characterized by orientation in life through subjective psychic contents. See *Extraversion*.

Mana. Melanesian word for extraordinarily effective power emanating from a human being, object, action or event, or from supernatural beings and spirits. Also health, prestige, power to work magic and to heal. A primitive concept of psychic energy.

Mandala (Sanskrit). Magic circle. In Jung, symbol of the centre goal, or of the self (*q.v.*) as psychic totality; self-representation of a psychic process of centring; production of a new centre of personality. This is symbolically represented by the circle, the square, or the quaternity (*q.v.*), by symmetrical arrangements of the number four and its multiples. In Lamism and Tantric Yoga the mandala is an instrument of contemplation (*yantra*), seat and birthplace of the gods. *Disturbed mandala*: Any form that deviates from the circle, square, or equal-armed cross, or whose basic number is not four or its multiples.

C. G. Jung: "Mandala means 'circle,' more especially a magic circle, and this form of symbol is not only to be found all through the East, but also among us; mandalas are amply represented in the Middle Ages. The specifically Christian ones come from the earlier Middle Ages. Most of them show Christ in the centre, with the four evangelists, or their symbols, at the cardinal points. This conception must be a very ancient one because Horus was represented with his four sons in the same way by the Egyptians . . . For the most part, the mandala form is that of a flower, cross, or wheel, with a distinct tendency towards four as the basis of the structure." (CW 13, par. 31.)

"Mandalas . . . usually appear in situations of psychic confusion and disorientation. The archetype thereby constellated represents a pattern of order which, like a psychological 'view-finder' marked with a cross or circle divided into four, is superimposed on the psychic chaos so that each content falls into place and the weltering confusion is held together by the protective circle . . . At the same time they are *yantras*, instruments with whose help the order is brought into being." (CW 10, par. 803.)

Neurosis. State of being at odds with oneself, caused by the conflict between instinctive drives and the demands of one's society, between infantile obstinacy and the desire to conform, between collective and individual obligations. Neurosis is a stop sign marking a wrong turning, a summons to be cured.

C. G. Jung: "The psychological trouble in neurosis, and the neurosis itself, can be formulated as *an act of adaptation that has failed*. This formulation might reconcile certain views of Janet's with Freud's view that a neurosis is, in a sense, an attempt at self-cure . . ." (CW 4, par. 574.)

"Neurosis is always a substitute for legitimate suffering." (CW 11, par. 129.)

Numinosum. Rudolf Otto's term (in his *Idea of the Holy*) for the inexpressible, mysterious, terrifying, directly experienced and pertaining only to the divinity.

Persona. Originally, the mask worn by an actor. C. G. Jung: "The persona . . . is the individual's system of adaptation to, or the manner he assumed in dealing with, the world. Every calling or profession, for example, has its own characteristic persona . . . Only, the danger is that (people) become identical with their personas – the professor with his textbook, the tenor with his voice . . . One could say, with a little exaggeration, that the persona is that which in reality one is not, but which oneself as well as others think one is." (CW 9 i, par. 221.)

Primordial image (Jakob Burckhardt). Term originally used by Jung for *archetype* (*q.v.*).

Psychoid. "Soul-like" or "quasi-psychic." C. G. Jung: "The collective unconscious represents a psyche that ... cannot be directly perceived or 'represented,' in contrast to the perceptible psychic phenomena, and on account of its 'irrepresentable' nature I have called it psychoid.'" (CW 8, par. 840.)

Quaternity. C. G. Jung: "The quaternity is an archetype of almost universal occurrence. It forms the logical basis for any whole judgment. If one wishes to pass such a judgment, it must have this fourfold aspect. For instance, if you want to describe the horizon as a whole, you name the four quarters of heaven... There are always four elements, four prime qualities, four colours, four castes, four ways of spiritual development etc. So, too, there are four aspects of psychological orientation... In order to orient ourselves, we must have a function which ascertains that something is there (sensation); a second function which establishes *what* it is (thinking); a third function which states whether it suits us or not, whether we wish to accept it or no (feeling), and a fourth function which indicates where it came from and where it is going (intuition). When this has been done, there is nothing more to say... The ideal completeness is the circle or sphere, but its natural minimal division is a quaternity." (CW 11, par. 246.)

A quaternity or quaternion often has a 3 + 1 structure, in that one of the terms composing it occupies an exceptional position or has a nature unlike that of the others. (For instance three of the symbols of the Evangelists are animals and that of the fourth, or St. Luke, is an Angel.) This is the "Fourth," which, added to the other three, makes them "One," symbolizing totality. In analytical psychology often the "inferior" function (i.e., that function which is not at the conscious disposal of the subject) represents the "Fourth" and its integration into consciousness is one of the major tasks of the process of individuation (*q.v.*).

Self. The central archetype (*q.v.*); the archetype of order; the totality of the personality. Symbolized by circle, square, quaternity (*q.v.*), child, mandala (*q.v.*) etc.

C. G. Jung: "The self is a quantity that is superordinate to the conscious ego. It embraces not only the conscious but also the unconscious psyche, and is therefore, so to speak, a personality which we *also* are . . . There is little hope of our ever being able to reach even approximate consciousness of the self, since however much we may make conscious there will always exist an indeterminate and indeterminable amount of unconscious material which belongs to the totality of the self." (CW 7, par. 274.)

"The self is not only the centre but also the whole circumference which embraces both consciousness and unconscious; it is the centre of this totality, just as the ego is the centre of the conscious mind." (CW 12, par. 44.)

"The self is our life's goal, for it is the completest expression of that fateful combination we call individuality." (CW 7, par. 404.)

Shadow. The inferior part of the personality; sum of all personal and collective psychic elements which, because of their incompatibility with the chosen conscious attitude, are denied expression in life and therefore coalesce into a relatively autonomous "splinter personality" with contrary tendencies in the unconscious. The shadow behaves compensatorily to consciousness; hence its effects can be positive as well as negative.

C. G. Jung: "The shadow personifies everything that the subject refuses to acknowledge about himself and yet is always thrusting itself upon him directly or indirectly – for instance, inferior traits of character and other incompatible tendencies." (CW 9 i, par. 513.)

"The shadow is that hidden, repressed, for the most part inferior and guilt-laden personality whose ultimate ramifications reach back into the realm of our animal ancestors and so comprise the whole historical aspect of the unconscious . . . If it has been believed hitherto that the human shadow was the source of all evil, it can now be ascertained on closer investigation that the unconscious man, that is, his shadow, does not consist only of morally reprehensible tendencies, but also displays a number of good qualities, such as normal instincts, appropriate reaction, realistic insights, creative impulses, etc." (CW 9 ii, pars. 422–3.)

Soul. C. G. Jung: "If the human soul is anything, it must be of unimaginable complexity and diversity, so that it cannot possibly be approached through a mere psychology of instinct. I can only gaze with wonder and awe at the depths and heights of our psychic nature. Its non-spatial universe conceals an untold abundance of images which have accumulated over millions of years of living development and become fixed in the organism. My consciousness is like an eye that penetrates to the most distant spaces, yet it is the psychic non-ego that fills them with non-spatial images. And these images are not pale shadows, but tremendously powerful psychic factors ... Besides this picture I would like to place the spectacle of the starry heavens at night, for the only equivalent of the universe within is the universe without; and just as I reach this world through the medium of the body, so I reach that world through the medium of the psyche." (CW 4, par. 764.)

"It would be blasphemy to assert that God can manifest Himself everywhere save only in the human soul. Indeed the very intimacy of the relationship between God and the soul automatically precludes any devaluation of the latter. It would be going perhaps too far to speak of an affinity; but at all events the soul must contain in itself the faculty of relation to God, i.e. a correspondence, otherwise a connection could never come about. This correspondence is, in psychological terms, the archetype of the God-image (*q.v.*)." (CW 12, par. 11.)

Synchronicity. A term coined by Jung to designate the meaningful coincidence or equivalence: (*a*) of a psychic and a physical state or event which have no causal relationship to one another. Such synchronistic phenomena occur, for instance, when an inwardly perceived event (dream, vision, premonition, etc.) is seen to have a correspondence in external reality: the inner image of premonition has "come true." (*b*) of similar or identical thoughts, dreams etc. occurring at the same time at different places. Neither the one nor the other coincidence can be explained by causality, but seem to be connected primarily with activated archetypal processes in the unconscious.

C. G. Jung: "My preoccupation with the psychology of unconscious processes long ago compelled me to look about for another principle of explanation, because the causality principle seemed to me inadequate to explain certain remarkable phenomena of the psychology of the unconscious. Thus I found that there are psychic parallelisms which cannot be related to each other causally, but which must be connected through another principle, namely the contingency of events. This connection of events seemed to me essentially given by the fact of their relative simultaneity, hence the term 'synchronistic.' It seems, indeed, as though time, far from being an abstraction, is a concrete continuum which contains qualities or basic conditions that manifest themselves simultaneously in different places through parallelisms that cannot be explained causally, as, for example, in cases of the simultaneous occurrence of identical thoughts, symbols, or psychic states." (CW 15, par. 81.)

"I chose this term because the simultaneous occurrence of two meaningful but not causally connected events seemed to me an essential criterion. I am therefore using the general concept of synchronicity in the special sense of a coincidence in time of two or more causally unrelated events which have the same or a similar meaning, in contrast to 'synchronism,' which simply means the simultaneous occurrence of two events." (CW 8, par. 849.)

"Synchronicity is no more baffling or mysterious than the discontinuities of physics. It is only the ingrained belief in the sovereign power of causality that creates intellectual difficulties and makes it appear unthinkable that causeless events exist or could ever occur ... Meaningful coincidences are thinkable as pure chance. But the more they multiply and the greater and more exact the correspondence is, the more their probability sinks and their unthinkability increases, until they can no longer be regarded as pure chance, but, for lack of a causal explanation, have to be thought of as meaningful arrangements ... Their 'inexplicability' is not due to the fact that the cause is unknown, but to the fact that a cause is not even thinkable in intellectual terms." (CW 8, par. 967.)

Unconscious, the. C. G. Jung: "Theoretically, no limits can be set to the field of consciousness, since it is capable of indefinite extension. Empirically, however, it always finds its limit when it comes up against the *unknown*. This consists of everything we do not know, which, therefore, is not related to the ego as the centre of the field of consciousness. The unknown falls into two groups of objects: those which are outside and can be experienced by the senses, and those which are inside and are experienced immediately. The first group comprises the unknown in the outer world; the second the unknown in the inner world. We call this latter territory the *unconscious*." (CW 9 ii, par. 2.)

... Everything of which I know, but of which I am not at the moment thinking; everything of which I was once conscious but have now forgotten; everything perceived by my senses, but not noted by my conscious mind; everything which, involuntarily and without paying attention to it, I feel, think, remember, want, and do; all the future things that are taking shape in me and will sometime come to consciousness: all this is the content of the unconscious." (CW 8, par. 382.)

"Besides these we must include all more or less intentional repressions of painful thoughts and feelings. I call the sum of all these contents the *personal unconscious*. But, over and above that, we also find in the unconscious qualities that are not individually acquired but are inherited, e.g. instincts as impulses to carry out actions from necessity, without conscious motivation. In this 'deeper' stratum we also find the ... archetypes ... The instincts and archetypes together form the *collective unconscious*. I call it 'collective' because, unlike the personal unconscious, it is not made up of individual and more or less unique contents but of those which are universal and of regular occurrence." (CW 8, par. 270.)

"The first group comprises contents which are integral components of the individual personality and therefore could just as well be conscious; the second group forms, as it were, an omnipresent, unchanging, and everywhere identical *quality or substrata of the psyche per se*." (CW 9 ii, par. 12.)

"The deeper 'layers' of the psyche lose their individual uniqueness as they retreat farther and farther into darkness. 'Lower down,' that is to say as they approach the autonomous functional systems, they become increasingly collective until they are universalized and extinguished in the body's materiality, i.e., in chemical substances. The body's carbon is simply carbon. Hence 'at bottom' the psyche is simply 'world.'" (CW 9 i, par. 291.)

Bibliography

1. Works by C. G. Jung

THE COLLECTED WORKS OF C.G. JUNG

The publication of the first complete edition, in English, of the works of C. G. Jung was undertaken by Routledge and Kegan Paul, Ltd, in England and by Bollingen Foundation in the United States. The American edition is number XX in Bollingen Series, which since 1967 has been published by Princeton University Press. The edition contains revised versions of works previously published, such as *Psychology of the Unconscious*, which is now entitled *Symbols of Transformation*; works originally written in English, such as *Psychology and Religion*; works not previously translated, such as *Aion*; and, in general, new translations of virtually all of Professor Jung's writings. Prior to his death, in 1961, the author supervised the textual revision, which in some cases is extensive. Sir Herbert Read, Dr Michael Fordham and Dr Gerhard Adler composed the Editorial Committee; the translator was R. F. C. Hull (except for Volume 2) and William McGuire was executive editor.

In the following list, dates of original publication are given in parentheses (of original composition, in brackets). Multiple dates indicate revisions.

1. PSYCHIATRIC STUDIES
   On the Psychology and Pathology of So-called Occult Phenomena (1902)
   On Hysterical Misreading (1904)
   Cryptomnesia (1905)
   On Manic Mood Disorder (1903)
   A Case of Hysterical Stupor in a Prisoner in Detention (1902)
   On Simulated Insanity (1903)
   A Medical Opinion on a Case of Simulated Insanity (1904)
   A Third and Final Opinion on Two Contradictory Psychiatric Diagnoses (1906)
   On the Psychological Diagnosis of Facts (1905)

2. EXPERIMENTAL RESEARCHES
Translated by Leopold Stein in collaboration with Diana Riviere

STUDIES IN WORD ASSOCIATION (1904–7)
The Associations of Normal Subjects (by Jung and F. Riklin)
Experimental Observations on Memory
The Psychological Diagnosis of the Criminal Case
An Analysis of the Associations of an Epileptic
The Association Method (1910)
The Reaction-Time Ratio in the Association Experiment
On Disturbances in Reproduction in Association Experiment
The Psychopathological Significance of the Association Experiment
Psychoanalysis and Association Experiments
Association, Dream, and Hysterical Symptom
PSYCHOPHYSICAL RESEARCHES (1907–8)
On Psychophysical Relations of the Association Experiment
Psychophysical Investigations with the Galvanometer and Pneumo-
    graph in Normal and Insane Individuals (by F. Petersen and
    Jung)
Further Investigations on the Galvanic Phenomenon and Respiration
    in Normal and Insane Individuals (by C. Ricksher and Jung)

3. THE PSYCHOGENESIS OF MENTAL DISEASE
The Psychology of Dementia Praecox (1907)
The Content of the Psychoses (1908/1914)
On Psychological Understanding (1914)
A Criticism of Bleuler's Theory of Schizophrenic Negativism (1911)
On the Importance of the Unconscious in Psychopathology (1914)
On the Problem of Psychogenesis in Mental Disease (1919)
Mental Disease and the Psyche (1928)
On the Psychogenesis of Schizophrenia (1939)
Recent Thoughts on Schizophrenia (1957)
Schizophrenia (1958)

4. FREUD AND PSYCHOANALYSIS
Freud's Theory of Hysteria: a Reply to Aschaffenburg (1906)
The Freudian Theory of Hysteria (1908)
The Analysis of Dreams (1909)
A Contribution to the Psychology of Rumour (1910–11)
On the Significance of Number Dreams (1910–11)
Morton Prince, "Mechanism and Interpretation of Dreams": a
    Critical Review (1911)

On the Criticism of Psychoanalysis (1910)

Concerning Psychoanalysis (1912)

The Theory of Psychoanalysis (1913)

General Aspects of Psychoanalysis (1913)

Psychoanalysis and Neurosis (1916)

Some Crucial Points in Psychoanalysis: The Jung-Loy Correspondence (1914)

Prefaces to "Collected Papers on Analytical Psychology" (1916, 1917)

The Significance of the Father in the Destiny of the Individual (1909/1949)

Introduction to Kranefeldt's "Secret Ways of the Mind" (1930)

Freud and Jung: Contrasts (1929)

5. SYMBOLS OF TRANSFORMATION (1911–12/1952)
    PART I
    Introduction
    Two Kinds of Thinking
    The Miller Fantasies: Anamnesis
    The Hymn of Creation
    The Song of the Moth
    PART II
    Introduction
    The Concept of Libido
    The Transformation of Libido
    The Origin of the Hero
    Symbols of the Mother and of Rebirth
    The Battle for Deliverance from the Mother
    The Dual Mother
    The Sacrifice
    Epilogue
    Appendix: The Miller Fantasies

6. PSYCHOLOGICAL TYPES (1921)
    Introduction
    The Problem of Types in the History of Classical and Medieval Thought
    Schiller's Ideas on the Type Problem
    The Apollonian and the Dionysian
    The Type Problem in the Discernment of Human Character
    The Type Problem in Poetry
    The Type Problem in Psychopathology

The Problem of Typical Attitudes in Aesthetics
The Type Problem in Modern Philosophy
The Type Problem in Biography
General Description of the Types
Definitions
Conclusion
Four Papers on Psychological Typology (1913, 1925, 1931, 1936)

7. TWO ESSAYS ON ANALYTICAL PSYCHOLOGY
    On the Psychology of the Unconscious (1917/1926/1943)
    The Relations between the Ego and the Unconscious (1928)
    Appendices: New Paths in Psychology (1912); The Structure of the
        Unconscious (1916) (new versions, with variants, 1966)

8. THE STRUCTURE AND DYNAMICS OF THE PSYCHE
    On Psychic Energy (1928)
    The Transcendent Function ([1916]/1957)
    A Review of the Complex Theory (1934)
    The Significance of Constitution and Heredity in Psychology (1929)
    Psychological Factors Determining Human Behaviour (1937)
    Instinct and the Unconscious (1919)
    The Structure of the Psyche (1927/1931)
    On the Nature of the Psyche (1947/1954)
    General Aspects of Dream Psychology (1916/1948)
    On the Nature of Dreams (1945/1948)
    The Psychological Foundations of Belief in Spirits (1920/1948)
    Spirit and Life (1926)
    Basic Postulates of Analytical Psychology (1931)
    Analytical Psychology and *Weltanschauung* (1928/1931)
    The Real and the Surreal (1933)
    The Stages of Life (1930–1)
    The Soul and Death (1934)
    Synchronicity: an Acausal Connecting Principle (1952)
    Appendix: On Synchronicity (1951)

9. PART I. THE ARCHETYPES AND THE COLLECTIVE
    UNCONSCIOUS
    Archetypes of the Collective Unconscious (1934/1954)
    The Concept of the Collective Unconscious (1936)
    Concerning the Archetypes, with Special Reference to the Anima
        Concept (1936/1954)
    Psychological Aspects of the Mother Archetype (1938/1954)

13. ALCHEMICAL STUDIES
Commentary on "The Secret of the Golden Flower" (1929)
The Visions of Zosimos (1938/1954)
Paracelsus as a Spiritual Phenomenon (1942)
The Spirit Mercurius (1943/1948)
The Philosophical Tree (1945/1954)

14. MYSTERIUM CONIUNCTIONIS (1955–6)
AN INQUIRY INTO THE SEPARATION AND SYNTHESIS OF
PSYCHIC OPPOSITES IN ALCHEMY
The Components of the Coniunctio
The Paradoxa
The Personification of Opposites
Rex and Regina
Adam and Eve
The Conjunction

15. THE SPIRIT IN MAN, ART, AND LITERATURE
Paracelsus (1929)
Paracelsus the Physician (1941)
Sigmund Freud in His Historical Setting (1932)
In Memory of Sigmund Freud (1939)
Richard Wilhelm: In Memoriam (1930)
On the Relation of Analytical Psychology to Poetry (1922)
Psychology and Literature (1930/1950)
"Ulysses" (1932)
Picasso (1932)

16. THE PRACTICE OF PSYCHOTHERAPY
GENERAL PROBLEMS OF PSYCHOTHERAPY
Principles of Practical Psychotherapy (1935)
What Is Psychotherapy? (1935)
Some Aspects of Modern Psychotherapy (1930)
The Aims of Psychotherapy (1931)
Problems of Modern Psychotherapy (1929)
Psychotherapy and a Philosophy of Life (1943)
Medicine and Psychotherapy (1945)
Psychotherapy Today (1945)
Fundamental Questions of Psychotherapy (1951)
SPECIFIC PROBLEMS OF PSYCHOTHERAPY
The Therapeutic Value of Abreaction (1921/1928)
The Practical Use of Dream-analysis (1934)

The Psychology of the Transference (1946)
Appendix: The Realities of Practical Psychotherapy ([1937] added 1966)

17. THE DEVELOPMENT OF PERSONALITY
Psychic Conflicts in a Child (1910/1946)
Introduction to Wickes's "Analyse der Kinderseele" (1927/1931)
Child Development and Education (1928)
Analytical Psychology and Education: Three Lectures (1926/1946)
The Gifted Child (1943)
The Significance of the Unconscious in Individual Education (1928)
The Development of Personality (1934)
Marriage as a Psychological Relationship (1925)

18. THE SYMBOLIC LIFE
Miscellaneous Writings

19. GENERAL BIBLIOGRAPHY OF C. G. JUNG'S WRITINGS

20. GENERAL INDEX TO THE COLLECTED WORKS

Other Writings

Memories, Dreams, Reflections (1962)
Recorded and edited by Aniela Jaffé; translated by Richard and Clara Winston. New York: Pantheon, 1962, 1967; Vintage, 1965, 1966. London: Collins and Routledge and Kegan Paul, 1963; Fount Paperbacks, 1977. (The later American editions include *Septem Sermones ad Mortuos*.)

Septem Sermones ad Mortuos (1916)
Translated by H. G. Baynes. London: John M. Watkins, 1967. In the USA: included in MDR, later editions.

The Freud/Jung Letters
Edited by William McGuire; translated by Ralph Manheim and R. F. C. Hull. Princeton University Press, 1974; second printing, with corrections, paperback, 1979. London: The Hogarth Press and Routledge and Kegan Paul, 1974; abridged, Picador, 1979.

C. G. Jung: Letters
Volume 1: 1906–50. Volume 2: 1951–61
Selected and edited by Gerhard Adler in collaboration with Aniela Jaffé;
translated by R. F. C. Hull. Princeton University Press, 1973, 1976.
London: Routledge and Kegan Paul, 1973, 1976.

See also
C. G. Jung Speaking: Interviews and Encounters
Edited by William McGuire and R. F. C. Hull. Princeton University
Press, 1977. London: Thames and Hudson, 1978; Picador, 1980.

C. G. Jung: Word and Image
Edited by Aniela Jaffé. Princeton University Press, 1979.

Man and His Symbols
By C. J. Jung *et al.* London: Aldus Books, 1964. New York: Doubleday,
1968.

2. Books about Jung and Analytical Psychology

Adler, Gerhard, *Studies in Analytical Psychology*. London: Routledge and
   Kegan Paul, 1948; new edition, Hodder and Stoughton, 1966. New
   York: G. P. Putnam's Sons, 1967
Bennet, E. A., *C. G. Jung*. London: Barrie and Rockcliffe, 1961
Bennet, E. A., *What Jung Really Said*. London: Macdonald, 1966
Brome, Vincent, *Jung: Man and Myth*. London: Macmillan, 1978. New
   York: Atheneum, 1978
Dry, Avis M., *The Psychology of Jung*. London: Methuen, 1962
Fordham, Frieda, *An Introduction to Jung's Psychology*. Harmondsworth:
   Pelican, 1953
Hannah, Barbara, *Jung: His Life and Work*. New York: G. P. Putnam's
   Sons, 1976
Moreno, Antonio, *Jung, Gods and Modern Man*. Indiana: University of
   Notre Dame Press, 1970. London: Sheldon Press, 1974
Odajnyk, Volodymyr Walter, *Jung and Politics*. New York: Harper and
   Row, 1976
Serrano, Miguel, *C. G. Jung & Hermann Hesse: a Record of Two
   Friendships*. New York: Schocken, 1968
Staude, John-Raphael, *The Adult Development of C. G. Jung*. London:
   Routledge and Kegan Paul, 1981

Stern, Paul J., *C. G. Jung: the Haunted Prophet*. New York: Braziller, 1976

Storr, Anthony, *Jung*. London: Fontana Paperbacks, 1973

Von Franz, Marie-Louise, *C. G. Jung: His Myth in Our Time*. New York: G. P. Putnam's Sons for the C. G. Jung Foundation for Analytical Psychology, 1975

White, Victor, *God and the Unconscious*. London: Harvill, 1952

Index

Born in 1920, Anthony Storr was educated at
Winchester, at Christ's College, Cambridge, and at
Westminster Hospital. After qualifying as a doctor in
1944, he specialized in psychiatry and held posts at
Runwell Mental Hospital and at the Maudsley Hospital.
He also trained as an analyst in the school of C. G.
Jung, though he prefers not to be labelled as an
adherent of any one analytical school. His publications
include *The Integrity of the Personality* (1960), *Sexual
Deviation* (1964), *Human Aggression* (1968), *Human
Destructiveness* (1972), *The Dynamics of Creation*
(1972) and *The Art of Psychotherapy* (1979). He has
contributed reviews and articles to many papers,
including the *Sunday Times*, *The Times Literary
Supplement* and the *Spectator*. At present, Dr Storr is
Consultant in Psychotherapy, Oxfordshire Area, a
Fellow of Green College, Oxford, and Clinical Lecturer
in Psychiatry, University of Oxford.